PATRICK PEARSE

THE TRIUMPH OF FAILURE

by

RUTH DUDLEY EDWARDS

LONDON
VICTOR GOLLANCZ LTD
1977

First published April 1977
Second impression August 1977

ISBN 0 575 02153 5

Printed in Great Britain by
Lowe & Brydone Printers Limited, Thetford, Norfolk

Some had no thought of victory
But had gone out to die
That Ireland's mind be greater,
Her heart mount up on high;
And yet who knows what's yet to come?
For Patrick Pearse had said
That in every generation
Must Ireland's blood be shed.

W. B. Yeats: *"Three songs to the one burden"*

To John

CONTENTS

LIST OF ILLUSTRATIONS

PHOTOGRAPHS
following page 206

IN THE TEXT

ACKNOWLEDGEMENTS

The material consulted during research for the book is widely scattered; as the net spread, I came into contact with an increasing number of institutions—mostly, of course, in Dublin. I wish to thank the following, or members of the following for their interest and help, and for the ready manner in which they gave their time and expert advice to me, or to my mother and my husband, my fellow researchers: the Director and staff of the National Library of Ireland (especially Alf MacLochlainn), whose active pursuit of material which might otherwise have eluded me went far beyond the call of duty; the Commissioner and many of the staff of the Board of Works, especially Mary O'Sullivan, who introduced me to people, places and material connected with St Enda's—on which imaginative and thorough restoration work is in hand; the National Museum; the Library of Trinity College; the Library of the Honourable Society of the King's Inns; the Registry of Deeds; the Public Record Office of Ireland; the Land Valuation Office; the Kilmainham Jail Restoration Society; Alexandra College; Clongowes Wood College; St Agatha's and St Andrew's Churches; the Bodleian Library, Oxford and Ms Heather J. Forbes; Mr P. J. McCullough of the Eastern Health Authority; Professor Ivor Brown; Rev. Dr K. Kennedy of the Dublin Diocesan Archives; Miss Esther Semple of the UCD Library; the Folklore Department of UCD.

I owe a special debt to the Director and staff of the UCD Archives Department. My thanks to Kerry Holland, Orla Green and particularly Seamus Edge, for unfailing help and hospitality.

Others, in a private capacity, were generous with their help. I enjoyed enlightening interviews with Mr Frank Burke, Mrs Eibhlin Tierney, Mrs Geraldine Dillon, Miss Sighle Bairead and several years ago, and on a different project, the late Senator Margaret Pearse. Fr Michael Hueston and John O'Beirne Ranelagh gave me helpful advice, and Miss Jeanne Sheehy of TCD put me in touch with some very useful material on James Pearse and his circle.

Brother W. P. Allen of the Christian Brothers School, North Richmond Street, treated me to his personal reminiscences of some of the characters in these pages, and to a guided tour of his historical documents and the school's most professional museum. I hope that his collection continues to flourish.

Mr Eamonn de Barra, a lifelong worker for the Irish language, has been personally responsible for preserving a valuable collection of Pearse papers, to which he allowed me unrestricted access. His kindness to me over many months was greatly appreciated.

Professor F. X. Martin OSA was very generous with his advice, and with the special knowledge he has accumulated in his tireless and effective pursuit of hitherto inaccessible material on the period.

I was fortunate in my first readers. Perhaps because they were all good friends, their comments were often of the cruel-to-be-kind sort, and I hope the final result will satisfy them that they did not completely waste their breath. Whatever flaws future readers may find will be the result of my own stubbornness; they will have already been pointed out to me by Ronan Fanning (whose remarks were particularly exhaustive and knowledgeable), Liam Hourican, James McGuire, Desmond Williams, and the other readers whom I thank elsewhere.

It would have been churlish to include my friend Oliver Snoddy, of the National Museum, simply in his professional capacity or as a first reader (both of which functions he fulfilled with remarkable dedication). I came to rely heavily on him for guidance at every stage of research and composition, and his knowledge of the complex affairs leading up to the insurrection was a crucible in which to test my assertions and opinions. We differed often, but not on important issues. Were it not to cast me in an unlikely rôle, I should call him Laegh to my Cuchulainn.

Tony Clare and my brother Owen suggested titles I found quite unusable; at the opposite pole, I enjoyed the moral support of Dermot Fenlon, Deirdre McMahon, Virginia Connolly and Neasa MacErlean.

In order to get some writing done, it proved necessary to quit Dublin occasionally. Sean and Rosemarie Mulcahy lent me their beautiful cottage in Wicklow for the purpose; I only hope they realize how close the book came to being dedicated to Clara Bridge.

My mother began to prepare the ground long before I came to Dublin, and provided constant support and encouragement at every stage. She sacrificed an immeasurable amount of her time, which would otherwise have been spent on her work on Yeats. I thank her not only for her selflessness, but also for all she taught me about the language she speaks so beautifully and the literature she knows and loves so well. Like her, my father advised me on my research, and read the text piecemeal as it was written; he did his very considerable best to prevent my losing an appreciation of historical context. He also provided the title. I shall always be grateful to both of my parents for the love, help and intellectual stimulation I have always received from them.

My husband, John Mattock, an Englishman, had never heard of Patrick Pearse when he met me first. He gave up a full six months to research with me, organize my complicated life pleasantly and improve my often erratic and impatient prose. He learned a lot about Ireland and came to love it. He gave me courage to continue with a project which had grown unexpectedly to frightening proportions. This book is dedicated to him.

Bridget Foley typed the manuscript with skill and speed, in the face of fearful odds.

Patrick Cosgrave and Giles Gordon persuaded me to take on the project in the first place. My publishers have been patient throughout. Kevin Crossley-Holland was always encouraging; my subeditor, Peter Day, weeded out many inconsistencies in the book and became a friend in the process.

Lastly, I give thanks to those of my ex-colleagues in the British Post Office without whose efforts on my behalf I might never have had the time to write this book.

For permission to quote material or publish photographs, I wish to thank the following (in addition to those already acknowledged above): Mrs Desmond Ryan; Senator M. B. Yeats; Miss Anne Yeats; Macmillan, London and Basingstoke.

R.D.E.

PREFACE

Patrick Pearse has been a contentious figure in Irish politics for over sixty years. Discussion of him has borne little relation to the facts of his life, since until very recently there were virtually no manuscripts available on which to base an interpretation. Ten years ago I hoped to make him the subject of my MA thesis, but had to give up through paucity of sources. With the deaths, in recent years, of many of his contemporaries, a great deal of material has come to light which made it possible to attempt a full biography. Furthermore, the political climate in Ireland now leaves room for hope that Pearse's admirers and detractors will be equally prepared to view him more objectively. The Irish have always tended to impose on their patriots, posthumously if necessary, impossibly high standards. (One historian has drawn the parallel with Caesar's wife.) To suggest that Casement was homosexual, or Tone amorous, has been to undermine all their beliefs and achievements. I hope that the original material in this book will show that Pearse, like them, was a human being, with considerable virtues, and faults to be seen in context. I have been uneasily aware while writing this book that some of my observations may cause pain to those who have a great reverence for the man: I can only hope that they will accept that I have tried to present a fair picture of a complex personality.

The variations on Pearse's surname which appear throughout the text may cause some confusion. The family name was spelled "Pearse", but many contemporaries were more familiar with other spellings of the name, so he appears variously as "Pierce", "Pierse" and "Pearce" in records, correspondence and reminiscences. I have avoided the [*sic*] convention in this and other matters.

Quotes followed by an asterisk are those which I have translated from Irish.

CHAPTER ONE

BEGINNINGS

I JAMES AND MARGARET

Patrick Pearse's father, James, was born in 1839 into an artisan family in Bloomsbury. With his two brothers, William and Henry, he lived with a free-thinking father and devout Unitarian mother in two rooms and a garret. Later, reminiscing about his early life, he would admonish his children: "'You must not forget the garret!' ... pretending that his susceptibilities were hurt if we left that important addition to their *ménage* out of consideration."[1]

James's father was a composition-maker, later a picture-framer, who spent his leisure hours constructing intricate and beautiful objects out of wood. In later years he visited his son and grandchildren in Dublin: "a little old white-bearded man, quizzical and original, who spent all his time making bird-cages of rare woods, and carving them exquisitely; he left us about twenty of them when he went back again to England."[2]

The family was happy, it seems, although very poor. While the boys were still young, circumstances forced a move to Birmingham. The children went to work, William in a gun factory, Henry at picture-framing and James, only eight years old, in a chain factory. While his brothers stayed at the same trades all their lives, James was more restless. He loathed the chain factory, and for some years he changed jobs regularly. After evening classes in drawing, he found release for his artistic aspirations as a sculptor's apprentice.

Despite his lack of schooling, James Pearse had a fierce appetite for knowledge. His only formal education had been at Sunday School, which he quit in disgust at the inadequate answers to his acute questions. He became an atheist in reaction to this experience, but he never ceased to read and question and the library he built up in his more prosperous years betrayed a wide interest in comparative religions, as well as literature, history and politics, the more usual diet of the self-educated.

As he grew up, the Gothic revival was in full flood, and he rode the wave to become a stone carver—a flourishing trade when no church or public building was complete without its ornate marble front or frieze. There is no record of his decision to leave England, but it was presumably out of economic necessity. Dublin firms were recruiting English talent, and James Pearse, still in his teens, went to Ireland.

Ireland offered exciting possibilities. Catholic Emancipation had increased the prosperity of middle-class Catholics in the cities and had brought some Catholic control of local government. A boom in church building was under way, and Irish taste adapted itself readily to the importation of flamboyant styles of building and decoration, which were expensive in the skilled labour of craftsmen in marble, stone, wood and wrought iron.

Halfway through the century, a community of English craftsmen had sprung up around Great Brunswick Street, Townsend Street and Westland Row, a hard-working commercial quarter between the quays at the Liffey's mouth and the lawns of Trinity College. James Pearse joined this community as a journeyman at the firm of Harrison in Great Brunswick Street, and by the early 1870s had set up, with another English immigrant, the firm of Neill and Pearse. He married early—a young girl, Emily Susanna Fox, who in 1864, at the age of eighteen, gave birth to their daughter Mary Emily, and later to two other children, of whom only one, James Vincent, survived infancy. They lived in a small terraced house off Great Brunswick Street (South Great Clarence Street—now Macken Street). While the children were still very young, about 1870, the family was received into the Catholic church. When, later in that decade, certain Catholic stone carvers were objecting on religious and racial grounds to church-work being given to him, James asked Father Pius Devine to testify to his conversion. Father Pius responded not only with a testament to that conversion but with a warmth which demonstrated the impact made on him by James's energetic mind:

> I recollect well your sensible objections and difficulties, whilst you were under instructions and the clearheaded manner in which you saw the answers as soon as they were proposed to you by me. Indeed I don't think I ever received a convert—and I received a good many—with whose disposition before and after reception I was so pleased with as I was with yours.
>
> I wish you every success in your business and if you continue to give in future the satisfaction you have given in the past I have no doubt you will. If anything comes in my way to suit you, you shall certainly have the preference.

James used the letter in his defence, and endorsed it: "Please be certain to return this, as I hold it to be very precious."[3]

The marriage of James and Emily was not a happy one; James claimed in later years that the infant's death was due to its mother's neglect. Emily died of an inflammation of the spine in 1876, at the age of 30, and James, now 36, moved with his children into the house of a friend, John McGloughlin.

For an artisan too poor to afford a housekeeper and nurse, remarriage was an imperative, and James was not long in finding a suitable wife. He had by now separated from his partner Neill, and had leased premises at 27 Great Brunswick Street. Every morning, on his way to work, he would stop at a stationer's shop to buy a newspaper from a pleasant, polite nineteen-year-old girl called Margaret Brady.[4]

It was not an untroubled courtship. James was an ambitious man of unusual intelligence, and personal reserve. Margaret was warm, impulsive, traditional in her Catholicism and very simple in outlook. Their love letters were often an attempt to reconcile head and heart;[5] Margaret poured out her love, and craved reassurance.

> My Dearest Mr Pearse
> ... I do be watching every post during the day to see if you are thinking of me ...
> I would like you to write them [letters] more affectionately.
> [And later:]
> I don't know if you are so anxious to see me as I am you ... I think every day a week thinking when I shall see you.

[James did his best:] "It strikes me I have not the power of writing so affectionately as you have but you know you must take the will for the deed sometimes. Any how I think you must know that I love you dearly and sincerely and I tell you, that you must not be doubting and fancying all sorts of things." He suffered from a badly infected throat throughout much of the courtship, and Margaret offered the best consolation at her disposal.

> My own Darling
> I trust and hope through the goodness of Almight God you will be all right in a few days I promise you I will pray to Him for you ... I will pray to the Blessed Virgin to intercede with her Divine Son for you and ask of him to restore your health to you for your dear children's sake and also darling for mine.

James's Catholicism was more cerebral, and he reacted impatiently:

"... my awful and most infernal throat, it is no use saying please God this nor please God that it never will be well and there is an end of it. It appears to me if he is pleased in the matter at all it is to keep it bad".

But even if James was conscious of the intellectual gulf between them, his letters displayed again and again his gratitude for her enthusiastic affection. Her attractions were obvious.

> The other day one of the men said he was worried to see me so poorly and then added jokingly, you want some one to take care of you ... I mean a wife, perhaps I said you know some angel in the form of a woman who would have compassion upon me. I don't know much about Angels said he, "but I have seen in at the paper shop below a grand looking young woman with dark hair and eyes, no nonsence about her plump and rosey she seems homely yet bright and full of life, that is the sort of woman I should go in for."
>
> See here I could not stand it any longer. I had to walk away wondering what he would say if he could only read what I had in my pocket.

He could not resist teasing Margaret over her religion, her most vulnerable spot. "... I do not mean to embrace you more than ninety times and kiss you a trifle over twice as many times during the whole afternoon, I hope it will not rain, but that the Gods will smile upon us. And I promise you his reverence shall have no cause to chide you when next you seek his ghostly pressence." His desire for simple domestic happiness was as strong as her own.

> I am shure the happiest part of my life, was spent with the "Old folks at Home", but that is all past and gone my dear Mother gone to rest and the old house we all loved so well filled with strangers who in their turn will have to give way to others and so it will be till the end of time I think it must be a great blessing and consolation to be permitted to pass through this world of change, with one who will be all to you at all times, one whom you can turn to when the world frowns. A house in which you can find peace and rest.

Despite some parental opposition to a quick marriage (which Margaret bitterly resented, but James quite understood) they were married within a year of his first wife's death.

Margaret's family was very different in tradition from James's, but materially there was not much to choose between them. She came of Catholic County Meath stock; two of her ancestors had died during the 1798 rising. Her grandfather, who could speak only Irish, was forced by the 1848 famine to move to Dublin with his five sons and two daughters; the boys became hackney-cab drivers, and the girls went into service. Three of the boys, including Margaret's father, Patrick, later bought some land with horses and cattle, but this new prosperity did not secure a leisured life for his two surviving children, Margaret and Catherine. When Margaret married James she was living in one of three small "cottages" belonging to her father (by now a "coal factor") in a tenement area off the North Strand. A widower with reasonable prospects, even with two children, was a good match. He was now calling himself a sculptor rather than a stone carver. The distinction was a fine one, especially in a century more ready to accept an overlapping between artisan and artist than is our own. A craftsman who carved to an architect's designs was a stone carver; if the design was his own, he was a sculptor.

James did have William Morris-like aspirations; in his son's words, he "entered on the hopeless task of trying to make Irish church-builders recognise what was beautiful and religious in sculpture".[6] Indeed, his involvement with the Gothic revival seems to have run deeper than mere acceptance of contemporary artistic convention. Among the artist-craftsmen of his acquaintance, it was he, even in his early days, "who had in him (atheist though he was) more of the religious mind of the middle ages than any other". It would be an exaggeration, however, to claim that these more high-flown concerns set him quite apart from the rest of his circle; many of his friends dabbled in the fine arts. On more than one occasion the infant Patrick was called in to model nude for them.

But family responsibilities kept James's feet on the ground. He undertook what design commissions were available, but much of the business that came his way was in the realization of others' ideas, and in stock carvings of established popularity and traditional design. He never lost his yearning, though, for creative fulfilment, and even allowing for filial pride, Patrick struck a sad note when he said, "If ever in an Irish church you find, amid a wildnerness of bad sculpture, something good and true and lovingly finished, you may be sure that it was carved by my father or by one of his pupils."

Margaret can have brought no dowry to speak of, and James was yet far from wealthy. He already had a lease on 27 Great Brunswick Street and the family moved back into three of its rooms; apart from the workroom in the basement, the rest of the house was initially sub-let. In that house, within six years, Margaret bore James four children.

II Childhood

Although the family lived "over the shop", their existence was comfortable. As business improved, less of the house was let to tenants. Socially, the family unit was self-sufficient to a large degree; James Pearse had the occasional visitor, Margaret none, other than her relatives. Although the two sets of children got on well, the step children did not stay long. Emily married Alfred, the son of James's friend John McGloughlin, when Patrick was just old enough to be a page at a big wedding. James Vincent married, had a family, and lived out his days in England, whence he maintained friendly relations with his father's new family.

Margaret's children were a mixed bunch. All the will seems to have gone into the two eldest, Margaret and Patrick, while the young pair, Willie and Mary Bridget (later Gaelicized to Brigid), were natural followers. Margaret emerges from family reminiscences as a bossy elder sister, who was not initially inclined to bolster Patrick's ego as did the other children. Patrick was an intelligent, industrious boy, accorded by his mother all the deference due to an elder son in an Irish Catholic home. Willie, two years his junior, imitated his brother in word and deed, although he had neither the intelligence nor the aptitude to emulate him academically. He was more gifted artistically than Patrick, and was therefore from an early age marked out as the natural inheritor of the family business. Mary Brigid was delicate, neurotic in later years, and a largely passive influence on Patrick—she was a willing audience for his readings, recitations and other youthful performances.

Patrick had an exceptionally vivid imagination. Mary Brigid's reminiscences and Patrick's own autobiographical sketch are filled with accounts of childhood games providing heroic rôles for Patrick—Patrick riding his wooden horse into battle, or in search of the Holy Grail. Patrick turning the living-room into his own ship or his own kingdom. Patrick receiving a present of a gigantic scrap book and living its contents:

> I began straight away to people our house with the creatures of that book, and to see myself going into the perils that were pictured there. This was my way with every book that was read to me; with every picture that I saw; with every story or

> song that I heard. I saw myself doing or suffering all the things that were dared or suffered in the book, or story, or song, or picture: toiling across deserts in search of lost cities; cast into dungeons by wicked kings; starved and flogged by merciless masters; racked with Guy Fawkes; roasted on a gridiron with St Laurence; deprived of my sight with the good Kent. When I heard of anyone's sorrow or of anyone's triumphs, I suffered the sorrow and enjoyed the triumph myself.[1]

As he grew older, he began to write plays for the junior members of the family, including a couple of Brady cousins. All these plays were in high romantic vein, full of love, jealousy and death. Willie, Mary Brigid and the cousins were a docile group, always happy to take direction, and flattered at the attention they were getting. Reading, writing and performing for his captive audience preoccupied Patrick to the exclusion of less earnest childish dabblings.

The children seem never to have had friends outside the family group. Their mother had aspirations to gentility which would have made contact with the children who haunt wharf and warehouse unlikely, and to a child as romantic as Patrick, family life must have been suffocatingly dull—barren of any fodder for his voracious imagination. His father, though kindly disposed towards his children, was too reserved to affect his son's development to any great degree: "My father came up to our room only once or twice in the day, and at evening. He was big, with broad shoulders that were a little round. He was very silent, and spoke only once or twice during the course of a meal; breaking some reverie to say something kind to my mother or something funny to one of us."[2] His mother, though a naturally happy woman, could flare into panics of distress which were made the more intense by her husband's stolid sense—she felt estranged from him at such times. After Patrick's birth, there was a rift, caused by an undisclosed indiscretion of Margaret's.

> ... God above knows if I am not a true and devoted wife and always will be no matter what comes or goes dearest Jim what in under Heaven am I to do darling with my unfortunate mind ... nothing will ease me now but death alone and only for me poor little ones I would be freely satisfied to go if my peace was made with God Almighty but alas it is not dear Jim I hope you are not angry with me about that afair but you must not mention it to me for I shall go deranged to think such a thing ever to be said about me but moreover darling to live knowing you are not fond enough to be jealous I wish to God I had that

to say of you if so I would think less of this afair ...[3]

Although their later letters were again affectionate, the difference in their temperaments could not be bridged. James became increasingly involved in his self-education, and left his children for most purposes to his wife's care.

Patrick's devoted mother cosseted his body and his ego, but offered no mental stimulation. The only one to bring news of a broader, more exciting world was his mother's octogenarian Aunt Margaret, who would tell him stories and sing him songs. She had spent her childhood in the country, and was a link with County Meath culture, and a revelation. As she related half-remembered tales about Tone, Emmet and the Fenians, she was planting in him attitudes and beliefs which were to remain with him for life. Her songs similarly gripped his imagination, songs of death and exile, mostly about Irishmen, many about Napoleon. Writing of her in 1906 he said: "She loved all who had striven for Ireland from the shadowy heroes of old to those of her own blood and ours who had died in '98 or been imprisoned in '67. Her heart had a corner for the Fianna of Fionn and another for the Fenians of John O'Mahony."[4] Even allowing for the effect of time upon his memory, there can be no doubt but that this old woman exerted a lasting spell on her rapt great-nephew. He could now stock his day-dreams with "real" people, but he was young, and for all the subtlety this lent the dreams, they might as well have been based round cut-outs of saints and wicked kings. And in these day-dreams he still found a prominent place for himself.

Apart from the visits of Great-Aunt Margaret and excursions to the house of Brady relatives, life in Brunswick Street provided only self-made diversions. One such was a pastime which was to persist into adult life—that of dressing up as a beggar or an old woman and wandering about the streets. It was not an uncommon game among children of that period, and Patrick enjoyed playing parts; his private incognito forays, when he was grown up, around the streets of Dublin, and, on occasion, Connemara, were no more than an extension of this. Apart from his child-like enjoyment of charade, he seems to have had a genuine desire to find out "what it was like" to be a beggar in Dublin or "a man of the road" in the West, and to have believed that he acted these parts convincingly. Mary Brigid describes occasional expeditions of Patrick and Emily's son, Alfred McGloughlin, dressed in old clothes, begging in well-to-do Donnybrook. The disturbing aspect of that image, like that of him going native in Connemara, is that he seems to have been satisfied not only that he was indistinguishable from the genuine article, but that he was experiencing the real life of the people. This respectable youth, who donned old clothes for a few hours before the family tea at six, had little understanding of life's realities as they were for the majority of his fellow-Dubliners, the unpalatable realities of the stinking slums, the realities of survival crowding out all concern for the glory of the Gael. And in Connemara, where life on the land was ugly and hard, and a knowledge of English offered a rare prospect of prosperity for the next generation, Pearse's vagabondings seem to have taught him little about harsh economics.

In 1884, when Patrick was five, the family moved to a modest but comfortable house in Newbridge Avenue, Sandymount. The accommodation in Brunswick Street had become a little cramped, with four children and a growing business; the stone-carving trade was thriving, and James had taken his foreman, Edmund Sharp, into partnership, drawing for himself the very respectable salary of £250 a year.[5] The previous year had seen James's sole excursion into print.

Thomas Maguire, professor of moral philosophy, fellow of Trinity College, had written a provocative pamphlet called "England's duty to Ireland, as Plain to a Loyal Irish Roman Catholic". The gist of his argument was that the Irish question could be answered by "consistent enforcement of the law, and the promotion of education". The Parnellites were "the most degraded section of the inhabitants of the British Isles.... The vast preponderance of intelligence and wealth is in the hands of the Protestants," he asserted. Home Rule would lead to the "boycotting and massacre of the loyalists". The national police would be "composed of the local idlers and village ruffians". The "corner-boy", wanting another glass "of protected red-headed whiskey", would "only have to discover that the umbrella of some inoffensive person is of English manufacture, and that person, if inoffensive, will be stoned and kicked to death". Strict law enforcement would solve "The Problem" because "no people improve more under steady discipline than the Irish". Engagingly absurd though this bluster might seem now, in the sensitive days of 1886 Maguire was successful in his determination to be offensive. Like other colleagues from Trinity College, notably professors Atkinson and Mahaffy in later years, he contrived to infuriate moderate men, among whom was numbered James Pearse.

According to family tradition, the Maguire pamphlet so enraged this normally taciturn man that he cried, "I'll teach the bloody fellow a lesson. He ought to rinse out his mouth." With speed born of righteous indignation, he produced (and published at his own expense) a 20,000 word reply—four times as long as the Maguire pamphlet—taking up every point and answering it at great length. The central argument was that of a solid constitutionalist of Parnellite sympathies. "England's duty to Ireland ... IS TO GIVE LAWFUL EFFECT TO THE WILL OF THE PEOPLE CONSTITUTIONALLY ASCERTAINED AND EXPOUNDED BY THOSE WHO ARE LEGALLY AND BY BRITISH LAW CHOSEN TO REPRESENT THEM." He concluded that Home Rule was inevitable.

Where Maguire's pamphlet is bigoted and boisterous, James Pearse's is fairminded and rather dull; he was the best kind of decent Englishman. There are extensive and rather self-conscious quotes from his very personal pantheon—Polybius, Gordon, John Bright, Gladstone and the Irish historian D'Arcy McGee, but he showed a concern for facts, and a desire to establish objective truth. For all its rambling prolixity, the pamphlet makes it clear that James knew a great deal about open-mindedness and objectivity.

James had in no way eschewed his nationality. In a letter defending himself against the attempts to have Pearse and Sharp blacked from Catholic churches, he pointed out that he and his partner were both converts to Catholicism, but refused to apologize for things he could not change.

> I am bound to admit that we are both guilty of being Englishmen, but as God in His wisdom thought fit to call us into existance upon the other side of the water, and as His will was done in the matter, and not ours; We think there needs no apology from us on that head ... although we are not Irishmen, and I avow honestly, we do not feel ourselves agrieved thereby; indeed I know we should earn your contempt if we said otherwise.[6]

He maintained a close interest in English politics, and became a supporter of Charles Bradlaugh, freethinker and radical MP. In 1888 James Pearse published, again at his own expense, a dialogue between Bradlaugh and the leader of the Marxist Social Democratic Federation, Henry Hyndman, in which Bradlaugh clearly got the better of the argument. (The essence of his philosophy was embodied in the motto of Pearse and Sharp—"*Self Reliance: Labor omnia vincit*".) Bradlaugh argued for a property-owning democracy against Hyndman's call for class warfare and the use of force. James advertised the pamphlet in *The Freethinker* and the *Agnostic Journal*. While he presumably kept up the practices of his adopted Church—business pressures made that necessary—the depth of his faith by the late 1880s is doubtful (he had invested £50 in the Freethought Publication committee),[7] but it is inconceivable that his wife, always a good Catholic, would permit the children's orthodox devotion to be undermined. It is easier, indeed, to see her growing increasingly protective of her brood, shading them from Papa's baleful spiritual influence.

The two pamphlets represent James's only forays into politics. Most of his energies went into the business. His reputation as a skilled and reliable architectural sculptor was growing, helped on its way by a first class award from the 1882 Dublin Exhibition, where Messrs Pearse and Sharp had proudly displayed exhibit 959 in the new Rotunda building: "High Altar, in statuary and foreign coloured marbles, sculptured subjects representing the Birth, Crucifixion and Resurrection; the carving on shields, the passion of Christ."[8]

He saved money from his income, and invested modestly in stocks and shares. He inherited from his father an interest in a Birmingham shop, and paid the mortgage: he had plans drawn up for restructuring the shop, and seems for a time to have contemplated moving back to Birmingham.[9] But whether because of family pressure, or the professional difficulties of abandoning a well-established business, the project never came off. Besides providing a good material existence for his family, James confined his attentions to his children to occasional expensive presents, and in their reminiscences he is a shadowy figure. Dominant though he was intellectually he was too distant from Patrick to counter-balance the narrow and often maudlin nationalism with which the boy was being fed through his maternal influences.

III SCHOOL

Patrick Pearse's first school was a private one, run by a Mrs Murphy. He was there for four years, until in 1891 he and Willie, eleven and nine years old, were sent to the Christian Brothers' School, Westland Row. Willie and Patrick were devoted. Family tradition tells of Patrick successfully defying teachers at both his schools when they attempted to chastise his brother. Certainly his attitude from the time Willie could walk into harm's way seems to have been one of great protectiveness. Patrick was idolized from the start, and his enthusiasms accepted uncritically—Willie acted as a sympathetic audience, and joined in all his brother's activities. In return for this, Patrick gave to Willie, from the outset, his complete confidence and affection. "As a boy he was my only playmate; as a man he has been my only intimate friend. We have done and suffered much together, and we have shared together a few deep joys."[1] Later acquaintances were to be classed as "friends" certainly, but Willie's position in Patrick's hierarchy of affections points to a deficiency in the language: comrade, confidant, intimate, support, mirror, doppelgänger, Willie satisfied all these needs, and nobody else came so close to Patrick.

The Christian Brothers' School, then, was not to have any marked effect on Patrick's emotional development; socially, he made no advances. His leisure activities were still almost totally confined to home, where, until the Intermediate examinations began to preoccupy him, he continued writing and producing plays, and began giving lectures to his assembled family, illustrated by an expensive magic lantern provided by his father. According to Mary Brigid, he was the only member of the family to perform on these occasions, and the audience appears to have been wholly admiring.

There is no record of why the Pearse brothers were sent to the Christian Brothers' School, but it was in keeping both with the social status of the family, and its image of itself. Although they were comfortably off, they were, by virtue of James Pearse's trade, anchored firmly in the lower-middle class. Genteel, they had now a firm hold on respectability and material prosperity, but no taste yet for further social climbing. Unsurprising then, that the boys should be sent to a school with a reputation for the best examination results. Sean O'Faolain's description of this secondary school, run by the Presentation Brothers, holds equally for the Pearses' new school:

> It provided some sort of religious education, and it was a useful cramming factory for the sons of less well-heeled parents—clerks, civil servants, lay teachers and the like. In this latter it sometimes succeeded to remarkable effect when it got hold of specially brilliant students. It was also the useful gateway through which a small number of youths entered the local college ... there—if they were industrious—to become doctors, engineers, secondary teachers and the like. The majority went into banks, insurance and the railways ...[2]

O'Faolain goes on to discuss the facts the teaching Brothers had to face under the empire—Irish education, like so much of Irish life, was "an imitation of something else, somewhere else", and it was necessary to shape pupils to fit the pattern if they were to succeed. The pupils at Westland Row were a mixture of the poor and prosperous—but they had all been sent to the Brothers to qualify for the best career possible. The teaching methods were dictated by the omnipresent spectre of the Intermediate examinations. A future biographer of Patrick Pearse, Desmond Ryan, who attended Westland Row in 1907, described the tyranny of the examination system: "... to gain results under the Intermediate system every subject had to be learned by heart, with the result that the majority of victims hated the sight of books for the rest of their days, although they mastered every text and knew every subject amazingly well until the examination lists gave the signal that Shakespeare and Milton and Racine were well and truly 'done' for ever".[3] The Brothers had no option but to *get results* in the most efficient way possible, and maximum efficiency was incompatible with explorations of the by-ways of the curriculum, or the patient inculcation of a love of books. Patrick Pearse was in later years to denounce with personal bitterness the Intermediate system and to describe it, with justice, as "instruction without education".

> It grinds day and night; it obeys immutable and predetermined laws; it is as devoid of understanding, of sympathy, of imagination as is any other piece of machinery that performs an appointed task. Into it is fed all the raw material in Ireland: it seizes upon it inexorably and rends and compresses and remoulds; and what it cannot refashion after the regulation pattern it ejects with all the likeness of its former self crushed from it, a bruised and shapeless thing, thereinafter accounted waste.[4]

The machine did not eject Pearse. He was an intelligent, exceptionally industrious boy, who adapted successfully to the system, whatever his later reservations.

Young Pearse became more and more introspective during his time at secondary school. Perhaps to be closer to the school, the family had moved back to the business address, but Patrick still did not mix with his fellows outside school, and little enough even inside. He was probably not encouraged to play in the streets, even if he had had the inclination to do so; Great Brunswick Street was on the edge of a red-light district. Not for the young Pearses the season's crazes for handball, marbles, spinning-tops, conkers and kites. Patrick preferred to read at home, while Willie spent some of his time learning about the mysteries of the workshop.[5]

Patrick rarely took part in games at school, though he had some enthusiasm for boxing and occasionally played football. Even allowing for its reverential tone, a reminiscence of one of his class mates is revealing—there was a more sturdy temperament beneath the reserve:

> Paddy passed through school a grave, sweet, silent boy. He never joined in the ordinary games at playtime. He often climbed up on the high window-ledge of the school-room and sat there reading. He did, however, play some school football. On one occasion we were challenged to play a "frelden match" (I remember well the spelling of the challenge) by a team of working boys from City Quay. Pearse was on the school team. It was anything but a friendly match and we schoolboys were kicked and bruised and badly beaten and my recollection is that only five or six of us were able to continue to the end. Among this few I well remember Paddy who played with a fierce tenacity we had not given him credit for. He was hot-tempered too. At another match he missed the ball badly and someone sitting on the ditch laughed at him. He left the ball, walked across and struck the lad on the ditch a resounding blow on the jaw.[6]

Even at home he began to devote himself almost full-time to school work, and grew increasingly withdrawn. He sat the four grades of the Intermediate—preparatory, junior, middle and senior—between 1893 and 1896, with results, as he later said himself, "respectable and never brilliant", though he managed to win an exhibition every year.

He was fortunate in some of his teachers. At a time when Irish was rarely taught in the schools, the Christian Brothers were almost alone in giving the language space in the curriculum—although, of course, in preparation for the inevitable Intermediate papers. Of Patrick's teachers at least two, Brother Maunsell, a native Irish speaker from County Kerry, and Brother Craven, with whom Pearse kept up friendly relations after he left school, communicated respectively confidence in spoken Irish and enthusiasm for literature to their pupil. Brother Maunsell's "vivid personality, understanding himself and his class"[7] won the affection of many of his pupils. Patrick was one of the four signatories to an elaborate illuminated address presented to him when he left Westland Row.

He began to learn Irish in 1893 and from then on showed more interest in it than in any other subject, although he continued to do well in English, French and Latin. The examination papers he sat, and the curriculum built around them, emphasize the deficiencies of the education he was receiving. He was reading Scott, Milton, Pope and Macaulay, true, but only for regurgitation, never for analysis. Caesar, Livy, bowdlerized Ovid and Horace yielded interminable passages for him to translate, but he was never taught the tools of literary appreciation. Racine and Corneille suffered the same fate. In Irish, rote translation from edited texts was the only relief from endless grammar, and history was endless dates and battles. Nonetheless, Pearse emerged from the system with a regard for the English classics and a passionate love of the Irish language and its literature. His affection for English literature had grown largely from his traditional position as reciter of the family—declamatory passages from Shakespeare and Milton were standard fare in parlour entertainments. Irish was, however, the focus of all those romantic yearnings which had been aroused by his aunt, whose death during this period must have made her medicine even more potent. When he first began to learn Irish, he said later, "The turf fire was back and the dead voice was speaking to us again."[8] Stories which she had told him were in the school texts; he could now read about Oisin and Diarmaid and Grainne. His own private researches, at the National Library, stimulated his appetite still further. There he read Douglas Hyde's collections of Irish folk tales. "Here we were in the very heart of the land of mystery and romance on which so many years before that kindly hand had raised the curtain, bidding us look with eyes of childish wonder ... all the time we were learning to realise ourselves as a child of our Mother [i.e. Eire] and the heir of a tradition."

Pearse's school had had neither time nor inclination to equip him with a critical faculty—no more would university or law school. He read and continued to read folk tales and legends with seriousness, conviction, and that same childish wonder of years before, and took them literally, in a way which would have shaken the sophisticated and subtle Dr Hyde.

For a book-prize won on Senior Grade Intermediate, in 1896, he chose *For the Tongue of the Gael*, by Thomas Flannery, whose name was familiar to him as the Intermediate examiner in Irish, and the editor of his school text, *The Lay of Oisin in the Land of Youth*. His chosen prize was a book of essays and reviews of Irish literature, and was a comprehensive introduction to the work being done by contemporary Irish scholars. Later, Pearse was to say: "Irish the lad had known in a way for several years previously, but the spirit of the Irish Revival first blew in upon him from the pages of Tomas O Flannghaile."[9] His enthusiasm for Flannery did not fade. He corresponded with him for years, and paid tribute to him publicly as late as 1907. This was the influence that was to lead him to the fledgling Gaelic League, which he joined in October 1896.[10]

He was now sixteen years old, free of the demands of the Intermediate and looking round for new worlds to conquer. He had been appointed a pupil-teacher of Irish at Westland Row, and was trying to decide on a career. He was too young for university, and was not to sit the Matriculation Examination of the Royal University until June 1898. Meanwhile Willie was still a pupil, and was having examination troubles. He had passed his preparatory examination in 1895, failing in Latin and algebra, scraping a pass in Irish (or Celtic as it was termed by the Intermediate Board), and not distinguishing himself in any other subject. He was now studying for the Junior examination.

Patrick had no exams ahead of him for two years, and—a great novelty—had time on his hands. Inevitably he was looking for an opportunity to indulge his two passions—performing before an appreciative audience, and Irish language and literature. At the school debating society he had gone in for what a fellow-student described as the "grand manner" in speaking, a style which from then on would characterize all his oratorical endeavours. With a handful of his contemporaries from school (including Eamon [Edward] O'Neill, who was as close a friend as Patrick ever made), he set up a society with the grandiose title of the New Ireland Literary Society. Whether they were unaware of the existence of the National Literary Society, led by such luminaries as Dr Douglas Hyde and Mr W. B. Yeats, or whether they were intending to offer a challenge to it by concentrating on Gaelic literature is unclear. If the title of the new society was pretentious, its launching was even more so. A ponderous circular letter was sent round to suitable contemporaries:

> Sir,
>
> It is an inexplicable fact that Dublin, which must necessarily contain many young men of ability and culture, should possess fewer literary and debating societies than any city of equal importance in Great Britain. In view of this, it is contemplated to establish a new literary and debating society, of a high-class, yet popular, nature: and we, on behalf of those who have initiated the project, beg to request your presence at a meeting which will be held at the Star and Garter Hotel, D'Olier Street, on Tuesday next, December 1st, at 7.30 p.m.
>
> To dilate on the usefulness of a really good and well managed

literary Society is needless, as there can be no two opinions respecting it.

It is confidently expected, then, that you will see your way to co-operate; and that the new society will be in full working order in the course of a few weeks.[11]

EDWARD O'NEILL
PATRICK H. PEARSE

Pearse was president of this small group, and he applied himself to his duties with his accustomed seriousness. He contributed frequently to the society's manuscript journal, where he wrote some poems which were no better and no worse than might have been expected from a sixteen-year-old of self-conscious talent and romantic bent. The only recorded sample is a translation of verses from his school text, Diarmaid and Grainne. The first two stanzas ran:

O, white-toothed one, the bright, the fair,
Thou of the curling dusk dark hair!
Alas! thine own strong spear is red
With thy brave blood so sadly shed.

Alas! the boar tusk's venomed flash,
Alas! the sore sharp gaping gash,
Alas! the malice of thy foe—
The falsely fair hath laid thee low.[12]

The members of the society used to meet weekly in the Star and Garter Hotel, there to read and recite from, and lecture each other on, Gaelic literature. They also held occasional social evenings—"high class, yet popular". A printed programme for a *conversazione* held in April 1897 gives the flavour of one. Dominated by Pearses, it included such items as:

1. Overture: "Killarney" ... Miss M. Pearse
6. Recitation: "The Celtic Tongue" ... Mr E. O'Neill
10. Recitation: "Mark Anthony's Oration" ... Mr P. H. Pearse
12. Duet: "Whispers from Erin" ... The Misses Pearse
21. The Ghost Scene from Hamlet: Hamlet: Mr P. H. Pearse, Marcellus: Mr E. O'Neill.

Accompanist: Miss M. B. Pearse[13]

Their president was more prolific than any of them. He read three lengthy papers to the society between March 1897 and January 1898—papers he was to publish in the spring of 1898.

They were the product of an industrious and ambitious schoolboy, and they still read that way. The first lecture, "Gaelic Prose Literature", is based largely on his Irish school textbooks, Flannery's work and a sketchy but precocious acquaintance with contemporary work of the Irish revivalists. It is derivative, and in putting forward the case for the glories of Gaelic literature he relies on assertion rather than logical argument, but for a seventeen year old it was an impressive production.

The second lecture, "The Intellectual Future of the Gael", has the same faults, and betrays in addition a juvenile's lack of understanding of contemporary literature: "... at the present moment no literature is being produced in Europe, or in the world, worthy of the name". The written word, to Pearse, must "make us better, holier, happier", but "the intellectual and literary tastes of the world have been carried away by a craving for the unreal, for the extravagant, the monstrous, the immoral". This narrowness of outlook, encouraged by his puritanical education, was to be modified somewhat as he grew older; for the moment, his love of literature began and ended with the heroic. The writers of the 1880s and '90s—men like Wilde, Zola, Henry James, Shaw, Chekhov, Maupassant—he presumably discounted as decadent. It would take him several years to see any merit in Yeats, and for some time he was not to go beyond the accepted schoolboy greats. Of English novelists he knew little—Dickens was about the mark. Literature to him was about appreciation of nature and hero-worship:

> Closely connected with, and indeed, directly dependent on this love of the Gael for nature, is his capacity for worshipping his heroes. Hero-worship, no doubt, is often carried to extremes; we are prone too frequently to mistake the hero for the cause, to place the man before the principle. But there can be no doubt that hero-worship, in its highest form, is a soul-lifting and ennobling thing. What would the world be without its heroes?

The mission of the Gael was to be the propagation of this spirit.

The third lecture, "The Folk-Songs of Ireland", once again heavily dependent on Flannery, is yet another paean of praise to the glories of the literature of the Gael. "Save the language, and the folk-tale, and the folk-song, and all the treasures accumulated in the folk-mind during three thousand years will be saved also. The cause is a holy one—God grant it may succeed." It was always to be a feature of Pearse's crusades that God was on his side—not only ratifying the Gaelic cause, but participating in its furtherance. Religion was to him an intensely personal matter. He enjoyed all the rituals of the Catholic church, but from the beginning his greatest devotional zeal was reserved for the Holy Week ceremonies and the crucified Christ.[14]

For a man from such a conventional family, with such a conventional education, he was surprisingly independent-minded when it came to the clergy. He had little of the automatic reverence for the priesthood common among his contemporaries. This may have had a great deal to do with the bitterness he and his father shared over the fate of Parnell—to Pearse, Parnell had been betrayed, and this seems to have left him with a somewhat jaundiced attitude to those of the Irish clergy who, he felt, had failed to put their country before conformism. He was only eighteen when he made his first public criticism of the clergy: in a speech to the Central branch of the Gaelic League he is described as "... alluding to the comparatively poor support which the Irish clergy as a body were extending to the movement, and hoping that something would be done on the night of the Oireachtas to point out to them their duty to the National language".[15]

IV The Gaelic League

While Pearse was still edifying his fellow members of the New Ireland Literary Society, he was already a very junior member of the Gaelic League. When he had joined the League, in 1896, it was only three years old. Growing scholarly interest in the language, and the realization that without help it would be dead as a spoken language within a couple of generations, had led many enthusiasts to call for dynamic action. Although since 1877 there had existed a Society for the Preservation of the Irish Language, it had never secured a popular following, and the early 1890s were a propitious time for a new attempt to halt the decline. Parnell was dead, his party had split, and the Irishmen were ready for a new enthusiasm, if there was the leadership there to fire and fuel it. Three men, Douglas Hyde, Eoin (John) MacNeill and Father Eugene O'Growney, provided that leadership when, at MacNeill's instigation, they and a few others founded the Gaelic League in July 1893.

Douglas Hyde was president, figure-head and chief spokesman of the League from 1893 to 1915. His pioneering work in editing Irish poetry had endeared him to all lovers of the language, who knew him by his pen-name—An Craoibhin Aoibhinn—The Delightful Little Branch. (Such pseudonyms were common among

Irish writers; one of the best-known was Beirt Fhear—Two Men—the *nom de plume* of J. J. Doyle.) Hyde gave the movement prestige from the start. He was a Protestant, with a Trinity College doctorate, and then president of the National Literary Society of Ireland. Although only 33 years old, he was cosmopolitan, with a widespread scholarly reputation, and influential friends among the aristocracy and intelligentsia of Ireland. His involvement with the language movement was to bring it from the outset the goodwill of the liberal Protestant establishment and the Irish *literati*. In the words of a jaundiced contemporary, Sean O'Casey, "he was rushing round, shouting in at the Dublin Castle Gates, It's a Gael I am without shame to myself or danger to you".[1]

Father O'Growney on the other hand gave the movement the stamp of clerical respectability. He had been working for years, often almost single-handed, to popularize the Irish language, and had produced a series of simple textbooks which were to sell in their tens of thousands as the popularity of the League spread throughout the country—but his health was suffering from years of overwork, and he had little time left to support the movement.

The third member of the triumvirate, Eoin MacNeill, was its moving force. Without him the Gaelic League could not have survived its early years. Content to work behind the façade of Hyde, he spent the 1890s in heavy drudgery for the Gaelic League, as its secretary, editor of the *Gaelic Journal* (a scholarly periodical which Father O'Growney brought as a dowry to the League), Irish editor of its first official newspaper, *Fainne an Lae* (Dawn), speaker at endless meetings, teacher of Irish classes and member of the inevitable committees. MacNeill was only 26 when the League was founded, and he was to spend the next decade working himself to the brink of exhaustion in its interests, while simultaneously advancing his own academic career.

When Pearse had his first contact with the League, it occupied two small rooms in Dame Street. He seems to have attended a few Irish classes there, and to have had a meeting with Canon Peter O'Leary,[2] a native speaker of Munster Irish, whose extended folk-tale, *Seadna*, was innovatory in its use of the speech of the Irish country people. Pearse began to attend meetings of the Central branch (Coiste Ceanntair) of the League, and by the end of 1897, while he was still only seventeen, he had achieved some prominence. The Central branch was the most vital throughout the League's history: it was also disliked and resented by many elements within the League. It attracted the most enthusiastic of the Dublin Irish revivalists, and so enjoyed a disproportionate representation on the Executive committee of the League. Its members included MacNeill and O'Growney, and for an ambitious youth, it was clearly the place to seek the limelight. And yet it was not a superficially glamorous world; Sean O'Casey, a life-long member, paints an acerbic and accurate picture of the Dublin Gaelic Leaguers: "... respectable, white-collared, trim-suited Gaelic Leaguers, snug in their selected branches, living rosily in Whitehall, Drumcondra, Rathgar, Donnybrook, and all the other nicer habitations of the city".[3]

In November 1897, at the Central branch annual general meeting,

> Mr P. Pierce proposed and Mr J. J. Kenny seconded: "That this General Meeting of the Gaelic League consider it advisable, for the purpose of rendering the weekly public meetings more popular and attractive than they have hitherto been, that the Executive Committee should at the Commencement of each session draw up a programme of original papers, readings, etc. to be delivered by the members during the session, and further that the General Meeting, recognizing the necessity of bringing the Irish language movement before the public in a *prominent and attractive* form, consider that the holding during the winter months of a series of lectures and concerts under the auspices of the Gaelic League would greatly tend to promote popular interest in and enthusiasm for the objects of the League, and that the Executive Committee be instructed to take steps for the carrying out of this proposal."[4]

The motion was carried, and Pearse was allowed to follow through, for the Executive committee invited him to sit on the sub-committee appointed to implement the programme. He was thus a prime mover of an important stage in popularizing Gaelic League meetings, which were for many years to add a new dimension to the social life of towns and villages throughout Ireland. It was characteristic of Pearse that he should recommend such a method of promoting the language. He was naturally didactic; everything he ever wrote was intended to inform his audience. But there was no harm in sugaring the pill, and he used every means at his disposal to render his lesson as palatable as possible. Music, dancing, drama, farce—any device was seized that might serve for the dissemination of the important message, which, at this stage of his life, was: The Gael can attain resurrection and immortality through a revived Irish language and literature.

Pearse was not slow to build on the early success of his motion.

The following month he wrote to Eoin MacNeill to ask him to speak at the New Ireland Literary Society, which was becoming anxious to enlarge its scope. It was the respectful letter of a very young man: "When the idea of organizing a public lecture was started, your name was the first that suggested itself to us; for we knew that a lecture by you on some phase of the Irish language movement, or, better still, on some phase of Gaelic literature, would not only be the most delightful of treats to us members, but would also attract a larger number of strangers than a lecture by any other available person."[5] MacNeill, ever generous with his time, gave the lecture in January 1898, and brought the society to public notice for the first time. Among the audience were Canon O'Leary and Dr Sigerson, Hyde's successor as president of the National Literary Society. Pearse's introduction was as enthusiastic and assertive as ever:

> a lecture entitled "The Gaelic Poetry called Ossianic" was delivered by Mr John MacNeill, B.A., under the auspices of the above Society, in the Molesworth Hall, Dublin. Mr Pearse, President, who occupied the chair, in introducing the lecturer, said the society were endeavouring to revive one of the oldest of European literatures, and that the unique and predominant glory of the Irish race was its literature. Mr MacNeill was one of the leading spirits in the Gaelic movements, and was well known as the editor of the *Gaelic Journal*.[6]

From January 1898, Pearse's activities can be followed from week to week in the bilingual newspaper, *Fainne an Lae*, founded at that time "to actively aid the Gaelic League in its great work of patriotism".[7] All Gaelic League meetings were reported in it, as were any other events of interest, and the officers of the New Ireland Literary Society were careful to send in reports of their meetings. The society emerges from these columns as virtually a three-man band. Apart from his friend Eamon O'Neill, Patrick Pearse, with Willie's loyal support, dominated the proceedings of the society almost to the exclusion of any other member. During the three months reported by *Fainne an Lae*, Pearse read two papers, led in two debates and spoke at length following the two other papers read, one by O'Neill and one by Willie. Willie's paper shows all the signs of Patrick's fine Gaelic hand. It concerned Cuchulainn and the Red Branch Cycle, and in seconding the vote of thanks Patrick "urged that the noble personality of a Cuchulainn forms a true type of Gaelic nationality, full as it is of youthful life and vigour and hope".[8]

Fainne an Lae also noted the publication of *Three Lectures on Gaelic Topics* in March, and reviewed it warmly: "this little volume ... is full of warm enthusiasm for the movement, and is, moreover, marked throughout by elevation of thought. We look forward with interest to further work from Mr Pearse in the cause."[9] The nationalist *Shan Van Vocht* agreed: "we can only say that if the society of which Mr Pearse is president is made up of any considerable number of persons capable of appreciating and discussing such purely literary and Gaelic topics, such a society may become a motive force in the education and literary movement."[10] The *Irish Monthly* was almost as kind: "He has worked up his subjects with the industry of enthusiasm, and he has a clear, correct and unaffected style."[11] Heady praise—even though it came from the obvious quarters. The only discordant note was sounded by the *New Ireland Review*, which remarked rather sourly that Mr Pearse failed to realize that material well-being was a higher priority for the Irish people than his high-mindedness would allow.[12]

Concurrently, Patrick was attending the meetings of the Central branch with great regularity. The recommendations of his motion of the previous year had now been put into effect, and the weekly meetings in the new League premises at 24 Upper O'Connell Street often consisted of readings, recitations, songs and lectures. Pearse was to the fore. Although he had nothing to offer in music and dancing, having no ear for music, and dancing with application rather than panache, he was always anxious to contribute. He gave readings, made speeches, frequently took the chair, and marked himself out as a young man of energy and boundless enthusiasm for the movement. Many of his contributions were juvenile—even embarrassing, like the speech in which he compared one of Horace's poems with a Connacht love song, to the advantage of the latter. He showed no signs of growing out of this habit of endlessly repeating a message that remained fresh only to himself. He was often banal. But his whole-hearted commitment was attractive, and was to bring him gradually to the attention of the Executive committee, which badly needed youthful talent and industry.

By the summer of 1898, Pearse had passed his Matriculation and was about to enter the Royal University and the King's Inns. He had not applied himself to the Matriculation with the same zeal and patience that had characterized his approach to the Intermediate. Apart from first-class honours in Irish, he did not distinguish himself, but the lack of scholarship or exhibition seems to have been no hindrance—there was money available to pay the heavy fees required by the King's Inns. In any case, he continued for a time to teach Irish at Westland Row. Family ambition was centred on Patrick. Willie had left school the previous year, after an unimpressive performance in junior Intermediate, and was now at the Metropolitan School of Art, where he was a student of average achievement. The girls had received in a convent the education expected of their improved social position, and showed few signs of further ambitions, though Margaret spoke adequate French and Mary Brigid had musical and literary aspirations. Like Willie, she was led by her admiration for Patrick to attempt to follow his interests for a time: she used to play the harp occasionally at Gaelic League social events. Patrick was generous to her, as always in relations with those for whom he felt affection. He gave her her first harp—one of many presents and a symptom of his engaging open-handedness and disregard for economic pressures.

He was no more accomplished socially than he had ever been. Physically he was fresh-faced, boyish-looking, with an eye-disfigurement of which he was always self-conscious. Observers differ as to what exactly was wrong with the eye, but it seems to have been a combination of a drooping eyelid and a squint. Adult photographs are almost always posed to show only a profile. As a child he wore spectacles, later replaced by *pince-nez*. He usually dressed in black, and this, combined with his natural earnestness of expression and his high smooth forehead, made him look like a young clergyman. He was slightly taller than average, and of sturdy build—later inclining towards stoutness, which caused him some unhappiness, since by all accounts he was rather vain. In his fragmentary autobiography, he notes the comments of those friends of his father's for whom, as a child, he used to pose as a model: "They said I had a thoughtful face, and was very finely shaped." His introspective nature and his obvious shyness put him at an immediate disadvantage in society, as did his total lack of small talk; he got on reasonably well with colleagues, but only in pursuit of some specific goal.

At seventeen, his reserve, his near-obsessive devotion to work, his disapproval of smoking, drinking and swearing combined to produce a priggish and intolerant young man, who was to take several years to mellow. University life might have been valuable for him, had he not viewed it only as a means of adding to his qualifications. The Royal University was not a teaching institution: it was merely an examining body. Students had the option of studying for their degrees by private study, with a tutor, or by attending courses of lectures at suitable educational institutions such as University College, Dublin. Pearse chose private study for his first two years as a student, although he was at UCD for a part of his third. For the King's Inns more social contact was necessary. Not only was he obliged to attend lectures in Trinity, but he had to keep terms at the King's Inns and frequently eat his dinners there. His courses in feudal, English, criminal and constitutional law made little impression on him, but his was not, and was never to be, a mind attuned to close logical argument. He achieved no success in the King's Inns debating society, where the "grand manner" was not enough; he had still learnt no method of argument beyond the emotional appeal. And even though he was much given in speeches to invoking the shades of patriots and writers as precedents, his appeals were scarcely founded on fact. The other undergraduate forum, the Literary and Historical Debating Society in University College, was a training ground for generations of speakers. But it always prided itself on its critical audiences, and Pearse, used to polite or adulatory groups, was not inclined to try his luck with such an unpredictable rabble. He occasionally attended, but made no mark on the society until 1902, when he went in the comparatively safe rôle of chairman.

CHAPTER TWO

ASPIRATIONS

1 THE COISTE GNOTHA

In the autumn of 1898 Pearse was co-opted on to the Coiste Gnotha (Executive committee) of the Gaelic League. He was already studying for arts and law degrees, teaching some classes at Westland Row, and religiously attending Central branch meetings and various social events proper to an enthusiastic young Gaelic Leaguer. Despite all this, he threw himself wholeheartedly into the activities of the Executive committee and attended more regularly than any other member. In his first two years on the committee, he missed only six out of 109 meetings, usually because other League business had called him away. His commitment was total. He and Eamon O'Neill had decided to bury the New Ireland Literary Society, due to begin its third session that autumn, to give them more time for the League.[1] The society's last mention in the public press was as a subscriber towards relief of distress in Irish-speaking districts—particularly severe that year.

Pearse found the League a sympathetic environment. It was full of respectable, middle-class Catholics—teachers, civil servants, and doctors—with a sprinkling of academics, priests and intellectuals—"white-collared, trim-suited". The Coiste Gnotha was composed of the most energetic and distinguished of them, and Pearse, despite his tender years, was now rubbing shoulders with men and women whose work filled the *Gaelic Journal* and *Fainne an Lae*, who lectured throughout the country, and whose names were familiar to all Leaguers. Even the great Dr Hyde occasionally graced a committee meeting with his presence. There was Norma Borthwick, a prolific writer, who brought dissension into many a committee meeting, and Mary O'Reilly, who with Pearse's old acquaintance from the Central branch, P. J. Keawell, was to give the League its first taste of serious dissension over the issue of Pan-Celticism. There were industrious senior men, like John Hogan, Thomas Hayes and Stephen Barrett, who had been working for the preservation of the language for many years. Above all, there were Eoin MacNeill and Dr O'Hickey, a professor from Maynooth elected to the Coiste

Gnotha on the same day as Pearse, but to fill a more august rôle. He was to take over from the legendary Father O'Growney, whose tuberculosis had exiled him to Arizona.

Hyde, MacNeill and O'Hickey were each essential for the League's success, and otherwise wholly unalike. Hyde stayed in the country in his Roscommon house, carrying on his correspondence in the interests of the League with the brains and wealth of Ireland, shooting for relaxation, dining at the best houses, and turning out to speak at meetings where a prestigious presence was called for. He was a consummate diplomat, determined to exclude political issues from the League, and so adept at fence-sitting that he managed to stay at the head of the League for two decades, while it was being infiltrated at all levels by the Irish Republican Brotherhood. MacNeill and O'Hickey between them took on the mundane work of the organization, which with the spectacular expansion of the League was growing heavier by the month. MacNeill was primarily a scholar, O'Hickey a fighter: "A lion's roar, a wolf-dog's bay beside the pigeon-cautious coo of Dr Douglas Hyde, and the scholarly and elegantly brushed phrases of Eoin MacNeill, an Aaron's rod that rarely bore a bud."[2]

Pearse made little contribution during the first few meetings of the committee, as befitted such a junior member, but his light was not long under a bushel. At his first meeting (at which W. J. Pearse's name came up for election to membership of the League) he informed the committee: "that the Christian Brothers in Westland Row were teaching Irish, the *Fainne an Lae* was read, and prayers said in Irish"; facts unlikely to be wholly unconnected with Pearse's employment there was an Irish tutor. He continued to play a prominent part in the gatherings of the Central branch. He had spent some time in Aran during the summer—and the experience had been exhilarating. The Gaelic-speaking west was to be his favourite place of retreat all his life, and the source of inspiration for his fictional writings. At this stage it was very new and exciting. He read a paper to the Central branch on his experiences in the west and published an article in Irish on the subject in *Fainne an Lae*.[3] This reads like a sound school essay. It is written in good, careful Irish, and, with his usual didacticism, he introduces unusual words and phrases at appropriate intervals. It describes the month and a day he spent in Aran, the people he met, and his success in setting up, in conjunction with a couple of League colleagues and the local parish priest, a branch of the Gaelic League. Like so many of Pearse's public writings, it contains unconsciously revealing remarks: "Be sure that I had little interest in the girls—I was listening to their conversation".* Otherwise, it makes dull reading. He had not yet learned how to communicate his own heartfelt enthusiasms.

In November the Coiste Gnotha came up for re-election, and despite his comparatively junior status, Pearse was successful, coming tenth of fourteen. He was still relatively silent at committee meetings, appearing mainly as a seconder of motions. His name was to be found in the columns of *Fainne an Lae* appealing for money for a library for Aran, attending various League meetings and giving readings at Central branch gatherings. At the beginning of January 1899, he gave a lecture at the Catholic Commercial Club on Irish saga literature which showed the same deficiencies as had so far characterized all his reported speeches and lectures. This lecture was attended by a sharp critic, Joseph Holloway, a Dublin architect who never missed a play or important lecture and who was unsparing in his comments on all performers when he reviewed them in his diary. Though Holloway was in later years to be a good friend to Pearse, he was unimpressed at first contact:

> The lecturer is quite a young man with a peculiar, jerky, pistol-shot-like delivery that becomes trying to listen to after a time, as it makes him hack his sentences into single words and destroys the sense of his remarks.... He was indiscriminately eulogistic to absurdity over his subject, and the adjectives he employed to describe the extracts which he read from the Sagas were beyond the bounds of reason when the stuff so praised became known to his listeners. Woeful exaggeration or absurd grotesqueness were the only merits they possessed as far as I could see, but then I am not a Gaelic speaking maniac (harmless but boresome) which makes all the difference in the world. With them art stopped short in the early ages and nothing outside the Irish language is worth a rap. Unfortunately I can see beauty and worth in many things written nowadays even outside our own country—which a true Gael could never see or if they did would never acknowledge that they did. Mr Pearse missed his mark in not being somewhat critical in his appreciation. If the extracts that he jerked out so inartistically were the best to be found in the Sagas few would care to dig deeper into them ... his overpraise of very ordinary exaggerated prose extracts killed the Goose.... It is this absurd unmeaning, almost fanatical, praise that makes the few lovers of the Irish language left to us so unbearable and impractical to all broad minded people.... I noticed that Mr Pearse used many words a-la Mrs Malaprop in most inappro-

priate places and made use of such remarks as "handed-down by word of mouth" etc. which struck me as funny.[4]

Harsh, but deserved by a lecture which showed all the naïveté of his earlier efforts. Still the reliance on assertion—still the emotional peroration: "[If the Irish people let the language die] they gained nothing—not even their pound of flesh; mentally, morally, physically, and pecuniarily they would be losers, and they would go down to their graves with the knowledge that their children and their children's children cursed their memory."[5]

Pearse was to have a fresh challenge that spring. Father Delaney, the president of the then Jesuit University College, Dublin, asked the Gaelic League to make Irish classes available to his students, and Pearse took the job on. It was a more unnerving prospect than tutoring in the Westland Row school; this time he was obliged to face his peers. It was a small class, which met weekly for an hour. Less than a dozen students attended, and even the most pious recollections agree on the shyness and earnestness of the teacher: "shy, somewhat awkward, earnest, studious-looking young man with pince-nez";[6] "shy, studious-looking, very earnest young man";[7] "pale young University man in pince-nez, to most of those who knew him a student and a dreamer, who dreamt of a new Gaelic world and a new Gaelic civilization".[8] A more severe critic, James Joyce, attended a few of the classes and found Pearse a bore. In the end he left and, influenced by Ibsen, took to Norwegian because he couldn't stand that same habit of Pearse's which had so irritated Joseph Holloway—the denigration of the English language in order further to elevate Irish.[9]

Although there was no sign of the inspiring teacher or orator of the future, the classes were popular and successful enough to be continued for another year, and to lead Father Delaney to invite Pearse to run a weekly class under University College rather than Gaelic League auspices in the academic year 1901-2.

The demands of his Irish class, his two degree courses and the frequent committee and branch meetings did not dull Pearse's appetite for work: he took on more with reckless abandon. He agreed to assist MacNeill in editing the *Gaelic Journal.* Acting as an adjudicator in two letter-writing competitions, he made free as usual with his superlatives, "reporting that all the letters submitted were excellent and that the work of the Kilmilkin students reflects the highest credit on their teachers and on the Branch".[10] He sat on the committee organizing the annual gala event of the Gaelic League—the Oireachtas—and took his first prominent part in that event. The previous year, 1898, he had been no more than a steward. This year he had the impressive title of "Conductor of the Competitions". He was also taking some part in the family business. James Pearse was now advertising regularly in the new Gaelic League organ, *An Claidheamh Soluis* (The Sword of Light) and offering a new service: "Irish crosses, with interlaced work, reproduced from ancient Irish crosses, shrines and MSS. Inscriptions in Irish a speciality." Patrick was closely involved with this facet of the business, even to the writing of letters, and he was making profitable contacts for his father through the Gaelic League. Even in the dry medium of a business letter, he could not resist overwriting: "You need, however, have no fear as to the correctness of the spelling, 'Liosdunain', which, I think is unimpeachable ['quite right' crossed out]."[11]

That spring he launched an ill-informed adolescent attack on Yeats, whose plays, poetry and Irish National Theatre were under constant attack by *Fainne an Lae* as un-Irish. Although MacNeill, the editor of *An Claidheamh Soluis*, was like Hyde on friendly terms with the leading figures of the literary movement, his supervision of his editorial board was at this time too mild to contain their hostility either. Lady Gregory wrote to MacNeill in early May 1899:

> I am a little anxious about the attacks that continue to be made by correspondents in the "Claidheamh Soluis" on the literary movement. I know so well what delight there always is across the channel when any new split or quarrel appears in Ireland and yet this can't be said to be a quarrel, for it is on one side only. I know with what constant and warm admiration Mr Martyn and Mr Yeats and others of our writers speak of the work of the Gaelic League, but these letters would give the impression that they kept aside from it. We all want each other's help in Ireland, and it will be a very great pity if such men are forced out of sympathy with the Gaelic movement.

Despite Hyde having written to MacNeill in similar terms, less than two weeks later the paper published the letter from Pearse, which he would regret when he came to know Yeats later:

> The "Irish" Literary Theatre is, in my opinion, more dangerous, because less glaringly anti-national than Trinity College. If we once admit the Irish literature is English idea, then the language movement is a mistake. Mr Yeats' precious "Irish" Literary Theatre may, if it develops, give the Gaelic League more trouble

than the Atkinson-Mahaffy combination. Let us strangle it at its birth. Against Mr Yeats personally we have nothing to object. He is a mere English poet of the third or fourth rank, and as such he is harmless. But when he attempts to run an "Irish" Literary Theatre it is time for him to be crushed.[12]

In June 1899 Pearse was re-elected to the Executive committee, and rapidly became involved in his first public dispute.

II The League and the Pan-Celts

The Pan-Celtic dispute had been going on for some time. The previous November, Dr Hyde had written to the Executive committee stating that he had been invited to attend the committee of the Pan-Celtic Congress, planned to be held in Dublin in 1900, and asking whether he should do so. The Pan-Celts were the subject of much controversy and the object of much ridicule. They believed that joint festivals of representatives of the Celtic races —Irish, Scots, Welsh, Manx, Cornish and Bretons—would be to the advantage of all and would promote a revival of the Celtic spirit. In Ireland their chief advocates were an emigré called Edouard Fournier, and Lord Castletown, president of the "Celtic Association". The movement had many friends, especially among the more broad minded of the revivalists—men like Hyde and MacNeill. But its enemies, who included members of the Coiste Gnotha, were vociferous and bitter, and their spokesmen prevailed. Hyde was informed that the committee did not wish to be represented at the congress. Though it placed no restriction on him in his private capacity, it "would be sorry that any of their members should give time or money to an enterprise that could not help the Irish language". Hyde, never a man to back an outsider, swiftly eschewed any involvement.

Two months later, MacNeill, supported by the Irish scholar, Tadhg O'Donoghue, proposed that Hyde be authorized to join the Pan-Celtic committee in his official capacity, and was shot down in flames by the opposition. The prime mover of the opposition was P. J. Keawell, who had been on the Coiste Gnotha for several years, and although a useful worker was an obstreperous personality. He exerted great influence over his colleagues, Mary O'Reilly and Norma Borthwick. Much valuable time had to be spent in trying to mollify the dissidents. O'Hickey's letters to MacNeill are full of despairing references to this group. "What is to be done now? Mr Keawell is in a sullen obstructive mood, and how is he to be got out of it?" The reasons for their lack of sympathy with the Pan-Celts were deep-rooted. The Pan-Celts were socially identified, in Ireland at least, with the aristocracy and the Dublin Castle circle; Lord Castletown was the main target for abuse in this respect. Besides, their more cosmopolitan attitudes were seen as a threat to a purely Irish political stance. Keawell had, in O'Hickey's words, an "unreasoning antipathy" towards Fournier. The Hyde-MacNeill position, on the other hand, was conciliatory for largely diplomatic reasons. The Pan-Celts were by and large Protestant, and the leaders of the League were anxious to keep the movement apolitical and non-sectarian. Happy relations with the Pan-Celts would do much to appease the Protestant minority in the League, some of whom, fearing clerical influence, were audibly muttering in favour of secession.[1]

The split in the League was soon taken up by the two rival chroniclers of the movement. *Fainne an Lae* had been founded with high hopes, but disputes between the publisher, Bernard Doyle, and the Coiste Gnotha had caused the Gaelic League to disown the paper, and it set up a rival, *An Claidheamh Soluis*, in March 1899. Doyle had reacted with resentment and increasing bitterness. Although MacNeill was editor of *An Claidheamh Soluis*, Keawell, O'Reilly and Borthwick were on his editorial board, and they swung the paper's policy to one of contempt for the Pan-Celts, who were either ridiculed or ignored. Doyle's *Fainne an Lae*, on the other hand, was fervently devoted to the cause, and quick to avenge insults. It was also on the look-out for any opportunity to publicize splits in the League, and in its self-imposed crusade to protect the great names in the Irish revival, its first victim was the unfortunate Pearse. In July 1899 it carried the following item:

> At the last public meeting of the Dublin Branch of the Gaelic League Mr P. H. Pearse presided. When one of those present proposed singing "The Memory of the Dead" (Dr Hyde's version) the Chairman objected, on the ground that "it was not Irish". Whether to look upon this as an insult to the President of the Gaelic League, or as a slight on the sentiment contained in the song, we know not, but perhaps this youth who has set himself up as censor of what "is not Irish" would explain.

This assault coincided with a minor success for the pro-Pan-Celtic lobby, which had succeeded in getting agreement to send a delegate—Pearse—to the Welsh Eisteddfod, though he was to be wholly independent of the Irish Pan-Celtic contingent and was to present a separate address on behalf of the League. This was Pearse's first trip outside Ireland, and he acquitted himself creditably. Even *Fainne an Lae*, though poised to deal him renewed blows, was complimentary:

> The Gaelic League was represented by Mr P. H. Pearse, and considering all the war and rumours of war emanating from 24 Upper O'Connell Street against everything savouring of Pan-Celticism, the address presented by him to the Eisteddfod was of a most advanced and encouraging character. Mr Pearse was in a difficult position as delegate to a Pan-Celtic Eisteddfod, and he acquitted himself with great tact and courtesy. On his return he will, no doubt, be able to clear up the situation considerably.

This, unwittingly, Pearse was able to do: his visit to the Eisteddfod was ultimately to act as the catalyst which resolved the situation. He came back full of delight at his stay in Wales, which had been characteristically productive. Not for Pearse the enticing social opportunities offered by a Celtic junket—his time was spent in making speeches, visiting the Cardiff branch of the League, collecting information for the League on a subject of abiding interest—bilingualism—interviewing the secretary of the Cardiff School Board, and visiting schools. He had also had two or three interviews with the Irish Pan-Celtic leader, Lord Castletown, who was still anxious for the League's co-operation. Pearse reported that the Cardiff branch of the Irish language movement believed that the Gaelic League could gain control of the Pan-Celtic movement. He had aligned himself firmly on the side of the Pan-Celts.

This was more than the anti-lobby could take. The next issue of *An Claidheamh Soluis* contained a no-holds-barred assault on the Pan-Celts. Typical was a jibe at the hardworking Breton secretary, Fournier, "an Englishman of Huguenot extraction now residing in County Dublin". Pearse sent a telegram to the Coiste Gnotha from Aran, where he had gone on holiday with Willie and Eamon O'Neill, protesting at the onslaught, but his anger was nothing to that of the paper's editor, MacNeill, who wrote to the *Freeman's Journal*, the Irish nationalist daily, disassociating himself from the article. This flaunting of the League's dirty linen was more than even *Fainne an Lae* could have hoped for: it joined battle with all guns firing and although Pearse had recently earned its praise, he was not spared in the new onslaught:

When a man of Mr MacNeill's position is forced to send such a letter to the papers it is time something were done to curb the wild and, we might say, belligerent spirits who have control of the League publications—the youths of both sexes who imagine themselves the Heaven-sent leaders of the Language Revival, and who are thoroughly unfitted to take any prominent or responsible part in the conduct of a great National movement. We have the spectacle of a boy named Pearse insulting Dr Douglas Hyde, the President of the Gaelic League, an Irishman and a scholar of whom the Irish nation is justly proud—a man whose name is synonymous with everything patriotic, whole-souled and learned. This stripling when presiding at a meeting recently stated that Dr Hyde's version of "Cuimhne na Marbh", "The Memory of the Dead", was not *Irish*. Up to the present he has not had the manliness to qualify or retract his assertion. And this is one of the shining lights of the "organ" of the Dublin Committee.... The League publications are kept afloat by public money, and not by an individual, as was the case with *Fainne an Lae*; and all who value the respectability of the language movement or hope for its permanency, should protest against the absurdities of the amateur journalists, incapable and irresponsible, who write without judgement or logic, and whose arrogance and egotism is fast dragging the movement into the mire.[2]

The Coiste Gnotha hastened to put its house in order. Keawell and Miss O'Reilly resigned from *An Claidheamh Soluis*, and Keawell from the Coiste, the members of which devised a long compromise resolution which eschewed any formal involvement with the Pan-Celtic movement but left individual members of the League "absolutely free" to involve themselves as they wished. The battle was almost over.

Pearse, who was still in Aran conducting examinations in written Irish and addressing the local League branch, and who would have been glad to escape the unpleasantness, was to be more closely involved with the Pan-Celts than any other member of the Coiste Gnotha. Hyde made timid efforts at a later stage to involve the League more closely, but was unsuccessful, and the issue faded into insignificance. Pearse, however, maintained his interest. In October he attended the Highland Mod in Edinburgh, and presented another illuminated address from the Gaelic League. He found the proceedings less impressive than the Eisteddfod, considering the Scottish movement too academic and "by no means popular in its methods". At the Mod, he was yet again keeping company with Lord Castletown and the Pan-Celts, and the same month he was co-opted on to the Irish committee of the Pan-Celtic Congress.

This smacked of divided loyalties to Norma Borthwick, who, incensed at the increasing strength of the Pan-Celts, instituted a new intrigue, this time recruiting the acerbic pen of Canon O'Leary, who wrote to MacNeill of Lord Castletown: "I have known that man for 15 or 16 years. I would not sit at the same table with him to save my life." Borthwick lodged a complaint with the Coiste Gnotha demanding Pearse's resignation. Although she was referred to the resolution of a couple of months before, she did not give up easily, but went to Hyde with further complaints. In a letter of January 1900 she levelled an accusation against Pearse which was unlikely to stir any passions in the heart of Douglas Hyde, but which was an emotive issue at a time when nationalist Ireland was taking a virulently anti-English and anti-monarchical line over the Boer war:

> Last summer, just after the anti-Pan-Celtic articles appeared, I was standing on a boat-slip in Inismeadhon, talking to a boy of 19 or 20. He could read both Irish & English, and he told me he had been asking Pearse, who was in the island at the time, was it true that he drank the Queen's health when he was over in Wales? Pierse said it was true. Then he said he asked him did he do it in his private capacity or as the representative of the Gaelic League? . . . and he couldn't get a satisfactory answer out of him! Of course not, because Pearse was invited to the Entertainment, whatever it was, simply and solely because he was the delegate from the Gaelic League. And my Inismeadhon boy said to me that if Pearse *did* do it as representative of the Gaelic League, he did what he had no right to do, and a thing that did *not* represent the Gaelic League, and the Gaelic League should not send delegates who would do such things in their name.[3]

But formidable influences were operating in Pearse's favour. After a journey to Roscommon to see Hyde, O'Hickey was able to tell MacNeill that he had soothed the "Keawell-Borthwick-O'Reilly-O'Leary intrigues". With the absorption of *Fainne an Lae* by *An Claidheamh Soluis* in 1900, passions were dampened, although a year later Hyde still felt unable to attend, in any capacity, a private entertainment given for foreign Pan-Celts. "I dare not appear even at a social function, in company with them while these furious partizans hang on our flank. It is, as you say, heart-breaking."[4]

Pearse, who saw how the wind was blowing, and gradually detached himself from the Pan-Celtic movement over the next few months, regretted the necessity to do so. As late as August 1901 he wrote to an Irish writer of his acquaintance: "I agree with you as to our proper attitude towards the Pan-Celts. The fact is that the League made a gigantic blunder two years ago in deciding to have nothing to do with the affair."[5]

For all the difference it made to his actions, Pearse might as well have been ignorant of the issues throughout the Pan-Celtic squabble. It was an initiation into the techniques of political in-fighting, and the less ethereal motivations of many of his colleagues. Politics loomed large in Irish Ireland at the turn of the century; many Gaelic Leaguers were privately active in the celebrations attending the centenary of the 1798 rebellion, nationalists in general were vocally pro-Boer, and Queen Victoria's lamentably ill-timed visit to Ireland in 1900 served to polarize opinion for months before her arrival. And yet Pearse maintained a conspicuous silence concerning all these matters. His uncritical and placid acceptance of the Gaelic League's apolitical *credo* placed him on the right wing of the League, but his real feelings were of bewilderment—why were they all getting so heated over irrelevancies, when the real work was still to be done—uplifting the soul of the Gael?

In September 1899, still in pursuit of this noble end, he read to the Central branch "a lengthy and original paper in Irish, entitled 'Brian Boroimhe' ", which was printed in the following issue of *An Claidheamh Soluis.*[6] This was a new departure, and reveals much of Pearse's current level of academic development. All his earlier efforts had been broad in scope—ranging over the entire *corpus* of Irish literature and the whole span of Irish history. He had shown, too, that his childhood preoccupation with heroes and great deeds was still in no way modified. Now he was writing about one specific hero—at that time his favourite.

Not until Eoin MacNeill began lecturing in early Irish history in 1904 was there much appreciation in Ireland of the necessity for applying certain scientific principles to its study. Pearse's knowledge of the subject was confined to the desiccated requirements of the Intermediate, and his own private reading, which was erratic and romantic. It could not be expected therefore that he would have other than the most unsophisticated view of the legendary Brian Boru, and this was manifest in his paper. Brian Boru was a great southern prince of the eleventh century who was the bravest of his race and made himself High-King of Ireland to rid Ireland of the Danes. But Pearse went further than this. In the battle order, God was ranged on Brian's side, the side fighting for Our Saviour's faith against the Gall (an Irish word meaning "foreigner", which was applied in turn to the various invaders of Ireland and which gained a pejorative sense, like Sassenach, as the years progressed. Pearse used the term extensively). Because his cause was righteous, Brian's personal ambition was justified. The end justified the means. This was a moral which was to recur with more force later in Pearse's career.

Father Eugene O'Growney died in the autumn of that year, and Pearse was one of those to pay tribute to him. They had been in correspondence shortly before his death. Pearse had published an article in the *Gaelic Journal* on "Names of Birds and Plants in Aran", and a letter from O'Growney to *An Claidheamh* a couple of months later on an allied subject had inspired Pearse to write to him. O'Growney, who spoke well of Pearse's Irish writings,[7] had written back very kindly, sending him lists of names.[8] Pearse's speech of tribute was brief but well received—he was to deliver a much grander panegyric some years later, and also, with the passage of time, to claim an intimacy which had hardly existed.[9]

Early in 1900 Pearse read another paper to the Central branch, on "Fiann and the Fiann Saga", which was published in June in the *Gaelic Journal.* For his first year examinations in the Royal University, in 1899, he had studied one of the texts relating to the Fianna, and the paper shows that he had done this with exemplary thoroughness. He had read all the contemporary writings on the Fenian cycle and was able to discuss them with some authority, but his emotional addiction to the heroic still clouded his judgement. The cycle of stories of Finn and his warriors was to have great significance for Pearse throughout his life. Finn was a legendary hero, the strongest, noblest, bravest and wisest leader of Irish mythology. His band of warriors, the Fianna, fought in countless battles throughout Ireland. The stories, which exist in many versions, revolve particularly around Finn, his challenger for the leadership of the Fianna, Goll Mac Morna, Finn's son Oisin and his wife Grainne, and her lover Diarmaid.

No modern historian would assert that these stories were other than fables, but pioneering Irish historians in the previous three centuries, including Keating, O'Donovan and O'Curry, believed them to be authentic. By 1900, the attentions of continental scholars had been turned on Irish literature and severe blows had been struck at the acceptance of stories of figures like Finn as historical fact.

Pearse had read these modern scholars, but he could not bring himself into line with their findings. He arraigned himself uncompromisingly alongside the "euhemeristic" historians—those who treated supernatural beings as real historical characters. Over 40 years later Thomas O'Rahilly summed up the reasons for the popularity of the euhemeristic method in Ireland: "It is easy to apply; it enables the uncritical writer to fill up the historical vacuum which he abhors; and it gives us the flattering notion that the records of our history reach back into a very remote past."[10]

All these aspects of the approach appealed to Pearse. He always liked fundamentally simple answers; he hated uncertainty about Ireland's history; and he was wholly convinced that Ireland had the longest and most glorious history of all. But more than that, Pearse *wanted* to believe in the great heroes of the past. He needed great symbols of nobility, courage and selflessness to compensate for the many self-seeking, weak and timid people who surrounded him. There were fine men and women in the Gaelic League, but to a romantic like Pearse most of them were dull; there were also many who were destructive and bitter and who caused Pearse great personal hurt throughout his decade of whole-hearted commitment to the League. In all his life's endeavours, people were to let Pearse down. He expected them to flock to his causes with the speed and abandon of the Fianna and to show the same uncompromising dedication that he possessed. That he was abnormal in his single-mindedness was something he could never accept. A friend recalls him almost weeping with vexation in the early days in the League when he heard that Eoin MacNeill was getting married: this might interfere with MacNeill's work.[11]

III THE LEAGUE'S NEW HORIZONS

The years 1899-1900 were to see a great upsurge in the fortunes of the Gaelic League, which was to give it the money and membership to expand its activities considerably. When Pearse had joined the Executive committee in 1898, the League was still a small-scale operation, growing steadily but slowly. The following year, however, professors Mahaffy and Atkinson of Trinity College mounted an attack on Irish which was to arouse popular interest in the language.

Mahaffy had opposed the Gaelic League from its inception, believing (quite correctly, as it was to turn out) that it would prove a dangerous threat to the Irish establishment. He was particularly bitter about its success in attracting Protestants into its ranks—this he saw as a betrayal. He also knew that to control the teaching of Irish in the schools would be to control its spread. "Give me a nation's examination papers and I defy the politicians to control its sentiments."

In 1899 a viceregal commission on Intermediate education was set up, and Mahaffy launched a campaign to have the number of marks awarded for Irish in the Intermediate reduced. Since Intermediate exhibitions were awarded on the basis of total marks secured in the whole examination, such a step would further weaken the position of Irish in the schools—already lower in importance than continental languages. As his chief ally he brought in Dr Robert Atkinson, professor of Sanskrit and comparative philology in Trinity and Todd professor of celtic languages in the Royal Irish Academy. Although Atkinson was a respected Irish scholar, he believed the language to be wholly unsuitable for schoolchildren, and its literature wholly devoid of "any elevation of thought or dignity". Hyde was brought into the battle on behalf of the Gaelic League, and by dint of securing defences of Irish from a cohort of distinguished foreign scholars, he managed to forestall Mahaffy's attempts further to weaken Irish, although he did not manage to improve its status.

Academic though this dispute was, Mahaffy, like Maguire thirteen years earlier, had awoken hitherto dormant public opinion through his intemperate language. "All the Irish language textbooks used in Irish schools are either silly or indecent . . . it is almost impossible to get hold of a text in Irish which is not religious or does not suffer from one or other of the objections referred to." This assault, and the dialogue which followed it, were to arouse the interest of a large section of the Irish public. A contemporary ballad ran:

> The Irish language, Mahaffy said
> Is a couple of books written clerkly
> A dirty word in a song or two
> "Matter a damn" says Berkeley.

The League's victory over Mahaffy gave it new importance in the eyes of many people who had ignored it previously, and during 1899 its branches more than doubled in number. Mahaffy also helped to unify the existing members; he claimed in a newspaper interview to have "restored harmony in the Gaelic family by drawing them on himself". By 1900 the League had an income of £2,000—a far cry from the £43 of 1895. It was employing a growing number of organizers and other paid officials, and extending its publishing activities to include more than its two papers and the occasional pamphlet.

Although the impetus towards growth was to be kept up for several years, Mahaffy had not lost the war, only the first battle. The League, confident that it had won its case over the Intermediate, began to concentrate its efforts in education on the introduction of bilingual education in schools in the Gaeltacht (Irish-speaking areas—where there were many non-Irish-speaking teachers), and on persuading school managers, usually priests, to put Irish on the curriculum. In both these aims it had a great deal of help from the Archbishop of Dublin, Dr W. J. Walsh, a League supporter. The Archbishop, who was on very friendly terms with both Hyde and MacNeill, even went to the lengths of having an address of his on bilingualism published as a League pamphlet—at his own expense. It was to be many years, however, before either aim was fully achieved. In the meantime, the League kept up a relentless campaign.

In 1901 it found itself attacked on another flank. Professor Mahaffy had been unexpectedly appointed to the Intermediate Board, and the new programme issued in 1901 showed signs of his influence. Irish had in no way improved its position: German and Greek were receiving even more favour than before. Dr O'Hickey was first into the fray, declaring that this was an attempt to squeeze Irish out while keeping the people blind to what was happening. Hyde claimed that this attempt to teutonize the Irish people was because Mahaffy and the king both spoke German. The rest of the League was also up in arms: but to little result. The campaign on the Intermediate front was to run as long as the other educational conflicts.

Pearse had been very much on the side-lines during the first of these confrontations—still too junior to have an important voice. Bilingualism was, however, a subject very dear to his heart. Education had always interested him greatly, and was to be a preoccupation in the future. Until he was old enough and experienced enough to join the mêlée on his own account, he fixed the bullets for others to fire. In letters to a Leaguer in the north:

> As regards bilingual fight, I am sure you are doing your best up north. The Commissioners are plainly wavering, and a fierce agitation now may win the fight ... Could ... a meeting be got together in Derry?[1]
>
> As regards education questions, do your level best, by hook or crook, to get up an agitation on the subject of the language. Leave

no stone unturned. Bring pressure to bear from all quarters.... This is the crisis in the history of the movement ...[2]

A letter of his on the subject was printed in the *Freeman's Journal* in April 1900, citing his Welsh experiences and the use of bilingualism in Cardiff schools with a "Bravo, Cardiff".[3] But though he was still too junior to have an important voice in the educational debates of the next few years, he was passionately involved with the controversies, which were shaping his future attitudes. In 1898 he had been a young student seriously considering a career in the profession most concerned with upholding the established order. By 1900, although he was still pursuing his studies, and was attending law lectures in Trinity College, side by side with his enthusiasms for the Irish language were developing new resentments at anti-Gaelic elements within Irish society. These resentments were not lessened by his brief experience of Trinity.

IV The Publications Committee

The new prosperity of the League at the turn of the century offered wide new opportunities to an energetic and ambitious young man. In June 1900 Pearse became secretary to the Publications committee, and over the next three years established the League as an important publisher. The range and scope of the Committee's publications over this period proved the universal truth that one man with determination can force his will on a group of less single-minded fellows. In July he wrote to J. J. Doyle:

> The object of the Committee is to place in the hands of students both of schools and colleges and in League classes, a series of carefully-edited and carefully-selected modern Irish texts, with introductions (where necessary), full vocabularies, and no translations. The idea is to give to students a scientifically-edited and up-to-date series of texts, similar in style and matter to those used in the study of French, German, etc. The series will comprise modern classics, prose & poetry, ... and also original modern Irish work.[1]

As an aim this was admirable, but the League's lack of experience in publishing, its reliance in its Publications committee on wholly voluntary labour, and its lack of extensive capital should have proved serious stumbling blocks. But the committee had Pearse, and he was determined. Despite the many other claims on his time, he flung himself into commissioning work, editing, proof correcting and endless correspondence. He had a great deal of help from colleagues, including O'Hickey, MacNeill, Stephen Barrett (by now the full-time paid treasurer of the League), J. H. Lloyd, and Tadhg O'Donoghue. But his was the day-to-day burden; he attended every committee meeting and wrote innumerable letters begging, pleading, encouraging, chivvying and expressing gratitude. His correspondents ranged from Archbishop Walsh, whom he addressed with youthful deference, to all the notable Irish writers of the period. But his ambition was not wholly disinterested. As in all his activities, he wanted to get his name known, and his correspondence shows that he rarely missed an opportunity to do so. His letters to Archbishop Walsh, although usually written at the behest of the committee, were always written much more neatly than usual and were more full and more personal than was strictly necessary. Where possible they gave the impression that the correspondence and decisions on publications were inspired by the secretary rather than by the committee. "I should be glad to have Your Grace's opinion on these circulars before getting them printed off."[2]

> I have the honour to acknowledge Your Grace's of yesterday. I am glad Your Grace has returned the proofs direct to Browne and Nolan, as it will save time. It is most desirable that these model schemes should be in the hands of the public as early as possible. Every day the necessity for something of the kind is brought home to members of the League Executive. At the last meeting, for instance, letters were read from two teachers asking us to draw up programmes for them! We replied that Your Grace's prize schemes would shortly be published, and that teachers should draw up programmes for themselves on the lines of those.[3]

He also took care to send Walsh his own first League publication, a penny booklet of suitable pieces for recitation which he edited with Tadhg O'Donoghue, and published in 1900. But although he never lost sight of personal ambition, there is no doubt that his work for the committee was prodigious. Within two years the League's output was provoking a private publisher, the Irish Book Company (of which Norma Borthwick was Irish editor), to invoke the aid of D. P. Moran's *Leader*. Moran was an old ally of Borthwick's. Before the anti-Pan-Celtic cabal had stopped kicking, it had tried to engineer the suppression of *An Claidheamh Soluis* and leave the field clear for a new weekly, anti-Pan-Celt in outlook, to be edited by Moran. The scheme foundered, and when Moran floated his own paper, the *Leader*, in 1900, he was too much his own man to give much space to the Pan-Celtic squabble, which was in any case cooling by this time. Moran now accused the League's Publications committee of competing unfairly with private publishers by not sticking to text-books.[4] A similar accusation later appeared in *Banba*, the organ of the Keating branch of the League —traditional critics of the Coiste Gnotha. The Keating branch was the stronghold of the Munster men—led by supporters of Father O'Leary, who were eternally petulant at the Dublin domination of League affairs, who championed Munster Irish to the detriment of all other dialects, and who were delighted at the opportunity for another jibe at the O'Connell Street monopolists:

> This spirit of reckless speculation directed against private enterprise is manifested in the work of the Publication Committee, or rather of a section of that committee, which has got hold of the wires and pulls them when opportunity offers. The books in which the League has a monopoly are sold at extravagantly high prices, and other publications are offered ridiculously low so as to kill competition. In this connection we consider the attitude of the Publication Committee towards the Irish Book Company to be unworthy and unbecoming.[5]

Pearse replied to the *Leader*'s complaints by denying that any unfair competition was intended and by incidentally making a sweeping claim. "[The] League's publications business, besides being propagandism of the best sort, is its main permanent source of revenue, and without it the League's general organising and propagandist work could not be carried on in anything like its present magnitude."[6] The *Leader* was not impressed.

> Mr Pearse's statement that the profit from its publications is the main source of permanent revenue for the League will come as a surprise to many. We should have thought that the affiliation fees from its large number of Branches, the delegate fees, and the Language Fund formed the principal revenue. Our view that the capital sunk in the League publications is a tax on the general revenue is borne out by the last appeal issued by the Executive Committee on behalf of the Language Fund, which states that "the different series of text books and booklets are issued at little over cost price, and could only be provided by the aid of the organisation".[7]

It went on to say, with much truth, that the League seemed unaware that it was now a large-scale business, which should be run in a business-like manner. "During the past two years the League ... has developed from being a huxter's shop into a great wholesale concern." The Coiste Gnotha should act like a board of directors, directing paid staff, with committees for finance, industry, organizers, education, and press. These books should be properly audited. New blood should be recruited on to the Coiste Gnotha.

Pearse's answer in the next issue was not wholly convincing. He claimed that the net profits on the publishing business during the year ending 31 March 1901 were about £360, as opposed to £211.2s. received from affiliation and delegates' fees. The penny booklets alone made 50 per cent profit on first edition, 250 per cent on second and other editions. The *Leader* found these claims extravagant—"we remain dubious of the soundness of the accountancy that brings out these results". Moran was of course right in principle. The League was now big business and needed to employ professionals. In fact, within a few months of this exchange, it had set up appropriate sub-committees for finance, industry, organization, education and press, employed professional auditors, and considerably increased the number of paid officials.

Nevertheless, even if Pearse's method of calculating profits was rather unsophisticated, he was correct in asserting that the League's publications were making money. They were also providing important help in the teaching of Irish, making cheap books available to a wide audience and encouraging Irish writers to publish—advances for which much of the credit must go to Pearse. His achievement was made all the more impressive when viewed against the other activities claiming his time from his election to the secretaryship of the publications committee in June 1900.

v New Responsibilities

James Pearse had died in September 1900, while visiting his brother in Birmingham. His obituaries showed the position of respectability and relative eminence which he had reached by the end of his long Dublin career. The *Irish Builder*, even if it got his name wrong, paid him generous tribute.

> Mr Pearce settled in Ireland very many years ago, and speedily established himself as a successful architectural and ecclesiastical sculptor. Works of his are to be found in well nigh every church in Ireland, and bear record of the sound and excellent work he did. Personally, he was of a courteous and affable disposition,

and will be regretted by all who had business transactions with him.[1]

The *Freeman's Journal* and the *Irish Independent* agreed that his most notable work was the heroic group crowning the façade of the National Bank in College Green.[2] The *Independent* paid him a compliment which he would hardly have appreciated, calling him the "pioneer of modern Gothic art, as applied to church work, in this country".

James's death posed problems for his family. He had steadily built up the firm while the children were growing up. Although he had split with his partner, Edmund Sharp, by 1892, his business continued to thrive. He leased ground-floor premises in 156, 160 and 162 Townsend Street, which had a common back laneway with 27 Great Brunswick Street. The lane was wide enough to take heavy traffic in marble and granite slabs, and the four buildings between them made up a substantial stone-cutter's yard. Although James never became rich, he was quite prosperous when he died, and had moved his family to a comfortable house once more in Sandymount, 5 George's Ville, four doors away from Yeats's birthplace. Their material position had been improved by the death of Patrick Brady, Margaret's father, in September 1894. From Brady's will it is clear that despite apparently losing his land in 1879 he had built up a small but profitable business over the following decade.[3] His whole estate was valued at £216.14s.6d. gross, made up of three cottages in Aldborough Avenue, and a house in North Clarence Street (both in the North Strand), and various cattle, horses, cars and carts. He left his sister Margaret (Patrick's beloved great-aunt) a life interest in his house property, and the residue of the estate to his daughter Margaret Pearse, who was to inherit everything after her aunt's death, subject only to £10 each "for the purpose of binding the two children of my deceased daughter Catherine Kelly to a trade".

Margaret Brady did not long survive her brother, and the resultant legacy, a substantial sum for a family of modest means, must have made a significant difference to the Pearse family. James and Margaret did their duty by Catherine Kelly's children, John and Mary Kate. Mary Kate was sent to boarding school; she later married a Fellow of Merton College, Oxford. John was set to a trade, but he was killed in an accident at the age of sixteen while cycling to work from the Pearse home.[4]

By 1900 then, when James died, the family was accustomed to a comfortable standard of living, a pleasant house and at least one servant. Patrick was still studying for his degrees and Willie, not yet nineteen years of age, had just finished his third year at the Metropolitan School of Art. Neither of the girls had been educated to earn a living. James's estate was valued at £1,470.17s. 6d.[5] but most of this was tied up in the business; to maintain their prosperity it was necessary to keep that business going.

Willie was the destined heir of the firm, but he was not yet fit to take over sole control. He had not particularly distinguished himself at art school, though his results showed him to have some talent in drawing and sculpting. He was still and, indeed, was always to be in Patrick's shadow. He had grown up to be a pleasant-looking, slender young man with sad eyes, a receding chin, a lisp, and a carefully cultivated artistic appearance, complete with flowing dark hair and a floppy tie. He was still dedicated to Patrick's enthusiasms, and had learned Irish sufficiently well to teach a class at the School of Art and at the Blackrock branch of the Gaelic League. He frequently wore a kilt, a garment of which Patrick approved more in theory than practice. Willie had the figure for a kilt; Patrick did not. He seems always to have felt rather ridiculous when obliged to wear one—he preferred a silk hat and frock coat for formal occasions. The brothers were as inseparable as their busy lives allowed. They went on holidays together to the west of Ireland, they spent much of their leisure time together, and they addressed each other often in baby talk—quite oblivious of the disconcerting effect this had on others, who found it impossible to reconcile with the reserved, serious Patrick Pearse. They now decided to run the business together. Patrick wanted Willie to have the opportunity for further study—he always maintained that sculpture was the noblest of arts, and now decreed, with typical grandiloquence, that at the first opportunity Willie should go to London and Paris to train for his unquestionably great future. In the meantime, together they took over the commercial reins. James Pearse gave way to Pearse and Sons, and Patrick described himself officially as "Patrick H. Pearse, Sculptor".

In a spirit of economy, perhaps, the family moved house again in spring 1901, from George's Ville to a smaller house in Lisreaghan Terrace. As if in compensation, the house was promptly christened and the number and street dispensed with: Liosan, Sandymount, was a little grander.

Patrick did not allow domestic grief or business problems to interfere with his main obsession. He was back at League committee meetings and law lectures within a week of the funeral,[6] and he seems to have kept his father's death so quiet that even the normal votes of condolence were not passed. He worked at the business; he continued to study for his two sets of final examinations, due in June 1901; he ran the Publications committee; he taught his Irish class; he was co-opted to serve on the committee of the Central branch; he attended virtually every meeting of the Coiste Gnotha; he made himself available to any branch in need of an official speaker, in Dublin or outside; he gave lectures, addresses, and never missed an opportunity to speak from the floor at the numerous meetings which he attended.

His anxiety to seize every opportunity to speak in public was symptomatic of his belief in the necessity for long, hard training before excellence can be achieved: "... even the most gifted have to be taught ere they can achieve ... 'Untaught genius' is a vile phrase —as vile as the thing itself is crude and ineffective ... true genius does not disdain training—does not even disdain the mere routine drilling in the techniques."[7] He was always intrigued by the power of the spoken word; he badly wanted to stir crowds by his oratory. But he knew he had first to serve an apprenticeship, and this he did during most of his career with the Gaelic League. He adjudicated recitation contests at feiseanna (local festivals), and he practised his public speaking on small audiences throughout the country. Whether disputing with his more sophisticated contemporaries at Central branch meetings in Dublin, addressing small provincial branches in Mullingar or Castleblaney, or mounting a soap-box outside Connacht churches to harangue the after-Mass crowds, Pearse was learning his craft. Manuscripts of his later spectacular speeches show a preoccupation with the *mot juste*, the balanced sentence, the well-judged pause, the reiterated motif. The adolescent orator whose best audience was his family gave way to a reliable League speaker, who became the man to have at your branch if Hyde, MacNeill and O'Hickey were too busy to come.The most striking feature of Pearse's self discipline at this stage of his life was his ability to combine multifarious activities without letting any of them suffer. In June he took his BA finals and the last of his law exams, and did well in both. His degree was in modern languages, and his results were in line with both his Intermediate and first and second year university performances. As in all those examinations he won an exhibition for a good but not brilliant performance. His subjects were English, Irish and French, and although he did not take first-class honours, he was second of the nine second-class honours. In his law exams he came near the top of the King's Inns group, and in June he was called to the Bar.

He had ambivalent attitudes to the legal profession. Once qualified, he missed no opportunity to sneer at lawyers, and later claimed to be "heartily ashamed" of his BL. Law was the "most wicked of all professions"; lawyers were parasites. This appeared in his writings as early as 1902. And yet he had invested a great deal of money in his legal studies, and no one could ever be prouder of his degree than the young Pearse. For an artisan's son, struggling to achieve middle-class status, the right to don a wig and gown was a privilege to be widely advertised. He always had a liking for titles, and unlike his more sophisticated colleagues in the League, he always described himself as P. H. Pearse, Hon. Sec. It was not long before the Publications committee had its own headed notepaper, emblazoned with the legend: "P. H. Pearse. BL, Hon. Sec.". More commonly he described himself as P. H. Pearse, BA, BL. His pride in his qualifications was not lost on his more malicious acquaintances. Father Dinneen, a sharp-tongued Munster priest who was one of the great League eccentrics, and later one of Pearse's chief critics, always referred to him either as "P. Haitch Pearse" or "B-A-B-L".[8] Although in later years Pearse admitted his youthful vanity, he never dropped his legal title.

Though he seems to have thought briefly about practising on the Connacht circuit,[9] he abandoned the law soon after being called to the Bar—as much because of his growing antipathy to the profession as because of a whole-hearted commitment to the League which would not allow for a career outside it. (His only case, in 1905, concerned League interests.)

Financially he was still sound enough in 1901 to enable him to continue without looking for full-time employment. The Irish classes for University College Dublin were undertaken more because of his interest in teaching than for the money they brought in. The firm was still doing reasonably well. He and Willie had been fortunate in inheriting a business in a flourishing industry. According to the *Leader* in September 1901, ecclesiastical sculpture was in a healthy state, with ample apprentices. Dublin alone had in the region of 60 carvers, 150 stone cutters, and 150 rubbers and polishers, and Pearse's yards employed the largest staff in Ireland. The same year they secured an important order for a high altar for St Patrick's Church, Trim, which was probably what they exhibited at the Cork Exhibition in 1902, an exhibit which showed how little tastes had changed since the 1882 Dublin Exhibition. "High Altar in Sicilian, Carrara, and Irish marbles; Baptismal Font and Credence Table in Sicilian and Coloured marbles; statue of the Sacred Heart in Oak, etc. All the work executed on our own premises by Irish artists." Pearse worked hard for the business, which required much travelling, and where possible, he combined business trips with Gaelic League activities. He contrived during the next few years to give Willie, as he had promised, the time and money to study in Paris and at the Kensington School of Art.

Despite his attention to the business, it was obvious that Pearse regarded his involvement with it as temporary. For the sake of his career in the League, P. H. Pearse, sculptor, was to follow P. H. Pearse, barrister, into oblivion; he even toyed, belatedly, with the possibility of becoming the League's first paid general secretary. In May, the Coiste Gnotha had decided to advertise for a general secretary, at a salary of £200 per annum. Pearse was on the sub-committee appointed to recommend a suitable candidate, who was to have fluent Irish, a good character and address, office training and experience, organizing ability and literary capacity and a wide knowledge of both the movement and the country. Not surprisingly, this paragon was hard to find, although applicants included several respected League members like Owen Naughton, Richard Foley and Piaras Beaslai. By October the unofficial view in the League's corridors of power was that the only likely candidate was a young countryman called Patrick O'Daly. At this stage, to his amazement, O'Hickey was informed by Stephen Barrett that Pearse "would not be averse to taking the secretaryship". He wrote to MacNeill:

> With regard to Pierse, I told Barrett that I did not see how his name could be at present entertained. He would have applied long ago, but thought the salary too small for him, stating that he could make more by paying close attention to his business at home. He hopes now that it would be soon increased, with the forward advance of the League. But it seems to me . . . that we are precluded from entertaining his name at present: as a matter of fact his name has not at all come before us. For my part if the applications sent in give us a man whom I should consider fully up to the mark and having all the qualifications agreed upon, I should consider myself bound in honour to vote for him. . . . If we fail to make an appointment as a result of the advertisement, then we should, I fancy, be quite free to consider Pierse's application. . . . About Pierse himself all I would say is this:
>
> (1) many people think him very haughty and proud; not, of course, those who know him, but people who meet him casually;
>
> (2) there is some danger, I fancy, of a cry getting out that posts are being made for members of the Executive, and it does not

> look well to have men appointed to offices of emolument whilst still on the Executive, or immediately after resigning to qualify.... There is the further point (which is mainly for Pierse himself), whether he is acting prudently in renouncing (even for a time) his chances of making his way in his profession.
>
> These points apart, I suppose there can be no second opinion about his fitness for the office. He certainly has been a great success as Secretary of the Publication Committee....[10]

O'Daly was appointed secretary, and for the moment, at least, Pearse had to forsake any hope of a paid position within the League. The other job which might have attracted him, but for which he was not qualified, the editorship of *An Claidheamh Soluis*, went to Owen Naughton. But he had thrown his hat in the ring; the next time he wanted a paid job he would not be dilatory in applying for it.

VI An Claidheamh Soluis

During 1902, Pearse's life followed much the same pattern as the previous year. The new feature was his mounting interest in journalism. He began to bombard *An Claidheamh Soluis* with articles and reports. Owen Naughton, though a literate native speaker of Irish, was not a success as editor. The paper was unexciting and editorially indecisive. Naughton veered between relying too heavily on Coiste Gnotha decisions to dictate the paper's policies, and impetuously taking up untenable positions which alienated important sectors of opinion—usually the clergy. He was friendly with Pearse and gave him a great deal of publicity and was glad to publish any material he had to offer, most of which concerned his experiences in the Irish countryside.

Pearse's first visit to Aran in the summer of 1898, when he began to study the living Irish language at the feet of J. M. Synge's first Irish teacher,[1] had left him with a passionate love of the Gaeltacht, and the west of Ireland Gaeltacht in particular was to be a life-long passion. From that time on he had contrived to visit the west three or four times a year, and he realized more quickly than many of his colleagues that the future of the language was in the hands of the native speakers rather than the Dublin enthusiasts. The language was dying rapidly, because its speakers associated it with poverty and famine; the most unsophisticated Connacht labourer realized that his children needed English to find jobs in the towns or, more probably, in America. Emigration was sapping the life of the countryside; Irish-speaking parents were sapping the life of the language by speaking English to their children. Most of the Gaeltacht schoolteachers taught only English to their pupils. The necessity of reversing this trend was to be a preoccupation with Pearse and with the League in general.

Pearse's love for the Gaeltacht was idealized. He would spend long evenings in the people's homes, marvelling at their language and their stories, and finding in them all the virtues of his beloved Gaelic civilization. It was a long time before he could see in them anything but purity and beauty. His prose often reached heights of absurdity when he fell to decribing his beloved "kindly-faced, frieze-coated peasants". This piece concerned a meeting at Carrick-on-Suir:

> What wonderful faces one sees in Irish-speaking crowds! Truly the lives of those whose faces are so reverent and reposeful must be beautiful and spiritual beyond your and my ken. A painter might find here many types for a St John, a St Peter, or a Mater Dolorosa. I often fancy that if some of the old Masters had known rural Ireland, we should not have so many gross and merely earthly conceptions of the Madonna as we have.[2]

In February 1902, he published the first in a ten-part serial in Irish about a recent visit he had paid to Connacht. Like most of the writing of this reserved, introspective man, it was highly self-revelatory. "La Fa'n Tuaith" (A Day in the Country)[3] was a story about a trip he took to an obscure village, miles from anywhere. When the priest he was visiting proved to be away, Pearse was obliged to seek the hospitality of the people of a wayside house. Although poor, they were happy and welcoming. Like their neighbours, they spoke Irish which was a joy to hear. They were an idealized family, consisting of a toothless grandfather, a fine giant of a father, a small bustling mother, a beautiful young girl and an intelligent, attractive boy, Padraig Ban (Fair Padraig). Their house was a social centre in the evening; neighbours called on them; the story-teller held them all spellbound with a tale of the Fianna. As a literary creation it was not impressive. Pearse was proud of his widening knowledge of the Connacht idioms, and he lost no opportunity to include, presumably for the edification of his readers, useful words and phrases. He followed, rather uneasily, many of the conventions of the Irish story-teller. There was far too much of the "And I can tell you I was not long in following him" kind of flourish, and it still smacked more of the schoolboy essay than of the serious literary effort of an adult. But as with oratory, so with writing. Pearse had to learn his trade, and he was only beginning.

Where the series was revealing was in Pearse's attitude to the people of the Gaeltacht, their children, and their poverty. It also betrayed great innocence. His idealization of the family with whom he stayed was one thing; his apparent total incomprehension of the unpleasant aspects of poverty was another. The story is set in winter, and there is frost on the ground, but Padraig Ban, his sister Maire and his mother are bare-foot, like all the children whom Pearse meets on his journey. There is no suggestion from this comfortably-dressed and well-shod observer that there might be the faintest discomfort in this. It is a fact of life, and a rather agreeable, romantic fact of life at that. It is echoed in another article written later that year: "A tidier, brighter set of Irish cailins I have never seen in a National School—albeit they had only three pairs of boots between them."[4] He eats a meal of potatoes and griddlecakes and greatly enjoys it, with no thought that it might be a monotonous diet for those obliged by circumstances to eat it most days.

It was not that Pearse was unsympathetic. His love for the Connacht people was wholly sincere: but he had no understanding of the poverty and the fears of famine that drove them to emigrate. To him they were the repository of the noble tradition of the Gael, and it bewildered him that they did not find complete satisfaction in the fulfilment of this sacred duty.

The children held for him a special magic. Pearse, the apprentice teacher, was always more at home with children; he could relax with them and show a gaiety and ease of manner he never displayed with any adult except Willie. The pleasure he took in their company shines through the otherwise rather run-of-the-mill characterization of "La Fa'n Tuaith". And although he describes the beauty of the young girl, Maire, his special pleasure is in the description of Padraig. "He was a comely little boy, about twelve years old, and it wasn't hard to see that he was a brother of Maire's. He had a face as bright as the sun, and no hunting-hawk had a clearer eye than had he. Maire was fair-haired, but if she was, Padraig was much fairer, and he had curly hair, like the coat of a March lamb. He was as slim as a weasel and probably as swift as a deer."*

Pearse found boys physically attractive: this emerges from many similar passages in prose and verse. As the tone of his later writing shows, this taste became more pronounced as he grew older, while remaining wholly innocent of lasciviousness. He never had an inkling that there was anything sexual behind it, and indeed no man of his reticence and obsessional purity of thought and deed could have written as he did otherwise. In the social sphere in which Pearse moved, relations between men and women could be viewed in a sexual light; homosexuality was so aberrant as to be almost beyond comprehension—liberal and informed opinion looked on it with a pitying revulsion otherwise reserved for leprosy.

Although society would have smiled on any properly-conducted heterosexual relationship this apparently eligible young man might have embarked on, Pearse was ill at ease with women—even Mary Brigid. He was not one of those men who crave the company of women, but are too shy to seek them out. Whatever sexual drive he had he sublimated through work. Before he reached puberty, he used to write plays dealing with heterosexual love and passion—formula stuff, presumably included to please the predominantly female cast. After adolescence passion between man and woman virtually ceased to figure in his writings. He was compelled to mix with women to some extent in all his enterprises. One of them, Mary Hayden, a Gaelic League colleague seventeen years Pearse's senior got to know him relatively well in 1903, better than most of her sex. She has written about his attitude to women:

> Their lower, or even their lighter side, he very little understood. He looked on the purity, the power of self-sacrifice, which is to be found more commonly in women than in men, as something divine. On this side he could understand them, for these qualities were strong in his own nature. Anything coarse disgusted him; from a doubtful story or jest he shrank as from a blow. Never, in all the years I knew him, did I ever hear from his lips even the mildest "swear-word".

This sensitivity made it unthinkable that any hidden and unacceptable sexual proclivity of Pearse's should find open or deliberate expression in a context superficially so normal as his early writing. Unfortunately for Pearse's memory, his ingenuous literary productions have survived into a less innocent age, and judged by modern standards they provoked reactions that would have shattered him. "La Fa'n Tuaith", for instance, ends with a sequence which caused great hilarity among the knowing pupils for whom the department of education, innocent in its turn, recommended the text in the 1920s. It occurs when Pearse realizes that he is being given Padraig Ban's bed.

"If you only have two other beds," said I, "there will not be room for the five of you. You must put little Padraig in my bed."

"God forbid," said Caitin, surprised. "Go up to bed quickly, Padraig."

Padraig was on his way to the loft, but before he reached the ladder I told Cait that I wouldn't go to bed at all unless she let Padraig sleep with me.

Although she was an obstinate woman, she had to yield to me.

"Everyone to his will," said she. "The loft is good enough for Padraig, but if you are determined to share your bed with him, I'll not go against you".

I think that Padraig was contented to be allowed to sleep with me. We went back to the room without delay, undressed quickly and into the bed with us. We stayed awake for about an hour talking together.*

Despite the naïveté of this series, and of some of his other writings, Pearse's command of Irish, his consistent concern for the Irish speakers, and his vigorous League missionary work were winning him increased respect.

By the end of 1902 he had become a force to be reckoned with. Apart from O'Hickey (for MacNeill, overworked, was beginning to withdraw gradually from the more extortionate demands of League business) there were few officers of the League so dedicated to its interests and so industrious on its behalf. And he was assiduous in ensuring that this was recognized. Any rural visit he made which was in any way outside the norm he wrote about at length for the *Claidheamh*, and was often made the basis for a paper to a Dublin branch. His enthusiasm was infectious; often the impression given was that he had "discovered" the places he visited. He went to Glasgow in June on behalf of the League, and the *Claidheamh* remarked that his visit was likely to strengthen the local movement considerably. There was a large attendance at one of his Glasgow addresses, "all heartily appreciating Mr Pearse's work of counsel". When the League set up its various committees, Pearse, adding to his already heavy burden of work, took seats on the Education and Finance committees. All this activity was helping to win him the praise of his colleagues, though Dr O'Hickey entered a *caveat*: "Pierse's opinion is always worth having, but he appears to lack imagination, and movements depend a good deal on imagination."[5] Of course O'Hickey was not talking about romantic imagination, which Pearse always had in superabundance, but political imagination. Pearse had little sensitivity about others; he was so unlike the average man that he found it impossible to understand what made him tick.

Pearse took a brief holiday at the turn of the year—in the west of course—surprisingly enough with a woman, his colleague Mary Hayden. The situation appears to have arisen accidentally. Mary Hayden, a history lecturer, was typical of the well-educated, serious-minded, Dublin Gaelic Leaguers. She was also typical of the kind of woman Pearse was mixing with in the course of his work. At this time, many of the prominent women in the League were either mannish or odd: it was an era in which professional ambition in women was considered an eccentricity at best, and those who worked in the upper echelons of the League often affected unfeminine traits in dress and manner, perhaps in an attempt to be taken seriously in a man's world. Certainly, Pearse met few who could have been described as eligible. Of his first female colleagues, Norma Borthwick was fractious, even venomous, by nature. Mary O'Reilly, who lived with her, was unhinged, and died in a lunatic asylum. His two reliable and diligent female colleagues were Agnes O'Farrelly and Mary Hayden. Both of them were academic spinsters, with more pretensions to intellect than personal charm.

The diarist Joseph Holloway was typically harsh in describing them. Of Agnes O'Farrelly, he wrote: "In her 'Empire' gown and strange little topknot of hair she cut a quaint semi-grotesque Dresden china-like figure on the platform."[6] She was, he said, "a young girl with an old woman's voice.... She is a very unattractive speaker with a strong weakness for hearing herself talk." About Mary Hayden he was hardly more kind. "How is it literary folk dress with so little taste? Misses Haydon, Louise Kenny ... were sights to see and marvel at."[7]

This "sight" was over 40 when she and Pearse spent their holiday together. She had been engaged for some years, but her fiancé was dying of consumption. Nobody could consider her a sexual match, and Pearse was proportionately at ease in her company. Her diary gives a third-party account of one of Pearse's Gaeltacht visits, of Pearse in relaxed mood—yet far from idle. It has a melancholy charm of its own as well.

Thursday January 1st

Here I am down at Letterfrack Co. Galway, trying to get practise in Irish speaking. Mr Pearse, an enthusiastic Gaelic Leaguer (BA, BL) is my companion and there is no one else except a young priest at the hotel. Mr Pearse is only 23, young enough, if I had married v. early indeed, to be my son. Yet Hester [her friend, Dr Sigerson's daughter] and I dare say others, didn't think my coming with him over proper: however—I came and *he* at least seems to have no hesitation about accepting the situation as a matter of course, which is a blessing. We talk a lot on all sorts of subjects and I find him most companionable, a really nice fellow. I am enjoying my holiday greatly—except when thoughts of poor Arthur come up.

This morning we both got drenched cycling from Mass and we did not go out at all again. I did some Irish in the evening.

Friday
We walked to Kylemore, which is beautiful even now in winter and wandered about the place, returning to potted salmon at 4 o'clock and to a long talk until 11.30.

Saturday
We had a very long walk today by a round to Recess. On the way we turned into numerous cabins. Mr Pearse talked to the people and I listened, putting in a word now and then. They are v. nice people, polite and courteous, though the pig *does* sleep in the living room. At Recess we had some food in the hotel.... Then we walked back; altogether we must have done some 14 miles....

Sunday
We were awfully late for Mass at Tully, it was disgraceful. After Mass we went into a cabin and talked to a v. nice woman. We returned, left our cycles at the hotel and had a stroll. We visited the Industrial school; the brother who showed us over it asked us to an entertainment tonight, and after dinner we went. There was dancing and singing and some acting; the two former very fair, the latter poor, except for an excellent little fellow, who seems to have real ability. The lads looking on seemed rather spiritless. Poor children, even in a poor home they would be happier, I think. We returned to tea and a long chat over the fire. Mr Pearse is returning to Dublin tomorrow.

Monday
The post brought two dismal letters—one from poor Arthur, who is distinctly worse.... It made things all the worse as I was alone to think them over, for after breakfast Mr Pearse started for Clifden. I saw him a mile or so on his way and then turned back. I felt very gloomy....

Wednesday
We reached Dublin at 7.12 and Mr Pearse met me at the train. It was really v. good of him; he wheeled the laden bicycle right across town.

Thursday
I had a distinct feeling that things were *flat* and I missed the long chats with Mr Pearse though I had them for less than a week—it's easy to get used to what you like....

Friday
Visited Hester ... [who] cannot get over the *solus cum solâ* nature of our sojourn in Letterfrack, yet she isn't a scrap conventional....

Monday
... over to the Gaelic League, where there was a concert and a couple of scenes from a play. Mr O'Neill acted. He did look funny with a flowing wig and long moustache dressed in a tunic and with bracelets on his bare arms. Mr Pearse walked to the tram with me. It is odd how one lives a little while in great intimacy with a person and then they drift away, perhaps altogether.

Mary Hayden was also to be an onlooker, but this time one of many, at the brutally efficient fight which Pearse put up during the next seven weeks for the editorship of *An Claidheamh Soluis*. His early departure from Letterfrack was due to his anxiety to be back in Dublin to intensify his campaign.

If the League was divided on many matters, it was united on one: Owen Naughton was a bad editor, and should be replaced. Following a particularly serious political error, which had compromised O'Hickey badly, the latter wrote to MacNeill in November 1902 in despairing tones.

> What on earth is to be done with O'Neachtain [Naughton]? Such an awful exhibition of vacillation, of alternate strength and weakness, finally ending in utter imbecility and making the League a laughing-stock before all men, has never before been seen ... here we have a fool after making a show of fight giving away the whole case.
>
> I am in utter despair about the *Claidheamh*.... As far as I can see there is nothing for me except to leave the League.... The first fight, in which, for tactical reasons, I have had to stand aside, has been bungled beyond all description.

Naughton's case was discussed by the Coiste Gnotha. In January he was given a two-month trial, but his fate was already sealed. O'Hickey for one was determined that he should go. "He will never *edit* the paper, make it a force, or cause it to be read.... Balance and sobriety of judgement are required in an editor of the *Claidheamh*, but not timidity and vacillation." The ideal editor, said O'Hickey, needed first-rate Irish, good English, journalistic instinct and aptitude, loyalty to the League and the Coiste, complete acceptance of its constitution (which at the time was under fire from the Keating branch) and its ideals, and well-balanced judgement.

By 8 January, candidates for the editorship were already under discussion. According to O'Hickey, there were only three available candidates: Pearse, W. P. Ryan (a London journalist and Gaelic Leaguer whose son, Desmond, would later be Pearse's first biographer), and Patrick MacSweeney, a Munster native speaker. "The only objection to Pierse would be that he is not a native speaker. I don't mind this very much; for he seems to me to write Irish very gracefully and idiomatically, and is a scholar. But I know that others mind it a great deal." O'Hickey was, however, already favouring MacSweeney, who, he said, was "well-educated, level-headed, determined and resourceful". There was some alarm when it became clear that the redoubtable Father Dinneen wished to be considered. A man so pugnacious, hyper-sensitive and intolerant, however fine a scholar, was "out of the question". Even Dinneen quickly grasped that he would be unacceptable, but he began to look round for another candidate to back. O'Hickey's position began to harden towards the middle of January, apparently in response to lobbying. "I am against advertising the post and will stand firm for a native speaker until it is proved that there is none fit. Nothing will induce me not to make that a '*sine qua non*'." Nor would he accept a compromise solution of two editors, dealing respectively with the Irish and English sections of the paper. "We must have one man—a native scholar if we can get him, or if not Pearse."

Although the League had had a rare moment of unanimity over the necessity to replace Naughton, the usual divisions were quickly intensified over the question of his successor. In response to a letter from the other sharp-tongued Munster cleric, Father O'Leary, O'Hickey wrote: "His letter is mostly abuse of the Executive.... Father Peter is not practical." O'Hickey in the same letter also showed that Pearse was not standing idly by. "Pearse is most anxious for the position, that is now clear. Failing a qualified native speaker, he is, I believe, the best candidate."

All these undercurrents were not lost on the unfortunate

Naughton. At the end of January he wrote a sad, dignified letter to MacNeill.

> I heard that you are on the sub-committee which is looking at the *Claidheamh*'s work.
>
> If you want to fire me I would be grateful if you would let me know in advance so that I can resign, because I would prefer to give up the job myself rather than have people throw it at me that I had been sacked.
>
> I know that I will get honest, kind advice from you at least.*

According to *Banba*, not predisposed in his favour, Pearse had been engaged in a vigorous canvass long before the middle of February, when Naughton officially resigned, and Pearse put his application before the Coiste Gnotha.[8] On 17 February its members discussed the three declared candidates, Ryan, MacSweeney and Pearse, and in Mary Hayden's words "each one voted as he considered journalistic training, full command of Irish or 'level-headedness' more important".[9] Her mind was made up. "I think Mr Pearse would be best. No decision was come to—they will advertise. It was 12.50 when we left. Mr Pearse walked home with me. He would be the man to make the paper succeed I think."

Pearse's band-wagon was rolling, and although there were a few attempts to stop him, they were sporadic and unco-ordinated. *Banba*, for instance, hampered by being a monthly journal, managed nothing more than a side-swipe at him in its February issue, in a review of the second penny booklet of recitations, *An tAithriseoir* (The Reciter), which he had again edited with Tadhg O'Donoghue, a Corkman. "What in the name of reason, is the meaning of having such a collection—a mere sixteen-page booklet—under joint editorship, with the names of the editors boldly set out on the title-page, especially when ... most of the work is the work of Tadhg? ... Aspiring editors should really have some sense of proportion, and what is even more essential, the manhood to strive after a reputation by legitimate means."

The *Claidheamh* editorship, worth £240 a year, was advertised on 21 February. It did not help to allay criticism of the Coiste Gnotha that it was a small advertisement, which demanded that applications be lodged by the 27th. Pearse was now able to canvass officially. Although the Dublin members of the Coiste Gnotha had been thoroughly lobbied, there remained the non-resident members, those who were full members but, living outside Dublin, rarely attended meetings. Letters to J. J. Doyle show how

Pearse set about rallying this support. He displayed no false modesty, and a much improved grasp of the prevailing politics of the League.

> I am applying for the editorship of *An Claidheamh Soluis* as advertised in the current issue. I don't know what your view may be with regard to the names ... which have already been informally before the Coiste. I find, however, that I am being actively and determinedly canvassed against, and am now obliged in self-defence to put my position before one or two members who, I believe, if placed squarely in possession of the facts, would be in my favour.
>
> My qualifications both in Irish and English, my long and close communication with the details of League work, both in the country and at Headquarters; my personal acquaintance with practically all the Irish-speaking districts:— all these are well known to you. My position for the past five or six years on the Executive, and for the past three years as hon. sec. of the Publication Committee has been, as it were, an apprenticeship for such a post, whilst my work on the sub-committee has brought me into touch with all the leading Irish writers and workers. I think, too, I may fairly claim to be above all petty provincial jealousies, and in a position to steadily regard the movement as a whole.
>
> It seems to me that whilst, of course, our editor must be a capable writer of Irish and English, he must also bring to the management of the paper a steady level head and a strong hand: clear sane notions of things; the faculty of grasping issues and facts, and being able to gather round him a loyal band of competent writers; he must be able to give a lead to the country, and inspire the country's confidence.
>
> If you are in favour of me, I frankly ask your vote (if present at the meeting), and in any case your influence. I do so with the less reserve inasmuch as I have reason to believe that I am being fought unfairly. Your own good sense will prompt as to what is best to be done in the circumstances. More may depend on this appointment than any of us yet see.[10]

Doyle was not convinced, and said as much in his reply. Pearse answered immediately.

> Many thanks for your prompt and honest reply. Of course, I see that a native speaker should get the preference, *other things being equal*. That, however, is the rub. It would be fatal to thrust an

untried man into the position simply because he is, or is alleged to be, a native speaker. I am, of course, an interested party, but for the sake of the League as well as my own, I hope the Coisde will not be guilty of the folly of taking on trust a man with no experience save that of a country town, and about whose general qualifications we have only the word of his own personal friends. We did that on the last occasion, and with disastrous results.

It seems to me that while a vernacular knowledge of Irish is important, it is by no means the most essential thing. After all, it is not the business of an editor to write his paper, but rather to get it written—to organise a staff of representative writers in whom he inspires confidence. Naughton writes practically none of "An Claidheamh". It is neither necessary nor desirable that the editor should, as a rule, write even his own leading articles. The same style, however good, would pall ultimately. On the contrary, he should command the services of the best writers in the country. His own duty should be to keep things going, to organise his forces, to keep in touch with all the workers and centres, to arrange and set in order.

We want a man who will make the best use of the writers at his command, and give the country a lead. That, I think, is far more important than a native knowledge. If we can combine the two, well and good. But can we?[11]

Nor did Pearse leave matters here. Two days later, he sent Doyle a circular which was, presumably, sent to all other interested parties. It was a comprehensive statement of his views on how the paper should be edited. News in Irish should have increased prominence, and should be written by competent writers from the various provinces. Every week there should be a leading article, by a leading writer of Irish, treating "from an Irish Ireland point of view the countless vital problems which confront the country, —such as the land question, emigration, industries, agricultural organisation, railway reform, the drink question, technical education, etc.... The object of these leading articles should be to lead the thought of the Irish speaking districts, and educate it on the pressing Irish problems of the day." There should be a students' section, "short bright stories or sketches", humorous, attractive and vivid, a column of "racy ancedotes", and at least one illustration in each issue, connected with a leading Irish-Ireland event. As for the English side of the paper, there should be a weekly leader "giving the country a lead as to the policy to be adopted with regard to the events of the hour". The English notes should have freshness and variety. A staff of local correspondents should be organized, book reviewing should be prompt and adequate, leading writers of English like Lady Gregory, W. B. Yeats and W. P. Ryan should contribute literary articles. The size and shape of the paper should if possible be increased, and its format made more rational and attractive. The editor should attend all important local celebrations, and should also attend the meetings of the Coiste Gnotha, and the Organization, Publications, Education and Oireachtas sub-committees. By any standards this was an impressive document, demonstrating that he had thought long and intelligently about the paper, and would bring to it a badly-needed freshness and energy.

Nor were Pearse's admirers idle. MacNeill received two letters by the same post from leading Leaguers advocating Pearse's cause, from two different standpoints. George Moonan, a Dubliner much disliked by the Corkmen, wrote on a slim pretext to savage Pearse's opponents.

> Mr MacSweeney has given no proofs of the breadth of view, the powers of insight, comparison and grasp that are the essential of an editor. On the contrary his circumstances appear to have been against the growth of such qualities and his public efforts have not displayed much depth or originality of thought ... my impression [at a recent meeting] ... was that he was slow of comprehension in following the proceedings of the committee and not very lucid in his ideas or in his expression of them—and certainly not forcible in the last. A nervousness and hesitancy that he showed I ascribed to character rather than to shyness or to a trick of manner, and such a fault in character would be fatal in an editor.
>
> ... Ryan is a good journalist but his method of arguing in generalities on imaginery premises makes me doubt his judgment and his involved journalese *in English* would scarcely arouse enthusiasm or direct it; and he has had *to force* his mind into the moulds of the movement.

Stephen Barrett, a gentler personality, took a more positive approach.

> Now I think you will agree with me that taking everything into consideration the one who would best serve the interests of the League and the one best entitled to the post is Pearse. His talents and abilities are of a very high order. He has done enormous work for the League during the past five or six years, for all of which he has received not a penny. His knowledge of Irish, spoken

and written, is very good. For these reasons I think his friends should leave no stone unturned to secure his election. I have been thinking that you might see your way to interview Dr Hyde . . . on his behalf. Pearse is to my mind so well suited and so well entitled to the post that it would be great hardship if he did not get it. Apart from his suitability in other ways his loyal services to the League, in a laborious office, for many years past should count for much.

When the Coiste Gnotha finally met to elect the new editor, it had a slightly revised range of options. W. P. Ryan had ultimately not applied, but J. J. O'Kelly, a Munster writer backed by Dinneen, was a late candidate. An unprecedented number of council members turned up for the meeting, some from as far afield as Belfast, Derry, Kerry, Galway and London. The result was a triumph for Pearse, who got nineteen votes against three for MacSweeney and four for O'Kelly, but at least two of the three most important men in the League—Hyde and O'Hickey—had voted for MacSweeney, and O'Hickey was furious at the annihilation of his own candidate.[12] For some time he had been toying with resigning from the League. This made up his mind. Pearse, rushing home to tell the news to his mother, who had been praying for his success, had unwittingly lost O'Hickey for the League.

An Claideaṁ Soluis

[An Claidheamh Soluis.]
Agus Fáinne an Lae.

[Registered as a Newspaper.]

CHAPTER THREE

JOURNALIST

I The New-Style Claidheamh

Pearse's editorship began with a row. The issue of the *Claidheamh* which had appeared on 7 March 1903, five days after his election, contained an anonymous article critical of the bishops' Lenten Pastorals for their lack of reference to the Irish language. The article's tone had offended the clerical elements within the League and alarmed the moderates. Furious letters appeared in the *Freeman's Journal* on the issue, mainly from clerics, including, of course, Father Dinneen. Their letters were full of phrases like "scandalous exhibition", "calculated insult to the Bishops of the Catholic Church", "dishonour and disgrace". It was difficult to establish whether Naughton or Pearse should bear the responsibility, but a compromise solution was reached: "... the Coisde Gnotha regrets that any article couched in such a tone as that signed 'Ua' in the last number of *An Claidheamh* should have inadvertently been admitted whilst arrangements for a change in the editorship of *An Claidheamh Soluis* were being completed."

Capitulation was necessary. The League, however it might regret lack of episcopal support, could not afford to alienate the clergy: it had to try to win them over to its cause. Pearse was not, however, frightened off by this reminder of clerical power. God was on the side of the Gael, and if the priests didn't realize it, it was time they did. Throughout his tenure of the editorship of the paper, the *Claidheamh* never ceased to summon the clergy to the cause of Irish Ireland, and to rebuke them when they appeared to dally or obstruct.

Before reorganizing the content of the paper, he had sweeping changes to introduce in its format. Although technically he did not take over responsibility until the tenth, he presented a *fait accompli* to the Finance committee at a special meeting on the sixth.

> Mr Pearse stated that he considered it advisable to make a change in the shape of the paper; and that having decided to do so he could not wait for the special meeting and the change had therefore been made.
>
> The committee approved of the change on condition that the additional cost would not be more than £2.10 per week; the ordinary tender to be submitted in writing.

This was to prove a pious hope.

A broadsheet was sent out with the paper to branches and subscribers on the twelfth, which outlined both Pearse's new mission and his proposals for its pursuit:

> It is felt that, with the nationalisation of the Gaelic League's work, the time has now come for the nationalisation of the League's weekly organ. On the other hand, the rising tide of native thought, now becoming for the first time in recent history an educated and disciplined force, demands an adequate outlet for its expression. To attain these two objects, and at the same time to more effectually cope with the present needs of the organisation, it has been decided to make a radical alteration in the character and appearance of *An Claidheamh Soluis*.
>
> In future, *An Claidheamh* will be an Irish-Ireland newspaper in the largest sense of the words. It will be issued in broadsheet form, the space available will be increased by one-third, and a still further economising will be effected by a new disposal of the matter. For the rest, as to our hopes and aims, we quote from our leading article in the current issue:—
>
> "Henceforward, current news in Irish will be the outstanding feature of our Irish department. Our news columns will be written by a staff of competent and representative Irish writers. Home affairs will naturally occupy the place of honour. Foreign events will be treated in due perspective, and will always, of course, be approached from the Irish side. Our ideal is to place in the hands of the Irish speaker in Glenties or Aran a newspaper

giving him, in vivid idiomatic Irish, a consecutive and adequate record of the home and foreign history of the week.

"The best writers of Irish Ireland will continue to contribute stories and sketches to our literary columns. We have opened a special section for students and propose to devote a corner to our juvenile Gaels ... Our editorials—Irish and English—will aim at leading the thought of the country and educating it on the countless vital problems which confront Irish-Ireland.

"As the organ of militant Gaeldom, this paper has a well-defined mission before it. It will be its duty to put clearly the point of view of the Gael: to make articulate the thoughts and hopes and ambitions of those who dwell in the Gaelic places. It has a further function as the first fighting line of an organisation which has become the dominant force in the land. As the Gael rises to the surface, and that organisation looms larger in the national life, this paper will gradually become the leading organ of opinion in the country."

An impressive programme, but an expensive one—and there was more to come.

The issue of 14 March included an illustration of O'Hickey and a pull-out picture of Hyde, and subsequent issues included illustrations and more elaborate design work. In October, Pearse asked for a private office to be set up for him, and also for funds to be made available for the payment of contributors to the paper. He was also given longer holidays than his predecessor, and extra staff was taken on. A new manager was appointed to the paper: Sean T. O'Kelly, who, five decades later, would be President of Ireland. These departures caused a major headache for the Finance committee. The *Claidheamh* was printed by the Clo-Chumann, the League's own printing company, which, by August, was losing heavily on the new *Claidheamh*. The reasons given for the loss were the unexpectedly large proportion of Irish (printed in Gaelic script), the weekly illustrations, duplicate lining on the first three pages, tabulated matter, expensive paper, and overtime due to the late arrival of copy.[1]

Pearse lost his illustrations and had to modify the format, but he was not yet out of the wood. A letter to O'Kelly in November 1903 shows how Pearse was having to face up to the financial facts of life:

I hope you will succeed in getting a sufficient number of good advts. at at least 3/- an inch to fill the two side columns of page 1 of "An Claidheamh", and that you will have them in time for the next issue. They should, if possible, be fairly permanent ads., so that they would not require to be changed frequently: An Clo-Chumann should, in spite of what Shanley may say to the contrary, be able to give a very appreciable reduction per week if this were effective.

I wish we could manage to fill page 7 every week. I also wish we could fill the bottom portion of page 6: we might have a sort of feuilleton of advts.... Have you asked the secs. of the Wexford Feis to give us their syllabus as an ad? You might also write to the secs. of the Mayo Feis for an ad. of their syllabus: I gave them a good puff last week, and it is only fair they should stand to us in return. You could put this point strongly in writing them.

"An Claidheamh" is really in a serious position: it was referred to at the Coiste Gnotha meeting on Saturday, and was also the subject of some strong remarks in a letter ... No effort must be spared to make it a paying property, and that depends entirely on the advts. As 100 copies costs practically as much as we get for them, mere circulation scarcely counts. The advts. must be worked up at all costs: not only the future of the paper, but in a large measure the future of the League depends on this. I tremble for the result at next Ard-Fheis [Representative Congress] if it is found that the League has spent nearly £1000 on *An Claidheamh* during the year, and *An Claidheamh* still a losing concern. They will possibly think of dropping the paper altogether.

... You and I must make a success of this thing at all hazards: our reputation depends on it, and much more, both for us & the League.[2]

In the same month he and O'Kelly put a brave face on the paper's position in a circular to the branches.

When, some eight months ago, it was decided to launch *An Claidheamh Soluis* on a new career as a militant Irish-Ireland newspaper, it was felt that while the step would necessarily involve increased responsibility, financial and otherwise, on the Coiste Gnotha, there would undoubtedly be a corresponding return in the shape of an increase not only in the influence and utility of the paper, but in the prestige of the movement as a whole. We are glad to say that this expectation has been to a large extent realised. *An Claidheamh* now occupies with regard to the Irish-Ireland movement at large the commanding position which rightfully belongs to the official journal of the Gaelic

League. Whether judged from the point of view of its value to the organisation itself, from that of its influence on contemporary thought in the country, or even from a point of view of mere circulation (not always an unerring index of influence), the position and prospects of *An Claidheamh Soluis* are, on the whole, encouraging. Since the change in its form and character the circulation of the paper has increased by more than 50%.[3]

The circular ended with an injunction to all members to help increase circulation and advertisements.

In March 1904, with the commencement of Volume Five, drastic economies were imposed by the Coiste. Pearse was obliged to admit to his readers that the paper was too large and too expensive, and was being reduced in size. The League did not again make the mistake of letting Pearse have his financial head, despite his pleas to them to set the paper up as a separate company with capital of £1,000, and the paper began to pay its way. By early 1905, it was making a small profit and it continued to do so for some years. It also steadily increased its circulation.

The episode is a highly significant one for a student of Pearse's psychology. As in all his enterprises, he started by reaching for the moon, and was bewildered at finding it unaccountably out of reach. Again people had let him down. Irish Ireland advertisers failed to buy it in appropriate numbers; and most disappointing of all, even Gaelic Leaguers failed to do their duty by it. He had started out by giving his public the best: the paper he redesigned so quickly was attractive and well presented. He did not count the cost (he never did in any of his endeavours), and was fortunate in the people who pulled on the reins. Again he had betrayed that serious flaw in his character—an inability to understand that such single-mindedness as his was not common among his associates.

There is evidence here of another, quite incongruous, trait. The printers had complained about the late arrival of copy, and the Finance committee had to tell Pearse to stick to agreed copy times. Curiously for such a disciplined and industrious man, Pearse was almost arrogantly unpunctual, most notably for meetings which he knew would wait for him. Mary Brigid has some stories which illustrate this irresponsible streak.

Regularly he would gravely warn his mother that if the tea were not on the table at six, *precisely*, his whole career would be blasted. The fond and trustful lady used to bustle round and have tea to the second. Yet at eight o'clock he would be leisurely drinking stone-cold tea and calmly perusing some book. When reminded of the time, he would appear mildly surprised, and then remark in the most casual manner: "How annoying! I ought to have been delivering a lecture in the city at eight sharp!" Then he would flash his mother a quizzical smile, and rush out like a whirlwind.

> It was literally true that he ought to have been lecturing at eight o'clock! I, myself, have sometimes been sitting in a crowded hall, waiting for this very casual lecturer, who, I knew, could not possibly arrive for at least half an hour, the reason being that I had left him at home peacefully drinking tea or correcting proofs.[4]

As with audiences, so with printers. Alfred MacGloughlin, the Pearses' cousin recalled:

> At this time he was editor of *An Claidheamh Soluis*. At 7.30 when the alarm rang out, he would start throwing pillows, books, boots—anything, in fact, at the clock, in order to stop the noise so that he might go to sleep again. At 8.30 he would reawaken, spring from the bed, and cry frantically: "There are twenty printers cursing me now!" Madly he would scramble into his clothes, bolt his breakfast, and rush from the house.[5]

Unpunctuality apart, as editor of the *Claidheamh* his single-mindedness never waned. His devotion is evident in every issue of the paper.

II Issues

Pearse had never lacked opinions; now he had a platform for their expression. His own contribution to the *Claidheamh* during over six years as its editor ranged over an enormous variety of topics: politics, education, history, emigration, literature, theatre, morality, religion and countless other subjects were handled, along with his own stories and poems. He had a natural facility for writing, honed by his years of apprenticeship, and allied to his formidable industry this enabled him to produce thousands of words every week, while continuing to make speeches and give lectures throughout the country. From his editorial pulpit he thundered against opponents of the Gaelic cause, and equally against its faint-hearted or self-seeking adherents, earning himself many enemies both within and without the League. On the other hand, his positive nature, his wholehearted belief in the League's work and his blossoming gift for communicating his enthusiasms gained him a great deal of respect.

Pearse set out to explain to his readers their duties to the cause, and reminded them of these duties throughout his period of office. In innumerable editorials he expounded his belief that the supreme calling was the preservation of the Irish language, an objective which should occupy the souls and minds of the Irish people: no other cause could even approach it in importance.

> When the position of Ireland's language as her greatest heritage is once fixed, all other matters will insensibly adjust themselves. As it develops, and *because* it develops, it will carry all kindred movements with it. Irish music, Irish art, Irish dancing, Irish games and customs, Irish industries, Irish politics—all these are worthy objects. Not one of them, however, can be said to be fundamental.
>
> When Ireland's language is established, her own distinctive culture is assured.... All phases of a nation's life will most assuredly adjust themselves on national lines as best suited to the national character once that national character is safeguarded by its strongest bulwark....
>
> To preserve and spread the language, then, is the single idea of the Gaelic League. While other causes are borne along by it as the water-fowl is carried by the current, it alone is our inspiration.... We have a task before us that requires self-sacrifice and exertion as heroic as any nation ever put forth.... Woe to the unfortunate Irishman who by his lethargy, his pride, his obstinacy, or his selfish prejudice, allows the moments to pass, or impedes this national work until it is too late.[1]

This total commitment to the language was not, of course, common to all *Claidheamh* readers. There were many fellow-travellers who believed that the language revival was only one of several important objectives. In a letter to the *Claidheamh* in 1905, a distinguished contemporary of Pearse's, Tom Kettle, then a journalist and supporter of the pro-Home Rule Irish parliamentarians, took issue with Pearse. Their exchange of views demonstrated clearly the essential simplicity of Pearse's mind—his inability to see the web of issues around his own prevailing obsession. Kettle had a subtle and wide intelligence, and in his sympathetic letter he challenged Pearse's narrowness.

> The life of a nation, or ... the battle of a nation for life, is complex and multiform, a web of very various functions and

activities, and to compress it into a single organisation is impossible. Many organisations are necessary, each of which operates in a definite and limited province....

But this specialisation has one bad result. Men who have put their lives into some one branch of national effort come to regard that branch as supreme in value, as *the* movement. Thus we have Mr Redmond speaking of "the work being carried on by the United Irish League as 'the National Movement' in contradistinction to the work of the Gaelic League." And on the other hand we have yourself, with all your largeness of view, writing, "The language movement is, of course, only a part of the national movement, but it is its most important part—the part which gives vitality and coherence to the whole." As a matter of psychology it is necessary if we are to do anything effectively that we should for a time believe it the only thing on earth worth doing; and we see how in due course everyone comes to consider his profession in life as the centre and indispensable hub of reality. But useful as this illusion is, we must not introduce it into our statements of public policy. All the leaders of all the movements should remember how the disciples disputed as to whom was the first among them, and what came of the dispute.

... since ... the Ireland of the future must be free as well as Irish, the political movement is indispensable.[2]

Pearse missed the point. In his reply, although he showed a courtesy which was typical of him in personal controversy, he clung resolutely to his original position: the language came first.

Mr Kettle thinks and writes so sincerely and, as a rule, so justly that we believe he will, on reconsideration, come to see our view that the language movement is the most important point of the whole national movement and "the part which gives vitality and coherence to the whole", is not to be lumped with the "illusion" commonly entertained by men who have devoted their lives to the serving of a cause. In truth, the language movement is not merely more important than the political movement, but it is on a different and altogether higher plane.... Political autonomy ... may ... be necessary to the continued existence of the Nation—in the case of Ireland it probably is—but it is not, in itself, an essential of nationality.[3]

It was years before Pearse modified this position; he was a very late convert to political rather than cultural nationalism. At the *Claidheamh* he used only one criterion in making judgements on contemporary events—did they help or hinder the language movement? He read a wide range of contemporary newspapers and journals—British, French and American—and missed few opportunities to comment on relevant affairs. He kept a close eye on the progress of cultural nationalism, especially in the Pan-Celtic countries, and drew parallels for Ireland. His imagination was fired by the publication, late in 1904, of Arthur Griffith's *The Resurrection of Hungary*. Griffith, the aggressive, harsh and very gifted editor of the weekly *United Irishman*, was an apostle of Irish political separatism who produced, in this book, a piece of inspired propaganda, drawing dubious lessons from resurgent Hungarian nationalism for the edification of Ireland. Pearse was entranced.

> We do not know that there has been published in Ireland in our time any book in English more important than "The Resurrection of Hungary".... [It] marks an epoch, because it crystallises into a national policy the doctrines which during the past ten years have been preached in Ireland by the apostles of the Irish Ireland movement.
>
> ... [The Gaelic League] must always continue to be the soul and nerve centre of the movement; but the movement is wider than the Gaelic League. There are departments of national life with which the League voluntarily precludes itself from dealing....
>
> The moral of the whole story is that the Hungarian language revival of 1825 laid the foundation of the great, strong and progressive Hungarian nation of 1904. And so it shall fall out in Ireland.[4]

But the sympathy with political nationalism which he intimated in this editorial did not affect his belief about what was really important. As he said at this time in a running controversy with the *United Irishman*: "Political autonomy ... can be lost and recovered, and lost again and recovered again. It is an accidental and an external thing—necessary, indeed, to the complete working out of a national destiny, necessary, in many cases, to the continued existence of a people, but not in itself an essential of nationality."[5]

Although his position in the League did not preclude him from joining a political party, he continued to stand aloof. The *Claidheamh*'s manager, Sean T. O'Kelly, became an active member of Sinn Fein, the political party founded by Griffith in 1905 on a platform of national self-reliance. Although Pearse applauded the work done by O'Kelly in his capacity as a member of the Dublin Corporation, he became distressed at his neglect of his League duties. By 1908 this was making him desperate. He wrote to ask MacNeill to bring O'Kelly to heel.

> The fact is that, as the auditor said a year and a half ago, "An Claidheamh" is not being managed at all. It is being allowed to manage itself. The advertisements have been let decrease to a lower point than ever. *Nothing* is being done to increase them. *Nothing* is being done to extend the circulation. *Nothing* is being done to collect the debts. At the present moment, there is far more money due to us than would pay all our debts, yet not a penny of it is being collected, and each month Barrett has to make an advance. What the Manager is doing I don't know. He is hardly ever at the office. Sometimes I don't see him for whole days. I don't think he spends more than half-an-hour a day on average at the office.... What occupies him or where he is all day I can't say. He may be at Corporation meetings. He may be doing Sinn Fein work. He may be doing Coiste Ceanntair [Dublin Gaelic League] work. He may be doing Vincent de Paul work. But I am perfectly sure he is not doing the work he is paid for—managing "An Claidheamh Soluis".
>
> ... The present situation is intolerable and is getting on my nerves.

To O'Kelly, of course, a member of the secret Irish Republican Brotherhood (IRB), the Gaelic League was only a means to the end—political independence. Not an excuse Pearse could swallow.

He maintained his non-political stance throughout his period at the *Claidheamh*, even praising the English administration when he felt it was deserved. His defence of Chief Secretary Bryce, a Liberal who gave practical support to the Irish language, provoked an attack by Griffith's new paper, *Sinn Fein*. Pearse replied "We said—and we repeat—that Gaels will retain kindly memories of the official who, in spite of all the forces against him ... has done these things."[6] He showed a similar open-mindedness over the Irish Council Bill, proposed by the Liberal government in 1907 as a partial answer to the demand for Home Rule. Although even the moderate Irish parliamentarians rejected the Bill because of its narrowness, Pearse supported it because it gave educational home rule. If it gets on to the statute book, he said, "we shall be on the eve of the greatest and most beneficent revolution in the modern history of Ireland. THE SCHOOLS WILL BE OURS."[7]

His colleagues felt otherwise. One of them said so in a letter to MacNeill (who himself opposed the Bill).

> ... wanted to talk to you re Pearse's articles. They are spreading consternation and dismay amongst rank and file and I think the Advisory Committee ought to intervene and stop any more editorials re the Bill until Coisde Gnotha has given him instructions and declared its view and policy.... I certainly am not going to leave the impression abroad that he speaks for the League as if the League had instructed him to write as he has done. There are calls far and wide for a change in the editorship and I think the circulation will go down 1000 a week soon, if he continues there. Anyhow I think the damage being done should be checked at once—things are bad enough as they are without being made worse.[8]

The total rejection of the Bill put an early end to the controversy and saved Pearse from further repercussions, but the personal nature of the attacks had distressed him greatly. Six years later he wrote about this period in *Irish Freedom*, urging the need to accept criticism as a spur to action rather than as a destructive force.

> You are a member of the Gaelic League. A friend and colleague writes to the press to point out that you are selling the League to the Liberals and that your reward will be a title. This is not a damned lie: it is his way of hinting that you ought to be a little more strenuous, to smite a little harder and a little oftener, to keep up perpetually a sort of Berserker rage or *riastra* in the way of the old heroes.[9]

Pearse's failure to make concessions to the clerical establishment did not endear him to more orthodox contemporaries. In 1907 Maynooth College, the national seminary, relegated Irish classes from compulsory to voluntary status, and Pearse went straight for the throat of the president, Monsignor Mannix (later a famous Archbishop of Melbourne). He blamed him for the decision, which was felt throughout the League as a serious blow to the policy of providing Irish-speaking priests for Irish-speaking districts. It was particularly hard to take from an institution which had been in the vanguard of the language movement. "Can it be that where Irish Ireland hoped to find a friend she has found an enemy who is in a position to do her untold harm?... What shall it profit

Maynooth to cut a fine figure in the Royal University Results List if the Irish language dies in the Gaedhealtacht and with it the old, pure, unquestioning strenuous faith of Ireland?"[10] Strong stuff—which was improved upon in successive weeks. "It is the beloved College of O'Growney that has declared itself with the Gall and against the Gael. Men whom we had thought trusty have failed us."

Mannix was undeterred by all the assaults of the League and its paper. He wrote an unrepentant letter in response to appeals from the Coiste Gnotha, putting it in its place: "it will be a day of joy and of hope for the friends of the national language when the Gaelic League, in its great work throughout the country, begins to follow the example and to rival the success of Maynooth. The Irish language will then be safe."[11]

Pearse's attack had meanwhile infuriated influential sections of Irish opinion. Archbishop Walsh, the old friend of the League, threatened to withdraw his support. In a letter to him Agnes O'Farrelly pleaded the League's case:

> I frankly confess I was both surprised and pained at Your Grace's letter of yesterday.... I need hardly say that I regret extremely that Your Grace disapproves of any action of the Gaelic League and that the organisation is in danger of losing your sympathy and friendly help....
>
> May I point out to Your Grace that Claidheamh Soluis has never advocated compulsion as such. It has only cried out against a retrograde step and one which may endanger all the hard work of years—and it has been cruelly hard work at times. The manner in which the details have been gone into has not pleased many members of the Coisde Gnotha—but a committee cannot edit a paper.[12]

Maynooth emerged triumphant, and the flow of Irish-speaking priests to the Gaeltacht was no longer guaranteed. Two years later there was a bigger fracas, big enough to bring O'Hickey out of the self-imposed retirement from League affairs which had lasted since Pearse's appointment as editor. It centred around compulsory Irish again—this time in the new university—and again Pearse was in the thick of it, wielding the *Claidheamh Soluis*.

There was no acceptable university for nationally-minded Irish Catholics. Trinity was still resolutely a Pale institution; the Royal University had no teaching facilities; the two Queen's Colleges at Cork and Galway were run on British lines and made few concessions to resurgent Irish cultural nationalism. Pearse had for years been a vociferous agitator for a truly national university. But he rejected the demand that the university should be instituted with government support—a vain demand, he believed, for something that was in any case undesirable: "Are the joint forces of the Church, of political nationalism, and of Irish Ireland unequal to the founding of a National University?"[13] He did not want a specifically Catholic university—Irish yes, but not "a water-tight denominational institution with doors rigidly barred against non-Catholics".[14]

As usual, his colleagues' selflessness did not meet his standards. Although the Gaelic League echoed his call for a university founded by popular subscription, it proved an impossible dream. Ultimately a government decision was needed to found a national university, comprising the Cork and Galway colleges, and setting up University College, Dublin, as the third constituent establishment.

The Gaelic League demanded from the outset that the National University should make Irish a compulsory—or as it termed it, "essential"—subject for Matriculation. Although it was initially unsuccessful, there was a long-drawn-out agitation on that and on the allied question of staffing and controlling the new university. Foremost in the campaign for "essential Irish" was Dr O'Hickey, who had lost none of his old *penchant* for polemics during his hibernation in Maynooth. To many his language seemed intemperate. In a pamphlet entitled *An Irish University, Or Else*— he railed against the opponents of essential Irish in a manner which did not endear him to the many clerics, including the Standing Committee of Bishops, who were in the opposite camp.

> If we tolerate this thing [optional Irish] we are still a race of helots, deserving the contempt and scorn of mankind. Let us brush flimsy arguments and peddling considerations and specious sophistries aside. Our difficulties are of our own making. More particularly, I grieve to say, are they the making of the class to which I belong, the Irish clergy, the one influential and educated class during the worst years of our national decadence.... Let us not suffer ourselves to be cajoled and wheedled out of it [a new university with essential Irish] by a section of the Irish population, who, though Catholic, are un-Irish, when not anti-Irish, in every fibre of their being, even in the innermost marrow of their bones.

In July 1909 he was dismissed from his chair at Maynooth by the trustees, the Irish bishops. Pearse, who hitherto had been relatively tolerant of the opposers of essential Irish, was furious, and outspoken in defence of his old opponent. He knew, he said, that Mannix would recommend O'Hickey's dismissal, but

> could not believe that the Bishops of Ireland would dare to lend themselves to the vile work of the suppression ... of Irish intellect and freedom of thought. There is ... no longer room for doubt. The Bishops have done their worst against Irish-Ireland. It is not Irish-Ireland who will suffer. Neither is it the noble priest whom the Bishops have turned out of their College—the bravest man of all the men of Maynooth who, from O'Growney to the young students so shamefully penalised today [i.e. deprived of Irish classes], have been building up the Gaelic League and the language movement. It is the good name of the Bishops of Ireland that will suffer; it is, we fear, the good name of the Catholic Church that will pay the penalty of the folly and shortsightedness of those who represented it in Maynooth on Tuesday last....
>
> The thing that amazes one most is the horrible fatuity of the men responsible for this piece of tyrannical blundering.[15]

Although the League condemned the dismissal, and although there was widespread condemnation of the bishops' action, Pearse's no-holds-barred style yet again caused alarm. MacNeill, who had since O'Hickey's resignation been a vice-president of the Gaelic League, and who was more approachable than Hyde, was often the recipient of disgruntled letters. One such came from the president of Sinn Fein, John Sweetman, a very orthodox Catholic, who had previously had brushes with Pearse. "For years I have thought that Mr Pierse as editor of An Claidheamh Soluis would bring the Gaelic League into difficulties. With the best intentions he has no prudence. The abuse of the bishops in his leading article this week 'The Dismissal of Dr O'Hickey' will do us no end of harm and will delight the enemies of the Gaelic League."

But Pearse was not silenced, even by a denunciation from the bishops themselves.

> Considering the course which, especially of late, is being pursued in this and similar matters by certain newspapers—including one which is generally reputed to be the official organ of the Gaelic League—the Bishops feel it to be a sacred duty to warn the people committed to their charge against allowing themselves to be misled by writings the clear tendency of which is antagonistic to the exercise of episcopal authority and which, in some

instances, are calculated to bring into contempt all ecclesiastical authority, not even excepting that of the Holy See itself.

(Signed)
MICHAEL, Cardinal Logue,
Chairman
RICHARD ALPHONSUS, Bishop of Waterford and Lismore
ROBERT, Bishop of Cloyne,
Secretaries to the Meeting.[16]

He replied to this with characteristic courage.

> We are the mouthpiece of a non-sectarian organisation, and as such we have no standing in any matter concerning the exercise of episcopal authority within its own sphere. But we claim and will always exercise the right to criticise any action of the Bishops, as of any other body of Irishmen, which affects the welfare of the Irish language.... The men and women of the League will ... stand by the man who has stood by them.[17]

Pearse was too industrious and effective an editor to be easily replaced, and he never pulled his punches. But neither he nor anyone else could save poor O'Hickey. He spent years fighting his case unsuccessfully at Rome and died unhonoured and unsung in 1916. Pearse's affirmation that "the noble priest" would not suffer was a reflection of his life-long belief that material or professional deprivation was irrelevant if a man knew himself to be in the right.

This failure to understand deprivation was fundamental to his attitude on another great issue of this period—emigration. It was not an attitude unique to him. Colleagues of his like Mary Hayden were equally innocent of the raw reasons for emigration—fear of a mean life on the land which provided subsistence at best, poverty and hunger for many. Pearse found the logic elusive—like so much about his countrymen. "Let us plainly tell the emigrant that he is a traitor to the Irish State, and, if he but knew all, a fool into the bargain."[18] He supported the viewpoint of the poet Alice Milligan that Irishmen should be content to stay at home as landless labourers and Irishwomen as domestic servants: "if the emigrants are still fleeing, a large proportion of them ... can scarcely be accounted a loss, for they are deserters who have left their posts, cowards who have refused to work in Ireland though work is to be had."[19]

He had harsh words too for the American Irish who encouraged their relatives to seek a better existence. "If our American exiles—

our 'deserters', as a prominent Gaelic Leaguer once called them—would let us alone, the matter [abandoning Ireland and Irish] would not be so bad; but their interest in Ireland is chiefly manifested in their efforts to induce the remnant of the population that remain in the country to leave it."[20]

His old belief that the natives of the Gaeltacht should be content to stay and preserve their unique heritage was manifested in an address to the people of Rosmuc on the need to uphold the language. A heckler shouted in Irish " 'It's not much use when you go past the Burned House!' "*[21] The Burned House was the landmark which marked the boundary of the Gaeltacht; beyond that point a knowledge of English was essential if a living was to be made. And despite all the best endeavours of Pearse and his friends, the native Irish continued to go past the Burned House.

Pearse's writings, of whatever period, make clear his energetic belief in the necessity for action. The people must act to save the language, the teachers must educate the children along Irish lines, the clergy must preach sermons against emigration, the League faithful must propagandize at every moment of their lives. He was no Hyde, no diplomat, no practitioner of masterly inactivity. The one and only court appearance of P. H. Pearse, barrister-at-law, was a result of his passion for action—however precipitate; it concerned the matter of painting Irish names on carts.

It was legally necessary for a cart-owner to put his name on his cart, and with the spread of the League's ideas on the use of Irish forms where possible, individual cart-owners began painting their Irish names in Irish characters. There were one or two prosecutions on this account, with small fines resulting, and these were faithfully reported, with appropriate editorial fulminations, in the *Claidheamh*. Douglas Hyde, with his usual political acumen, believed that softly-softly was the way to secure widespread use of Irish names—a matter of symbolic importance. He wrote about this episode years later, in an unpublished memoir, with unconcealed irritation.

> When I was going to America in 1905 [an inaccuracy—this was before his American trip—his diary shows that this was a lengthy trip to England] I left the strictest orders that the question should not be opened in the law courts. I wanted the placing of the Irish forms on carts to become so common that it could not be interfered with, and the government was not interfering. To my great annoyance this plan of mine was knocked on the head

> by Pearse, who being a barrister appealed to the higher courts against a fine [on Niall Mac Giolla Brighde—Neil MacBride], and argued the case before the Lord Chief Justice Peter the Packer [Lord O'Brien] and another [Mr Justice Andrews] who complimented him on his knowledge of Irish and his conduct of the case—and promptly decided against him, as any fool with half an eye must have foreseen that they would do. Thus it was made illegal not only to have the name in Irish letters but to have it in any form except the correct English form. I heard Pearse was quite pleased with the compliment the judges paid him, but that was poor compensation for bolting and barring the door against Irish names for ever, or at least from that day to this.[22]

Pearse of course saw the matter differently. He had been strongly supported on the Coiste Gnotha by such militants as Sean T. O'Kelly,[23] and in his view it was a glorious assault by the Gael on the bastions of English law in Ireland.

> On Tuesday last the language movement marched boldly into the King's Bench Division of the High Court of Justice in Ireland, and for five hours counsel discussed with the Lord Chief Justice, Mr Justice Andrews, and Mr Justice Gibson, various questions ranging from the origin of the Irish alphabet to the position of the Pan-Celts with regard to the Irish language.[24]

The wide-ranging arguments were indeed put with knowledge and skill. (Pearse had not expected to lead for the appellant—he had been retained as second fiddle to a greatly distinguished barrister, Tim Healy KC, the Irish parliamentarian, but Healy had failed to turn up.[25]) But the arguments were irrelevant. The judges were kind to the inexperienced counsel and the young solicitor, his friend Louis Walsh. Lord O'Brien noted that the case had been "most elaborately and interestingly argued". Andrews referred to "the very ingenious, interesting, and, from a literary point of view, instructive arguments of Mr Walsh and Mr Pearse".[26] Gibson was more blunt: "The interesting antiquarian discussion on the history of the form of Saxon and Keltic letters does not help. The statute refers not to prehistoric or obsolete shapes of letters, but to living symbols."

Pearse had not argued as a lawyer—his mind was not attuned to it. The notoriety of the case resulted in a flood of prosecutions of cart-owners, which gave Pearse great delight. He urged them to further intransigence.

> We are only carrying out the spirit of the resolution of the Ard-Fheis when we advise all Gaels to simply ignore the British Law that makes it penal for them to use their own language to the exclusion of English. If they are summoned and fined, let them refuse to pay; if they are sent to prison, let them go to prison. The question can be brought to a head no other way.[27]

He showed no concern about, and possibly was unconscious of, the difficulties which this policy brought on its followers. At the end of 1905 he announced triumphantly: "By its spirited action in the Niall MacGiolla Brighde case the League placed British Law and Order on the horns of a dilemma; and the case of the language has benefitted hugely by the prosecutions which have since ensued."[28] It is not immediately clear how the prosecutions had aided the language. Many cart-owners who had had Irish names on their carts for years were now being prosecuted. With a change of administration in 1906, which brought Ireland a liberal chief secretary and attorney general, the prosecutions virtually ceased and the issue died down. But Pearse never had any doubts—any action was better than no action. He was prepared to fight to the last cart-owner.

III DISCORD

As O'Hickey had pointed out, Pearse was not an imaginative man. But however insensitive he was to the human strife around him, in his position as the *Claidheamh*'s editor he could not fail to be increasingly aware of the dissensions within the League. The unpleasantness over the Pan-Celts had been his first introduction to this unhappy reality; the row over his election was the second. At the end of the first year of his editorship he was already commenting sadly on the great flaw in the Gaelic League—its lack of cohesion. He desperately wanted to see a united organization fighting its enemies as one man. Every year he waxed lyrical about the League's great show of force—Language Week. During this week, usually held around St Patrick's Day, there were nation-wide festivities, a national collection which raised thousands of pounds for the cause, and the climactic Language Procession through Dublin. Those who marched represented every section of society sympathetic to the aspirations of the League, from school-children to industrialists, temperance societies to political nationalists. To Pearse, it was a soul-stirring sight.

> For three long miles the host of the Gael extended through Dublin streets....
>
> Dreamers of dreams, perhaps, were they who marched there, but stern purposeful men nevertheless—dreamers who have made their dreams into facts.[1]

He waxed lyrical about the great men of the organization.

> Carriages drive up—it is the Coiste Gnotha, with An Craoibhin, the beloved, amongst it, and Eoin MacNeill, the quiet, forceful man in whose brain the idea of a popular movement for the salvation of the Irish language first crystallised, and whose keen northern mind, sane and practical, has given the whole movement which he created its characteristic trend of thought.[2]

Certainly, for dedicated Leaguers, the procession was the high spot of their year. The vast crowds taking part and looking on bore heady witness to the growing prestige of the movement. To those involved, all goals seemed achievable in such an intoxicating climate. But there were those who saw in it a complacency which made it ridiculous rather than glorious. Sean O'Casey, a language enthusiast who gradually became involved in the labour movement and republicanism was, as usual, a sceptical onlooker, who wrote later (with ample poetic licence and layers of puns):

> Here come the carriages holding the neatly-clad forms, trim beards, set faces, sober-hatted, silently-jubilant, respectomissima members of the Gaelic League's Central Executive, the Coiste Gnotha, their whole demeanour making all men aware of their non-political, non-sectarian natures, each bluffed out with a pride of his own, for the money the crowd was giving was rattling into the collecting-boxes, the chink-chink of the falling coins loud above the methodical medley of the rolling drums.
>
> In a leading carriage rode Dr Douglas de Hyde, with a pleasant little branch of bells in his hand, and a barr buadh [trumpet of victory] a thousand times the size of a bucina on his lap, and he looking, in his innocent happiness, like a bigger Boy Blew. By his side sat a mauve-soutaned, crimson-girdled Domestic Prelate of the Vatican, who laughed, and slapped the Doctor affectionately on the back all the way along, calling him a jolly good fellow, and appealing for confirmation from a tinker and

a flapper fairy who sat on the opposite seat. Beside them, on a prancing white horse, went Oona Ni Merrily, [Una Ni Fhair-cheallaigh—Agnes O'Farrelly] with rings on her fingers and bells on her toes, followed by Mary Ni Hayadawn, [Maire Ni Aodhain —Mary Hayden], in a pony and trap, her tender voice ever calling on the Irish people to come to these yellow, white and green sands, catch hands, and sing, The cuckoolin is icumen in in Gaedhilge. Next came the biggest carriage Dublin could supply. In it were two men, the sweat rolling off them, counting the money the collectors were pouring in on to the floor of the vehicle, with Stiffun Barrett, [Stiofan Bairead—Stephen Barrett] the official treasurer, holding an umbrella over them to keep the sun off their heads so that they could count calmly an tawn bo cooly. Then came Eoin Mac Neill aswing in a sedan-chair carried by an Ulster man, Connaught man, Leinster man, and a Munster man, one at each corner.... Trudging along in a wide space by himself came Padruig Mac Pirais [Padraig Mac Piarais —Pearse], head down, dreaming a reborn glory for Ireland in every street-stone his foot touched; followed by vis-à-vis, landau, brougham, and victoria, containing the rest of the Central Executive, sleek and sleepy-looking, crooning quietly to themselves. We are all nodding, nod, nod, nodding; we are all nodding, so Irish and so fey![3]

Pearse's dreams of a reborn glory for Ireland were sadly bruised by his experience of Gael's inhumanity to Gael. As P. S. O'Hegarty later wrote, the executive "was composed of a number of strong-minded people divided into groups, who hated each other like poison, and would almost have assassinated each other if it would advantage the victory of the particular dialect of Irish in which they believed as the master dialect."[4] The squabbles were endless and acrimonious, and they left Pearse, a man without venom, bewildered and hurt. He wrote frequently in the *Claidheamh* of the need for unity—with little result, since his guileless words were taken as veiled attacks on individuals. In an editorial in 1904 he condemned the wranglers. "Any man who, while professing to support the Irish language, would for personal or extraneous reasons estrange from the movement the support of any person or class, or who would waste the strength of the movement on subsidiary or non-essential matters, must be regarded as a conscious or unconscious traitor."[5] This elicited a defensive reaction from one pseudonymous correspondent, who saw it as an impertinence.

Is it brave, or Irish, for anyone to shelter himself behind your desk, and thence hurl insults at men, who have given their whole lives to every Irish work, to keep our people pure, to elevate them from the foul ways of Saxon civilization?

You have no right to denounce those who condemn the shams, and shoneens [apers of English manners].... You have no right to call those with keener sensitiveness and clearer vision of what such a sham leads to, "traitors".[6]

But Pearse went on with his sermons to the faithful. In one of his Christmas editorials he wrote about a worker's duty to the cause.

What is patriotism but a pure and disinterested philanthropy, a charity embracing every known and unknown member of the nation's household, and extending to every one of God's creatures, animate and inanimate, which claims with ourselves the motherland as a home?...

One of our duties to Ireland is to be good and pure, kindly and true.

... Do we always show sufficient of that spirit of kindly Christian charity which should characterise the mutual dealings of ordinary Christian men, let alone of workers in the same cause, and that cause so sacred as ours? Are we sufficiently tolerant of one another's opinions? Has the movement given rise to as many fine and steadfast friendships as, all things considered, it might be expected to have done? Has it not, on the other hand, been rather prolific, we will not say in enmities, but in estrangements, in misunderstandings, in suspicions?[7]

If Pearse thought that appeals, however high-sounding, would shame such Leaguers as Father Dinneen, Father O'Leary and their fiercer colleagues in the Keating branch, he was to be disappointed. The bitter factionalism did not abate. Stephen Gwynn, the Irish parliamentarian who served for a time on the Coiste Gnotha later referred to the "cantankerous spirit" of the League, of which he said justly that both Hyde and Pearse were innocent.[8] No eloquence could sweeten that cantankerousness. But Pearse, dogged to the last, kept trying.

We plead for the return of that old spirit [of comradeship]. What we ... deplore is the concurrent existence of a spirit of mistrust which separates district from district, province from province, native speakers from non-native speakers, the supporters of one policy or organisation from the supporters of another, the favourers of one mode of spelling from the favourers of another ... do we not, by our lack of toleration and generosity, by the lightness with which we speak and write hard things of one another, by the readiness with which we take offence and the slowness with which we forget, often make work in the movement unnecessarily unpleasant for ourselves and for others? There is need in the Gaelic League for more broadness of view, for a greater fineness of feeling, above all for a more carefully-adjusted sense of humour.[9]

There was little enough humour in 1908 over the question of paying teachers' fees for teaching Irish during school hours. Pearse opposed this—Irish should be integral to the system. Dinneen responded with vindictive relish. As his biographer justly said: "Dinneen was as amicable a man as one could meet so long as he got his own way—but he thought that the man who did not agree with him was witless and culpable."*[10] His style of invective was summed up in an earlier grumbling letter to Pearse, in which he denounced the hapless secretary of the Gaelic League, O'Daly, as "ignorant and crooked".[11] He initiated a series of attacks on Pearse in the *Leader*, which had for years been a persistent critic of the *Claidheamh.*

No one would care much what the *Claidheamh Soluis* says if the Coiste Gnotha weren't paying for it. People think it is the *official organ* of the Coiste Gnotha and Connradh na Gaedhilge [Gaelic League] ... many people will think that this *organ* thinks more of Cherry and Starkey [the National Board Commissioners] than of the Coiste Gnotha ... but these paragraphs are not the opinion of the Coiste, perhaps it derives from two or three members, or from Cherry and Starkey, but not from the Coiste Gnotha.[12]

He called for Pearse's replacement as editor and took issue with other aspects of his educational policy. Dinneen's attitude was supported by furious letters to the *Claidheamh* from such future political allies of Pearse as Cathal Brugha and Piaras Beaslai.

This controversy led to a number of resignations from the Coiste Gnotha, including those of Dinneen and O'Leary. Pearse, as on other occasions, had alienated important figures from the League in spite of his self-imposed duties as peacemaker.

His distress at the turn of events led him to publish a full-page rebuke of the "Wrecker Party", which had called a special meeting of the Ard-Fheis (League Congress) to vilify the Coiste Gnotha, and the *Claidheamh* editor. Pearse called upon the League as a whole to rally to its executive. He traced the growth of opposition in the League.

> For years past, as most of those who have to any extent shared the inner councils of the movement are aware, there has been an official "opposition" in the Gaelic League. This little band, including some Gaels undoubtedly honest but also others who in the pursuit of their propaganda have never hesitated to follow indirect and crooked paths—men not without talent and dowered with quite an unusual share of energy and pertinacity—this little band, we say, has impartially opposed everything that those at the head of the movement have done or endeavoured to do, and just as impartially urged the doing of everything which the leaders of the movement have felt it to be unwise and impolitic to attempt. At each Ard-Fheis these malcontents have mustered in force. Every year has seen them with a new grievance and a fresh shibboleth.
>
> ... Enmities have grown up; ugly wounds have been given and have festered; bad blood has crept into the system of the movement, welling up from time to time and subsiding only to well up again ... the whole movement suffers from it as from a foul disease.
>
> During the past two or three years, but more especially during the past twelve months, the ulcer has been coming to a head. Pretext after pretext has been seized or invented for virulent attacks on the Coiste Gnotha and on individual members of it. Provincial bias has been attributed to it; corruption has been imputed to it; misuse of funds has been broadly hinted at; its members have been accused of climbing backstairs to Government patronage, and finally the whole body has been charged by the leader of the Wrecker Party with "trimming its sails in sympathy with the wishes of a Castle Department".[13]

The Wrecker Party had persuaded *Sinn Fein* to back its actions.

> It is stated that there is an implied understanding, if not an express agreement, that at the Ard-Fheis the Sinn Feiners are to support the malcontents on the Fees Question ... that the whole party, embracing as it does many earnest and able Gaelic Leaguers, is willing to wreck the language movement at the bidding of a disaffected handful within the movement itself, is, we hope and believe, untrue

He ended with a paragraph intended to win over the undecided.

> We must not be taken as imputing unworthy motives to all, or even to the majority, of those who are taking part in this attempt on the independence and integrity of our movement. Most of them we believe to be honest and earnest Gaelic Leaguers. They have, however, been fed for years on unwholesome suggestion, innuendoes, and downright falsehoods by the little group which has apparently set itself the task of throwing down the edifice so slowly and painfully built up by the life-work of An Craoibhin, An tAthair Eoghan [O'Growney], Eoin MacNeill, and the other young men and women who fifteen years ago commenced to toil at the foundations of the Gaelic League. Even to this little group—even to its head and leader—we do not attribute base motives. When Father Dinneen says that the League has been trimming its sails in sympathy with the wishes of a Castle Department; when he hints at corruption and malversation of funds; when he allows it to be understood that he would be glad to see An Craoibhin ousted from the leadership of the movement, and states bluntly that it is his object to capture AN CLAIDHEAMH SOLUIS and to drive Una Ni Fharily and An Dr Mac Enri [Dr Henry] from the Coiste Gnotha—when he says all this he may be actuated by motives the most lofty and altruistic. It is not for us to probe his conscience: we have merely to state the tenor of his words and to draw attention to the trend of his policy. That trend is, we firmly believe, towards the destruction of the movement.

He subscribed to the view of W. P. Ryan, the editor of an anti-clerical weekly paper the *Peasant*, which had accurately summed up Father Dinneen. "It would not be unfair to say that for some years past Father Dinneen has been *in* but not *of* the Gaelic League. We admire his gifts and do not doubt his sincerity, but we mistrust his imagination, question his judgement, dislike his plan of campaign, and declare that his position ought to be made perfectly clear."[14] But he did not go along with Ryan's view that the campaign was a clerical conspiracy against a lay-dominated organization. Dinneen's attitude "has ... a much more personal and a much less recondite significance than that". He ended his editorial with a direct appeal for unity in support of the Central Executive at the special Ard-Fheis.

Unsurprisingly, although the League moderates rallied, Dinneen and his adherents were unaffected by any appeals. Cathal Brugha wrote to Pearse what the latter described as an abusive letter, saying he could convict him of a string of "absolute falsehoods".[15]

Dinneen repeated his charges and inspired the Keating branch to propose to the Ard-Fheis "That we direct the Coiste Gnotha to form a new sub-committee the duty of which will be to carefully examine the leading and sub-leading articles of the editor of *An Claidheamh Soluis* before they are printed." This drew from Pearse probably the bitterest personal invective of his career. Dinneen, he said, was either deliberately seeking to bring the leaders of the language movement into bad odour, or his words "are the mere meaningless ravings of a diseased imagination".[16] The Central Executive won the encounter at the Ard-Fheis, but nothing could heal the wounds.

Hyde wrote ten years later, in his unpublished memoirs, about this aspect of League politics. His career in the League was by far the longest of all its major figures. He was president from 1893 to 1915, when the IRB takeover finally forced his resignation. During the last ten years he was the victim not only of the tactics of the Keating branch and its allies, but of Sinn Fein—and particularly Arthur Griffith—which sought to infiltrate the organization and force it into a political mould. Hyde was not discouraged as easily as O'Hickey had been, or as Eoin MacNeill was in the early 1900s, but he could not forgive the personal vilification which he had had to endure.

> When a person is working unselfishly for any cause, it is perfectly easy to drive him out of it by getting some one to abuse him for what he is doing or has done. A man finds it much easier and much smoother for himself to simply drop the work he was doing. He says to himself "Why should I expose myself to abuse for others? If that is the way I am to be treated let them do without me." I have seen this in the Gaelic League time and again. It was the personal abuse that was showered on Dr O'Hickey by Sgeilg (O'Kelly) [Sean, not Sean T.] and his friends of the Keating Branch in that narrowest, meanest and most bitter of all Irish publications Banba that drove him out of the Gaelic League, the election of Pearse to the editorship of the Claidheamh being only the last straw. Dr O'Hickey called these men footpads so incensed was he at his treatment by them. The same thing happened with John MacNeill.... He was attacked ... in the most monstrous and violent language, and not in the Gaelic League Journal alone but in other papers ... holding him up as a renegade and a traitor and I don't know what else.... Those attacks had their natural consequence, MacNeill gradually dropped out of the League, ceased apparently to take any interest

> in it, and finally although he was Vice President deserted the meetings altogether.... He was the longest-headed and most clear-sighted man in the G. League and had great moral influence with the members....
>
> The G. League, which was really a delightful body of men and women so long as it was actuated by only one desire, that of restoring the Irish language, began to lose its charm when it became powerful. It was then worth capturing and people, notoriously Griffiths, set about to do so.[17]

Pearse was as sickened by the new trend of the League as anyone. Although much later he dismissed it as a spent force when he opted for political rather than cultural nationalism, he admitted to close friends that he had been greatly hurt by the abuse lavished on him. He was accused of snobbery for wearing morning clothes at League formal functions, of pride because of his reserved manner, of anti-clericalism, and of sucking up to Dublin Castle. His Irish, so painfully acquired by long years of industry, was scoffed at by native speakers. Although he was scrupulously fair in the *Claidheamh* in giving equal treatment in the Irish pages to the various dialects, he was abused for giving prominence to non-Munster Irish. And mud thrown at the Coiste Gnotha as a group ("corruption and malversation of funds ...") adhered equally to him. Revival of the language was his passion throughout the decade, but internecine strife was hastening his disenchantment with the League and leading him to consider ways to work for that revival as an individual, rather than as a member of an unwieldy group.

IV PROSE AND POETRY

In Pearse's new expanded *Claidheamh* much space was devoted to Irish literature and in many ways it was in this area that he achieved his greatest editorial success. He wanted to make progress on two fronts—in editing and popularizing Irish classical texts and in stimulating an indigenous modern literature. Although he had resigned from the secretaryship of the Publications committee when he became editor of the *Claidheamh* in 1903, he kept a close interest in its activities and resumed the secretaryship in September 1905. He was not wholly disinterested. He published in the *Claidheamh* (and persuaded the committee later to publish in book form) his own versions of two Irish folk-tales, *Bodach an Chotha Lachtna* (The Rustic in the Drab Coat) and *Bruidhean Chaorthainn* (The Enchanted Hall of the Rowan-Tree), both of which were competently edited. In the *Claidheamh* he also published, with Owen Naughton, an edition of *Toraidheacht Fhiacail Riogh Greag* (The Quest for the King of Greece's Tooth). All this work was later praised by Hyde.[1]

An aspect of contemporary Irish scholarship which affected the Pearse edition of *Bruidhean Chaorthainn* was the necessity for bowdlerizing the text. Conan, the hero, in the original manuscript loses the skin of his buttocks; in Pearse's version, it is the skin from his heels, the back of his head and his shoulders. Not that Pearse would have had any choice in the matter: because of the staunch respectability of Irish scholars, and because of their uncomfortable awareness of critics of the vulgarity of Irish folk literature, bowdlerization was automatic. But in any case Pearse was himself, as he showed in an embarrassing later episode, unappreciative of the earthy and bawdy in native Irish humour. It was a manifestation of his beloved Irish culture that he failed to absorb or even understand.

His love for native literature appeared again and again in his paper. Early in his editorship he set up a fund for Colm Wallace, a Connemara folk-poet, who had been discovered in an Oughterard workhouse at the alleged age of 107. With his usual indefatigable energy he sent letters appealing for money for Wallace and organized his transfer to a private house. It was a feature of his appeals in the *Claidheamh* that he demanded rather than requested contributions; in his later financial difficulties this was to be a recurring motif: "We are not appealing to the charity of the Gaels, we are asking them to perform an act of duty."[2] Although Wallace died in 1906 in a workhouse hospital, he had had two years of relative comfort, was not treated as a pauper, and finally had his funeral paid for out of Pearse's fund. The League also published a book of his poems.[3]

Pearse was still a great admirer of the pioneer literary work of Father Peter O'Leary, "perhaps, the most striking and picturesque figure of our movement: its sinewiest writer, its raciest speaker, one of its most masculine thinkers".[4] At this stage he still believed, as he had written in a university magazine in 1901, that the source of creative Irish writing must grow from the Gaeltacht rather than from English models:[5] writers must have a sound knowledge of old Irish literature. As late as 1904, in an admiring review of O'Leary's *Seadna*, he wrote,

> Irish prose of tomorrow, whilst retaining much of the lyric swing and love of melody of later Irish prose, will be characterised by

> the terseness, the crispness, the plain straightforwardness, the muscular force of what is best in mediaeval Irish literature.... It will be founded on the speech of the people, but it will not be the speech of the people; for the ordinary speech of the people is never literature, though it be the stuff of which literature is made.[6]

Although he had considerably modified his position on the Anglo-Irish contribution to literature, and had asked Lady Gregory to write for the *Claidheamh*,[7] he still believed that it provided no real alternative to the development of native literature. "While personally we have a high admiration for much of Mr Yeats' work, we agree ... that the movement of which that work is a product is 'a movement of defeat'."[8] And two years later, in 1906:

> Unlike most Gaelic Leaguers, we have a sincere admiration for much of the work of Mr Yeats, Mr Russell [George Russell—AE], and the other poets and dramatists of what, without irreverence, we may call the Celtic Twilight School.... But do Mr Yeats and his fellows hold a place in the intellectual present of Ireland comparable to that held, say, by An tAthair Peadar [O'Leary] or Conan Maol [Patrick O'Shea—the Gaelic League writer]? ... The Twilight People will pass with the Anglo-Irish Twilight.... The future is with the Gael.[9]

Unfortunately, the Gael failed to flock to this call with a new vital literature. Although there was some talented work being produced in Irish, it was poor stuff beside the luminous creations of the galaxy of Irish writers in English. No amount of exhortation could produce literature of the calibre of Yeats, Lady Gregory, AE, or George Moore. Pearse applied himself with his customary thoroughness to the analysis of contemporary Gaelic literature, and to concocting the recipe for a renaissance; by 1906 he had begun to realize that mediaeval Irish literature was not enough.

> ... a little more originality, a little more boldness, a little more ambition on the part of Irish writers ... [is] both necessary and desirable ... a living modern literature ... cannot ... be built up on the folktale.... Irish literature gave models to Europe. Is it not high time that it should give models to Ireland? ... We must get into touch also with our contemporaries—in France, in Russia, in Norway, in Finland, in Bohemia, in Hungary, wherever, in short, vital literature is being produced on the face of the globe. Two influences go to the making of every artist, apart from his own personality—if indeed, personality is not

only the sum of these influences: the influence of his ancestors and that of his contemporaries.[10]

Pearse was benefiting from a wider range of acquaintances. His interest in the theatre, in particular—an interest fostered by Willie, who had a taste for the stage—brought him into contact with Leaguers who looked to different horizons. Men like Edward Martyn, a cultured, patriotic Catholic landlord, and Tom MacDonagh, a young schoolmaster with poetic ambitions, could not fail to have a seminal influence on a mind as susceptible as Pearse's. He was developing a position on literature far more modern in outlook than most of his League colleagues—he had one foot in the literary world outside.

> We would have our literature modern not only in the sense of freely borrowing every modern form which it does not possess, and which it is capable of assimilating, but also in texture, tone, and outlook.... We would have the problems of today fearlessly dealt with in Irish: the loves and hates and desires and doubts of modern men and women. The drama of the land war; the tragedy of the emigration-mania; the stress and poetry and comedy of the language movement; the pathos and vulgarity of Anglo-Ireland; the abounding interest of Irish politics; the relations of priest and people; the perplexing education riddle; the drink evil; the increase of lunacy; such social problems as (say) the loveless marriage.
>
> ... There would seem to be an amazing conspiracy amongst our writers to refrain absolutely from dealing with *life*—the one thing with which, properly considered, literature has any concern.[11]

A little later, he wrote that literature is "the author's *view* of something ... It is the revelation of the artist's soul ... *his* interpretation of a fragment of life".[12] Irish writers, he observes, are just photographic. In the same issue he paid tribute to Ibsen, who had just died and for whom he had developed a great respect. "We hail him, dead, as one who showed the world what the 'little' nations can do."

Such comments, although they represented orthodox contemporary literary opinion, were heretical to many Irish Irelanders, who were hostile to the very idea of modernity in literature. D. P. Moran's *Leader* missed no opportunity to ridicule and revile members of the Irish literary renaissance, particularly Yeats, as unIrish, untalented, and decadent. Pearse, despite his restrictive education and stultifying home life, was painfully broadening his mind. Many of his prejudices were founded on ignorance, and he was prepared to learn. Towards the end of his editorship, although he still had reservations about the Anglo-Irish *literati*, he was able generously to admit his debt to Yeats. "We may not all agree with his theories on art and literature, but we cannot forget that he has spent his life in an endeavour to free our ideas from the trammels of foreign thought, or that it was through his writings many of us made our first acquaintance with our early traditions and literature. He has never ceased to work for Ireland."[13] Pearse was still restrained from personal excess by domestic gentility, and the ultra-respectability of many of his colleagues, but he applied to art his belief that free speech was a natural right. He intervened briefly in an unsavoury League row centring around a member of the Coiste Gnotha, the Protestant clergyman, J. O. Hannay, better known as the novelist George Birmingham. In *The Seething Pot* and *Hyacinth*, Hannay tilted impartially at such varying targets as misuse of clerical power, and fatuous imperialism. Although no intelligent reading of these novels could have found them offensive, they were assailed, mainly by people who had never read them, as anti-clerical and showing "a virulent hatred of the Irish people".[14]

Hannay's authorship of these books was a secret until 1906, and when it came out the popular outrage reached a crescendo with the refusal of Canon Macken of Tuam to allow Hannay to sit on the committee of the Connaught feis. Pearse was unequivocal on the issue. Hannay, he said, was "as good a Gaelic Leaguer as the best of them". "We should be untrue to ourselves and to the trust reposed in us by the organisation if we did not protest with all the vehemence of which we are capable."[15] Hannay, though he survived this row, lost confidence in the League. In 1907 he said "I find of late that some of its leaders are becoming cowardly and truckling to priests and politicians."

Certainly the League was no place for a controversial writer. Even Pearse, however much he might defend Hannay from intolerance, was unhappy about his books. He disagreed strongly with many of the views expressed in them, and found that in *Hyacinth*, Hannay was "frequently unjust and occasionally ungenerous". Nevertheless, he was very much more mature in his literary judgements than the young man who thirteen years earlier had found contemporary European literature extravagant and immoral.

Pearse was disappointed in the response to his call for a new modern literature in Irish. There were no really promising young Irish writers emerging,[16] and he began to experiment in the medium himself under the pseudonym Colm O Conaire. He was in a difficult position. Any book in Irish written by a non-native speaker would immediately be ridiculed by the inevitable Dinneen and O'Leary. Although Pearse had still the greatest respect for those born to the tongue, he felt that with application and intelligence a non-native speaker could learn to speak and write good Irish. By 1905 he had been a dedicated student of the language for fifteen years, and he felt qualified to make a contribution. He wanted to be taken seriously, so he published his own pseudonymous work in his newspaper, and kept his secret well.

In March 1905 he published a full-length adventure story for boys in three issues of the *Claidheamh.* Called "Poll an Phiobaire" (The Piper's Cave), it was an adventure story about two boys who spend two days and nights exploring a cave on the western coast. It owes a good deal to the *genre* of Mark Twain, although the humour is absent, and it has a number of rather harrowing scenes. It was published in book form the following year by the Publications committee. As he had advocated, he relied on the speech of the people rather than on traditional Irish literary conventions. It was predictably well-received in reviews in the *Gaelic Journal*, the *Irish Peasant* and the *Irish People*. The *Claidheamh* reviewer, unaware of the author's identity, wrote a piece that must have made Pearse uneasy:

> It is most gratifying to find a young talented Irish speaker like Colm O Conaire suddenly blossoming into an author. I have not had the opportunity of knowing his circumstances, but it appears to me that his inspiration to write has come from *An Claidheamh Soluis.* I notice several points in his style to which I have at one time or another seen something similar in its pages. Colm, being young and receptive, has unconsciously assimilated these points, and with true literary instinct brought them into living organic connection with the language of his native district.[17]

There was trouble brewing elsewhere. Sgeilg (Sean O'Kelly) reviewed it extremely favourably, under the name XYZ, in the *Irish People*, describing it as "the most artistic and suggestive publication of its kind yet issued by the League—easily the most vigorous and idiomatic piece of Modern Irish that has so far been given to us by the Western writers".[18] But Dinneen was not taken in. Although he did not know the identity of the author, he smelt a rat. He wrote in response to Sgeilg's review:

> I can hardly bring myself to think that XYZ who showed up *Amhrain Chlainne Gael* [The Songs of the Gaelic tribe—a collection by western writers whom Dinneen despised] a few weeks ago in your indispensable paper is the same individual who reviews a certain Irish storyette with a nauseous name in the current issue.... I have tasted Connemara butter before now: it has its defects ... but in colour and taste it is natural.... It may at times be over-salted and over-dosed with the water of "bearlachas" [anglicization] but it is genuine mountain butter all the same and not clever margarine. I am afraid the storyette about the *Piobaire* smacks more like the margarine of the slums than pure mountain butter.[19]

Dinneen was wounding not only on linguistic grounds. His reference to the "nauseous name" was particularly embarrassing. Pearse, with his idealization of Irish speakers and his antipathy to vulgarity of any kind was not quick to see double meanings. "Poll an Phiobaire" to the knowledgeable also meant "The Piper's Hole", and the slip must have greatly amused Pearse's critics. Even the Publications committee had tried to effect a change of name, but the minutes record that the author did not wish it changed. Dinneen, though a great defender of respectability in literature, could not resist ending his letter with a pun of withering vulgarity. "It is to be hoped that the Piobaire will continue to draw from the stores of his capacious and well-filled arsenal." *Banba* rallied to Dinneen's support with an attack on O Conaire's *bearlachas*.[20] Nevertheless, "Poll an Phiobaire" sold well, and benefited from being put on the Intermediate Examination curriculum.

In 1905 and 1906 Pearse also published four short children's stories, issued in book form by the Publications committee in 1907, under his own name, with the title of *Iosagan agus Sgealta Eile* (Little Jesus and other Stories). The first "An Sagart" (The Priest) concerned a little boy, Patrick, who liked to dress up as a priest and say mass, and his mother's frightened reaction—quelled by the priest, who makes young Patrick an altar boy. The inspiration was drawn from Pearse's own childhood, for this was another of those dressing-up games of which he was so fond. The second, "Eoghainin na nEan" (Little Owen of the Birds) was about a child who loved the swallows and who used to talk with them about their travels. The story ends with his death, and his mother's painful grief. "Barbara" was a doll, rejected by its owner, Brighdin (little Bride) for a new glamorous Dublin doll, but which eventually saved the child's life by falling off a dresser and breaking at an opportune moment. *Iosagan* was about an old man, Matthias, who was won back to God on his death-bed by his love for little children and the appearance of the child Jesus.

All the stories were over-sentimental, and they still reflected Pearse's absurd idealization of the Connacht people. Nor were they particularly original: *Iosagan* has close affinities with Oscar Wilde's "The Selfish Giant", and "Eoghainin na nEan" echoes Hans Christian Andersen. But they showed some talent, they faithfully applied Pearse's stated precepts about modernizing Irish literary conventions, and they were written in a fluent Irish, which, although open to criticism by native speakers, was idiomatic and readable. They could not justly be called creative; they were the product more of conscientious application and verbal fluency. But they were a brave effort: there was little material in Irish suitable for children, and they were immediately popular. Like the "Piobaire", they were added to the Intermediate Examination curriculum, and their critical reception was even warmer. The *Claidheamh* reviewer was ecstatic—and surprised.

> This little book is one of the best attempts at creating a modern Irish literature that the language movement has yet inspired. It is a veritable gem ... unspoiled Children of the West ... [The author shows] an artistic power in dialogue and description, a sympathetic appreciation of character, and an all-round literary taste which is full of the richest promise, and which we confess we hardly credited Mr Pearse with possessing to such a degree before.[21]

Other glowing reviews appeared in such disparate papers as *An Connachtach* (the *Connachtman*) and the *New Ireland Review*.

Pearse was not averse to publicizing his own work. As secretary to the Publications committee he sent it to *An Connachtach*, urging it to review it in English,[22] and large advertisements for it appeared in several issues of the *Claidheamh*. His efforts were successful; sales for *Iosagan*, as for the "Piobaire", were among the highest ever recorded by the League. Since contributors received a flat rate, Pearse did not reap proportionate financial benefits.

Iosagan was not proof from assault. Dr Richard Henebry, who believed that modern Irish literature should be strictly modelled along traditional lines, began a series in the *Leader* in November 1908 attacking the modernists. Before he got round to singling out

Iosagan, Pearse had taken up the cudgels in defence of his literary beliefs.

> It is high time to protest against the oft-reiterated parrot-cry of his personal friends and exploiters that the Irish of An tAthair Peadar [O'Leary] is the only "Irish Irish" that is being written at the present day. We believe ... that An tAthair Peadar's Irish is the most vivid and vigorous Irish that is being written today. But there are dozens of people who write, and thousands of people who speak, Irish quite as *Irish* as An tAthair Peadar's.
>
> ...
>
> If Dr Henebry thinks he is going to impose dead linguistic and literary forms on a living language, then he is mistaken. Irish literature has taken its path—the path of the living speech ... [Present writers] may not be producing very exalted literature but at any rate they are answering the cry of the awakening thousands of Irish speakers for something to read in their own language—something that they can understand, something that is pleasant and familiar and homely, something that is capable of filling a place in their daily lives.[23]

Pearse had good grounds for citing this need. His early device of including a good deal of news in the Irish section of the paper had proved unpopular. The call from Irish speakers had been for songs and stories—not news. Although Henebry spent three issues in early 1909 specifically attacking *Iosagan*, his comments were predictable and petty. Neither these nor Pearse's later short stories deserved their subsequent inflated reputation, but they lived up to his own desire to provide unpretentious readable prose.

Pearse published two more stories in the *Claidheamh* during his editorship, "Brighid na nAmhran" (Brigid of the Songs), and "Brighid na Gaoithe" (Brigid of the Wind)—later called "The Keening Woman". He had clearly taken account of criticisms of sentimentality, and he moved with these tales into an adult world. "Brighid na nAmhran" was an effective story of an old woman who walked across Ireland to sing at the Oireachtas, only to die from exhaustion during her second song. "Brighid na Gaoithe" showed a new trend of thought. It was about a woman whose son was executed by the English for a murder he did not commit, and it ended with a threatening statement from the narrator within the story: "'Maybe, little son,' says he, 'we'll all be taking tally-ho out of the black soldiers before the clay will come on us.'"

Both of these stories showed the darker side of Pearse's

imagination. His wide reading, and increasing absorption with contemporary Irish drama was having an effect. Tragedy was to be the keynote of many of the poems, plays and stories which he would write during the rest of his short life. Too much must not be read into the ending of "Brighid na Gaoithe". Pearse's admiration of the military heroes of Irish history was not new; the story's conclusion did not yet herald his conversion to the need for physical force in contemporary Ireland. But it did demonstrate that his was a mind susceptible to such a philosophy. He revealed this also in a series of prose poems which he wrote as Colm O Conaire. From the earliest of these, published between August and October 1906, it can be seen that he was undergoing an emotional crisis. They betray a deep sadness with the condition of Ireland, and a desperate fear that all his work is being wasted. Although often trite, they are packed with images of torment and grief.

> It has long been night in Ireland. The sun set hundreds of years ago. The beautiful clouds of day departed and darkness spread over the land. The song of the birds and the sound of harps and the laughter of children was quenched. The country is silent. She is asleep.
>
> Will the day ever wake in Ireland? Will the wonderful light of the morning be ever seen on the summits of the hills and the face of the waters? Will the song of the birds and the music of harps and the laughter of children be again heard?
>
> And a voice spoke in my heart and said: "That light will not be seen. That music will not be heard. Any country or nation is promised only one time of glory. And that has gone in Ireland. It will never come again."*[24]

But Pearse had an answer to these self-questionings. Writing in an editorial around this time he had said "Let everyone take up his allotted and definite task, let him concentrate himself upon it, empty his best powers into it, and feel that he is responsible to Ireland and his comrades for its success."[25] Or, as he said later, in his prose poem: "No nation is snuffed out except by its own will. If the glory of a nation is extinguished by its own cowardice or by its own despair, a second age is there if it strives properly for it. God never abandoned the nation that did not abandon itself."* Another in the series shows the same preoccupation with the will.

> God promised intellect and will to every one of us.... If we do not work to fulfil the counsels of God, He cannot fulfil these counsels for us.

> We do not know what God has intended for us, but we can be sure of this: that He has appointed for us no trifling work. This is the Island of Destiny. We are as certain, as we are certain that God exists, that the Gaels of this land will do great deeds yet, and that these deeds will be lasting and fine.*[26]

He urges the study of the ancient heroes, and particularly Cuchulainn, the mythological young warrior from the north. "The story tellers say that Cuchulainn said once when he was only a boy: 'By the oath my people swear, I swear,' he said, 'that my deeds will be told amongst the great deeds that the greatest and strongest warriors did.' And they are told."*

Whichever single pressure, or complex of pressures, from his remorselessly busy life had occasioned the crisis of confidence so plainly set out in these lines, Pearse had set himself back on the trail of glory. Cuchulainn was to be a vital influence throughout the rest of his life.

He also experimented with conventional poetry during this period, and published four efforts in the *Claidheamh* under another pseudonym—Cuimin O Cualain. The first of these was written to express his loneliness when Willie was away in Paris. Entitled "Ar Thraigh Bhinn Eadair" (On the Strand of Howth), it offers the poet's friend memories of the places which they used to visit together.

> What I ask
> Of you, my dear
> Now that you are far away:
> That you will sometimes think
>
> Of the note of the corncrake
> Beside Glasnevin
> From the heart of the meadow
> Speaking in the middle of the night*

The second poem, "Betlehem", is a Christmas poem about the poverty and hardship endured at the nativity. Pearse had given excellent coverage to both of these poems in the *Claidheamh*; "Betlehem" was resplendent with decorative borders. Nor was he less modest about the third, which was announced in advance as a new national hymn written by a young Connacht poet. This is a song of praise about Ireland, "Mora Dhuit a Thir ar nDuthchais" (I hail thee, O Land of Our Heritage), which was later set to music. It is a tribute to the beauty, the literary and heroic traditions of Ireland and promises her eternal love. A four line poem, "A Ein

Bhig" (O Little Bird), heralded two of Pearse's dominant themes—innocence and death.

O little bird!
Cold to me thy lying on the flag:
Bird, that never had an evil thought,
Pitiful the coming of death to thee!

Additionally, "Brigid of the Wind" included a very promising four stanza poem, "Bean tSleibhe ag Caoineadh a Mic" (A Woman of the Mountain Keens her Son)—a vivid dramatization of maternal grief.

I called to you and your voice I heard not,
I called again and got no answer,
I kissed your mouth, and O God how cold it was!
Ah, cold is your bed in the lonely churchyard.

Of the others, none shows any particularly striking qualities: two are almost unacceptably derivative. "Betlehem" owes its inspiration and style to a nativity poem, "Noël", by Théophile Gautier. The hymn of praise is directly modelled on a poem by one of Pearse's favourite poets, Geoffrey Keating, called "Mo Bheannacht Leat, 'a Scribhinn" (My Blessing with Thee, Writing). But they represent another effort to introduce some modernity into Irish poetry, and from a novice they show courage, not least in their defiance of the normal Irish insistence that poetry should be impersonal. Pearse had still to reach the emotional maturity necessary to write self-revelatory poetry, and his comments on contemporary verse owed much to his old prejudices.

> When all is said and done, a Roibeard Weldon making homely rhymes by a fireside in the Deise is nearer the heart of Ireland, is accomplishing a nobler work for Ireland, is, from every point of view, of greater moment to Ireland than a W. B. Yeats trying over elaborate cadences to the accompaniment of a zither in a Dublin drawing room.[27]

But later, when he came properly to appreciate Yeats and his associates, and when he began to mix regularly with the younger Irish poets, he would develop greatly both as a critic and as a creator of poetry.

V The Irish Theatre

Pearse's early interest in the theatre remained rudimentary until he was 25 years old. His heavy work load did not allow for much leisure, and in any case, his free time was always spent in serious pursuits. Although Willie was personally involved in the dramatic efforts of the College of Art, Pearse seems to have remained uninspired until 1905, when he came to see drama's importance for the Irish-language movement. His growing admiration for Yeats had led him to the Abbey, but he took issue with him on the question of drama for its own sake. Commenting on Yeats's belief that propaganda should have no place in the dramatist's thinking, he wrote: "If he has a message to deliver to the world he delivers it, and his work, if great enough, is true art whether the artist was most concerned for the advancement of a cause or for 'art for art's sake'."[1] Molière and Shakespeare, he said, were propagandists. "As for writers in English, they interest us only when they directly or indirectly help on our work, as, we think, Mr Yeats himself has done in 'Cathleen Ni Houlahan', and, to a certain extent, in 'On the King's Threshold' and 'On Baile's Strand'." No other contemporary dramatist satisfied him. Writing of Yeats's lament about the decadence of young Irish drama, he observed, "We sympathise with him to a certain extent, though we think that the divergence between the ideal and the actual is at least equally marked in the case of the Irish Literary Theatre itself, always excepting Mr Yeats's own work."[2]

He was unimpressed by J. M. Synge, then reaching the peak of his popularity in the Abbey. *Riders to the Sea* he described in the *Claidheamh* as being too sad, and not really a play.

> Except for a strange infatuation which makes him see a great dramatist in Mr Synge, Mr Yeats' views on the position and purpose of his Theatre are entirely sane.
>
> We recognise in the Irish National Theatre, so long as it is true to its best instincts, not a danger to, but an ally of, the language movement. We thus go almost as far as Mr Yeats has gone in any recent utterance—there *were* days in which he put forward lofty claims which Irish-Ireland was compelled to disallow.[3]

Yeats was now making anything but lofty claims. Bludgeoned by the Irish Irelanders, he had made endless concessions to them and since he now acknowledged that there was a need for the development of drama and literature in Irish, Pearse was fair-minded enough to accept his work on its merits. He had been further won round by the courtesy of such doyens of the Irish literary scene as Lady Gregory and AE. By 1906 he was confessing an admiration for many other contemporary dramatists, and lamenting the poor quality of Gaelic playwrights. "There is little or no characterisation in our Irish plays.... There is in our playwrightship something of the naïveté of the Moralities and Mysteries, in which, too, the characters were all types or abstractions rather than individuals."[4]

But prejudices died hard with Pearse, and like so many other Irishmen, he was appalled by Synge's *The Playboy of the Western World*, first staged in 1907. His belief in free speech led him to condemn the riots during performances of the play, but he had little to say for Synge, and the whole episode had temporarily soured his view of the Abbey Theatre. His editorial on the *Playboy* riots was called "The Passing of Anglo-Irish Drama": he now called urgently for the foundation of a truly Irish Theatre. (It was an editorial which later greatly embarrassed him: by 1912 he was claiming the *Playboy* as a masterpiece.)

> Mr Synge's play was indefensible. But it was defensible—and was ably defended—on almost every ground on which it was attacked. The objections to certain plain-spoken expressions which occurred in the dialogue as it was originally spoken were simply puerile. The serious resentment of the play as a libel on Irish character was almost as inept. Irish character does not have to be vindicated against Mr J. M. Synge; and if it did, the audience went a passing strange way about vindicating it. But we do not believe that Mr Synge intended his play either as a picture or as a caricature of Irish life. The charge we bring against him is graver. Whether deliberately or undeliberately, he is using the stage for the propagation of a monstrous gospel of animalism, of revolt against sane and sweet ideals, of bitter contempt for all that is fine and worthy, not merely in Christian morality, but in human nature itself ... it is not Ireland he libels so much as mankind in general, it is not against a nation he blasphemes so much as against the moral order of the universe.
>
> In "The Shadow of the Glen" we find Mr Synge preaching contempt of what he would doubtless call the "moral convention"; in "The Well of the Saints" he railed obscenely against light, and sweetness, and knowledge, and charity; in "The Play-

> boy of the Western World"—not so much in the mere story or plot as in the amazingly powerful dialogue—he has produced a brutal glorification of violence, and grossness, and the flesh. In these three plays humanity is in savage revolt. In the beautiful and wonderfully impressive "Riders to the Sea" humanity is represented as passive and despairing in the hands of some strange and unpitying God. A sinister and unholy gospel, truly.
>
> The Anglo-Irish dramatic movement has now been in existence for ten years. Its net result has been the spoiling of a noble poet in Mr W. B. Yeats, and the generation of a sort of Evil Spirit in the shape of Mr J. M. Synge.
>
> ... Mr Yeats triumphs for the moment, but he has lost far more than he has gained. As for Anglo-Irish drama—it is the beginning of the end.[5]

He immediately set to work to plan his proposed national theatre. Less than a month later he had produced a scenario guaranteed to scare off the most starry-eyed patron. He had made a brief trip to Paris some time earlier, and was greatly impressed by its theatre. A national theatre should be based on the French model, having a school of acting like the Conservatoire and a theatre like the Comédie Française, the former to require, as in France, three years of study and stiff examinations, and the latter painstaking standards, slow promotion and long contracts. The theatre should be under institutional rather than individual management.

> A national theatre in Ireland should be the exponent of the country's soul. Its pieces need not be panegyrics of the Irish people, but neither should they be travesties representing them in a false light. Problem plays, of the kind seen in Paris and London, with nothing Irish about them but the names of the characters and the turn of the dialect are hardly suited to an Irish national theatre.... We should have our own plays, historical ones, comedies, tragedies, Irish, Anglo-Irish, plays that appeal to all kinds and degrees of Irish Irelanders.[6]

This programme would, he felt, squeeze out the vulgar music-hall productions which revolted him. His management proposals showed a touching faith in his already creaking organization. "The national theatre and the dramatic school should be under the Gaelic League. A committee from it would be formed for the management of both."[7] He went on the following month to point up the deficiencies of current acting in Irish. He urged on players the need for a sound training and high standards. "Shakespeare had to learn stagecraft—and he was quite a long time mastering it."[8] Gaelic actors should study the Abbey and Cluithcheoiri-na-hEireann (The Theatre of Ireland—a group set up a short time earlier under the patronage of Edward Martyn, and supported at its inception by Pearse and MacNeill). The latter featured two actresses Pearse particularly admired, Maire Nic Shiubhlaigh (Mary Walker) and Sara Allgood. "To an exquisitely poetical temperament in the one case, and to a rich and very versatile personality in the other, are super-added rare and charming gifts of voice and manner."[9]

In lampooning the ham acting common in Gaelic plays, Pearse for once displayed a sense of humour. (Although in the columns of the *Claidheamh* he very occasionally aired a kind of heavy whimsy, his sense of humour—always limited—was very late in developing. As a child it had been limited to the odd practical joke: as a young man his unrelieved seriousness was oppressive.)

> It is not a characteristic of Irish people in real life to walk and stand with bent knees ... folk sitting in a kitchen or a parlour do not invariably rise from their seats when they have a casual remark to make and immediately resume them as soon as they have finished speaking ... it is only people who have an impediment in their delivery, or who are in a certain stage of intoxication, that speak in disjointed, staccato sentences, or rather segments of sentences, and even these do not, as a rule, bob up and down from their chairs as each segment is ejected ... at least obvious and glaring anomalies in costume ought to be avoided ... cycling-knickers should not be worn by eighteenth-century peasants; nor should portmanteau-straps be worn for binding the hose of gallow-glasses.[10]

He supported Martyn's suggestion, in a letter to the *Freeman's Journal* in 1907, that a troupe of Irish-speaking players be sent throughout the Gaeltacht. Pearse wanted to see this combined with the plan for funding a national theatre, which he calculated would cost about £2,000. This kind of money just was not available. The Theatre of Ireland, although most of its work was in English, put on plays in Irish occasionally, as did some amateur groups, but Pearse's national theatre was a pipe-dream. Typically, although he was disappointed at the outcome of his grand plan, he did not give up completely. In the school which he was shortly to found, acting had a very important part, and its amateur performances attracted large and distinguished audiences. His blossoming interest in the professional theatre led him to apply high standards to costume and design as well as acting and production, and the stage remained one of his preoccupations over several years.

At this period he also made an attempt at writing a play (only recently discovered)—*Eoghan Gabha* (Owen the Blacksmith). It was set in the seventeenth century, and featured the Irish military hero, Patrick Sarsfield, a blacksmith, his apprentice and the blacksmith's daughter. The apprentice, apparently of humble origin, woos and wins the girl, and is finally shown to be worthy of her when his noble ancestry is revealed. It was a rather pedestrian and inadequate play, which Pearse never finished—a sure sign with him that he was dissatisfied, since he rarely failed to complete any undertaking. It is illuminating in two ways. It is the only known play of Pearse's written during his period of apprenticeship. His later plays, for all their defects, have a sureness of touch and a maturity lacking here. It is also unusual in its treatment of romantic love. Later plays were moulded in a convention which did not require such love as an ingredient, and its inclusion in *The Blacksmith* had been purely a concession to tradition.

VI THE SCHOOLS

The *Claidheamh* between 1903 and 1909 logged the development of Pearse's views on education, and his growing conviction that in the schools lay the raw material for good Irish men and women. In a man of less prolific enthusiasms, Pearse's zeal would have been accounted obsessive; yet in the early stages at least, his devotion to the cause of education simply earned it a high placing among his numerous interests. His incessant reiteration of his educational ideas was to have a decisive effect on the standpoint of the League, though it was often wearisome for those of his readers who were not involved in the contemporary controversies. P. S. O'Hegarty was a reader of the *Claidheamh*, whose memories of Pearse's editorship were dominated by the endless articles on education. "On the *Claidheamh Soluis* . . . one got the impression of a mere automaton, whose one strong passion was bilingual education. In season and out of season he urged bilingualism, and in season and out of season he brooded on the question of Irish education, seeing in that, as so many have done, the spear-point of English influence in Ireland."[1]

"As so many have done"—Pearse did not have an original mind.

None of his educational ideas was his own, but he studied Continental educational thinking, and applied it intelligently to the Irish situation. He had also benefited from the educational ideas of men like MacNeill, Hyde and O'Hickey. In an editorial of November 1904 he laid down his fundamental philosophy. "The aim of education is not the imparting of knowledge but the training of the child to be a perfect man or woman.... The real education consists in the forming of the child's character, the drawing out of his faculties, the disciplining of his intellect."[2] His resentment over the deficiencies of his own schooling was evident. He noted that Irish children hated school, and he strongly condemned prevailing Irish teaching methods and the brutal use of corporal punishment. "To inflict corporal punishment *for a mistake* is surely the very acme of stupid and purposeless folly."[3]

He believed that conditions were infinitely better on the continent, and was particularly attracted by three aspects of their schools: the prevalence of bilingualism, the Direct Method of teaching languages and the use of modern teaching aids. Articles on continental education had appeared in the *Claidheamh* even before Pearse's editorship, but he took up these ideas with a fervour which made the subject almost all his own. He had already taken a brief look at bilingualism in Welsh schools; in June 1905 he went to Belgium for a month to study its educational system at first hand. His visit was, of course, organized to utilize his time to maximum advantage. In a letter to Sean T. O'Kelly, he said, "I am working the whole day from eight o'clock in the morning to six or seven in the evening."*[4] He visited schools in Brüssels, Malines, Antwerp, Ghent and Bruges, and his spare time was filled with museums, art galleries and national monuments. Even here he was not free of family shackles. Margaret was with him, brushing up her French. He wore her out. "I often got tired, passing from room to room, when he would advise me to sit and rest whilst he continued his tour of the gallery, because, as he said, he went abroad to see 'pictures and people'."[5] His companion was not avid for new sensations. "Following this tour we entered a Chinese restaurant for lunch. I took a strong dislike to it so we left, he rather reluctantly."

Even the heady delights of foreign travel did not make Pearse forget his national responsibilities. An enthusiastic convert to D. P. Moran's "Buy Irish" industrial philosophy, "... he did not approve of buying abroad what could be got at home. He advised me to buy only small souvenirs or works of art. 'We must not unnecessarily spend our money outside our own country', he would say to me ...".

No such restrictions applied to journalistic material; he brought back enough ideas to fill pages of the *Claidheamh*. Throughout his editorship he displayed the editor's gift for converting experience into column inches. Holidays and business trips yielded endless copy. The month in Belgium formed the basis for nearly 50 separate articles and editorials. They showed that he had read widely on Belgium's history and institutions, as well as on its education, and covered the spectrum from the general philosophy of education to the *minutiae* of language teaching. Bilingualism as a concept was not new to the League, which had officially supported it for years, but until now attention had been focused on the needs of the Gaeltacht areas, where native speakers of Irish often went to schools which taught no Irish—frequently finishing their schooling illiterate in their own tongue. Pearse saw a broader need: bilingualism should be in operation throughout the country. In September 1906, he formulated a set of proposals which was to be his inspiration in setting up his own school:

1. Every child has a right to be taught his mother tongue.
2. Every child ought to be taught at least one other language, as soon as he is capable of learning it.
3. Such second language should be gradually introduced as a medium of instruction in other languages.
4. All language teaching should be, as far as possible, on the Direct Method.

The two languages concerned were, of course, Irish and English.

Pearse expected of teachers a totally unrealistic level of commitment, but he was sensible of the fact that they were ill-equipped to introduce new teaching methods to Irish schools. For instance, the Direct Method, a technique of teaching a language through conversation, required the setting up of specialist training courses. The League established evening classes in modern Irish-language teaching, and Pearse was intimately concerned with the organizing of the Leinster College. Now he turned to the problem of suitable texts and instruction manuals for live teaching. He followed his usual approach of identifying the need in editorials, defining what was required, and finally producing an example of the *genre*. In June 1907 he began a series in the *Claidheamh* called "An Sgoil" (The School), which ran for about ten months, and offered a comprehensive Direct-Method course for teaching Irish to beginners. With other specimen lessons published in 1909, and with his question-and-answer column for teachers, Pearse made a solid personal contribution—the fruit of several years of part-time teaching.

He had come a long way from those first hesitant days as an Irish teacher. He had been employed as a part-time Irish lecturer (at university examination level) by Alexandra, a Protestant girls' college, and by Westland Row Christian Brothers, and was an examiner in Irish history for the Jesuit College for boys, Clongowes Wood. Additionally, from January 1906 he was running two weekly elementary and advanced classes in Irish language and literature for University College, Dublin—in parallel with MacNeill's series on Irish history. In 1905, he applied for an assistant Intermediate examinership in Irish, but although he was backed strongly by Hyde as having "a profound and extensive knowledge of the Irish language, spoken and written",[6] he was unsuccessful. He taught with dedication, reflected a great deal on the duties of the teacher; as he grew older, his love for children deepened, although it was tempered with a knowledge of their failings.

> The two gravest faults of Irish children, as we have known them, is a certain lack of veneration for the truth, and a certain thoughtlessness in their treatment of weaker or more sensitive companions, as well as of dumb animals, often amounting to primitive cruelty. We do not think that the two mighty virtues of truth and of loving kindness are sufficiently taught either in Irish homes or schools.[7]

These faults in children sprang from their education. Irish-speaking children in their natural state were quite free of original sin and moved him to flights of idealized fancy. "He [the Irish-speaking child] is the fairest thing that springs up from the soil of Ireland—more beautiful than any flower, more graceful than any wild creature of the fields or the woods, purer than any monk or nun, wiser than any seer."[8] Children learned to lie and be cruel at school, in reaction to the frightening atmosphere. "The teacher should not be a man of terror to his pupils [but] ... a wise and tolerant friend."[9] And to those who thought this unrealistic, he could say with some justice "we have ourselves, as a teacher in an Intermediate school, practised everything that we here preach".[10] As the sentiments were fine and wholly sincere, so this claim was unexaggerated.

However, Pearse was an exceptional man and, in his maturity, an exceptional teacher; through the exercise of his remarkable will he had conquered the bad temper of his childhood. He was by nature kind and unselfish, though insensitive. His reading and journalistic experiences had broadened his horizons. He was too industrious and too interested to find the preparation of lessons a chore, and found pleasure in the use of modern teaching aids—like the magic lantern of his childhood. He had little in common with the average teacher in an Irish school, badly trained, miserably underpaid and governed by the examination system (results often affected payment). Pearse was right. Irish schools were, by and large, primitive, the teaching they offered pedestrian—even brutal. The prevalence of corporal punishment in schools and homes frightened children into mendacity. But this was a situation which could only be improved by a vast injection of money into the system and by a change in educational policy from the top; not simply by an act of will. But Pearse, ever hopeful, went on with his propaganda to fellow teachers. In 1905 he wrote:

> Our Intermediate teacher must, in the first place, be a man (or woman) of fine character and lofty ideals. He must, in the next, be warmly Irish in sympathy. This does not mean that he must of necessity be a rampant politician. It means only that he must know Ireland and love her with an intimate and discerning love; that he must regard himself as a worker for Ireland; that he must realise the awfulness and the responsibility of his position as one into whose hands it is given to mould for good or ill the characters of future Irish citizens.[11]

Two years later the standards laid down were even higher.

> ... it is only by making his own life a thing of grace and beauty that the teacher will gain the happiness of seeing successive generations of good men and women grow up around him. The teacher whose every act does not show that to him untruth and injustice, unkindness and meanness are things unholy and abhorrent, will preach and teach in vain.[12]

Like most of the Irish people, the teachers failed to meet Pearse's expectations. Although some of them showed an interest in bilingualism and the Direct Method (encouraged by the Intermediate commissioners of education), and also in the teaching of the Irish language, their enthusiasm was not entirely disinterested. Irish was worth teaching while fees were paid for the extra work involved. Numbers dropped dramatically when the treasury abolished the fees in 1904. The League—and the *Claidheamh*—applied pressure for the restoration of the fees, held public demonstrations, and made allies of a large section of the teachers. Unfortunately for Pearse's faith in the "lofty ideals" of the teachers, he ultimately incurred their wrath. Fees were restored through the good offices of Chief Secretary Bryce, whom Pearse described as "a scholar and gentleman", but a row then broke over the question of fees for teaching Irish inside rather than outside school hours. Pearse argued reasonably that there should be no extra payment for teaching Irish as part of an ordinary day's work. The dropping of Irish as an *extra subject* and its inclusion in the *normal* curriculum of the national school would be an advance for the national language. No one could think otherwise, he said. But the teachers did: they were too badly paid to be high-minded. Pearse did not consult the Coiste Gnotha on the question, but pre-empted its decision by ranging the *Claidheamh* against the teachers, and with the commissioners of education—an exercise in open-mindedness which was appreciated by few. Pearse went on with his appeal to the teachers to be less mercenary and more reasonable. "Some of us are in danger of yielding to the vulgar notion prevalent in pre-Gaelic League days that the whole duty of an Irishman is to be 'agin the Govirmint'."[13] Piaras Beaslai, writing to MacNeill, was made furious by Pearse's cavalier attitude. "If you think we should leave the editor of the 'Claidheamh' to settle the policy of the League according to his own wishes, without permission from anyone, 'what is the point of you or me' being on the Coiste Gnotha, 'or of the Coiste itself' existing at all?" [punctuation Beaslai's][14]. Cathal Brugha, writing to the *Claidheamh*, lamented Pearse's insolent tone and stressed the need to induce—not compel—teachers to teach Irish.[15] Pearse, he said, could hardly have done the work of the National Board better had he been in its pay. Although the Coiste Gnotha later backed Pearse on this issue, it led to the traumatic feud with the Keating branch which so distressed him. It also contributed to his disillusionment with his teaching colleagues. He had already said of them in 1907, "The teachers of Ireland have not yet, we fear, nailed the colours of the Irish Nation to their masthead. They are wont to regard themselves as the civil servants of a foreign power, rather than as 'captains in Israel'."[16]

But if exhortation could not rouse the teachers of Ireland, perhaps example would succeed. As with poetry and prose, as with journalism and League work, so with education. He saw the need and would attempt to lead the way. In September 1908 he opened his ideal school.

Courage in our hands
Truth in our tongues
And purity in our hearts

CHAPTER FOUR

ST ENDA'S

I PLANS

Pearse's idea of setting up an Irish-Ireland school in Dublin, under lay management, was not an original one. The need for such a school had been seen for some time by certain prominent Gaelic Leaguers, including, at one time, Archbishop Walsh. In January 1906 a distinguished Leaguer, Thomas P. O'Nowlan, wrote to the archbishop to explain his plans for setting up a lay secondary school of Catholic boys the following October: his vice-president was to be one Patrick Pearse, BA, Barrister-at-Law.[1]

O'Nowlan was a man of impeccable academic record. He had been a Jesuit novice for fifteen years, but had quit the order in 1903, on conscientious grounds which left him on good terms with his ex-superiors. An ex-fellow of the Royal University, and UCD professor of Latin, he was known also as an Irish scholar of some distinction. By 1906 he was teaching in Mount Melleray, in Waterford, and was dissatisfied with his lot. He told the archbishop so in his letter: "The salary given to lay masters in our Catholic Colleges in Ireland is not a living wage to enable a man to settle down. So I must strike out for myself. The teaching profession is the noblest of all, except the sacred ministry, and perhaps the worst paid." By this time, the archbishop's enthusiasm had waned. The scheme fell through for other reasons, and O'Nowlan became professor of Irish at Carysfort Training College, marrying a prominent Leaguer and Sinn Feiner, Mary Butler. The collapse of this project may have contributed to Pearse's depression during the latter part of 1906. The delay between the identification of a need and the satisfaction of that need was always a purgatory for him. If nobody would do the job, he would do it himself. He had no doubts about his own qualifications to set up the right kind of school. But the financial demands of such a venture were great, and Pearse was personally in no position to provide the necessary capital; his father had left a prospering firm, but had not bequeathed to his sons his own business talent.

Willie had done his best with the gifts he did have, attending the College of Art on and off, full-time and part-time, from 1898 to 1910, with moderate success.[2] He had begun to exhibit the occasional piece of sculpture at Oireachtas and Royal Hibernian Academy exhibitions, and they showed a genuine, if slight, talent. Patrick's plans to send Willie to London and Paris for the best artistic training had materialized, and Willie consequently had a wider view of contemporary art than many of his contemporaries. His theatrical interests, and his involvement with a group called the Irish Art Companions (who sold works by Irish artists and craftsmen in their shops in Dublin and London), gave him in many ways a more liberal view of the world than his brother. Throughout their adult lives, although Willie tended always to the rôle of acolyte, he had an important part to play—like such later friends of Patrick as Thomas MacDonagh and Joseph Plunkett—in moderating his brother's priggishness. But Willie was no businessman, and that shortcoming, allied to a depression in the building trade, meant that Pearse & Sons in 1908 was a failing business, which on its dissolution in 1910 was worth only £500, and this despite considerable League business which Patrick has been able to put in Willie's way.

The League income was respectable—£240 from the editorship, and after 1906, there was £30 from the Publications committee secretaryship. Pearse also had a useful income from his lecturing and teaching work, and from his books. But expenses were high. He had a taste for gracious living, which required that the family move frequently to better and better houses. In 1904 they had moved from Lisreaghan Terrace to 39 Marlborough Road, and in 1907 to Brookville, Sallymount Avenue, which was swiftly renamed Cuil Chrannach and transplanted to the adjoining Leeson Park–a much more socially acceptable address. This concern with the niceties of prestige was not uncommon in middle-class Dublin, and subsequent evidence shows it to have been more a characteristic of the female members of the Pearse household than the male, but Pearse himself was certainly not innocent of all snobbery.

With Willie, Patrick was supporting a mother, two sisters, and, as time went by, fluctuating numbers of relatives. Their gentility was too far ingrained to allow either of the sisters to enter paid employment, although Margaret in 1907 founded a short-lived infants' school.[3] The expenses of the house, domestic servants, Willie's education abroad, and rebuilding the little cottage in Rosmuc which Pearse bought in 1907 were all heavy. He had nothing left over to put towards his new project, except £150 which his mother could raise on the lease of 27, Brunswick Street.[4] But Pearse would not be deflected by such a difficulty. If he could not adequately finance a school, then it was up to the Gaels. His position in the League had put him on friendly terms with most of its prominent figures, and it was to them that he appealed. In February and March 1908 he began writing to likely benefactors, in Ireland and abroad. MacNeill was an obvious choice.

> I wonder whether I can interest you in a project which, as I think you know, I have had at the back of my head for the past two or three years and which, if I can see my way clear, I am now more than ever anxious to proceed with? It is the project of a High School for Boys in Dublin on purely Irish Ireland lines. The arguments in favour of the establishment of such a school are irresistible. There is no *Irish* High School in Ireland. There is no High School for Catholic boys conducted by laymen in Ireland. My idea is, if possible, to fill this two-fold need.

The school was to incorporate Pearse's pet educational theories.

> I feel that I have ideas on the subject of the education of boys which are worth putting into practice. Among the features of my scheme would be:- (1) an *Irish* standpoint and "atmosphere"; (2) *bilingual teaching* as far as possible; (3) all language teaching on the *Direct Method*; (4) special attention to science and "modern" subjects generally, while not neglecting the classical side; (5) association of the pupils with the shaping of the curriculum, cultivation of observation and reasoning, "nature study", and several other points to which I have devoted a good deal

of thought; (6) physical culture,—Irish games, etc; and (7) above all, formation of character.

From MacNeill he wanted advice and a promise to send his sons to the school. These he got. He also asked for money, but like so many other Leaguers, MacNeill was being hard hit financially by his League responsibilities. "How is the capital to be found? You appeal to me. I have just pledged the last penny of my *credit* and burdened myself with heavy debt to complete the capitalisation of the Clo-Chumann, this burden being entailed on me mainly by the failure of Gaelic Leaguers to pay their debts." But he was in favour of the idea, though warning Pearse to suppress any odour of anti-clericalism—of which he was so often accused. He included two other main *caveats*. The school should be a junior rather than a senior school, since this would be much cheaper to found, and a senior school could follow naturally if the venture succeeded. He also took issue with Pearse's belief that a school could turn out fluent Irish speakers.

> I cannot at all agree with you that any course of instruction at school will produce really Irish-speaking children, unless there is a domestic foundation, or its equivalent, to build upon. I fear you have in your mind some imaginary state of things which does not exist. Nothing but *life* can teach a whole live language, though an intellectual medium of communication like Esperanto may be thoroughly taught by instruction. You cannot live life in a day-school. You cannot have passions, emotions, cares and endearments, you will not put the children to bed or give them their meals or do the thousand petty things and great things that occur in every normal home, nor will you be able to reproduce the contact with the outer world that a full-blooded language must have. Your school-taught language will never be more than a simulacrum of the living thing. The contrary notion is a fatal delusion, especially for us. If it is persisted in, it is certain to ruin most of our work.

Pearse had a way with advice like that. He absorbed those elements that ran with the grain of his convictions, and ignored the rest. Desmond Ryan, his best biographer, notes the important exception: "Pearse listened most courteously to all critics and went on doing as he liked until Willie lisped his fierce word."[5]

So he interpreted MacNeill's advice freely; he would open both an elementary *and* a senior school. If he could not teach languages properly in a day school, he would have a boarding school. Caution was thrown to the winds. It seems he planned initially to replace

Margaret's school at Cuil Chrannach by one of his own: instead, he would find bigger and better premises, with ample residential accommodation, all of which would be "decorated and furnished artistically, and as far as possible on Celtic lines".

As Pearse himself said later, the response from his correspondents was almost universally to argue against the project. But he had had enough encouragement—and he never needed much—to go ahead. Early promises of pupils came from an eminent northern Leaguer, Peter McGinley, from William Bulfin, editor of the Buenos Aires Irish exile paper, the *Southern Cross*, and from MacNeill. Although Pearse was not showered with money, Stephen Barrett, a close friend, and father of his godchild Sheila, acted as a guarantor, as did a rich northern merchant and philanthropist, Joseph Dolan of Ardee. That was enough to make the project feasible, and it blossomed. From the first modest plans of February and March there grew a more luxurious and infinitely more expensive reality. Although Pearse did not make his intentions generally known until June, when he resigned as editor of the *Claidheamh*, and although no advertisements for the school appeared for a month after that, he already had a full prospectus in proof by July, when he wrote to ask Archbishop Walsh's blessing on the project. His earlier hopes that Walsh might be prepared to be a patron of the school had been dashed by a letter to MacNeill from Monsignor Curran, the archbishop's secretary, who was himself sympathetic to the Irish-Ireland movement.

> His Grace is persuaded that there would not be sufficient support in Dublin for schools of either kind [O'Nowlan's or Pearse's] to make them a success. In these circumstances he is obliged to decline to have any personal responsibility in their establishment. However much he would like to see such a school succeed, he can do nothing to lead either founders or parents to what he believes will end in failure.

Pearse could now hope for little more than Walsh's passive acceptance of his foundation, and his approval of the appointment of a chaplain. Walsh wrote to him kindly, and although his first letter went astray, Pearse was eventually given permission to appoint a chaplain of his choice.[6]

The draft prospectus sent to Walsh was little modified later. To any parent concerned about the grinding, examination-orientated, colonial nature of contemporary Irish education, the philosophy propounded in the prospectus must have been encouraging. Apart from the familiar aspects of Pearse's educational thinking which it incorporated, there were plans for half-holiday lectures by such noted performers as MacNeill, Mary Hayden, Agnes O'Farrelly and Dr Henry. Throughout it breathed a spirit of commitment to Irish Ireland, respect for children as individuals, love of learning for its own sake, and concern with the broader issues of character building. Children were not to sit the Intermediate examination unless their parents specifically requested it. But there was an aspect of the prospectus which must have raised doubts in the minds of the less committed—and which as time went on, and the idea gained more practical expression in the school, was to alienate both actual and prospective patrons. Pearse outlined his beliefs on character training in the English section of the prospectus in an unobjectionable way:

> The School staff will constantly exert itself to promote amongst the boys an active love and reverence for the Christian virtues, especially for the virtues of purity, temperance, fortitude, truth, and loving-kindness. A spirit of chivalry and self-sacrifice; gentleness towards the weak and courtesy and charity towards all; kindness to animals and respect for their lives and well-being, as well as a love of inanimate nature and of everything in the world that is fine and beautiful—these are amongst the virtues and sentiments which the teachers of St Enda's will endeavour to implant in the hearts of their pupils. A manly self-reliance and a healthy ambition to plan and achieve will be not only inculcated in theory but fostered in practice by the system of organisation and discipline which will be adopted in the schoolroom and on the playground. Patriotism will be systematically taught, and an effort will be made towards the formation of a sense of civic social duty.

But in the Irish version, there appeared a more controversial line. "It will be attempted to inculcate in them the desire to spend their lives working hard and zealously for their fatherland and, if it should ever be necessary, to die for it."* This rather abrupt development in Pearse's gradual elevation of nationalism to the status of a religion must have had a disconcerting ring to others. Even in a Catholic country, where the catechism taught that at confirmation children became soldiers of Christ, who must be prepared to die for their faith, dying for one's country was another matter. Certainly for a hundred years it had not been a respectable end for any man of good family. Irish Irelanders like D. P. Moran, and they were in the majority, regarded the revolutionaries of 1848 and 1867 as dangerous fanatics. Pearse, though still no revolutionary, had romantic and mystical conceptions of duty to Mother Ireland, closely bound up with his personal, rather exotic religion. But such ideas were seen by many as "mad bloody fanaticism".[7] One such disturbed observer was the artist Beatrice Elvery, later Lady Glenavy.

> I had painted an allegorical picture of a seated, hooded figure of Cathleen ni Houlihan, with a child on her knee, presumably Young Ireland, stretching out his arm to the future, and behind her a ghostly crowd of martyrs, patriots, saints and scholars. Maud Gonne bought this picture and presented it to St Enda's College, the school for boys which Patrick Pearse started. Some time later I met one of the boys from the school and he told me that this picture had inspired him "to die for Ireland!" I was shocked at the thought that my rather banal and sentimental picture might, like Helen's face, launch ships and burn towers.[8]

Beatrice Elvery was only one of a band of artists whose work appeared in St Enda's, and had their influences on the boys and their headmaster. Sarah Purser, the stained-glass artist, was another. She had doubts about Pearse's influence on the boys,[9] but her work still appeared in the school when it opened in September, in an old Georgian mansion, Cullenswood House, in Oakley Road, Rathmines. Originally conceived as St Lorcan's School,[10] it took its new name from the patron saint of Pearse's beloved Aran. Pearse's friends and relations had worked with professional builders to produce a uniquely beautiful school. It boasted original pictures by such popular artists as Jack B. Yeats and George Russell, friezes by Edwin and Jack Morrow (prominent stage designers) and Willie Pearse, and sculptures by him and others. One of Edwin Morrow's works was a panel showing the boy Cuchulainn taking arms, framed in his most famous words: "I care not though I were to live but one day and one night provided my fame and my deeds live after me." This *ethos* had always appealed to Pearse's romantic temperament: its effect was to manifest itself in more practical ways.

Cullenswood House matched Pearse's promise. Set in mature gardens, it was a far more beautiful school than many of its Irish contemporaries. It remained to be seen how the pupils would react.

II The First Year

Pearse had been persuaded by the Coiste Gnotha to take a few months' leave of absence rather than to resign finally as editor of the

Claidheamh, and to return as soon as possible. He did not hesitate to use his position to ensure a great deal of publicity for his new school. His assistant editor, a League organizer, John Henry, did him proud after the opening, announcing with triumph that 40 pupils had arrived—"a guarantee that the success of his new establishment is assured". "With such an ideal master, a beautiful school, an original and up-to-date system of Irish education, Sgoil Eanna [St Enda's] will be a nursery of character, intellect, patriotism, and virtue, which may eventually exert a benign influence on the private and public life of our country."[1]

Certainly the opening of the school was all Pearse could have wished for. Besides the 40 boys who had arrived in the first week, there were 30 smaller children in the mixed preparatory school. The pupils came from among the most notable families in Irish-Ireland circles, including three sons and a nephew of MacNeill, a son of Stephen Gwynn (Coiste Gnotha member and parliamentarian), two sons of Peter McGinley, a son of William Bulfin, a son of W. P. Ryan of the *Peasant*, a daughter of D. P. Moran, and various young relatives of Agnes o' Farrelly, Mary Hayden, Stephen Barrett, Sean T. O'Kelly and Padraic Colum, the rising young Irish poet and dramatist. As Pearse himself said in the *Claidheamh*: "It is obvious that such children and lads as these are splendid material in the hands of a sympathetic teacher, and that to work with and for them is a perennial delight."[2] He gave himself a warning which the pages of the *Claidheamh* for that period showed to be necessary. "*An Claidheamh* must remain the organ of the Gaelic League—tempting as it might be to us personally to make it the organ of Sgoil Eanna."

From 8 September, when the school opened its doors, it was to engage a larger part of Pearse's prodigious energies than any activity so far, and to do so for nearly four years. P. H. Pearse, headmaster, who met his new pupils in the hall of St Enda's, was an imposing figure. The shyness of the youth had given way to the aloofness of his maturity. His black gown, over his black clothes, set off to best advantage his grave, handsome face, with its strong jaw and high white forehead, marred only slightly by his squint and receding hairline. Flanked by his black-clad mother, his plain squat sister Margaret and Willie, slight with flowing hair, he was not an approachable figure. But the boys were quickly put at ease by the ebullient, laughing man who swept quickly on the scene and had the apprehensive newcomers feeling at home within ten minutes—Thomas MacDonagh. For Pearse, with all his reverence for qualifications and professionalism, had fallen under the spell of this unorthodox young schoolmaster, neither BA nor BL, whose departure from the novitiate of the Holy Ghost Order had been followed by his abandonment of the practices of his religion, and whose main characteristics as a teacher were a love of ideas and imagination, rather than success in leading his pupils to examination glories.

MacDonagh was Pearse's right-hand man during the best years of St Enda's, and he, with the boys, helped to release in Pearse a sense of fun and an appreciation of gaiety and laughter which had been suppressed in him for so long. For St Enda's was a school which owed nothing to contemporary views of discipline. Pearse's ideas of education were based not only on his glimpses of the bright, happy classrooms of Belgium, but also on the old Irish tradition of the boy-corps of Eamhain Macha (Armagh) the band of children of the famous, who sat at the feet of their king and teacher and learned how to construct a happy and united society. In St Enda's, corporal punishment was unusual, silence was rarely enjoined. A great contrast from the silent dining rooms of the average Irish school, with a lone voice reading from an improving text, was the noisy, laughter-filled eating place of the St Enda's boys, who were turned out at the end of meals to work off their high-spirits on the playing-field. There were those who disapproved, and felt that the boys ran wild, but there were more who found it refreshing.

It was hard, gruelling work for the teachers, for the school was understaffed; there were few suitable applicants for such a shaky enterprise. Pearse was still searching for teachers shortly before the opening, but he succeeded in enlisting a number of like-minded recruits. The third resident master, in charge of dancing, music and athletics, was Tomas Mac Domhnaill (Thomas MacDonnell), ex-professor in the League's Connacht Training College, and well-known musician. Michael Smithwick, a Leaguer and mathematician of note, and rather later, the grave Dr Patrick Doody, classics master, lent support. Other visiting professors included O'Nowlan, John Henry and the popular Irish harpist, Owen Lloyd, of the staggeringly long finger nails. Other friends and supporters of Pearse swelled the ranks of the half-holiday lecturers. Such names as Yeats, Hyde, Padraic Colum, Standish O'Grady, Edward Martyn and the historian Alice Stopford Green came and went, and added to the glamour which St Enda's had at that time in abundance.

Pearse's family rallied round, although only Willie was qualified to speak the official language of the school—Irish. Mrs Pearse was pleasant and motherly, and with Margaret and Miss Brady, a cousin, she acted as matron and housekeeper, providing a maternal ear for the boys' troubles. Margaret ran the preparatory school, taught junior French, and kept up a correspondence with pupils when they went on holiday. She was a worrier, but conscientious and hardworking, at last finding an outlet for her busy nature. Willie, during the first two years of the school, was still running the family business and studying, but he taught art in the school, and was a constant support to his harassed elder brother. Even Mary Brigid did her share. Her relations with the family were mercurial. With adulthood she had become something of a hypochondriac, always needing a companion, financed by the family. She is remembered as an excitable woman, always swathed in coats in the hottest weather, while complaining incessantly of the heat. The family seemed rather embarrassed by her, and she elected not to live with them; but she taught music competently, wrote plays and stories and had a small literary reputation. They were an oddly assorted group. Mrs Pearse, at 50, almost eight years a widow, had a jolly, though limited, sense of humour. Margaret shared her anxieties about life, but could never see even the most obvious joke, and was mutually out of sympathy with Mary Brigid. Willie was always on good terms with everyone, but he felt some emotional gap in his life which his family could not fill. He was deeply attached to his favourite model, Mabel Gorman, with whom he corresponded regularly from the time she was eight years old.[3] (She apparently modelled nude for one of his best sculptures, "Eire Og"—Young Ireland.) He showered her with expensive presents and invitations to modelling sessions and social outings. It seems to have been a Lewis Carroll-Alice relationship, simple and innocent, but finally disappointing for both parties: Mabel's later letters to Willie show a diminishing gratitude for his acts of kindness. To the eight-year-old he was a pleasing adult patron; to the fourteen-year-old he became a bore. Her excuses for missed appointments became more and more frequent, and Willie retreated further into the predictable comforts of his family.

Over them all towered the commanding figure of the gifted and determined elder son, and they were all happy to serve him. Indeed, once St Enda's opened, Patrick had little private life outside the family. Still, and always, a devout Catholic (a daily communicant when possible), a non-smoker, a non-drinker (he abhorred pubs), and indifferent also to food, he had set himself firmly against marriage, or any relationship unconnected with his causes. In answer to a letter from Mary Hayden, his closest woman friend, he had made clear his attitude to marriage. She was distressed by his remorseless dedication. "No, I don't want you to have such a future as you plan for yourself.... There is a part of human nature that asks for human relationships and human sympathies. If I go to Rosmuck as a white haired old lady (the white hair is coming fast already) I hope it will be to find you settled as a paterfamilias, with children not adopted. However, there is time enough."[4]

The first year of the school was very hard going for Pearse. He had kept on the editorship of the *Claidheamh*, and despite his assistant, he was seriously over-worked. In October 1908 he said in a mock-petulant editorial, the response to an injunction from the *Peasant* to be more mellow:

> For ourselves, our editorial and sub-editorial work is got through either in a crowded class-room where we are supposed to be presiding over study, or else after midnight in a certain very icy apartment in the lower regions of Sgoil Eanna, some hours after the professors and pupils have gone off on their nightly visits to Tir na nOg [Land of Youth]. To be continuously "mellow" under these circumstances is a height of heroism towards which we aspire, but which we have not yet attained.

But even two full-time jobs could not quite contain his thirst for activity. Close association with MacDonagh brought him into increasing contact with theatrical circles, for MacDonagh's first play, *When the Dawn is Come*, was performed in the Abbey in November 1908, and he was becoming a well-known Dublin literary figure, rubbing shoulders with Yeats, AE and Padraic Colum. St Enda's boys attended Abbey plays, and the school began to plan its own dramatic productions, Willie and MacDonagh staging, Patrick producing (and later writing). Their first production was in March 1909, and to a Dublin obsessed with theatre-going, it was a great attraction. Two plays were presented, Hyde's *An Naomh ar Iarraidh* (The Lost Saint), a story in Irish about a meeting between a saint and a group of children, and Standish O'Grady's *The Coming of Fionn*, which describes the young Fionn's deliverance of his clan. They were an intelligent choice for a group of youthful, inexperienced actors, and the occasion began a tradition of acting in the school which, according to the distinguished actress, Maire Nic Shiubhlaigh, was on a par with that of many good companies in Dublin producing Irish plays. Joseph Holloway was, of course, at the performance:

> Mr Thomas MacDonagh was in the Hall welcoming the guests ...

> William Pierce presided over the tea and Mr Pierce made himself generally useful in making everyone at home, in a beautiful room newly decorated.... I noted what a distinguished company had come—Stephen Gwynn, ... Edward Martyn, Padraic Colum, John MacNeill, Mary Hayden ... Mr and Mrs Standish O'Grady, Miss Agnes O'Farrelly ... W. B. Yeats (who had a great chat with O'Grady who was seated just before him at the plays) etc. The stage was erected in a little corrugated iron shed in the grounds and when the company squeezed in they certainly were a tight fit. Amongst the company were some friars in their habits and some priests in ordinary everyday attire. Those who sat near me enjoyed the performance keenly and applauded heartily.... Yeats ... found it hard to secure a seat.... Mr Pierce, politely asked the ladies to remove their hats "in Gaelic", and seeing that his words had not the desired effect he had to repeat them in brutal English.... A young man attired in antient Irish costume treated us to a violin solo, to a pianoforte accompaniment, and after that the sound of distant pipes was heard and the entire company of youthful players headed by the piper marched up the centre of the hall into the stage where they formed into an effective tableau. Shortly afterwards Douglas Hyde's little play commenced and all the youthful players let fall from their lips in slow measured tones the "honey sweet speech of the Gael". There was a strange fascination about their crude boyish playing that I cannot account for.[5]

He liked both plays and was particularly impressed by the staging of *Fionn*.

> The setting was picturesque and the boys ... though they chanted their words in a style outside nature created an impression not easily forgotten. The torches gave an element of danger to the scene not wholly peaceful to the minds of the spectators. Loud calls for author at the end brought Standish O'Grady to his feet and ultimately he mounted on a chair and held forth in one of the most deliciously fresh impracticable speeches I have ever heard spoke. The men of old in Ireland did nothing only enjoyed "a simple life" and he hoped that Ireland would come to that again and take to the hills and the open air and sunshine like Fionn and his companions. Imagine such advice being given by one of our leading literary men in the twentieth century with all seriousness and an air of conviction not to be gainsaid. He hoped that Yeats and other great literary folk around him would bring the heroes of our antient literature more before the people

of today. A piper piped his lay and the entire audience arose to its feet when he had finished and sang right heartily the Rallying Song of the Gaelic League before dispersing. Each and all felt as they left the hall that they had just witnessed a unique and inspiring show and one that promises great hope for the Ireland of the near future.

If Pearse had succeeded in firing the imagination of his audience, he had no less fired his own. His theatrical sense, considerable even in childhood, had at last found room for expression, and over the next few years he poured this talent into the St Enda's plays, coloured by his romantic imagination. With every performance the mythological heroes of his youth assumed for him a greater significance. Excellent press notices for his first effort, in such disparate publications as the *Irish Independent*, the London *Sphere*, the *Leader*, and *Sinn Fein*, were a spur to greater efforts, and the June pageant, *Mac-Ghniomharta Chuchulain* (The Boy-Deeds of Cuchulainn), was a much grander affair than its predecessor. Pearse modernized the prose, but kept closely to the original story, and it was another success. Holloway was there again, and although he had certain reservations about the staging, regretting that acting and speaking always suffer in the open-air, he was moved. Three of Pearse's favourite pupils were the stars—the school captain, Denis Gwynn, Eamonn Bulfin and Frank Dowling. In Pearse's words, young Dowling realized

> in face and figure and manner, my own high ideal of the child Cuchulainn; that "small, dark, sad boy, comeliest of the boys of Eire", shy and modest in a boy's winning way, with a boy's aloofness and a boy's mystery, with a boy's grave earnestness broken ever and anon by a boy's irresponsible gaiety; a boy merely to all who looked upon him, and unsuspected for a hero save in his strange moments of exaltation, when the sevenfold splendours blazed in his eyes and the hero-light shone about his head.[6]

A year as headmaster had in no way disillusioned Pearse: his idealization of boys was unabated.

There was again a glittering audience, to pay tribute to the achievement of the school. Holloway, although no language enthusiast, was not immune. "It was a cheering sight to see those notable people present to do honour to the occasion—the first anniversary of the opening of the school. There is hope yet for Ireland when so many feel enthusiastic over an event like the school break up!"[7]

Pearse wanted the pageant to affect more than the audience: "we are anxious to crown our first year's work with something worthy and symbolic; anxious to send our boys home with the knightly image of Cuchulainn in their hearts and his knightly words ringing in their ears. They will leave St Enda's under the spell of the magic of their most beloved hero."

Press reports were again glowing, not only about the pageant but also about the first issue of the school magazine, launched at the same time. *An Macaomh* (The Youth) was a better-produced and more ambitious publication than the average school magazine. In it Pearse poured out his hopes and plans for his school and summed up his motivation.

> I am conscious of one motive only, namely, a great love of boys, of their ways, of their society; with a desire, born of that love, to help as many boys as possible to become good men. To me a boy is the most interesting of all living things, and I have for years found myself coveting the privilege of being in a position to mould, or help to mould, the lives of boys to noble ends. In my sphere as journalist and University teacher, no opportunity for the exercise of such a privilege existed; finally I decided to create my opportunity ... my school should be an Irish school in a sense not known or dreamt of in Ireland since the Flight of the Earls.

His more devoted supporters had no doubt that this had already been achieved. William Bulfin wrote of the St Enda's pageant in the *Claidheamh* "Irish work; Irish play; Irish mind; Irish thought; Irish heart; Irish emotion; Irish faith; Irish purpose; Irish education; Irish character. This indeed is Ireland."[8]

With the applause ringing in his ears, Pearse ended the school year in triumph. The success of St Enda's he felt to be assured. As term ended an army of builders had already been ordered to start work on improvements. Pearse's summer of planning for the new school year and running the *Claidheamh* was marred by a personal blow—the death of Eveleen Nicholls, an admired friend. She was a young girl, newly elected to the Coiste Gnotha, who had secured a wide reputation in League circles for her academic achievements and high-minded devotion to the Irish language, and had died in tragic circumstances.[9] While she was swimming in the treacherous seas off the Blasket Islands, with a friend, Cait Ni Chriomhthain (Kate Crohan), both girls got into difficulties. Kate's brother Donall tried to rescue Eveleen and died with her. Padraig

O Cearnaigh (Patrick Kearney) succeeded in rescuing Kate. Dublin heard a confused version of the events, and believed that Eveleen had drowned trying to rescue the other girl. There was public mourning.

Holloway wrote of the funeral, "Rare sorrow was felt at the loss of this fine young girl and wonderfully clever scholar—many looked on her death as a national loss she took such a practical interest in the Gaelic movement and was becoming such a power in the organisation ... a solumer funeral I never was at—an Nation wept for her lost child as well as those who knew her in life."[10] There were many who shed tears—and Pearse was one of them. He wrote an editorial in which he showed his distress.

> There are times when journalists and public men experience a trial more cruel than others can easily imagine. It is when they are called upon in the course of their duty to write or to speak in public of things that touch the inmost fibres of their hearts, things that to them are intimate and sacred, entwined, it may be, with their dearest friendships and affections, awakening to vibration old chords of joy or of sorrow. The present is such an occasion for the writer of these paragraphs.... It is not in human nature to write a glib newspaper article on a dead friend. One dare not utter all that is in one's heart, and in the effort at self-restraint one is apt to pen only cold and formal things.[11]

He went on to write briefly of Eveleen:

> Her grand dower of intellect, her gracious gifts of charm and sympathy, her capacity for affairs, were known to all, but those who knew her best know that these were the least of her endowments. What will stand out clear and radiant in their mental picture of her is the loftiness of her soul, the inner sanctity of her life.
>
> The close of that life has been worthy of it. If she had been asked to choose the manner of her death she would surely have chosen it thus. She died to save another, and that other a young Irish-speaking girl.... Her life was consecrated to the service of higher things.

Other friends and admirers wrote of her in similar terms, and her mother wrote to quote a recent statement of Eveleen's which had a Pearse-like ring: "I realise that for nations, as for individuals, true greatness lies in goodness. The Gaelic League is training the people to lofty ideals, to temperance, to industry, self-respect and self-reliance, and when their character is moulded on this basis, God will send freedom in His own good time."[12]

If a wife had to be chosen for Patrick Pearse, his contemporaries would have chosen Eveleen Nicholls. She was one of the few young women to reach a high position in the League; her sense of mission seemed as great as his (she had spent a French holiday revitalizing the Paris Gaelic League); her feminism would have been far more attractive to Pearse than to most of her other male colleagues, for his sense of natural justice had made him an early sympathizer with the movement for equal opportunities and pay for women. All the available evidence shows that Pearse had not the slightest inclination to take a wife. A posthumous romance was devised for Eveleen and Patrick, however. Desmond Ryan, his young pupil and protégé, was convinced of Pearse's emotional involvement by his tears at the funeral—but there were many others crying. It was not until years later, when Pearse was dead and a love interest was being sought, that relatives discovered a romance. Eveleen's brother claimed that she had rejected Pearse's proposal because she did not want to abandon her mother to the problems caused by alcoholism in her home.[13] This did not convince even the susceptible Louis Le Roux, Pearse's hagiographer of 1932, who could find no evidence of any attachment even in the hearsay of the 1920s.[14] But in the English version of Le Roux's book, his friend and translator, the same Desmond Ryan, altered the sense of Le Roux's account, and so the story of Eveleen Nicholls took up a permanent position in the Pearse legend. Natives of the Blaskets were told of the "engagement" by visitors from Dublin, and the story grew in the telling.[15]

The only basis for marriage with Eveleen would have been mutual respect, not sexual attraction. As Mary Hayden's evidence suggested he tended to put women on a pedestal. He knew nothing of homosexuality. When he wrote of beauty, he was inspired by the descriptions, so frequent and so elaborate, of characters in the old Irish sagas. Of course, any respectable man would have been careful not to write too eloquently of the female form, but Pearse went further. As he had shown particularly in "La Fa'n Tuaith", his delight in physical beauty was wholly reserved for his own sex, for boys or boyish young men. An obituary which he wrote of Michael Breathnach (Michael Walsh), president of the Gaelic League's Connacht College, who died of consumption in his early twenties (only nine months before the drowning) demonstrates this characteristic. Walsh he described as having "a figure slender and almost boyish but held erect with what a grace and dignity!

Recall then the kindling red in the pale cheek, the light in the large soft eye, the spirituality of the whole countenance, the noble gesture of the shapely head with its crown of dark brown clustering hair."[16] He waxed even more eloquent about Walsh in his youth: "He was only a boy then, very straight and slender and comely, with a virginal face and a voice that we thought was the softest and sweetest we had ever heard."

Pearse was an innocent, but there can be little doubt about his unconscious inclinations. His prose and poetry sing when he speaks of young male beauty. He had by now surrounded himself with the sons of many of the best families, and he delighted in them, as in all children. His innocence survived—with embarrassing consequences. In the second number of the *Macaomh*, published in December 1909, he published a poem in Irish, "A Mhic Bhig na gCleas" (Little Lad of the Tricks). Although it was well received and reprinted in the *Claidheamh* under the new editor who took over on Pearse's departure in November 1909, the English version which Pearse produced a few years later aroused alarm among his more worldly friends.

Little lad of the tricks,
Full well I know
That you have been in mischief:
Confess your fault truly.

I forgive you, child
Of the soft red mouth:
I will not condemn anyone
For a sin not understood.

Raise your comely head
Till I kiss your mouth:
If either of us is the better of that
I am the better of it.

There is a fragrance in your kiss
That I have not found yet
In the kisses of women
Or in the honey of their bodies ...

MacDonagh, and his great friend the young poet, Joseph Plunkett, were appalled. They explained to him the ignoble construction with might be placed on the poem, and the harm it could do his school.[17] Pearse was bewildered and hurt: his lifetime quest for purity, chastity, and perfection had blinded him to the instincts reflected in his poetry.

Contemporaries have remarked that his mother was a vigilant guardian of her sons' purity, and the aloofness of his father's virile influence left her in control. No interference, either, from his plain spinster sisters or his gentle admiring brother, to encourage the formation of healthy heterosexual relationships. But it is inconceivable that a man of Pearse's conventional mores and high code of chivalry could have lived with conscious homosexual inclinations. Certainly, with such knowledge, he could not have gone on writing as he did. Though he never again offered such ammunition as in "Little Lad of the Tricks", many of his later writings are a muted revelation of the same proclivities.

But in 1909 this distressing episode was in the future. Pearse's grief for Eveleen was not great enough to affect his work in any way. As W. P. Ryan had once said, "Pearse can always touch Heaven."[18] In his school he was almost in Heaven, full of hope and confidence in greeting its second year.

III 1909-1910

The St Enda's premises had almost doubled in size when the boys returned in September 1909. Pearse wrote of the improvements with pride.

> ... except that one kind friend has undertaken to provide us with a School Chapel, we have been left the proud privilege of carrying out our new building scheme unaided. We have now our Study Hall, built to hold thrice fifty with room and verge to spare; our Art Room; our Physico-Chemical Laboratory; a new Refectory, the old Refectory having been converted into a Library (where we have already 2,000 volumes); and a new Museum. I do not know that we need much else in the way of accommodation or equipment for teaching, except perhaps a special room for Manual Instruction. That will doubtless come in good time.[1]

The first year had been a year of experiment: the second was one of consolidation. The teaching staff was strengthened by the addition of classics and science masters, and there was occasional teaching from MacDonagh's brother Joseph, from Padraic Colum, and others. Numbers had increased, from the previous year's total of 20 boarders and 50 day-boys and girls.

There were now 30 boarders and 100 day-boys. Because of the large numbers, girls were no longer accepted in the preparatory school. Although Pearse was interested in female education, his boys took priority. With the discontinuance of the girls' school, the preparatory and senior school were brought under the same management, with Margaret Pearse and her assistant, Miss Browner, attaching themselves to St Enda's proper.

This was a time of jubilation for Pearse. He had committed himself to accepting no more than 150 boys at St Enda's, and it looked as if that target would be soon met. Plans were afoot for a series of St Enda's textbooks, to which Pearse was to contribute three—two volumes on the Direct Method of teaching Irish, and a school anthology of Irish Verse. And although he finally resigned from the *Claidheamh* in October, he intended to replace it with the *Macaomh* as a personal vehicle. As he said in the December 1909 issue, some such outlet was necessary for him and the *Macaomh* would be a welcome change from the polemical environment of the *Claidheamh*.

> It is a luxury to feel that I can set down here any truth, however obvious, without being called a liar, any piece of wisdom, however sane, without being docketed a lunatic. *An Macaomh* is my own, to do with it as I please; and if, through sheer obstinacy in saying in it what I think ought to be said, I run it against some obstruction and so wreck it, at least I shall enjoy something of the grim satisfaction which I suppose motorists experience in wrecking their thousand-guinea Panhards through driving them as they think they ought to be driven.

Pearse could not easily operate without a public platform. Both as a speaker and a writer, he communicated most easily with large groups. His letters are, by and large, disappointing. For self-revelation, one usually has to look to his public utterances.

The *Macaomh* was to be published twice yearly—and no longer as merely a school magazine, but a review, containing contributions by some of those in any way associated with St Enda's. "Nearly everyone in Ireland whose name stands for high thought or achievement in any sphere of wholesome endeavour will in his turn address our boys in their Study Hall; and these addresses will find a place in AN MACAOMH along with the work of the masters and pupils." This issue contained six items by Pearse, two by MacDonagh, one by Padraic Colum, three others, and attractive artistic illustrations. Although it was a step towards a literary review, it was a long way yet from Pearse's startling objective: "a rallying-point for the thought and aspirations of all those who would bring back again in Ireland that Heroic Age which reserved the highest honour for the hero who had the most childlike heart, for the king who had the largest pity, and for the poet who visioned the truest image of beauty".

It was admittedly an unusual school magazine, but Pearse was intoxicated by his school's *succès d'estime*, and had lost his sense of perspective. While the Irish language was still important to him, his school, designed to serve the language, had now usurped its place in Pearse's crusading heart. But he was not content with making St Enda's merely a good school. It had to be the best, the most enlightened, the most successful and the most beautiful of all schools. His boys were not just to receive a good education; each soul amongst them was to be brought to perfection, "because for every soul there is a perfection meant for it alone, and which it alone is capable of attaining".[2]

For a short time he was content; for a couple of months more he worked towards achieving perfection in Cullenswood House, before his restlessness prevailed. For the first time in several years he was not overwhelmed with work. Although he had been co-opted on to the Coiste Gnotha on resigning from the editorship, and still worked hard for the League, his days were no longer filled with the grinding, dispiriting jobs of proof-correcting, and filling up the empty spaces in the paper. He was also, for quite the first time, his own master, free of pettifogging disputes and endless bickering. His time was spent in teaching, improving the school, writing for his boys, taking them on excursions, addressing them in the daily assembly, and enjoying his first substantial home. His evenings were spent at the theatre, doing the books (in a meticulous hand), or in the company of like-minded teachers and pupils, all sharing his visions and pursuing them with the same spirit, if not the same dedication. Every night he would sit on the bed of one or another of the boarders, chatting to him and getting to know him as an individual whose mind he might influence. For weeks at a time he would be bound up with the excitement of staging a new play or pageant. There was another successful production in February 1910, this time of two plays specially written for the boys—a dramatization of *Iosagan*, and a play by Padraic Colum, based on an old Irish tale, called *The Destruction of the Hostel*. Pearse's right-hand man in the venture provided a contrast to his own reserve as headmaster and producer:

> Pearse took much pride in his players whether he saw them in their hero-garb in Cullenswood's pleasant field or ... in the small theatre he built on occasion in Cullenswood. Thomas MacDonagh was his stage-manager, the most exacting and competent Bully of a stage-manager imaginable, reducing stolid youth to the verge of tears and more excitable youths to rage, going his way genially insistent and implacable. The curtain rises and Thomas watches, unless he is acting himself. The curtain falls and Thomas leads or shares the applause and then wears a sack-cloth and ashes. He does a tremendous penance for his criticisms, apologising, eulogising, and taking it all back and calling himself all the names he can think of with a wave of his flowing tie and sweeping gestures.[3]

They were an effective combination. The St Enda's production of *The Destruction of the Hostel* was in April given the honour of a performance at the Abbey. As with the earlier plays, its effect was greatest on its producer, for the Pearse of Cullenswood House continued to experience in his maturity the same exhilaration which heroic tales had produced in him as a child. These two plays represented what he called then his "gospel of patriotism", *Iosagan* representing the spiritual and *The Hostel* the heroic. MacDonagh joked that Pearse had founded a school to give himself unfettered opportunity to make speeches, and the speeches he made were not about revolutionaries, but about Fionn, Cuchulainn and the flower of Ireland's great spiritual generation—saints like Enda and Columcille. To the boys he talked endlessly of the need for an Irish-speaking Ireland—Gaelic, but not necessarily free; a land of heroes, owing more to the influence of men like Standish O'Grady, than to Arthur Griffith.

These two years were the happiest of his life. St Enda's—a small school—was triumphant in the hurling and football championships of Dublin and Leinster; there seemed no limit to the potential of the young Gaels. Pearse and MacDonagh were both inspired teachers, and were winning the love and admiration of their pupils. In general, Pearse's code of chivalry prevailed in the school. One pupil, who had previously been at Jesuit schools, recalls St Enda's discipline.

> At other schools I had perpetually one eye on a Prefect and the other on what I wanted to do. It tended to give me a squint. The Prefect had one already. That is why he was a Prefect. In St Enda's there were no Prefects in that sense of the word. You were not watched, or kept under constant observation. You were put on your honour. And on your first transgression Pearse

> called you to his study; you gave your word not to offend again, and you usually kept your word. If you didn't, you knew somewhere at the back of your mind that you were doing something shabby on the Ard-Mhaighistir [headmaster]; that you were letting down him, letting St Enda's down, and letting yourself down too.... The discipline at St Enda's was good. And we mostly told the truth. Even I did.[4]

This might seem pious, but it has been borne out by many other ex-pupils. Pearse's notions of schoolboy honour owed as much to the English children's stories he devoured in his youth as to the boys of Emhain Macha. The code was effective because his pupils responded to his innocence and his faith in them. They took responsibility for much of the day-to-day running of the school, helped design the syllabus, and elected their school captain and other officers. In following his precept of appealing to the best in them, Pearse usually enjoyed a positive response. They found it difficult to deceive cold-bloodedly a man who believed in their uprightness and honesty. Nor did he inspire fear, for however close he got to the boys he always inspired awe and respect. A rare recorded case of corporal punishment was on one of the handful of Gaeltacht boys (several of whom were at St Enda's on scholarships which Pearse could ill afford). Pearse was cut to the quick when one of them admitted stealing a cake; he could not come to terms with such behaviour from the heir to all that was glorious in the Gaelic past. But he regretted even that solitary lapse, for which Margaret rebuked him.[5]

His gentleness imposed itself on the school. He was without cruelty himself, and often in his *Claidheamh* days deplored the primitive and callous attitude of the Irish people to children and animals, and praised the enlightened approach of the English. Great efforts were made at St Enda's to instil in the children a love of nature and animals. The only child ever expelled was sent home because of cruelty to a cat.[6] Desmond Ryan tells the story of the vicious turkey-cock which terrorized the school (in a later home).

> Sometimes in the summer there are open-air classes and Pearse holds a group of boys under his spell until a magic and angry bird more mighty than any headmaster arrives and swoops down to put to ignominious flight with strange cries from its scarlet and wrath-swollen gizzard all invaders of the small hilly green it regards as its own. Once Pearse held a raffle to raise funds for the school and saw an opportunity of ridding himself of this beloved but too militant turkey. He offered it as one of the

prizes and it was duly won by a very learned man who waited in vain for the prize. When he complained, Pearse wrote to tell him that if he wanted his bird he would have to come out . . . and capture it himself. Some sixth sense had told it that it was under banishment and its temper and speed increased amazingly. So the turkey lived with Pearse till it died, a despot to the end on its own hard-won green hillock.[7]

And there was always a menagerie in the agricultural part of St Enda's, where the boys were taught husbandry.

The end of the second, and last, year at Cullenswood was as glorious as the first.

Sir Henry Bellingham invited us all down to Castle Bellingham Feis to act once more the Cuchulain pageant. It was a glorious Sunday of brilliant sun, and the countryside was clothed with the fresh green and the wild flowers of June. We were a noisy crowd of irresponsibles as we marched from the train along the dusty road, led by Pearse, MacDonagh and a piper. William Pearse was in his element arranging and seeing to the transport of our costumes and our stage equipment—such as it was. In the distance we glimpsed the outline, jagged—and that day very blue—of the Mourne Mountains. These mountains, we were told, Cuchulain once knew as a boy. I have never heard how our pageant impressed our audience on that day; though we ourselves felt very satisfied, as we marched away when the long shadows of evening fell across the meadows at Castlebellingham. That night we arrived after dusk at Amiens Street [Station], and we formed into marching order behind our school banner of blue poplin, adorned with the gold sun disc of the Fianna. Some of us carried battleaxes borrowed from the school museum, others held tall gilded spears which glinted like polished bronze in the lamp-lit streets. A crowd gathered round, wondering at our strange weapons and our dusty faces. They followed us, and soon they were singing "Who Fears to Speak of '98" [a popular ballad about the United Irishmen's rebellion of 1798] as they tramped and surged round us. MacDonagh was delighted at the commotion we had raised. "Egad!" he said, as the crowd swelled to the dimensions of a riot, "they expect us to lead them against the Castle".[8]

But Pearse's contentment did not have deep roots. The restlessness which demanded ever-fresh ambitions had taken hold of him by the spring of 1910. All his initial good resolutions about keeping the school small had gone by the board. Now he wanted a bigger school, an environment worthy of his boys. He wrote of this decision in the next issue of the *Macaomh*, which, despite the high promise of December 1909, did not appear until the following Christmas. The journal ran to only four issues.

> ... very soon afterwards [after the previous number] I had convinced myself that the work I had planned to do for my pupils was impossible of accomplishment at Cullenswood. We were, so to speak, too much in the Suburban Groove. The city was too near; the hills were too far. The house itself, beautiful and roomy though it was, was not large enough for our swelling numbers. The playfield, though our boys had trained themselves there to be the cleverest hurlers in Dublin, gave no scope for that spacious outdoor life, that intercourse with the wild things of the woods and the wastes (the only things in Ireland that know what Freedom is), that daily adventure face to face with elemental Life and Force, with its moral discipline, with its physical hardening, which ought to play so large a part in the education of a boy. Remember that our ideal was the playgreen of Eamhain, where the most gracious of all education systems had its finest expression. In a word, St Enda's had the highest aim in education of any school in Ireland: it must have the worthiest home.

And once he had decided that a worthy home was necessary, a worthy home was procured. It was a disastrous step, both for Pearse and his school, for it took him from the realm of minor money worries to the verge of financial catastrophe. But Pearse's great virtue, which was also his serious flaw, was an inability to recognize the impossible. "I have constantly found that to desire is to hope, to hope is to believe, and to believe is to accomplish." He accomplished his new ambition when he discovered the Hermitage.

IV THE HERMITAGE 1910-1912

Pearse fell in love with the Hermitage at first sight. For a man with a taste for formal and dignified beauty it was an overwhelming temptation. He saw it before the end of the last term at Cullenswood House, and from then on financial consideration ceased to matter. Dominated by Kilmashogue Mountain, it was a large and beautiful eighteenth-century house, set in 50 acres of woods, parkland and orchards, enhanced by bridges, arches, grottoes, stone walls and, above all, by the river and lake near its boundary. Although he admitted that its gracious charm was largely that of Anglo-Ireland, it had historical connections with Robert Emmet, the leader of a pathetically ineffective rebellion in 1803, which had ended with his public execution. It was in the grounds of the Hermitage, tradition told, that Emmet used to walk with his ill-fated love, Sarah Curran. In this house and these grounds, Robert Emmet began to take hold of the eclectic imagination of Patrick Pearse, and displace his more ancient heroes. By the end of the first term there this was obvious.

> I am not sure whether it is symptomatic of some development within me, or is merely a passing phase, or comes naturally from the associations that cling about these old stones and trees, that whereas at Cullenswood House I spoke oftenest to our boys of Cuchulainn and his compeers of the Gaelic prime, I have been speaking to them oftenest here of Robert Emmet and the heroes of the last stand. Cuchulainn was our greatest inspiration at Cullenswood; Robert Emmet has been our greatest inspiration here. In truth, it was the spirit of Emmet that led me to these hillsides.[1]

His new preoccupations were no "passing phase". Emmet, and with him a whole revolutionary tradition, came to dominate the new St Enda's, as well as its suggestible head teacher. Desmond Ryan put it well in his memoirs.

> If a locality can preserve the past and haunt a receptive mind with past good or evil, assuredly the Hermitage haunted the mind and personality of Pearse.... Robert Emmet's memory haunted Pearse, and this haunting is clamant throughout Pearse's later speeches: he seems to see Emmet tapping his cane along the Rathfarnham roads, rambling through the Hermitage grounds and plucking grapes from the vines or lying hidden among the heather on Kilmashogue Mountain, which Pearse could see from his study windows, or standing on a scaffold before a silent Dublin crowd.[2]

St Enda's was to become increasingly politically minded during its Hermitage years, but Pearse still had many practical problems to occupy his mind. He had not only the boys' school to worry about. He had established a combined girls senior school and mixed preparatory school in Cullenswood House—St Ita's. Financial problems apart, he had difficulty in staffing both schools and in finding sufficient pupils. His main support, MacDonagh, had left the school to study for university examinations, and MacDonnell had left at the same time. Although the conscientious and serious-minded Dr Doody and Michael Smithwick were still with him in their new surroundings, the loss of MacDonagh's sunny optimism was a great blow. Other teachers were recruited, but payment of their salaries was so erratic that the turn-over throughout the years at the Hermitage was to be a constant headache. Even though MacDonagh returned for the 1911-1912 school year, he then left again for a university job. Without the solicitude of Willie, who finally dissolved the family business both to provide some capital for the new school and to free himself to help Patrick full-time, the burden would have been crushing. Willie had had some personal ambitions of his own, before the opening of the Hermitage. Frustrated in his creative endeavours by his other commitments, he had applied for a job at the School of Art.

> I am a practical worker in marble and stone and besides my work at my place of business at Brunswick Street I here execute some small commissions on my own responsibility—so that I am not an amateur but one with the earnest intention of pursuing my craft as a practical sculptor.
>
> It is for this reason that I would be anxious to obtain the appointment I ask for—as up to the present I feel I have not been able to do justice to myself or my work—my time being too much divided between this or more places and things.
>
> . . .
>
> Of course I know I have not much to boast of in awards or results of examining—as I did not make a practice of sitting for these examinations and this for more than one reason.
>
> Firstly my temperament would not allow me to go thro' such things with any degree of comfort or success. And I never saw sufficient reason why I should do violence to myself by so doing. Besides I have had so much to do both at school and at my work here that I never felt inclined. Of course things might be different if I was under service to you.[3]

His hopes came to nothing. Instead of developing as a sculptor (almost all his best work was done before 1910), he gave up all his ambitions for Patrick. Willie, although he had few gifts as a teacher, and none as a businessman, had an unswerving loyalty and determination to help his beloved brother which made him invaluable. "He it was who made the young idea wipe its boots on the mat and keep its fork in its left hand and answer all bells promptly.

He it was who managed plays and pageants and guided clumsy fingers round circles and curves in the drawing class."[4] The pupils appreciated his unassuming nature, and resisted the schoolboy temptation to put obstacles in its path.

Mrs Pearse, and more particularly Margaret, were also a source of strength, and with Patrick and Willie they preserved some element of continuity in the school. The gardener, Michael Mac Ruadhri (Michael MacRory), who was with St Enda's throughout its life, was another important link for the generations. He was a native speaker of Irish and winner of many Oireachtas medals. Ryan remembered Mac Ruadhri thus: "Micheal can dictate a history with only one pause for breath and chant a Rabelaisian or reverent Gaelic rann in his greenhouses as the mood takes him, and well deserves every one of the seven gold medals he has won for oratory, and if Michael prefers to wear all seven medals on a velvet board pinned to his lapel on feast days, that is his affair."[5] Mac Ruadhri's influence on the boys—especially those from the Gaeltacht—was considerable. The Gaeltacht boys had not been as successful an element in St Enda's as Pearse had wished.[6] He believed that they would help the others with their spoken Irish, while themselves benefiting from a broad education which they could not hope to get at home. But he had reckoned without the feelings of a minority, and without that inbred sense of shame which so many Irish speakers—despite the League's best efforts—still felt over their lack of English. MacDonagh realized the extent of the problems and spoke sadly to Yeats of it.

> Says that he [MacDonagh] finds a barrier between himself and the Irish-speaking peasantry, who are "cold, dark and reticent" and "too polite". He watches the Irish-speaking boys at his school, and when nobody is looking, or when they are alone with the Irish-speaking gardener, they are merry, clever and talkative. When they meet an English speaker or one who has learned Gaelic they are stupid. They are in a different world.[7]

But a versatile groundsman and staunch family support were not enough, Academic standards inevitably slipped. The endless changes in teaching staff were unsettling for the boys, and they were not to emulate the academic achievements of the first generation of St Enda's boys—to whom Pearse was always much closer than to successive generations. Besides, numbers had dropped because of the school's new location. Rathfarnham was a long way from the city, and many parents removed their boys rather than send them as boarders. From 130 boys in the 1909-10 session, the numbers had shrunk to only 70 in 1910-11. Pearse's increasing public involvement with politics from 1913 also took its toll of boys with disenchanted parents. After 1912-13 the numbers never reached 60, and in the final year of the Hermitage, 1915-16, there were only 28 boys over fourteen who stayed for two terms—a drop of twelve from the previous year.

A great deal of the teaching in those later years was done by local survivors of that first generation of St Enda's some of whom were now students at the National University, but chose to board at their old school. Three of them, Desmond Ryan (by now Pearse's secretary), Frank Burke and Eamon Bulfin he specially loved. Known as "The Dogs" (probably because one of Willie's nicknames for Patrick was "Mr Dog"), they had a room off the kitchen in which the Pearse brothers spent much of their leisure time, and there they used to talk late into the night, while Pearse listened and laughed, and drank tea from the great willow-pattern cup which enabled him to keep a much-regretted vow never to drink more than one cup of tea.

Pearse was styled "Director" of the sister-school, and although his heart was with his boys, he took a great interest in its beginnings. He was fortunate in the headmistress, Mrs Gertrude Bloomer, a musician, who was prepared to carry not only the responsibility for the day-to-day running of the school, but part of the financial burden as well. Unfortunately, she was little known, and parents reacted less well to St Ita's than to the boys' school. Also, as with St Enda's, staffing was a problem, in the early stages especially. MacDonagh was friendly with her and, despite what he called his "defection" from St Enda's, corresponded with her regularly from June to September 1910, talking over plans and offering her advice and encouragement about the obstacles that beset her.

> Surely when people like you want a thing and are brave enough to challenge destiny as you are doing, destiny must come to you. I find that it always does. Your estimate of £600 looks terrifying, but Pearse who started without estimates really and with more headshakes than handshakes from his friends, has really succeeded. By the way, in talking to you of your prospects I may seem to you to have lost faith in St Enda's, just a little. That is not so. I am quite assured that taken as it is it is the best school for boys in Ireland and will turn out the best Irish men. It is worth while sending boys to it to put them under Pearse who is the noblest man they will ever meet, I think. I was dissatisfied in certain things in the teaching and the staff, but I should be

dissatisfied in Heaven, you know, and I have the problems of seeing things from everybody's point of view.[8]

He was very keen that she employ a close friend of his, Mary Maguire (who later married Padraic Colum). She was one of those prepared to risk involvement with Pearse's enterprises for the sake of the intangible rewards:

> ... eventually I went to teach in one of Padraic Pearse's two schools. I knew nearly everybody connected with them: the teaching staff was young, and we seemed, all of us, to be travelling on the same road.
>
> ... Looking back, it seems incredible that so many young people were eager to devote their lives to the service of causes and ideals rather than to the normal things of youth. That they should take on themselves the arduous task of running a school, of bringing up and educating boys and girls, a task so full of drudgery and routine, seems unbelievable. But then it seemed equally incredible to some that parents would want to entrust their children to a group of young people whose chief recommendation was their ideals, their scholarship, their sense of art, and in other ways their lack of experience.[9]

In that memoir Mary Colum caught the elation of Pearse's schools. "Prudence," he used to say, "is the only vice." And to a generation craving adventure, trained to the missionary ideals of self-sacrifice, his novel ideas were a great attraction. It was his ability to excite such enthusiasms in others that carried St Enda's and St Ita's through their difficulties. MacDonagh was irate at the negative advice offered on all sides: Mary Hayden provoked his especial anger.

> I up and told her that it is very easy for people to talk and throw cold water on things but we have got practical good advice from no one and no one has proposed to us the name of a mistress who would satisfy their requirements.... I had wanted to settle with her for some time. Now it does not matter a straw whether she gives us her name or not [as a patron]. She told Mrs Gwynn [Stephen Gwynn's wife] that she takes no interest in girls.[10]

St Ita's, although compelled to offer girls many hours of domestic economy, needlework, drawing, dancing and other training in lady-like accomplishments, was more academically orientated than most Irish girls' schools. Pearse was consistent in his views on women's rights. He saw women primarily as moulders of the next generation, but he championed their fight for recognition as useful members of society. (He had strongly urged, for instance, the appointment of more women to the Senate of the National University.) He believed that they should be given maximum educational opportunities. He and Mrs Bloomer tried hard to find the best teachers, and he insisted that they be offered good salaries; as MacDonagh said to Mrs Bloomer, "that should be the last department in which to economize".

St Ita's began reasonably auspiciously. Pearse himself was little involved with the girls, but he used to come to see them every Wednesday afternoon and make to them the same speeches as he made to the boys. Mary Bulfin, sister of Eamon, recalled later: " 'Live up to the best that is in you,' he said; 'and if your way of life or your profession in life does not allow you to live up to that best that is in you, then you must *change* your way of life, or your profession.' "[11] This was the philosophy which had sent Pearse from his law studies to the Gaelic League, and, when disillusionment set in, from the League to his school. It won him respect at St Ita's as it did at St Enda's, but he could not quite achieve the same ease with the older girls. Although the senior boys were his favourites, it was with the smaller girls he felt most at home. "There was one, a little, fragile pale child, of whom he was especially fond ... although she was extremely shy and silent with the mistresses, and even with the girls, she always found plenty to say to Mr Pearse. Often the two might be seen having quite an animated chat, especially if no one else were around."[12]

St Enda's and St Ita's combined to mount what was probably Pearse's finest dramatic production—a passion play, in the Abbey, in Holy Week 1911—inspired by his personal devotion to Christ in his Passion and Crucifixion. He was at his best when he was at his most simple, and in this play he succeeded through the straightforward adaptation of the dialogue of the Gospels to an Irish social ethos. One of the features of the interpretation was the keening women who meet Christ on the road to Calvary. Pearse was helped in the production by two of his ex-masters, MacDonagh and MacDonnell, the former stage-managing and the latter composing the music. Although there were some who found the whole idea improper, especially on a public stage, it was a resounding success. Maire Nic Shiubhlaigh said of it: "Probably the most outstanding Gaelic production seen in Dublin before 1916 was Padraic Pearse's Passion play.... In its own way this created something of a minor sensation in Dublin, reports of it travelling across the Atlantic, and some of them finding their way into the continental press....

It was probably the first really serious piece of Gaelic dramatic writing produced."[13] Joseph Holloway was also deeply impressed.

> I went down to the Abbey to see a *"Passion Play"* in 3 acts by P. H. Pearse.... The pit was full when I got down to the theatre and the stalls and balcony rapidly got busy looking. Mr Pearse stepped from between the curtains and addressed the house first in Irish and then he explained the nature of the piece we were soon to behold and the way he wished us to receive it.... It was all most impressive and very beautiful to behold.... [At Calvary] the grouping was perfect and the "picture" created undying. The lighting of the whole scene from beginning to end could not be more effectively managed and the colour scheme was of unsurpassed beauty ... all who had followed the incidents were deeply and wonderfully moved. The students of St Enda's and St Ita's had in a simple and unaffected way recreated the tragedy of the King of the World for us again and we felt all the better for the sight. Never had I seen a more profoundly impressive and beautiful picture than that I beheld at the foot of Calvary during the Crucifixion! William Pearse was excellent as Pilate. I was greatly struck with by what simple means great effects can be produced and illusion intensified on the stage.[14]

Again, the play was a personal statement which served to reinforce the attitudes which lay beneath. Pearse's mystical love of the symbolism of Christ grew after the performance, and he began to identify himself more closely with Him in his remaining few years. Political burdens in the next few years were to prevent him again staging a passion play, although he had resolved that it should be a triennial event. Padraic Colum's belief that this performance had sown the seeds out of which a Gaelic drama might arise was not justified.[15] Pearse had not time to follow up his first attempt and there was no one else to take up the challenge.

There were other highlights in the first two years of the Hermitage. One was the visit of Roger Casement, who spoke to the boys about the Irish revival and left a spectacular penknife as a prize for the author of the best essay in Irish on his address.[16] He was greatly impressed by the school. He even contemplated sending to the school one of his adopted Indian boys whom he had rescued from the horrors of Putumayo. But though Pearse was enthusiastic, Casement changed his mind.[17] Still, in 1912, writing to refuse help to his old school, Ballymena Academy, he wrote that he preferred to contribute to a school which "trained its youth to know, love and respect their own land, before all others".[18] St Enda's, he said, was the only Irish school doing this. "I was taught nothing about Ireland in Ballymena School—I don't think the word was ever mentioned in a single class of the school . . . we shall see our country possessing inhabitants fit to succeed and prosper in every country but their own."

If Pearse could help it, St Enda's would provide more patriotic citizens. He wanted to train the men of the future, men to raise the country from what he was beginning to see as timidity bordering on corruption. But he could no longer envisage a smooth transition; some kind of catharsis was necessary. At the end of the first two years at the Hermitage, this belief was given form in his first real play—a Morality called *An Ri* (The King). The story was set in a monastic school in medieval Ireland, where the boys were discussing their king's successive defeats. The abbot explains that these are the fruit of the king's own guilt—God will not accept an offering from "polluted hands". When the king approaches, after another battle with the enemy, the abbot tells him that he must give up his throne to the righteous ruler, and offers as successor the purest among his group—Giolla na Naomh (Servant of the Saints). Although this little boy is without ambition, he accepts the burden, and although he himself dies in the ensuing battle, he leads his troops to victory. The play embodied three important aspects of Pearse's thought at this period. First, it showed his growing preoccupation with the sacrifice of Calvary, for Giolla is the embodiment of the Christ-child who must die to save his people. Second, it was a reaffirmation of his belief in the essential purity of childhood. Third, it stated the necessity of sacrificing the young and the sinless to save a decadent nation.

It is too easy to see all Pearse's literary writings as autobiographical, but many of them are a key to his prevailing convictions. The redemption brought by Christ's death, and the heroism of the child-king, appealed to the same element in Pearse's nature that had so readily responded to the shade of the martyr Emmet. He was not training revolutionaries, but his urgent desire to induce in his boys a sense of service was developing into a belief that they should be ready for self-sacrifice. In the *Macaomh* of 1910 he had written of them: "sometimes I wonder whether, if ever I need them for any great service, they will rally, as many of them have promised to do, from wherever they may be, holding faith to the inspiration and the tradition I have tried to give them."

In the last issue of the journal, published in May 1913, he showed an increasing awareness of the themes which were knitting together in his subconscious. He described a vivid dream of four years previously.

> I dreamt that I saw a pupil of mine, one of our boys at St Enda's, standing alone upon a platform above a mighty sea of people; and I understood that he was about to die there for some august cause, Ireland's or another. He looked extraordinarily proud and joyous, lifting his head with a smile almost of amusement; I remember noticing his bare white throat and the hair on his forehead stirred by the wind, just as I had often noticed them on the football field. I felt an inexplicable exhilaration as I looked upon him, and this exhilaration was heightened rather than diminished by my consciousness that the great silent crowd regarded the boy with pity and wonder rather than with approval —as a fool who was throwing his life away rather than as a martyr that was doing his duty. It would have been so easy to die before an applauding crowd or before a hostile crowd: but to die before that silent, unsympathetic crowd! I dreamt then that another of my pupils stepped upon the scaffold and embraced his comrade, and that then he tied a white bandage over the boy's eyes, as though he would resent the hangman doing him that kindly office. And this act seemed to me to symbolise an immense brotherly charity and loyalty, and to be the compensation to the boy that died for the indifference of the crowd.
>
> ... what recurs to me now is that when I said [to the boys] that I could not wish for any of them a happier destiny than to die thus in defence of some true thing, they did not seem in any way surprised, for it fitted in with all we had been teaching them at St Enda's. I do not mean that we have ever carried on anything like a political or revolutionary propaganda among our boys, but simply that we have always allowed them to feel that no one can finely live who hoards life too jealously: that one must be generous in service, and withal joyous, accounting even supreme sacrifices slight. Mr J. M. Barrie makes his Peter Pan say (and it is finely said) "To die will be a very big adventure," but I think that in making my little boy in "An Ri" offer himself with the words "Let me do this little thing," I am nearer to the spirit of the heroes.

Or, as the abbot said in the play, "Do not keen this child, for he hath purchased freedom for his people. Let shouts of exultation be raised and let a canticle be sung in praise of God."

On its production in June 1912, it does not seem to have been recognized as anything other than a straightforward Morality, without political significance. But then Pearse was not generally seen as a political figure. Yeats was impressed by the play and Holloway, who saw it later, found it "interestingly enacted and made for agreeable tableaux". But then it was played in Irish, and few of the audience would have been able to do much more than follow the basic plot. Yet it marked a new and important development in Pearse's thought: the boys, when they broke up shortly afterwards, left in the Hermitage a man very different from the creator of the adventurous, heroic and high-spirited Cuchullain pageant.

V FINANCES 1908-1912

St Enda's was founded in 1908 on little more than high hopes and £100 from the mortgage on 27 Great Brunswick Street. Pearse's early expectations that Irish Ireland would immediately fill his coffers were quickly dashed, but this did not deter him from charging low fees and spending money which he did not have on refurbishing Cullenswood House. It was not that his friends were mean, but most of them were poor, and even though many sent him pupils, his accounts show that there were those who did not pay all the fees. His main hopes lay with the richer elements among League sympathizers. He had taken on a bank loan to buy the school premises, and by February 1909 he was already in financial difficulties. Hopes of a substantial cheque from a South American Leaguer had come to nothing, and he wrote to Joseph Dolan, who had already advanced him money, and who was to be his greatest benefactor. Dolan was an Ardee merchant, an unpretentious man of great generosity, who has received little recognition for his philanthropy towards many Irish causes. Pearse wrote:

> The bank bill of which I spoke to you will be presented for payment in a few weeks, and some of the contractors who carried out the additions and improvements here are also pressing for a settlement. In the circumstances, it becomes necessary for me to avail of your own most generous and welcome offer. If you can advance me £300 at 5%, I will give you a promissary note for that amount plus the amount already advanced by you—i.e. £350 in all, or, with interest on that sum for one year, £367.10s. This to be re-payable in a year, but if I am unable to re-pay it in full in a year you would, as I understand, be willing to renew

> the bill at interest. This will relieve me from the possible pressure of unfriendly creditors, while your money will be safe, for the house and premises will always be to the good, and the prospects of the school are looking brighter and brighter....
>
> As one of the contractors is becoming threatening, it would be the greatest boon if you could let me have the £300 this week....
>
> With a thousand thanks for your confidence in me and in the future of my effort.[1]

Dolan replied by return of post with £367.10s., and immediate disaster was staved off. Pearse, as MacDonagh later remarked to Mrs Bloomer, had not really estimated his expenses: in his optimism he decided what the school needed, committed himself for it, and then looked for the money. He was spending all his own cash on the venture—even his unpretentious little cottage in Rosmuc suffered. "The building has been complete for more than twelve months past, but some flooring and plastering remain to be done and there is no furniture in it. The fact is that I have spent on St Enda's the money I meant to devote to completing and beautifying this cottage."[2]

By May he was in difficulties again. On top of his school and *Claidheamh* responsibilities he had what he called "a multiplicity of pressing and worrying affairs"—in short, creditors. Dolan came again to his rescue, with a further £105, but this only helped with existing debts—not with those new bills incurred by the refurbishing of Cullenswood House during the summer of 1909. These he paid off with a further £400 bank loan, for which his friend, Stephen Barret, a long-time admirer, stood as co-guarantor, as he had at the school's inception.

Pearse's worries were now somewhat abated. The resounding success of the first four terms augured well for the future, most of the improvements had been carried out, and with time he hoped to pay off the sundry loans from the school's profits. But his own impatient nature could not leave well alone. He counted on the growing reputation of the school as a bait for further financial assistance, and plunged into plans for finding grander accommodation.

As a first step, he secured an advance from the Intermediate Board in April 1910. Although at the school's foundation Pearse had wanted to stand back from the Intermediate rat-race, parental pressure and his own ambition led him to instate St Enda's as a fully-fledged Intermediate school, and to secure from the Board an advance of £300 on the next ten years' grant of £44.5s.6d. *per annum*. In May he distributed widely a circular listing the achievements of St Enda's, describing the newly-discovered Hermitage, and asking for funds. The wording of the appeal, as usual, stressed duty rather than charity.

> The effect on the whole future of Irish education of an Irish Ireland College, housed and equipped as St Enda's will be under these new conditions, will be incalculable. It is hoped that the Irish Ireland public has sufficient faith in the possibility of regenerating Ireland through her schools to endow this great undertaking in such a manner as shall ensure its permanent success.
>
> The house and lands can be had subject to a small rent for £6,000, or can be rented on lease at £300 a year. The balance of £10,000 is required for the necessary additions and the equipment of the place.
>
> It is believed that all friends of education in Ireland who recognise the importance of placing St Enda's in the position of a permanent national institution will be prepared to subscribe for that purpose.
>
> If the total subscribed should amount, as is hoped, to £10,000, it is intended to purchase. If it should not amount to that sum, the place will be leased, with the option of purchasing later on.
>
> The repayment of the sum will be secured either by Debentures in a company which would be formed, or else by a charge to trustees on behalf of the subscribers and which would be a first claim upon the property as acquired with all additions made to it, and to bear interest at £4 per cent. per annum.

A board of Governors was to be set up to administer the finances of the school: Joseph Dolan, Mary Hayden, Dr Henry (a lecturer in University College, Galway), Mrs Stephen Gwynn, the writer Shane Leslie and Seumas MacManus (a northern writer, Leaguer and political nationalist).

Pearse the optimist did not even allow for the possibility of an insufficient response even to lease St Enda's comfortably. But that was what happened. By 15 July, when he signed the lease for the Hermitage, he had received only £2,356.3s.8d. (despite a second appeal)—not even enough to pay the rent and carry out essential repairs. And he himself had contributed £500 to this—presumably the proceeds of the dissolution of Pearse & Sons. Joseph Dolan had subscribed another £600, Seumas MacManus £350, Alec Wilson of Belfast £200 and Dr Henry £130. The rest had been donated by 69 people, who gave sums varying from five shillings to £50, and less than £100 came in over the next six months. The total sum subscribed was wholly inadequate for Pearse's commitments. He had failed to anticipate that the rich were by and large unsympathetic to his aims, while the poor could do little to help. His old friends in the League, the merely prosperous, had so many calls on their purses that they could spare only small sums. Mary Hayden and Hyde gave £5 each, Agnes O'Farrelly £2. Many others gave nothing.

Joseph Holloway had become Pearse's architect, and that stocky little man, of the bushy moustache, with hair sticking out at all angles from beneath his inevitable bowler hat, was to stand by him loyally. He was with him the day the lease was signed, and witnessed the meeting of two cultures as William Woodbyrne, who in the ensuing conversation condemned the Abbey for opening on the day after the king's death, handed over the lease of the Hermitage to the Gael.[3]

Pearse's correspondence with Holloway over the next few years chronicled the struggles of the new St Enda's. There were difficulties with the landlord, squabbles with the builders and incessant financial pressure. In July 1911 he wrote sadly:

> I feel very much that I have not yet been able to let you have any of your fees. You know the great struggle I have to carry through my tremendous undertaking and to make it a success. Just now I have to provide for the half-year's rent and for a further payment to Messrs Farmer [builders]. As soon as I can I must let you have at least something on account. Meantime I appreciate very much your great consideration in not even asking me for a payment, as well as your great care of my interests.

But not all the creditors were so understanding. Pearse would recall to Desmond Ryan the similar trials of Sir Walter Scott, who paid off his debts by the production of endless romantic novels. Ryan was a witness to his sufferings.

> Pearse was a proud man and his pride was sorely tried in these days. I remember once in the Hermitage study while both of us were wrestling with accounts and lists and appeals and articles on the school written by us and others, an angry tradesman came in shouting and garnishing his shouts with lurid oaths about a certain account. *Fear an-droch-mhuinte*, (a very ill-mannered man), said Pearse with a sigh when the ill-mannered creditor vanished at last down the avenue.[4]

Pearse could not see grounds for complaint; could they not understand that they were contributing to a great national work? Most of them couldn't, and they forced him to further action, the setting up of Sgoil Eanna Ltd in January 1912. It was to have a capital of £8,000, made up to 8,000 shares at £1 each. The directors were Pearse, Dolan, Wilson, Barrett and the mathematics master, Michael Smithwick. In the company prospectus, Pearse's liabilities were listed: they now amounted to £6,685 against assets of only £566. The two schools were just paying their way; an annual surplus of £128.13s. was estimated. The directors were less sanguine than Pearse had been in 1910; it was no longer thought possible to find the £6,000 necessary to buy the Hermitage. Although various creditors had agreed to accept shares in the company in lieu of £1,990 worth of claims, more than £4,000 would be required to pay off the rest of the debts. Therefore, even if the whole 8,000 shares were taken up, there would be less than £2,000 over for improvements and repairs at the Hermitage. It was proposed that the company would engage Pearse as headmaster for ten years, at £150 *per annum*, giving him full educational control of St Enda's, while the directors would have business and financial control.

The idea was a sound one. With a group of hard-headed business advisers to bridle Pearse's impetuosity, St Enda's and St Ita's might have been viable. But the device of the limited company failed, primarily because there just was not that kind of money available in Irish Ireland, but also because Pearse himself during the first five months of 1912—when the school's fate was hanging in the balance—allowed himself to get distracted. Instead of devoting himself with his usual single-mindedness to extricating St Enda's from its desperate position, he had become increasingly involved in politics and had set up his own short-lived paper, *An Barr Buadh* (The Trumpet of Victory). By the summer of 1912, bankruptcy was staring him in the face: the directors of St Enda's Ltd, despondent at the inadequate subscription to the company and the ever-mounting debts, recommended voluntary liquidation. Pearse was in agony. If the school were to fold, he swore that rather than be pointed at in the streets of Dublin as a failure, he would go to America and work until he had paid off all his debts. But meanwhile he killed off *An Barr Buadh*, and threw all his energies and persuasive gifts into a last effort to snatch St Enda's from the jaws of its creditors. One of the directors, Alec Wilson, was moved by Pearse's plight and tried to help. In June 1912 he received from Pearse the full accounts of St Enda's and St Ita's and an impassioned plea. "I hope in God that this effort of yours will be successful. It looks our last hope —and yet we have turned the corner. It would be a tragedy if we were to go down now."[5]

Wilson had his work cut out. In a memorandum on the state of Sgoil Eanna Ltd he summed up the situation.

> Mr Pearse estimates cost of buildings, equipment, and other costs of starting the two schools at £5,036.... This is probably underestimated.
>
> I have not seen accounts for the two years 1908-9 and 1909-10, but have no doubts that money was lost, since the number of pupils was so small at the outset. I estimate the total capital sum that has been spent on getting the schools on their present footing at £8,000.
>
> Of this, (which cannot be considered too large an "endowment" even if it were treated as such), approximately £3,000 has been contributed by about 200 persons nearly all poor people, and for the most part without any expectation that the money would ever be repaid. Mr Pearse has sunk every penny he possesses in the enterprise. The Prospectus did not hold out any hope that shares applied for would earn a dividend.
>
> It is quite impossible to carry on the Schools any longer unless a further sum of £3,000 be immediately available, to pay off the capital cost of starting. The remaining £2,000 is not urgent at present.
>
> Unless by some means, such as a loan at low interest, or guaranteed bank overdraft, (or, best of all, donation), this sum of £3,000 be forthcoming, it will be necessary to close the Schools now. They cannot be reopened for the autumn term without clearing off these debts.
>
> I can speak of personal knowledge of the excellent work being done by the schools. They are fully equal to the best English private schools. Their reputation is already, after only four years, second to none. And I share Mr Pearse's opinion that it would be a calamity if lack of financial support should now force them to close down. I am ready to help in whatever scheme be devised, but am not able to do, singlehanded, all that is needed.

Even though Alec Wilson could not save the schools singlehanded, he found a stop-gap solution. He promised £300 on the condition Pearse be offered enough money by other friends to buy out the school from Sgoil Eanna Ltd, and that all creditors agree to accept a small payment on account and hold off pressure for the coming school year. This was a great deal to expect of Pearse's much-neglected creditors, who now numbered over 120, including most prominent Dublin merchants, and the best part of his staff. Mac-

Donagh was owed over £30, and the unfortunate Dr Doody over £80. One of his many grocers had had the lack of foresight to grant him over £200 worth of credit, and from the few scraps of correspondence from firms which remain, it is clear that Pearse had used his literary and personal gifts to cajole them into giving him time. He owed £106 to M. H. Gill, who complained: "You have treated us very badly and for no other reason that we can see but just because we have been too lenient with you."[6] All had been promised payment in full within a reasonable period, and now they were being asked to agree to a proposition which for many of them was an insult, for many more a serious hardship. Bolands, which was to suffer much greater calamities four years later, when the 1916 rebels took over its premises, wrote to him in honest indignation.

> ... we are sending to refresh your memory, a brief abstract of our correspondence with you in the pursuit of our fruitless endeavour to induce you to pay your account. The position appears to be that your friends will provide 2/- in the £ but that you yourself will undertake nothing. Looking to our experience of you, we submit that such a proposition on your part goes beyond all reason. We have nothing to add to our letter of the 13th inst. [threatening legal action].[7]

Despite such protests, the creditors were left with no option. Two shillings in the pound was better than nothing, and they settled for it. Enough money was raised from friends to set Pearse up for a new school year. He bought Sgoil Eanna Ltd from the Liquidator and was back in complete control, but he realized that he could do little more than stave off financial collapse, unless a new source of capital could be found. In his optimistic heart he understood at last that he could expect no more from Irish Ireland. Even those sympathetically disposed had become perturbed by Pearse's extravagances of later years. Edward Martyn voiced common doubts when he wrote to him in September 1912. "... I feel that whatever you get now will be only staving off the inevitable, since your Committee has gone.... I am sorry you would never listen to prudent advice ... you have now made impossible what with care and foresight might have become a permanent success."[8]

No amount of advice, complaints or threats could make him regret his decision to move St Enda's to the Hermitage. Vision was more important than financial competence, and his motives, he felt, had been wholly noble and disinterested. Although he rebuked himself for not giving enough attention to the school while he was editing *An Barr Buadh*,[9] he felt no blame otherwise for the school's financial straits. A shrewd commentator later summed up his attitude.

> His schoolmasters did not always receive their salaries with regularity. The reason that he did not pay them was the simple one that he had no money. Given another man this explanation would be uneconomic, but from him it was so logical that even a child could comprehend it. These masters did not always leave him. They remained, marvelling perhaps, and accepting, even with stupefaction, the theory that children must be taught, but that no such urgency is due towards the payment of wages.[10]

Although he spent much time looking into his own soul, and criticizing his own short-comings, he was never able to question his judgement. His causes were always beyond criticism, and commanded his formidable energies, but he would accept no advice that might steer those energies, or modify his conception of how best to apply them. Martyn was right in his criticism. Pearse could have made a modest financial success of St Enda's if he had stayed in Cullenswood House and trimmed his sails. Instead, partly because he believed it necessary for the boys, partly because it fitted his personal vision of his task and flattered his personal vanity, he had invited ruin by the move to Rathfarnham. Although his conscience was occasionally troubled by the financial burden he had placed on some of his friends like Dolan, Barrett, and Mrs Bloomer, his strongest tendency was to condemn those who had not helped, or not helped enough.

History was repeating itself. As the majority of the nation had failed to learn Irish; as the Irish Irelanders had failed to make the *Claidheamh* the most successful paper in Ireland; as the teachers had proved mercenary; as Ireland had failed to finance its own university; as the Gaeltacht had failed to produce great Irish writers; as the Gaels had failed to found a national theatre; so too, the country had failed to rally sufficiently to what was still the most glorious cause of all—a fine Irish school for Irish children. Perhaps he might find a more unstinting support across the Atlantic. Within a few years he was to go to America in search of funds; he would find as well a new political inspiration.

CHAPTER FIVE

POLITICS

I 1910-1912

The first decade of the twentieth century was a period of intense political activity in Ireland, but most of it passed Pearse by. James Pearse had been a supporter of the parliamentary Home Rulers, and his son had shared his admiration for Parnell. It says much for Patrick Pearse that he kept his reverence for the constitutional nationalists even after he was committed to a revolutionary path. His only criterion was that a man should have worked for Ireland, and, accordingly, just as in his constitutional days he had an affection for the Fenians and the rebels of 1848, so in his revolutionary period he could still find praise for O'Connell and Parnell. Certainly he was always a nationalist. His devotion to the Gaelic League was anchored in a strong belief that cultural nationalism would save the soul of the country. Like many of his generation, the fall of Parnell had left him disenchanted with politics and he sought an outlet elsewhere. He had little faith in Irish political parties, but neither was he hostile to them; he suffered no discomfort in following the League's non-political policy of supporting candidates, of any party, who embraced League objectives. He took a keen passive interest in Irish politics throughout his editorship of the *Claidheamh*, but he was regarded even by many respectable Leaguers as being dangerously right-wing because he was prepared to give credit, where credit was due, to the British government, the National Board and other Aunt Sallies. He seemed hardly conscious of the growing Labour movement. The resurgent revolutionary Irish Republican Brotherhood held no appeal for him—if indeed he even knew of its arcane existence—although he worked closely with one of its oath-bound members, Sean T. O'Kelly. He had some sympathy for Sinn Fein, having been deeply stirred by Griffith's *Resurrection of Hungary*, and he attended in his private capacity the national convention which set up the party in November 1905.[1] But although Sinn Fein was supported by such respectable League colleagues as Edward Martyn, John Sweetman and Mary Butler, and although it showed itself deeply sympathetic to the Irish language, Pearse did not become a member. Indeed Griffith's attacks on *Claidheamh* editorials and his general pugnacity held Pearse at a distance. The personal abuse to which Pearse was subjected by Sinn Feiners over his soft line on the Council Bill of 1907, when he stood to the right of even the parliamentarians, disillusioned him further, and since he was gradually losing faith in the League, he found in the autonomy of St Enda's the scope to exercise his nationalistic soul, free of the strait-jacket of organizational policy.

He was not cut out to be a faithful follower of a political party. During his six years as editor of the *Claidheamh* he had shown more inclination to lead than to follow. Even his great admiration for Douglas Hyde was not enough to keep him in line with League policy on all issues. The lack of such personal respect for Griffith was enough to keep him out of his party. At St Enda's he was carried along for a time by the widespread publicity and accolades he received. W. P. Ryan wrote of him in his book, *The Pope's Green Island*: "The most courageous pioneer in the realm of Irish education is a young man of thirty-two, Padraic MacPiarais (P. H. Pearse, B.A., B.L.). He is a scholar with a child-spirit, a mystical temperament, and a Celtic nature, in the heroic and constructive sense."[2] This was a generous and remarkably accurate tribute for the period, but when Ryan wrote those words, in 1911, Pearse's heroic ambitions were already reaching for further stars. The boys were rewarding, but training young minds for a glorious maturity requires a patience which Pearse did not possess. From the time it moved to the Hermitage, the foundering St Enda's was moving too slowly for him. Once more he was ready for a new enthusiasm.

It was the shade of Robert Emmet which wrought the most fundamental change in Pearse's political attitudes, but other mentors were to follow, more articulate than Emmet, who had left no written testament. During his early years at the Hermitage, Pearse steeped himself in the writings of revolutionaries, particularly in Wolfe Tone's *Autobiography* and John Mitchel's *Jail Journal*.[3] Both of them, and later the Young Irelanders Thomas Davis and Fintan Lalor, were to inspire his most impassioned political writing, but it was Tone whom Pearse loved, for from his *Autobiography* Tone emerged as a kindred spirit. Like Pearse, Tone was a disenchanted barrister, a frustrated man of ambition, a man capable of singlemindedness and self-sacrifice. But most of all, the appeal of Tone and the other revolutionaries was that they had *acted* in support of their beliefs, undeterred by overwhelming odds. A craving for action came to dominate Pearse's thinking, and combined with his literary and oratorical gifts, it made him an object of interest to revolutionary groups.

By 1910 Pearse was a public figure in Dublin. Through the Gaelic League he was well-known to many prominent politicians and on friendly terms with such dissimilar people as Stephen Gwynn, MP, a member of the Irish parliamentary party (father of Denis, Pearse's most brilliant pupil), Arthur Griffith, and Sean T. O'Kelly, who though best-known as a Sinn Fein Dublin councillor, was now in his tenth year of secret IRB activity. None of these tried to recruit Pearse; but there were others more alive to his possibilities, and he did not long remain outside the notice of the IRB leadership.

One of the many to whom Pearse wrote for help with St Enda's in 1910 was Patrick McCartan, a man of 32, prominent in Sinn Fein, and a dedicated IRB man.[4] He was an Irish-language enthusiast, who admired Pearse's work and suggested to him that it might be worth his while seeking the financial support of the AOH (Ancient Order of Hibernians) in America. He would himself, he wrote, seek the advice of Tom Clarke on the matter. Clarke was an ex-Fenian, who had served fifteen bitter years in an English prison for his part in a dynamite plot, and at 52, he was the doyen of the IRB. He sat in his tobacconist's shop in a shabby Dublin street, content to stay behind the scenes of political activity, while exercising effective control over the nation-wide network of IRB activity. It was to Clarke that the young, vigorous men of the movement, like McCartan, Bulmer Hobson and Sean MacDermott came for advice and instructions. On this occasion, he showed little enthusiasm for McCartan's protégé. He had heard rumours about Patrick Pearse which led him to question his brand of nationalism, and Pearse was obliged to write to McCartan in self-defence. Although McCartan seemed convinced by Pearse, Clarke maintained that the very rumours would poison Pearse's chances with the AOH. Pearse was always hurt by this kind of response, and as time went on, and Emmet and Tone took their hold on him, he came to resent fiercely accusations that he was a political right-winger. He was beginning to attend occasional public meetings run by republicans, who, he felt, were capable of only talk—never action. Desmond Ryan recalls such a meeting, where Pearse spoke from the floor about the separatist tradition in Irish literature, and with his usual fairmindedness criticized some of the speakers for their anti-Redmond gibes.

> ... Pearse's plea for a charitable attitude towards the Irish Parliamentary party drew taunts that he was a moderate very boorishly and ignorantly expressed with all the crudity of ex-

asperated doctrinaries. Pearse made a remarkable reply which ended: "Yes, give me a hundred men and I will free Ireland!" ... The faith behind his words silenced the critics and commanded respect, for a few days later the most outspoken of Pearse's opponents at the meeting sent him an unreserved apology for any rudeness. As we left the meeting Pearse's eyes burned and he talked all the way to the Rathfarnham tram at the Pillar, saying intensely: "Let them talk! I am the most dangerous revolutionary of the whole lot of them!"[5]

Tom Clarke was not so easily impressed. In 1911 his closest friend, 28-year-old Sean MacDermott, the IRB's national organizer, suggested that Pearse might be the man to deliver the oration at the Emmet commemoration meeting in March. Clarke, who had met Pearse in February, expressed doubts but MacDermott assured him that, properly primed, Pearse would say the right things. MacDermott knew his man, and Pearse was given his opportunity. It was his first truly nationalistic speech, and although it sprang from his devotion to Emmet rather than to any revolutionary programme, it demonstrated to the IRB men that he had talents which could be useful to them. McCartan was particularly moved by a part of Pearse's speech where he said: "Dublin would have to do some great act to atone for the shame of not producing a man to dash his head against a stone wall in an effort to rescue Robert Emmet."[6] Clarke, too, was much taken with the performance of his new spokesman: "I never thought there was such stuff in Pearse."

Although the memorial committee had specified that there should be no political resolutions passed at this meeting, Pearse's words inspired McCartan to defy IRB discipline and propose a resolution, seconded by Clarke, that Loyal Addresses should not be presented to the King of England on his forthcoming visit to Ireland. This speech, and others made during the next few years, crushed the reservations of some IRB members concerning Pearse; but in others' eyes he could not live down his political history, and they blocked attempts to recruit him into the organization until late in 1913. Cathal Brugha mistrusted him because of his record of bad debts,[7] but there were other reasons for opposition. Pearse's political position was still equivocal. As late as 1912 he spoke in favour of Home Rule, and his romantic praise for Tone and Emmet was still a long way from the secret oath and dry machinations of the IRB. But he was thinking more and more deeply about politics in his self-imposed isolation in the Hermitage, where he read and brooded over Ireland's past and future, immersing himself in the words of his personal heroes.

Pearse seems to have had little energy or inclination for literary composition during this period of transition. Between September 1910, when he moved to the Hermitage, and March 1912, when he threw himself into *An Barr Buadh*, his only literary publications (apart from prose writings in *An Macaomh*) were two Irish poems, which show the extent of the change in his attitudes. The first, published in December 1910, was "Nior Cruinnigheadh Liom-sa Or" (I Have Not Garnered Gold). Despite its melancholy tone, it showed that his pupils still embodied his most passionate aspirations.

I have not garnered gold;
The fame I found hath perished;
In love I got but grief
That withered my life.

Of riches or of store
I shall not leave behind me
(Yet I deem it, O God, sufficient)
But my name in the heart of a child.

The other poem, "Fornocht do Chonnach Thu" (Naked I Saw Thee —*renamed* Renunciation), was very different in its resolution. It concerned the poet's renunciation of beauty, music, and the other objects of desire, to set out on a fatal course.

I have turned my face
To this road before me,
To the deed that I see
And the death I shall die.

Death was becoming a preoccupation with Pearse. His mysticism, already shown in his attitude to religion, was to manifest itself from now on in his developing political philosophy, a philosophy which called for the final sacrifice in the holy cause of Ireland's freedom. These disparate elements were soon to crystallize into a conviction that only through death—Pearse's own death, at that—could Ireland live again.

II AN BARR BUADH

Pearse's growing interest in matters political demanded a public platform, and since he was not yet prepared to compromise his independence by joining any existing group, it had to be a platform of his own building, for the broadcasting of his own beliefs. In so far as these had solidified by the spring of 1912, they were: that the Irish people had lost their souls; that they must forget their differences to confront the British Lion; that Home Rule was worth accepting because it was a step towards complete freedom, but that if it were denied, the people, and especially the young, must be goaded into war—even a hopeless war—to restore national self-respect. With these convictions he retained the fundamental belief that political freedom was not enough—the Irish language and its literature were essential to the soul of Ireland.

To promulgate his views to the best of the people—the Irish speakers—Pearse launched his own newspaper, *An Barr Buadh* (The Trumpet of Victory), on 16 March 1912. If the enthusiasm, energy and industry shown in this new venture were typical of Pearse, so too was the financial irresponsibility and lack of common prudence; he had no money and little journalistic help available to him. Bulmer Hobson, years later, recalled the *Barr Buadh* as a prime example of Pearse's disturbing attitude to money:

> In financial matters he was certainly impractical, and possibly dishonest. He began a Gaelic journal, *Barr Buadh*, and when he found that he was in deep financial waters he came to me for advice. I asked him with what money he had begun the paper; he said "none". I could hardly credit this, and asked him to explain. He said that one evening when walking around St Enda's he had got the idea of such a journal, had gone into Dublin, and given the contract to a small printer, Curtis. No payment was ever made. It was a heavy loss for Curtis, but this did not bother Pearse.[1]

His will, a quality which Pearse always regarded as an infallible asset, was virtually his only resource. He had so much to say, and wanted so badly to say it, that he could not be contented with a monthly journal, though even that would have imposed an impossible strain: *An Barr Buadh* had to be a weekly. The new paper was announced in the columns of *Irish Freedom*, an IRB publication, whose editor, McCartan, and manager, MacDermott, were sympathetic towards Pearse. Its purpose was to preach "the elementary political truth that the liberty of a people can only be guaranteed by its readiness and ability to vindicate it in arms".[2]

Though *An Barr Buadh* only ran to eleven issues, and had only four pages, it was a rather tired publication. While Pearse could often rise to rhetorical heights, most of his articles were reiterative, and since he limited his canvas to Irish politics, and the Home Rule Bill in particular, his efforts had little of the breadth or content which had made his *Claidheamh* contributions so lively. The paper was written wholly in Irish, so its contributors were restricted to the few men who shared Pearse's idiosyncratic political principles and could also write adequately in Irish. Of these, the most prolific and significant was a frustrated young Dublin clerk, Eamonn Kent (Ceannt), who though a prominent Sinn Feiner had many grounds for difference with Griffith. Kent, a long-standing member of the Gaelic League, was almost fanatically devoted to the cause of the Irish language and Irish music, and had a son at St Enda's. Other important contributors were Peter Macken (Peadar O Maicin), a Sinn Fein city councillor, Cathal O'Shannon, a young Belfast journalist, Thomas MacDonnell, one of Pearse's ex-assistant masters, and Brian O'Higgins, who wrote for the paper a few of the many thousand pieces of Irish patriotic doggerel which he was to pen during his long career.

These contributors were loyal, but they were all busy men and none of them very gifted writers, so their pieces were rarely inspiring. The paper had to stand or fall by Pearse, who contributed about two thirds of the copy, drafting it in his scanty leisure time. He was neither famous enough, nor sufficiently popular in his views to command a wide public, and the paper was hampered from the start by its tiny circulation and consequent paucity of advertisements. *An Barr Buadh* was sometimes vigorous, and plucky in its attacks not only on the Irish lay establishments, but also on the bishops, of whom he was as little fond as he had been in his *Claidheamh* days. Yet its effects on its butts were negligible, and its chief value rests in its week-by-week revelation of Pearse's political thinking in a time of flux.

The new excitement in the political arena was over the Home Rule Bill, which had at last been offered for that parliamentary session. The Bill came at a time when Irish political parties were low in the public estimation. The parliamentary party was split, and the respective followers of John Redmond and William O'Brien seemed to many onlookers to be quarrelling over trifles. Sinn Fein, although it had had early successes in local elections, was steadily losing its impetus, and Griffith's suspicious nature and difficult personality were losing him many former admirers. A new spirit arose in the country with the news that Asquith was committed to Home Rule, for it looked as if Redmond, at last, was going to pull off the victory to which his life had been dedicated. The militancy of Orange Ulster in the face of this threat added another level of excitement, and passions became higher still when Griffith announced that the Bill as proposed was unacceptable, and demanded complete separation from the United Kingdom.

Pearse's attitude to the Bill was strangely compounded of moderation and extremism. He praised Redmond for his achievement, and called on all interested parties to submerge their differences and stand united with Redmond in the struggle for a better Bill. At the same time, he used language as powerful as that of *Irish Freedom* to describe what should happen if the Bill were not passed. Asquith and Redmond were to be supported if this would bring the Bill: otherwise, only the sword or the gun would save Ireland.

Pearse was a man of great moral courage, and although he knew the expression of such views would aggravate his unpopularity with many Sinn Feiners and republicans, he stuck resolutely to his convictions in his paper, and on a public platform at the great Home Rule Rally in Dublin on 31 March 1912. This rally was boycotted by Sinn Fein, the O'Brienites and the republicans, so the four speakers, Redmond, Joseph Devlin MP, Eoin MacNeill and Patrick Pearse were a curiously unrepresentative group. While Redmond, on one platform, was promising eternal loyalty to the English crown, Pearse was on another, speaking in Irish, and threatening revolution if the Bill were not passed. In Stephen Gwynn's words, Eoin MacNeill's speech, also in Irish, "went, as its speaker was destined to go, half the way with Pearse".[3] Pearse's was a speech unlikely to endear him to any political group in Ireland, but it ended on an uncompromising note.

> Let us unite and we will wring a good measure from the Gall. I think a good measure can be gained if we have enough courage. But if we are tricked again, there is a band in Ireland, and I am one of them, who will advise the Irish people never again to consult with the Gall, but to answer them with violence and the edge of the sword. Let the English understand that if we are again betrayed there shall be red war throughout Ireland.*[4]

He took up the same theme in a leader in *An Barr Buadh*, in a piece about honour and advantage, arguing strongly that both would be served by supporting the Bill.

> The Gael who would take the settlement that the foreigners are now offering us as a full settlement and who, because of that settlement, would make friends with the foreigners, would surrender his honour for his advantage. But the person who would refuse the present Bill which is before the British Parliament because that Bill denies the complete supremacy of the Gael in his own territory, or because he did not think the freedom under such an act would be sufficient for us, would in our opinion postpone unnecessarily his own advantage and the advantage of his people. He would deserve the Frenchman's praise "c'est magnifique, mais ce n'est pas la guerre". He would be doing as did the prisoner who refused to have one of his manacles taken from him when his oppressors would not remove the second one too. That prisoner did not understand that to remove one of the manacles would make it easier for him to escape, and perhaps it would be a weapon in his hand given him by God. It is clear to us that, not only is this a proposal to take a manacle from the Gael, but it is putting into the hands of the Gael a weapon. Our honour and advantage are on the one side this time.*[5]

Arguments like this had an impact on some of the young people who constituted Pearse's main readership, particularly those who had drifted into nationalism through love for the Irish language, but these were the junior and less influential element in the IRB—men like Ernest Blythe[6] and Richard Mulcahy, whose contribution to Irish history would be made after Pearse's death. (Mulcahy records that this leading article was later quoted as proof that Pearse would have supported the Treaty—at the same period when de Valera was claiming Pearse as an uncompromising republican.)[7] But for the senior men among the republicans—most of whom pushed cultural nationalism firmly into second place—such a philosophy was dangerous. They wanted revolution, and they realized that Home Rule would kill such a prospect. For Pearse was a rudimentary revolutionary still. While Clarke, MacDermott and Hobson were spending their energies in preparing an organization to fight a winning battle, Pearse stood apart. The rôle for which he was promoting himself in *An Barr Buadh* was that of Fionn, who blew the trumpet of victory and raised the hosts of the Fianna. Corrupt though he believed the bulk of the people to be, he was certain that there were those who would follow his summons. And it was rhetoric, not steady organizing by faceless men, that would bring the host of the true Gaels from all the corners of Ireland.

Pearse was in a peculiar state of mind as he edited and wrote his paper. There were those who, in retrospect, believed that by this period he was unbalanced, his reason toppled at last by his own vanity and arrogance.[8] To many he must have seemed an absurdity, the Messianic headmaster of a small and insecure private school, threatening the British empire with a sword which only he could see. But Pearse was often, throughout his life, verging on the absurd. He had spent years on the *Claidheamh* tackling giants, from the National Board to the bishops, speaking to them as if from the head of a superior force. Despite his Trumpet of Victory, he was now, if anything, less powerful than he had been in his League days. But what distinguished Pearse from many of his contemporaries was his awesome sincerity, and a growing nothing-to-lose attitude which sprang from frustrations and disappointments he was suffering as much as from the martyr's example set by Tone and Emmet. In the cleansing revolution he had to be the leader, for his temperament demanded it. Other men, with more to lose, might fear death; to Pearse it was an intoxicating idea. The more he thought about it, spoke about it, and wrote about it, the more it attracted him. His intellect might lead him to support right-wing politicians, but his emotions led him to promise and glorify the ultimate sacrifice of death. In *An Barr Buadh* then, Pearse was trying to balance his intellect and his emotional instincts.

Emotion's portion was best embodied in his two literary productions in the paper. The first, "Mionn" (Oath), was a declaration of his determination to keep the faith of the saints and patriots of Ireland, from Saint Patrick to Tone and Emmet. It graphically symbolized Pearse's interweaving of traditional Christian beliefs and revolutionary nationalism into a new mystical doctrine, which for him was replacing the orthodox apostolic creed of the Catholic church.

In the name of God,
By Christ His only Son,
By Mary His gentle Mother,
By Patrick the Apostle of the Irish,
By the loyalty of Colm Cille,
By the glory of our race,
By the blood of our ancestors,
By the murder of Red Hugh,
By the sad death of Hugh O'Neill,
By the tragic death of Owen Roe,
By the dying wish of Sarsfield,
By the anguished sigh of Fitzgerald,

By the bloody wounds of Tone,
By the noble blood of Emmet,
By the Famine corpses,
By the tears of Irish exiles,
We swear the oaths our ancestors swore,
That we will free our race from bondage,
Or that we will fall fighting hand to hand*[9]
Amen

The second, "Mise Eire" (I am Ireland)—later shortened in the *Collected Works*—personified Ireland as an old woman who spoke of her shame, her glory, her pain and her sorrow. Her glory was in Cuchulainn, her shame in those who sold her, her pain in the persecution of her enemies and her sorrow, the death of those in whom she had hope. Ireland was ever becoming a more and more real presence to Pearse, and in his emotions she represented a victim who must be avenged by the present generation, before it became old and fearful. (Old age he feared. A recurring theme in his writings is the timidity of old age.) The hope of the country lay in its youth. To his desire for action was added a growing urgency and impatience.

Pearse's intellect was still an important factor, however, and he was still generous; he hoped for unity and sanity in Irish politics, and again appointed himself a scourge for those leaders who, in his view, put their private feuds above the national interest. As editor of *An Barr Buadh*, and also under his pseudonym of Laegh Mac Riangabhra (Cuchulainn's charioteer, who goaded him to greater efforts with taunts of cowardice), he addressed such men as Redmond, Griffith, Hyde, Devlin and William O'Brien and urged on them courage, tenacity and unity. He chastised those Leaguers—at whose hands he had suffered—who put provincial interests, spelling reform, intellectual snobbery and preoccupations with the rule-book before the bringing of Irish to the people. He condemned Redmond's loss of courage, Griffith's paranoia and O'Brien's personal rivalry with John Dillon (a Redmondite MP). He condemned also those leaders of particular pressure groups, champions of women's suffrage and the Labour movement, who put their own causes above that of Irish freedom. (Yet strenuous effort in any cause could excite his admiration; he praised the suffragettes, with whom he had always been in sympathy, for their positive actions, though he deplored their destruction of property.) Such condemnations were always constructive, however, and he would give credit for a sound motivation and well-intentioned advice as to how the individual or group under fire might better achieve its ends. He was never dismissive or contemptuous.

In *An Barr Buadh*, Pearse displayed, through a new breadth of knowledge about the personalities and parties in Irish politics, a new sophistication and commitment. He might, as yet, be proudly independent, but by 1912 he was well-informed about the activities of everyone from the IRB to the Redmondites. Although in his "arm yourselves" speeches and writings he was speedily moving closer to the rhetoric of the militant left, he deplored its meaner manifestations, like the attempt to take over the Gaelic League and drive out Hyde, whom he still admired greatly. Most of the IRB men who opposed his recruitment did so on the basis of his support of the Council Bill (which he still retrospectively defended) and his prominent attendance at the Home Rule rally. They had still more ammunition from the columns of *An Barr Buadh*. If the IRB was not yet ready for Pearse, Pearse was not yet ready for the IRB.

Despite his relative political sophistication, Pearse betrayed in his paper a remarkable naïveté in economic matters. Although he rarely strayed on to such subjects, for they held few charms for him, he made several untutored contentions popular at the time; for instance, that Ireland could support a population of 20 million, and that it might be economically preferable to import coal from the US than from the UK. He also showed his characteristic ignorance of the horrors of poverty. Among those measures of which he voiced his disapproval was the granting of old age pensions. As far as he was concerned, the pensioners were selling out to the enemy. He still had to receive his education in social and economic matters. For the moment his mind was focused on politics, an area in which he again overestimated the generosity and enthusiasm of his fellows.

The paper charted the progress of a new political society Pearse launched—Cumann na Saoirse (The Society for Freedom), whose name embodied its objective. The society, like the paper, was short-lived: neither was to survive the May crisis of St Enda's. Its members were all Irish speakers and they were pitiable in number. They included Kent, O'Higgins, MacDonnell and other *Barr Buadh* contributors, Desmond Ryan and Con Colbert (the drill instructor at St Enda's—a leader of the Fianna, a militant Irish equivalent of the boy scouts) from his school, and Cathal Brugha and The O'Rahilly from the Gaelic League. The majority of these were in the IRB. One of those who attended the first meeting (Peadar O Cearnaigh—Peter Kearney) records the unease generated by the realization that Pearse was not speaking empty words.

> The proceedings were entirely in Irish, Pearse being the principal speaker. The keynote of his address was that a rifle should be made as familiar to the hands of an Irishman as a hurley. The audience appearing to agree, it resolved itself into a question of ways and means. But it was plain to be seen that those present were growing uneasy as the evening advanced when it dawned on them that Pearse was determined to carry out his policy. The mere academic discussion of revolutionary methods and their practical application were two different things.[10]

At the few remaining meetings of the society the audience had dwindled to a handful. Pearse had yet to learn that Irish speakers by and large were not radicals, and that it was not under their leadership that a revolution could be launched. But the society had had its effect. It established Pearse in the minds of a small but influential circle as a potential revolutionary, and his speech was reported to the ever-watchful Tom Clarke.

Pearse was much chastened when he realized at the end of May 1912 that in his involvement with the new excitement of politics he had almost let St Enda's die. At the end of the summer term his farewell to the boys showed that he knew he might well not be opening in the autumn. He confessed to his intimates that he had for once found that will was not enough. In trying the will on impossible objects you made a fool of yourself, he admitted.

> "I was mad!" he said to me [Desmond Ryan] after this same school crisis and his suppression of his above-mentioned *Trumpet of Victory*, "to start such a paper when the school was trembling in the balance. Why didn't you stop me?" This very question he had asked me when we visited a printing office to look over the proofs of the first issue, but he asked the question highly delighted with the appearance of the paper and with a joyous anticipation of the furious letters certain Gaelic enthusiasts would bombard him with for printing his paper in Roman type and his caustic open letters to political celebrities.... Pearse in his dashing moods struck you as quite insane, but as one who knew he was and one with whom it was pleasanter to go mad than with all the solid, sensible folk in the world.[11]

But for a while Pearse set out to be sensible. For the rest of 1912, and most of 1913, he would put politics in second place and concentrate, as far as he could, on saving his school.

III 1912-1913

The summer of 1912 was devoted to a last-ditch attempt to keep St Enda's going. Pearse had hoped to sell his interest in St Ita's to Louise Gavan Duffy, one of the teachers, but the scheme fell through, and the girls' school collapsed, leaving behind a pile of unpaid bills, at the end of the school year. The burden was still great, for Pearse had achieved only a stay of execution on St Enda's. His creditors were bound to leave him in peace until the end of the 1912-1913 school year, but renewed appeals, to a public for whom St Enda's glamour had faded, had brought only a small fraction of the amount needed to clear his debts. The prospects for an American tour, which he had been meditating for a couple of years, were not yet good, for as Shane Leslie said in a sympathetic but realistic letter that August, "You must remember that you cannot get Americans to subscribe for anything that is not a success—anything approaching bankruptcy they flee like plague."[1]

Nearer home, too, omens were gloomy: there had been many discouraging reactions to the new school crisis. Pearse's richer friends, like Joe Dolan and Seumas MacManus, had already backed him to their limit. Others, like Edward Martyn, who had been initially sympathetic, had learned to distrust Pearse's judgement. Douglas Hyde, prompted to write to Patrick MacManus of Argentina, long a prospective donor, praised the school in the warmest terms, but added an honest rider—the school must be run "on business lines".[2] And Shane Leslie's warm letter contained a barbed compliment. "Whatever your business methods may be your spiritual and intellectual work are invaluable to Ireland." His reputation deterred others from investing. MacDonagh, ever generous to a friend (although he had suffered himself from Pearse's insolvency), tried to persuade the rich Countess Plunkett, mother of his erstwhile pupil, Joseph, to help, and got a dusty answer. MacDonagh wrote: "I had already spoken to the Plunketts privately of the school, and got less than sympathy. Madame has some grievance about some money due to some friends of hers from St Ita's."[3]

Pearse was, however, doing his best; the accounts were still meticulously kept. Beleaguered by thousands of pounds in debts, he noted down religiously every penny he spent, and on himself he spent pathetically little. He was extravagant only in things that mattered, the grand things. He retained his old disapproval of drink and tobacco, and gave addresses, both formal and spontaneous, on the virtues of temperance. He travelled little, and then usually on business, except for holidays in his little Connemara cottage with members of his family and various pupils, and even from Rosmuc the unpaid accounts run up on holiday pursued him. His only luxury was books, which he coveted guiltily. Ryan describes his temptations. "He loved his books: that much-read edition of the *Cattle Spoil of Cuailgne* and his many editions of Shakespeare, all of which he had watched in the booksellers' windows, nobly renounced, entered, fingered, steeled himself, fled whole streets away, lingered, wavered, turned back and purchased, radiant and ashamed until he saw the next."[4] Like Willie, Mrs Pearse and Margaret, he never drew more than a small part of his salary from St Enda's. His account books are full of tiny sums being drawn for immediate expenses by his family, £1 here for Margaret, two shillings for Willie. Certainly, whatever the failing of the Pearse family, they showed little mercenary instinct where St Enda's was concerned. Every penny of James Pearse's legacy had been lost, and even his books and furniture graced the school.

Pearse's financial troubles were compounded by the attempts of his family to raise money for him. Willie and Mary Brigid had formed a small company, the Leinster Stage Society: he acted and she and Alf McGloughlin, and others, wrote the plays. It had been modestly successful, and like other small amateur companies, had put on plays at the Abbey from 1910-12, for which it enjoyed kind reviews,[5] although Joseph Holloway, who had admired Willie in the Passion, was privately unimpressed by one production he saw. Writing of the staging of AE's *Deirdre*, he praised the beautiful design, but "much of the acting was crude and restless, and many of the minor parts 'fluffily' filled. William Pearse, looked like an Indian chief, as Naisi. He speaks with a sort of inanimate monotone that never suggests manliness."[6] Maire Nic Shiubhlaigh, also, reluctantly withheld praise of Willie's acting, and she felt deeply for his desperate attempts to learn the craft.

> It seems a hard thing to say that he was never terribly successful as an actor. He never lost his self-consciousness on a stage. He was acutely aware of the unsuitability of his speech, and though he worked hard to perfect it, his voice never completely became his servant. But what he lacked in ability he made up in enthusiasm. At rehearsals he obeyed every command with humility. Often he would draw one aside and whisper: "Do you think I was good? I'm doing my best...." One could always gain his gratitude with advice.[7]

Willie loved acting too much to give up trying. "Apart from his work and his preoccupation with his family, this appeared to be his great interest in life. He gazed at the stage and at actors with a sort of awe." He got enough bouquets to encourage him to go on, and into the theatre he concentrated most of his frustrated artistic aspirations. Mary Brigid did a little acting too, but most of her creative energies went into her writing, and her adaptations of Dickens and some of her original plays were given restrained praise. She had a quaint style and peopled her plays with a stage peasantry which must have had poor Patrick squirming in the stalls. Her only novel, *The Murphys of Ballystack*, published in 1917, was an excruciating piece of sub-Somerville and Ross, which reflected an urban mind's notion of rustic frolics. But to produce even weak novels and plays requires some literary skill, and she gained some recognition.

Emboldened by their successes, Mary Brigid and Willie decided to take their company (including Desmond Ryan and Maire Walker) to Cork in May 1912, and there they met disaster. Their mother was with them to witness the fiasco. The Cork Opera House had been booked, at considerable expense, but the few patrons were unimpressed. To the bruises of bad reviews and tiny audiences was added the catastrophe of heavy financial loss. An SOS had to to be sent to Patrick, who had already put up the money for the venture, and his mother wrote distractedly to Margaret.

> I don't know what is to be done. Poor Willy is to be pitied I feel for him and he doing everything for the best and after all his hard work.... The worry of this disappointment has knocked all the worry of home off me I suppose both together make it all the worse Poor poor Pat how I feel for him and he so good to us Willy is in a state about him even poor MB said the first night when we heard only £5 our share Ah Lord what will we do about Pat's money ... two pounds for us and last night £3 odd so you may imagine our feelings will we get home at all we would not care if we did not make a penny if we got poor Pat's money [which] paid the people and expenses but I am afraid it is hopeless....[8]

"Poor Pat" indeed. Penniless, with his paper and his school collapsing about his ears, and his beloved family and their strolling players stranded in Cork, he rose to the crisis yet again, bailing the family out with some St Ita's fees which arrived fortuitously.

The Cork débâcle only deepened slightly the blackness of that May, but Pearse's indomitable spirit rose above it all. In that month he wound up his paper and his political society, and in June he successfully produced his play, *The King*. His summer was spent finding money, and it was not until a couple of days before the date set for re-opening St Enda's that he knew definitely that he had another year's grace. He quickly set about planning fund-raising activities for the school year, and, as usual, this was only part of a crushing work-load. He had few staff left, so he had to do much of the teaching himself: neither his sister nor his brother was qualified beyond elementary level, part from their respective specialisms in French and art. Although he had a good secretary in Desmond Ryan, he was not adept at delegation; he had too much interest in detail, and composed even the most trifling letters himself. Nor were his literary and journalistic talents idle. During the school year he wrote articles and a lecture on education, and a scenario for a school pageant. He delivered a lecture to the National Literary Society in December, published in *Studies* the following March. This lecture, "Some Aspects of Irish Literature", was of a different order of achievement from his "Three Lectures on Gaelic Topics" of fourteen years earlier. By 1912 Pearse was a mature commentator on literature, and his lecture was the distillation of many years of conscientious reading in Irish and European letters. As in his leaders of some years previously, he still championed contemporary European literary standards against the majority of living Irish writers, who, as he justly said, clung to outworn forms and were afraid to break new ground. Although he was still making sweeping claims for the old Irish literature, he showed a new discrimination. He could now compare Irish and Greek cultures from a position of knowledge which ruled out immoderate claims for the former. If Celtic rather than Greek literature had been unearthed during the fifteenth century, he said, there would have been a Celtic rather than a classical revival.

> I do not say positively that literature would have gained, but I am not sure that it would have lost. Something it would have lost: the Greek ideal of perfection in form, the wise calm Greek scrutiny. Yet something it would have gained: a more piercing vision, a nobler, because a more humane, inspiration, above all a deeper spirituality. One other result would have followed: the goodly culture and the fine mysticism of the Middle Ages would not have so utterly been lost.

He made a subjective attempt to define the greatness of poetry.

> The clear sheer detection and statement of some naked truth, the touching of some deep bedrock foundation, the swift sure stroke at the very heart of a thing: that is what I mean. There is

sometimes a harshness in the relentlessness of this truth-telling, a pain in the pleasure of this revelation. The heart shakes, because for a moment one sees with the awful clearness with which God sees.

Pearse was not original in his pronouncements on literature, but he had studied hard. He acknowledged gratefully and gracefully the inspiration he owed to Yeats, Ibsen, and, in a more personal but no less important way, Thomas MacDonagh. His own literary talent was not genius but he tried always to apply it in a "swift sure stroke at the very heart of a thing", and to avoid sentimentality.

A speech he made late in 1913 showed how far he had travelled since his youth. He was no longer dubious about Yeats and critical of Synge, and the reception given to his speech showed that Dublin had him catalogued with the literary radicals. Holloway is again the source.

He was speaking of art of expressing yourself—There was no such thing as bad art—all art was beautiful—beauty was art. Yeats and Synge would be the names of present day Ireland remembered hereafter and not the Gaelic League—Yeats did not write "Kathleen ni Houlihan" for propagandist purposes—he had a beautiful vision and recorded it. All art comes so from the person himself. Then he touched on Synge and said other of Synge's plays than Riders to the Sea were works of art and therefore of beauty—*The Playboy* for instance was a thing of beauty as at present played. All Dublin now accepts it as such—At this statement a few in the house called out "question!" and Lawrence who stood on landing of steps told the speaker to speak for himself—his statement wasn't true and then followed an exciting "scrap" between the speaker and Lawrence. Pierce went on to say that perhaps some things in *The Playboy* on the first night were not beautiful, like the bleeding head of the father; and on that occasion the piece wasn't properly played—Lawrence replied to this that he didn't know what he was talking about—it was played as Synge wished it. Undaunted by those richly deserved interruptions Pierce went on with his remarks, but hedged in a bit and said he spoke for himself—before he had been speaking for all Dublin—very different thing. He at last concluded a very long speech by telling all to express themselves and not mind what anyone said to the contrary and then they could be on the high road to creating art....

Lawrence told me he took an instinctive dislike to Pearse the first time he ever saw him and could never get over it since—there is something repulsively animal about his appearance which probably accounts for his seeing beauty in *The Playboy*.[9]

Pearse's literary conversion was startling in its magnitude. Over fourteen years he had made a sedate, but complete, *volte-face*. Where in 1899 he had had every aspect of the respectable Dublin middle-class prig, he was now in advance of the generality of Irish and Anglo-Irish opinion. It was one of his peculiarities that, while he always stated his convictions as absolute truths, he could nevertheless change his mind—with literature, as with politics. In this there was no opportunism or sleight-of-hand—rather his changes displayed a brave and flexible mind, often twisted by emotion, trying to shake off the shackles of his narrow experience, a feat in which he was not always successful. His family ties were too strong, and so was his desire to be a person of consequence. The snobbish house names and the pretentious notepaper which he always affected were symptoms of a personality which clung obdurately to many of the trappings of gentility. At this period, he still had little or no understanding of the scandalous social injustices rife in Irish society; despite his love for the Connemara peasantry, in Dublin he retained the world-view of his class. Mary Brigid, demonstrating Pearse's sense of humour, tells a story of unintentional significance:

Willie and I were producing at St Enda's a farce.... Before the curtain rose I was near the stage in the big Study Hall, dressed as a rough old countrywoman, my face very dirty and greatly changed with grease paint.

Pat came swinging along in his best Head Master style and stopped short when he saw the strange figure. Then he demanded with great indignation: "Who is this woman?"

I knew that my disguise was fairly good: but I never imagined that it could be as effective as it apparently was.... I was too amazed to speak, and Pat again inquired in still more truculent tones: "Who is this woman, and what does she want here?"

Willie, who was passing, dressed still more preposterously than I, found voice to say: "Why, it's Mary Brigid!"

Pat uttered a sudden exclamation, something between a chuckle and a war whoop, and faded away from the hall. When he reappeared he was exhausted and very red, and his eyes were moist. He had been seized with irresistible mirth, which had necessitated his strict seclusion for a time.[10]

Though Pearse retained some of his gentility, he occasionally kicked against the stiff social *mores* of his time. In *An Macaomh*, in the fourth and final issue of May 1913, he set down the commandments of "Respectable Society".

> ... these are chiefly six: Thou shalt not be extreme in anything—in wrong-doing lest thou be put in gaol, in right-doing lest thou be deemed a saint: Thou shalt not give away thy substance lest thou become a pauper: Thou shalt not engage in trade or manufacture lest thy hands become grimy; Thou shalt not carry a brown paper parcel lest thou shock Rathgar; Thou shalt not have an enthusiasm lest solicitors and their clerks call thee a fool; Thou shalt not endanger thy Job.... Those things about the lilies of the field and the birds of the air, and that rebuke to Martha who was troubled about many things are thought to have no relevancy to modern life....
>
> The great enemy of practical Christianity has always been respectable society.

These were, as yet, lightweight gibes at a system in whose coils he was entangled. It would be some time before he stood back far enough from the machine to observe its more elemental workings and purpose.

The only big literary production of the year was *The King*, and the piece was staged in aid of St Enda's. Payments to creditors had crept forward by only another sixpence in the pound, and Pearse went to Yeats for help, accompanied by Mrs Reddin, the wife of his solicitor and a well-known figure in Dublin theatrical circles, who had at least two sons at St Enda's. One of them, Kenneth, tells of the interview.

> My mother and Pearse went in to see Yeats. They were both nervous and pessimistic. It happened that at that time Yeats had discovered the Indian Poet and Mystic, Rabindranath Tagore, and a play of his called *The Post Office*. It was providential. The play is virtually a children's play. Having heard their story, Yeats rose smiling.
>
> "Of course I shall help you and your boys at St Enda's," he said. "We'll do Tagore's *Post Office*, and I'll give you two-thirds of the profits. And you, Mr Pearse, will you produce that little play of yours, *The King*? The two plays should go well together!"
>
> When they reached the street, Pearse turned to my mother and said: "It's true, you know. Only a great artist can afford to be greatly generous."[11]

The plays were a successful combination, and were well-attended: Pearse gave heartfelt thanks to Yeats for his kindness in *An Macaomh*.

The second big fund-raiser of the year was a much greater challenge—a fête in the park and stadium in Jones's Road. It lasted from Monday to Saturday, and included three pageants, one based on *The King*, one on the Cuchulainn saga and one on the ancient Fianna. It featured choirs, brass and pipers' bands, displays by the Fianna Eireann, and side-shows elaborate in conception, and expensive in production. Money had to be found for transport, lighting, printing, bill posting and other incidental expenses, but Pearse was fortunate in his friends. *Irish Freedom* gave extensive publicity to the event, and Sinn Fein, through the intercession of Eamonn Kent, lent Pearse an ass and cart for the week, provided Pearse undertook to see "that the ass was cared for during that time".[12] The Labour leader, James Larkin, supplied turf and paraffin for the camp-fires.[13] Others provided free entertainment and assisted in the preparations. But the plans were rather too ambitious, and rain fell for most of the week, dispiriting the performers and keeping potential revellers at home. Sean O'Casey was an enthusiastic helper, and in his autobiography he gives several pages to a glorious picture, full of wit and pathos, of Pearse's struggles to surmount the problems posed by the rain, by a noisy fun-fair organ which drowned the performers' voices, and finally, in the final tragedy of the week, by a fire which broke out on the last night. His account of the opening could not be bettered.

> ... the opening night was one of torrential rain, so that all who came crowded into the large hall of the grand-stand, to crouch there, saturated, gloomy, and low in heart as man could be. Pearse sat, the nadir of dejection, his grieving figure telling us that once more the damned weather had betrayed the Gael; while Douglas Hyde, who came to open it, roared out eulogy and boomed out windy joy, all the time the wind shook the sodden wooden walls, and the rain slashed down on the roof above them.[14]

Joseph Holloway, who came on one of the dry nights, was less sympathetic.

> There was a want of organisation about the Fete that depressed me—it lacked the dignity that should halo such an occasion—an Irish Fete got up for the maintenance of an Irish College! It was more on a level with a fair green on a market day! It did not inspire! Irish Ireland entertainments, sad to relate, seldom do!

How is it? What is wrong with them? Now Gaels dont all answer at once![15]

This was hardly fair to Pearse, who had successfully organized other dramatic functions, but he had overreached himself on this occasion, and made only a pittance for the Building Fund. When the school year ended, the debts were only very slightly reduced, but Pearse tried again. In August he held another ambitious event—an Aeridheacht (open-air entertainment) in the grounds of St Enda's—which raised another small sum, and there were other events during the winter term of 1913. But he knew that his best hope lay in America, and he spent much of the rest of the year seeking help and advice on the planning of a tour.

IV The Volunteers and the IRB

Although Pearse had set politics aside during the 1912-13 school year, he had maintained his interest. Gradually during that period he had become more intimate with the IRB men through activities not overtly political. He was involved with MacDermott in an attempt to set up an Irish-Ireland benefit society, an enterprise inspired by a new Insurance Act under which many working adults had to take out cover. Willie was on the executive committee of the Wolfe Tone and United Irishmen Memorial Committee, in company with Hobson, MacDermott and McCartan, with Clarke as chairman. Con Colbert was still organizing the St Enda's branch of the Fianna, and, unknown to Pearse, was recruiting some of the older boys into the IRB, while Hobson was a member of the Jones's Road Fête organizing committee. In February, March and April 1913 Pearse published three articles in *Irish Freedom*—publicly marking his association with that republican journal, in which from June 1913 to February 1914, there appeared another series—*From a Hermitage*—which stands among his finest writings. It records, month by month, his new political enthusiasms. In that short period Pearse was to develop a new social awareness, act as co-founder of the Irish Volunteers, and join the IRB. He reasserted his reverence for Wolfe Tone in a speech at his grave in the IRB-organized commemoration ceremony in June; although he had not reneged on his support for the Home Rule Bill, its slow progress through parliament had made him tired of the subject, and a political and practical desire for revolution began to reinforce his mystical yearnings for martyrdom.

The speech at Tone's grave was no masterpiece, for he was still learning the orator's craft, but it had moments of power which held promise of more potent rhetoric, and it set the tone for *From a Hermitage* by sketching his ideal of manhood. "Try to get near to the spirit of Tone, the gallant soldier spirit, the spirit that dared and soared, the spirit that loved and served, the spirit that laughed and sang with the gladness of a boy."[1] He spoke of Tone's great generosity of spirit, and, in terms strongly reminiscent of his own poem "Renunciation", of his willingness to face death for his country. Tone's great achievements were to articulate the gospel of Irish nationalism, and to arm his generation.

> This man's soul was a burning flame, a flame so ardent, so generous, so pure, that to come into communion with it is to come unto a new baptism, unto a new regeneration and cleansing. If we who stand by this graveside could make ourselves at one with the heroic spirit that once inbreathed this clay, could in some way come into loving contact with it, possessing ourselves of something of its ardour, its valour, its purity, its tenderness, its gaiety, how good a thing it would be for us, how good a thing for Ireland; with what joyousness and strength should we set our faces towards the path that lies before us, bringing with us fresh life from this place of death, a new resurrection of patriotic grace in our souls!

To his audience this was but the grandiloquence appropriate to the occasion, but to Pearse it was a creed; from this time his political writings show him striving to emulate the man he loved above all others. His accustomed tolerance blossomed into a compassion and charity for his fellows that read strangely to a generation used to the bitterness of Irish polemics. His pleas for unity became more intense, and he begged his contemporaries to stop questioning motives.

> I propose that we take *service* as our touchstone, and reject all other touchstones; and that, without bothering our heads about sorting out, segregating, and labelling Irishmen and Irishwomen according to their opinions, we agree to accept as fellow-Nationalists all who specifically or virtually recognise this Irish nation as an entity and, being part of it, owe it and give it their service.[2]

He stated a personal precept: "when a good man does an inexplicable thing there is always a motive creditable to his goodness". In this light all who appear to be hindering are in fact, for their own reasons, trying to do good. Those who had attacked him in the Gaelic League he now saw as playing Laegh to his Cuchulainn. And even if a man's motives proved false, there was always laughter to fall back on.

> Laughter is the one gift that God has given to men but denied to brutes and angels. Laughter is the crowning grace of the heroes. The epic tells how the dying Cuchulainn noticed that a raven which had stopped to drink his blood, becoming entangled in the clotted gore, was ludicrously upset. "Then Cuchulainn, knowing that it was his last laugh, laughed aloud". I think that Emmet, I am quite sure that Tone, would have laughed in similar circumstances.

As Pearse said himself, he had learned from teaching that laughter was a salvation. He had learned it too from friends like MacDonagh and, latterly, Joseph Plunkett, both of whom used to tease "P.O.P." —"Poor old Pearse".[3] Their bantering ridicule was an attempt to reconcile two Pearses. There was the dour, single-minded Gael, incapable of social chit-chat, unable to relax in company, who, as he said in an open letter to himself in *An Barr Buadh*, avoided or inhibited his fellows. "Pearse, you are too dark in yourself. You don't make friends with the Gaels. You avoid their company. When you come among them you bring a dark cloud with you which lies heavily on them. The fellow who was talkative before you came falls silent. The fellow who was merry and laughing before falls into a melancholy fit. Is it your English blood that is the cause of that, I wonder?"[4] This was the "sombre and taciturn" side known to most of his contemporaries, but his few intimates knew a more ebullient Pearse lay beneath the reserve, although he appeared rarely. "However, you have the gift of speech. You can make your audience laugh or cry as you please.... The gay and sunny Pearse is seen too seldom, and generally at public meetings and in Sgoil Eanna.... I don't like that gloomy Pearse. He gives me the shivers. And the most curious part of the story is that no one knows which is the true Pearse."

Pearse's penchant for public self-analysis disarmed criticism—he was aware that his social deficiencies were deep-rooted, and that he was doomed to failure in his attempt to emulate the gaiety and recklessness of demeanour of his heroes. He remained for most people the same shy and almost repellant personality he had always been. They respected, feared or admired him, but he inspired little affection—apart from the crowd, head bent, brows knitted, inarticulate to the last. Only on platforms could he show his mettle and, even then, the people saw the visionary, the fanatic he was becoming—not the laughing, careless spirit of his dreams. And in private, his laughter had a different quality from that of his irrepressible friends. The jovial Pearse recalled in family reminiscences was a man reacting to freak situations with a fierce, elated shout of laughter. While he was fighting a small fire in Brunswick Street, his laughter dominated the event. Mary Brigid analysed this aspect of him with unusual perception.

> My brother's laugh was ringing with exultation. Always a good fight—whether moral or physical—was a sheer joy to him: a kind of intoxication; a glorying in danger, and in the *testing* of his own powers to *meet* danger. His laughter at those times was deep and strong; the careless laughter of a sportsman, whether he wins or loses, so long as the *combat* is good![5]

His taste for moral combat he had indulged for years, with zest and enjoyment, sublimating his physical pugnacity through his reading and his St Enda's pageants. Certainly there was no reason to doubt his bravery; at the Jones's Road Fête, he faced fire once again.

> One of the stands was full of boys who were not taking part in the pageant. The stand caught fire. Pearse was off the field in a moment and had flung himself into the midst of the flames almost before anyone knew what was happening. He was shaking all over, not from fear, but from anxiety for the safety of the boys who were trapped, yet he climbed to the top of the flaming structure handing the smaller children to safety and calling for an orderly withdrawal. The boys heard his voice, lined up, and walked quietly to the ground through the flames. When it was all over he leaned against a nearby railing, the grease-paint smeared down his face from the heat, his head bowed. In a moment he was back with the boys on the field, clapping his hands for order, calling names, making jokes. That was the Pearse his pupils knew.[6]

As the new disciple of Tone and Emmet he felt his longing for physical action—a joyous, exhilarating action—become a necessity. Moral combats held less and less satisfaction. No one could question his moral courage any longer, and the arenas in which he had proved himself were growing shabby and sordid. At best, he envisaged a future of undignified financial worry, and the mockery of the unsympathetic. His early hopes that a Home Rule parliament would be a Gaelic institution were vanishing as he realized that Home Rule, if it ever came, could not change the character of the country: he could envisage no place for himself in a Home Rule parliament. So he came to dream of a revolution, in which he would walk gaily to his death, an ideal described in his article in *An Macaomh*, in June 1913.

> Here at St Enda's we have tried to keep before us the image of Fionn during his battles—careless and laughing, with that gesture of the head, that gallant smiling gesture, which has been an eternal gesture in Irish history; it was most memorably made by Emmet when he mounted the scaffold in Thomas Street, smiling, he who had left so much, and most recently by those Three who died at Manchester. [The Manchester Martyrs—executed in 1867 for killing a policeman in an escape attempt]. . . . I know that Ireland will not be happy again until she recollects that old proud gesture of hers, and that laughing gesture of a young man that is going into battle or climbing to a gibbet.

If the tone of such statements is idiosyncratic, it was not extravagant in the Ireland of 1913: nor were the ambitions that set the tone. Ulster Unionist opposition to Home Rule had taken an ugly turn the previous November, with the establishment of the Ulster Volunteer Force, dedicated to resisting the imposition of Home Rule, by military means if necessary. Nationalist Ireland, content for decades to believe in the virtues of constitutional rather than military action, reacted in general with disbelief and anger, although many of the republican elements, including *Irish Freedom*, welcomed Ulster militarism as a spur to the widespread arming of the Irish people, many of who were clamant for a response in kind to the sabre-rattling from the north (D. P. Moran's *Leader* among them).

By July 1913, the IRB had decided that the time was almost ripe to found an Irish volunteer force. In October 1913 its opportunity came. Eoin MacNeill published in *An Claidheamh Soluis* an article called "The North Began", which, in discussing the rise of the Ulster Volunteers, suggested that he might be in sympathy with the formation of a balancing force. MacNeill was no republican, but a long-time Redmondite. Through the Gaelic League and his professorship in the National University, he enjoyed a reputation as a man of moderation and integrity, and so was an ideal leader for an army which would rely for its strength on thousands of constitutionally-minded people determined to see the Home Rule Bill implemented in the teeth of the Ulstermen's opposition. The IRB leaders were politically astute, and realized that a respectable façade could usefully shield their infiltration of the organization. Hobson made contact with the

Claidheamh manager, The O'Rahilly (a member of Pearse's Society for Freedom), who proposed to MacNeill that he should preside at a meeting to discuss the formation of a volunteer force. MacNeill later claimed to have guessed at the inspiration behind his invitation. In his memoirs he wrote, "I had no doubt that both these men [O'Rahilly and Hobson] came to me from the old physical force party whose organisation was the IRB [O'Rahilly was an active Sinn Feiner, but not in the IRB] and I also had little doubt of the part I was expected to play."[7]

On 11 November the meeting was held. Eleven men were invited to attend. Pearse was now a political figure of sufficient importance to be one of them; the others, apart from MacNeill and O'Rahilly, included MacDermott, Eamonn Kent and Piaras Beaslai. Hobson, conscious of his reputation as an extremist, did not attend. At this, and subsequent meetings, a Provisional committee of 30 was appointed to set up a force to be called the Irish Volunteers. A public rally was organized for 25 November to inaugurate it.

Excitement in Dublin ran high when the meeting was announced. The Rotunda Rink, capable of holding 4,000 people, was booked, although the organizers feared they might not be able to fill it. In the event, there was an overflow of 3,000. The speakers included MacNeill and Pearse, and the warmth of their reception reflected the mood of the country. The Volunteers got off to a flying start, with 3,000 recruits signed up at the first public meeting.

Pearse's prominence was no accident. Apart from his recently-established reputation as a political commentator, he had given vent to his instinct for publicity by following MacNeill's article with one of his own in the following week's *Claidheamh*. Called "The Coming Revolution", it seized attention with its first sentence, "I have come to the conclusion that the Gaelic League, as the Gaelic League, is a spent force; and I am glad of it." This is often quoted as an attack on the League, but it was not so conceived, nor so explained in the rest of the article. Pearse's thesis was that the League had done great work, but that the great actions of the future would lie with those men, matured in their service in the League, who were now moving on to greater things. Parts of the article were disingenuous: Pearse disliked being accused of inconsistency, and here claimed that his League career had been a conscious and deliberate apprenticeship for the vital work of political nationalism. His own writings in the *Claidheamh* belie this, as do his admissions to friends that in his youth he had been "a harmless cultural nationalist", but few people resist the temptation to rewrite their own history when they have the opportunity, and the Pearse of 1913 had to justify the Pearse of 1907. Before he died he would go to the lengths of claiming distorted childhood memories as proof that he and Willie had been embryo freedom fighters from their toddler days. The *Claidheamh* article, like so many of Pearse's in this period, rose to a peak of enthusiasm about arms and blood.

> I am glad that the Orangemen have armed, for it is a goodly thing to see arms in Irish hands. I should like to see the AOH armed. I should like to see the Transport Workers armed. I should like to see any and every body of Irish citizens armed. We must accustom ourselves to the thought of arms, to the sight of arms, to the use of arms. We may make mistakes in the beginning and shoot the wrong people; but bloodshed is a cleansing and a sanctifying thing, and the nation which regards it as the final horror has lost its manhood. There are many things more horrible than bloodshed; and slavery is one of them.

Pearse's words must be seen in the context of their time. His rhetoric of blood was in keeping with much of contemporary political writing, in republican and socialist papers, whose tone had to compete with the growing hysteria of British army recruitment propaganda in the face of the German threat. Besides, arms were a gentleman's birthright, and an inveterate romantic like Pearse saw weapons as he saw uniforms and military bands—as an assertion of a nation's virility. His was a common view. It would take the war in the trenches to teach his generation that war meant filth and squalid death, far removed from the poetry of Rupert Brooke, or the Cuchulainn epic. The Irish were long accustomed to bloody revolution as a romantic convention in the written and spoken word, so most saw Pearse as typical of that tradition. They failed to sense the sincerity behind the words.

The Volunteers were determinedly non-political and, although Redmond withheld support, they had members reflecting virtually every shade of Irish nationalist opinion, from parliamentarians to republicans. Pearse was in his element, throwing himself enthusiastically into the organization of the Volunteers, whose numbers grew apace. Plans for his American trip were well advanced, but his zeal did not suffer from the essentially temporary nature of his involvement. He was still politically uncommitted in November 1913, and indeed seems to have warned MacNeill to be wary of Hobson's extremism. But circumstances were driving him into the meshes of the IRB. He joined in December at the instigation of Hobson.

> The circumstances leading to this were as follows: Being in financial difficulties with his school, St Enda's, Rathfarnham, and being afraid of bankruptcy, Pearse came to me in December 1913 with his problem....
>
> I arranged a lecture tour for him in the United States.... When these arrangements were made, and in view of the fact that Pearse would almost certainly have been brought into the IRB at a very early date, I swore him in before his departure for the states.[8]

St Enda's may well have been the catalyst. He would have had no chance of raising money among the rich and virulently republican Irish Americans without IRB help, but as Hobson said, it was only a matter of time in any case. Pearse was already, in the December issue of *Irish Freedom*, speaking with a new reverence of the Fenians and the Manchester Martyrs and citing them as precedents for armed revolution in this generation. Of the latter he wrote: "that ring of Irishmen spitting fire from revolver barrels, while an English mob cowered out of range, might well serve as a symbol of the Ireland that should be; of the Ireland that shall be. Next Sunday we shall pay homage to them and to their deed; were it not a fitting day for each of us to resolve that we, too, will be men?"

The oath Pearse took on joining the IRB demanded no further move to the left, although it involved a promise of obedience that might have troubled him had he not quickly reached a position of authority within its councils.

> In the presence of God, I ... do solemnly swear that I will do my utmost to establish the national independence of Ireland, and that I will bear true allegiance to the Supreme Council of the Irish Republican Brotherhood and Government of the Irish Republic and implicitly obey the Constitution of the Irish Republican Brotherhood and all my superior officers and that I will preserve inviolable the secrets of the organisation.[9]

From December on he, like the other IRB men in the Volunteers, was committed to a policy of infiltration of the Volunteer positions of power, under the unsuspecting nose of Eoin MacNeill. Pearse was a valuable asset to the IRB; he was quickly involved at a high level in the problems of organizing and drilling the swelling army. By January his prominence was established. He and Casement were selected as the two Volunteer spokesmen at a great public meeting in Limerick, one of the many gatherings of that period where Pearse, to tumultuous applause, praised the revolutionaries of the past and argued for an armed Ireland. The ready response of large, sympathetic audiences was adding polish to his rhetoric, and he began to overtake orators of greater repute. (At another Limerick meeting, indeed, Roger Casement ceded first place to Pearse, in contradiction to the advance publicity.)[10] The changes in his public statements were characteristically gradual; the respectable front of the Volunteers remained intact; and his IRB membership was a clandestine matter. The rôle of the Volunteers, he said at Limerick, was "to give Mr Redmond a weapon which will enable him to enforce the demand for Home Rule". But in private, his frequent exposure to more revolutionary spirits was adding fuel to his impatience with constitutional methods. In Limerick he was greatly affected by his encounter with the old Fenian John Daly, uncle-in-law of Tom Clarke.

During the latter half of 1913, personalities of a different stamp were also having their effect on him. Hitherto he had had no interest in the labour movement, being more suited to battles against the spiritual and cultural deprivation of the Gael than as spokesman for the materially poor of the cities. Communism repelled him; Socialism he distrusted. But he was always susceptible to men of energy and reputation, and began to fall under the sway of the two giants of the Irish labour movement—James Larkin and James Connolly. Larkin, the founder of the Irish Transport and General Workers Union, was a tempestuous man, powerful in impact, well able to arouse the largest audiences by the sheer energy of his performance. He had come to Dublin in 1907, and found there conditions which inflamed his compassionate soul—the slums housed 30 per cent of the Dublin people, infant mortality was higher than in any other part of the British Isles. Larkin was, initially, immensely successful as a union organizer. Pearse met him through his sons, who were sent to St Enda's, at a time when his reputation was at its zenith, and was attracted by his rumbustious personality. Douglas Hyde wrote later, with some bitterness, about being forced by circumstances into sharing a platform at the language procession with Larkin and Pearse.

> He [Larkin] mounted the wagonette and spoke from beside me. A tall blackhaired powerfully built man, with a great resounding voice and much fluency and energy, seeming to say a lot with great emphasis but really speaking platitudes, the gist of his speech being that if Irishmen really wanted Irish taught to their children there was no power on earth that could stop them! Patrick Pearse, who spoke also, pronounced a great eulogy on

> Larkin, *he* at least he said was *doing something*, he was making history. So he was, for he had closed the port of Dublin, and the workers of Dublin have not yet got over the effects of the general strike into which he plunged them—apparently without counting the cost. It was characteristic of Pearse that he never stopped to inquire if the *something* that Larkin was doing was good or bad. It was sufficient that he was *doing something*.[11]

Hyde was right about Larkin's platitudes, and his failure to count the cost of some of his strategies. He overreached himself when, in August 1913, he brought the tramwaymen out, and spread the strike to other industries belonging to the owner of the Dublin United Tramways Company—the arch-conservative among employers, William Martin Murphy, who persuaded the Employers' Federation to lock out all members of the ITGWU. English union solidarity with the Irish workers was shortlived, and by the beginning of 1914 the employers had triumphed. Larkin left Ireland later in the year and did not return till 1923.

No one with any interest in affairs could have remained untouched by the events of the autumn and winter of the lockout. There were about 25,000 men out of work, and the misery and starvation endured by their families were plain throughout the city, as were the effects of police brutality. For the first time Pearse was forced to recognize that there were great social injustices which could not be ignored. He was not quick to decide where his sympathies lay. Sean O'Casey claimed at the time that Pearse rode on trams worked by blackleg labour, but this could have been out of naïveté rather than any deeper motive.[12] In October 1913, however, his *From a Hermitage* column showed that he had decisively taken sides in the dispute.

> I would like to put some of our well-fed citizens in the shoes of our hungry citizens, just for an experiment.... I would ask those who know that a man can live and thrive, can house, feed, clothe and educate a large family on a pound a week to try the experiment themselves.... I am quite certain that they will enjoy their poverty and their hunger ... they will write books on "How to be Happy though Hungry"; when their children cry for more food they will smile; when their landlord calls for the rent they will embrace him; when their house falls upon them they will thank God; when policemen smash in their skulls they will kiss the chastening baton. They will do all these things —perhaps; in the alternative they may come to see that there is

something to be said for the hungry man's hazy idea that there is something wrong somewhere.

Moved as Pearse was by the horrors of the lockout, it is unlikely that he would have taken any more active an interest in the labour movement without the advent of its second great leader, Connolly, who took Larkin's place at the head of the ITGWU. Connolly had spent many years in Edinburgh, Dublin, America and Belfast, and unlike Larkin, who was essentially a practical man, he was an intellectual. By 1914 he had published widely in socialist newspapers and produced *Labour in Irish History*, a Marxist view of Ireland's past. He revitalized the shattered Labour movement and welded into a potent force one of the relics of the lock-out—the Irish Citizen Army. Composed of those prepared to arm in support of public ownership, the Citizen Army was resuscitated by Connolly and Sean O'Casey, and side by side with the Irish Volunteers (with which it was often out of sympathy) it brought a new militarism into Irish politics. Connolly was a political nationalist, but his socialism ran deeper.

> I have always held, despite the fanatics on both sides, that the movements of Ireland for freedom could not and cannot be divorced from the world-wide upward movements of the world's democracy. The Irish question is a part of the social question, the desire of the Irish people to control their own destinies is a part of the desire of the workers to forge political weapons for their own enfranchisement as a class.[13]

Of course Pearse did not see things Connolly's way. To him, the newly discovered injustice of Irish society had a simple solution. Ireland was capable of supporting twenty million people, and could not at present support four million decently. The reason was obvious.

> Before God, I believe that the root of the matter lies in foreign domination. A free Ireland would not, and could not, have hunger in her fertile vales and squalor in her cities. Ireland has resources to feed five times her population: a free Ireland would make those resources available. A free Ireland would drain the bogs, would harness the rivers, would plant the wastes, would nationalise the railways and waterways, would improve agriculture, would protect fisheries, would foster industries, would promote commerce, would diminish extravagant expenditure (as on needless judges and policemen), would beautify the cities,

would educate the workers (and also the non-workers, who stand in direr need of it), would, in short, govern herself as no external power—nay, not even a government of angels and archangels —could govern her.

Utopian promises were unlikely to influence a man of the intellectual stature of James Connolly, who had a great deal to teach Patrick Pearse. Within his emotional limits, Pearse was ever open to intellectual argument, and Connolly was to have a profound impact on him. They would dispute with each other the relative priorities of nationalism and socialism until they joined together in insurrection: it was Pearse who gave most ground in the battle, although his magnetism asserted itself on Connolly's emotions. But before Pearse had breathing-space to contemplate further the socialist dialectic, he had first to live through the most formative three months of his life—in America.

V The American Tour

Irish America had for some years been a source of financial and moral support for language and political movements in the old country. But it was as divided in opinion as was Ireland itself, and in preparation for a successful fund-raising tour Pearse had to gain the interest of one of the two most influential groups—the Redmondites, or the Clan-na-Gael, the old Fenian supporters who now backed the IRB. At the time when Pearse first showed interest in an American tour, his knowledge of the complexities of Irish-American politics was slight. He had a romantic attachment to the old Fenians, of whom John Devoy was the most famous American survivor, but his only personal contact with any of the influential Irish Americans had been an encouraging letter in 1910 from Judge Martin Keogh of the New York Supreme Court, who was considering sending two of his sons to St Enda's.[1] Pearse had written some time later to another wealthy patron of Irish movements, John Quinn, also a lawyer, and (like Keogh) a political moderate. Quinn's reaction had been disappointing. Like many Irishmen, Pearse believed the streets of Brooklyn were paved with gold, but Quinn, who had been instrumental in organizing Douglas Hyde's successful tour of 1905, had had his fill. He refused absolutely to arrange a tour for Pearse, who wrote back saying he would come anyway, testily doubting whether native Irish generosity lived on in the emigrés.[2] Quinn made his disenchantment clear when

Pearse addressed another financial appeal to him after the outbreak of war: he composed for a friend a lengthy piece of vituperative doggerel.

Damn, damn, damn the Gaelic Leaguers,
Damn the Parliamentarians too,
Damn, damn, damn the Clan-na-Gaelers
Damn all the Irish missions through and through.
I am sick and tired of their stories
Of all their hard luck tales and plaints;
I think that they have become a race of spongers,
And have long since ceased to be the land of saints.
. . .
Redmond is senile,
Carson's heroics a bore,
The Volunteers are flabby
The Parliamentary Party a whore.
. . .
Perhaps Dr. Wilson
Ought to be told
That the way to make peace
Is for Germany to hold
The land of the saints
When they will speak only Dutch,
And won't dare to breathe in Irish,
Which they all love so much.
Then the Casements, the Crowleys, the Pearses,
The Redmonds, the Carsons, the Healys, the Kellys and all
Can send their appeals in high and low Dutch
To Berlin and Cologne and Munich and such.
And thank God and the saints that we here
in benighted U.S.A. will be free
From their damned appeals by night and by day.[3]

With Quinn, the traditional holder of the keys to the moderate's vaults, in this frame of mind, Pearse had little hope of support from that quarter. In any case, by late 1913 his new political stance, and his prominence as a Volunteer leader, made him a natural protégé for Clan-na-Gael. Its organ, the *Gaelic American* (edited by Devoy), had already shown some interest in the new Pearse, and his fiery article in the *Claidheamh* sanctifying bloodshed had been reproduced in full in its columns. The *Gaelic American* was an unpleasant paper, with "a narrow, conspiracy-dominated outlook expressed in tones of habitual rancour. One campaign of that publication was to prove Synge's 'Playboy' part of a British plot aided and abetted by the Jews of Broadway."[4] It was anti-British to the point of absurdity. Typical was its joyous exploitation of a speech by Lord Ashbourne, a fanatical language enthusiast (and a member of the re-formed St Enda's Council), who described the dominant racial characteristics of the Gall: "thin, prominent lips, long front teeth, and the general appearance of a measly rabbit".[5] It was not a matter of genetics: such deformities were the inevitable result of speaking English.

The readers of this newspaper represented Pearse's best chance of raising money, as became apparent when he appealed for Hobson's intercession. Hobson was very close to Joe McGarrity, another giant of Clan-na-Gael, and an intimate of Devoy. He wrote to him for help in July, and to Devoy, Keogh and Quinn.[6] Although Pearse was not yet a fully-fledged member of the IRB, a preparatory step only taken once the tour was a certainty, Hobson had already assured Devoy at least of his soundness. "As to Pearse himself, he is all right and in line with us here, and is a regular contributor to *Irish Freedom*. ... I showed this letter to Tom [Clarke] and to J. MacD[ermott] before posting, and they agree thoroughly with what I have written."[7]

The response from America was slow in coming, and the proposed autumn tour moved to winter, and ultimately to February 1914. Pearse was promised help by the Clan-na-Gaeler, Judge Cohalan, whom he met in Dublin in September, and a fairly encouraging response from McGarrity added to his confidence, which must have been shaky by this time.

The *Gaelic American* spared no effort once the decision was taken. Pearse received a great deal of publicity in its columns in January and February for his Volunteer speeches, and enough lectures were arranged to keep him busy for a few weeks. While McGarrity was sympathetic to St Enda's, he knew that to pull in the crowds Pearse would have to be advertised as a left-wing Irish nationalist; he would have strong competition from simultaneous fund-raising efforts on behalf of the Gaelic League and the dying Fenian, O'Donovan Rossa. Nevertheless he set off with high hopes and higher sense of purpose.

He was to embark at Queenstown (Cobh) on 8 February 1914, and he wrote an unusually warm eve-of-departure letter to his mother from there (from Brady's Hotel, chosen because that was his mother's maiden name—an unaccustomed piece of sentiment). Normally his correspondence with his mother—or indeed his friends—was stiff and reserved. She was used to short, informative postcards with a blunt "P. MacPiarais" and no valediction. This letter, written before leaving for his first long period away from the bosom of his family, was full of solicitous enquiries and advice. He was sending her six shillings to take herself and Miss Byrne (her cousin) to the pantomime. She was not to worry about him, and was to go to the doctor if she felt unwell. More typically, there were instructions to Willie about dealing with pressing creditors. The card sent the next day was more typical still. "Am on board the tender and will soon be going on board the *Campania*. Good bye. P."

Poor Pearse was a notoriously bad sailor, quite capable of getting seasick in a rowing boat, and his sufferings on board ship, in heavy gales, were intense. He commenced a diary, *The Voyage of Patrick*, a week after departure when his worst torments were over.[8]

> Until this morning I have eaten practically nothing since breakfast in Queenstown at 5.45 Sunday morning last. Nothing would stay in me, so there was not much use in putting anything in. I have lain the whole week, half-dozing, and sipping milk and water occasionally. It was very dreary. I was too weak and sick to think of what I should say or do in America, or to think of the future at all: but everything that has ever happened to us in every place we have ever lived in since we were children passed before my mind....
>
> When I was not remembering old things I had nothing more intellectual or spiritual to do than to imagine dainty and rare repasts which I promised myself in the future: delicate flavours of peaches and apricots and roast apples; ... iced lemonade drunk through a straw like the iced lemonade for which we paid a franc a glass in the Paris Opera. In future I propose not to be so gross in my appetite as formerly, but to caress and woo my palate with delicious flavours of fruits and cool drinks and all things rare and *recherché*.

By the fifteenth, however, he had the strength to go on deck, where the "pure and cold" wind revived him. "I saw for the first time the face of the ancient sea as God saw it when His spirit brooded over the waters. And I heard for the first time the voices of the sea.... 'I have supped full of horrors' and nothing on the sea or under the sea can any longer terrify me." He began to consort with other passengers. "Most of the young people are very free and easy. They evidently regard me as a serious & important person charged with some weighty mission. There are practically no Irish people on board, except in the steerage." On the last night of the voyage he performed, at the celebratory concert, material which must have baffled the majority of the passengers.

> I recited in Irish "M'ochon 7 m'ochon o" [Alas and Alas] & told them it was a keen made by an Irish mother for her son hanged by the English. The blizzard raged during the concert. I was sitting on the floor & had to keep my feet against the legs of the seat to prevent myself sliding across the room. Two or three men had to lean against the stool on which the pianiste was seated to keep it from skeating away. Everyone gay. We have got our "sea legs" and only laugh at things which would have set us heaving a few days ago.

On the day he landed, Tuesday, 18 February, he dispatched to his family the diary of the voyage, and a letter pressing them to send him a "full account of *everything*". His confidence that Willie would do his best with the school was not matched by any great faith in his competence. Pearse's letters home show great fear lest his absense affect St Enda's adversely, and it was constantly impressed on his family that no mention was to be made that he had gone to America to raise money. He had not yet decided how long he would stay away, but everyone—boys, parents, creditors—was to be told that it would be only for three or four weeks.

Pearse was never given to false modesty. His printed appeal to Irish America, published during his tour, made claims for St Enda's even more dramatic than those of the Volunteers.

> I believe that in appealing on behalf of St Enda's I am appealing on behalf of the most important thing in Ireland. *Our work is radical: it strikes at the root of anglicisation.* Infinitely the most vital duty of the hour at home is to train the young in an Irish way for the service of Ireland. It is to this we have set our hands. The work of St Enda's, be it remembered, is not confined to its own sixty pupils, but, through the influence it has already had on the spirit and curricula of the other schools and colleges, extends to every boy and girl in Ireland. It is the literal truth to say that the whole experiment of Irishising education in Ireland must stand or fall with St Enda's.[9]

This paragraph was lifted from his relatively unsuccessful American appeal of October 1912, with a change in the text symbolic of the school's steady decline.[10] In those days he had referred to its 70, not 60, pupils.

Pearse was not totally ignored by the moderate Irish Americans, but his politics were not attractive to them, and their weekly, the

Irish World, reported only one of his lectures—on the safe topic of Irish literature.[11] Otherwise, although they printed his appeal and publicized one function in aid of St Enda's, they showed little interest in him. He was entertained by some of the Redmondites, including Robert Emmet's great-nephew, Dr Thomas Addis Emmet,[12] and even Quinn spent an evening with him. But for almost all his tour he flew the *Gaelic American* banner, and that journal faithfully reported most of his activities, though, as McGarrity wrote long afterwards, the appeal of St Enda's was limited. "I did not grasp at the time the real importance of St Enda's. The uppermost thought in my mind was the growth and equipment of the Volunteers. Every news item from Dublin, Belfast or London concerning the arming of the Ulster Volunteers was eagerly read by both the organised and the unorganised Irish in America."[13]

In that climate, Pearse was guaranteed attentive audiences, but only if he said the right kind of things. He offered a varied package of lectures: "The Heroic Literature of Early Ireland: Its Scope and Value"; "Irish Folk Songs"; "Wolfe Tone and '98"; "John Mitchel and '48"; "The Irish Volunteers: 1778-1914"; "The Fight for the Language"; "An Ideal in Education"; and "Ireland To-day: the People and the Movements". Engagements to deliver non-political lectures were very few: with the Gaelic League mostly. So Pearse began early in the tour to rely heavily on his association with the Volunteers, producing St Enda's propaganda as an end-piece to lectures.

His first engagements were in New York. The day after his arrival, he spoke at a Shamrock Club banquet on Gaelic League work, the condition of the "Ireland of today", education—and the Volunteer movement.

> It was a real treat [said the *Gaelic American*] to hear of the progress of that movement from a man active in its formation from the day it was started at the great Rotunda meeting in Dublin to the very eve of his departure for America. He was listened to with the greatest attention, for Irishmen in America were never more interested in anything than they are in the present Volunteer movement, and at the close of the address he was applauded very heartily, and after the meeting every man in the room shook hands with and congratulated him.[14]

Other New York meetings were no less successful. He spoke to the United Irish-American Societies of Greater New York and on the following day inspected the dress parade of the First Regiment,

Irish Volunteers. There were several Emmet commemoration meetings being held in New York at the time, and Pearse spoke on 1 March at the celebration arranged in Brooklyn by the Long Island Clan-na-Gael. It was the first really big event at which he featured, and had been planned before he began to make an American reputation as an orator, so he was lucky to be second on the bill. He followed the Governor of New York State, Martin H. Glynn, an Irishman who produced the extravagant claim that the round towers of Ireland were architectural wonders comparable to the Egyptian pyramids. The audience, all 2,500 of them (a vast number, considering that New York was suffering its worst blizzards for 25 years) responded with equal enthusiasm to both Glynn and Pearse, who gave a sanguinary speech, and raised the roof with his references to the growing might of the Volunteers. Understatement was not the keynote of the evening: Pearse's Emmet was developing divine attributes. "No failure, judged as the world judges these things, was ever more complete, more pathetic than Emmet's. And yet he has left us a prouder memory than the memory of Brian victorious at Clontarf or of Owen Roe victorious at Benburb. It is the memory of a sacrifice Christ-like in its perfection."[15] His promises about Volunteer policy were very different in emphasis from those given so recently at home.

> You ask me to speak of the Ireland of to-day. What need I say but that to-day Ireland is turning her face once more to the old path? Nothing seems more definitely to emerge when one looks at the movements that are stirring both above the surface and beneath the surface in men's minds at home than the fact that the new generation is reaffirming the Fenian faith, the faith of Emmet. It is because we know that this is so that we can suffer in patience the things that are said and done in the name of Irish Nationality by some of our leaders. What one may call the Westminster phase is passing: the National movement is swinging back again into its proper channel.
>
> ...
>
> After all, there are in Ireland but two parties: those who stand for the English connection and those who stand against it. On what side, think you, stand the Irish Volunteers? I cannot speak for the Volunteers; I am not authorised to say when they will use their arms or where or how. I can speak only for myself; and it is strictly a personal perception that I am recording, but a perception that to me is very clear, when I say that before this generation has passed the Volunteers will draw the sword of

> Ireland. There is no truth but the old truth and no way but the old way. Home Rule may come or may not come, but under Home Rule or in its absence there remains for the Volunteers and for Ireland the substantial business of achieving Irish nationhood. And I do not know how nationhood is achieved except by armed men; I do not know how nationhood is guarded except by armed men.

Pearse's only chance of money was to continue giving his audiences what they wanted (he was developing a taste for it himself) and to hope for some spin-off for the school. He was already rather discouraged. In a letter to McGarrity, written just the day after his highly successful Emmet speech, he sounded depressed. "My task here is hard. I have not yet made much progress, but people are working for me in various directions, and I am hopeful of getting enough to stave off a calamity until I am able to make a detailed tour, perhaps next autumn and winter." McGarrity did his best to help. The *Gaelic American* ran a long item on the St Enda's appeal, which was now adopting American gimmicks. Substantial donors would have the study hall and classrooms named after them: smaller sums would secure bronze plaques. The paper also gave a trailer for his next important speech, to be given at another Emmet celebration —a concert—on 8 March, again in New York. This time Pearse was to share the platform with two others, Colonel Richard O'Sullivan Burke of Chicago, and Bulmer Hobson (styled "vulgar" Hobson in a letter from Willie), who had arrived unexpectedly in America on a secret IRB mission. (He was to pass to Devoy a memorandum written by his close friend, Roger Casement, which Devoy in turn was to give to the German Ambassador. Casement was at this time already preoccupied with the forthcoming war, and was anxious to begin negotiations with Germany.) Hobson was well known in Clan-na-Gael circles as the long-standing Irish correspondent of the *Gaelic American*, and he was a support for Pearse while he remained in America. But as a speaker he was only a foil for Pearse, whose speech—sandwiched between two songs, "Memory of the Dead" and "Mother Machree"—was from the same mould as that of a week before, though even more uncompromising and messianic in its imagery.

> We pursue her [England] like a sleuth-hound; we lie in wait for her and come upon her like a thief in the night; and some day we will overwhelm her with the wrath of God.
>
> It is not that we are apostles of hate. Who like us has carried Christ's word of charity about the earth? But the Christ that

> said "My peace I leave you, My peace I give you", is the same Christ that said "I bring you not peace, but a sword". There can be no peace between right and wrong, between truth and falsehood, between justice and oppression, between freedom and tyranny. Between them it is eternal war until the wrong is righted, until the true thing is established, until justice is accomplished, until freedom is won.[16]

His reverence for Tone was set aside, for it was Emmet's evening. Although Tone remained the ideal, a personal identification with a more accessible type attracted Pearse.

> It is easy to imagine how the spirit of Irish patriotism called to the gallant and adventurous spirit of Tone or moved the wrathful spirit of Mitchel. In them deep called unto deep; heroic effort claimed the heroic man. But consider how the call was made to a spirit of different, yet not less noble mould; and how it was answered. In Emmet it called to a dreamer and he awoke a man of action; it called to a student and a recluse and he stood forth a leader of men; it called to one who loved the ways of peace and he became a revolutionary.... For Emmet, finely gifted though he was, was just a young man with the same limitations, the same self-questionings, the same falterings, the same kindly human emotions surging up sometimes in such strength as almost to drown a heroic purpose, as many a young man we have known. And his task was just such a task as many of us have undertaken: he had to go through the same repellant routine of work, to deal with the hard, uncongenial details of correspondence and committee meetings; he had the same sordid difficulties that we have, yea, even the vulgar difficulty of want of funds. And he had the same poor human material to work with, men who misunderstood, men who bungled, men who talked too much, men who failed at the same moment....
>
> Yes, the task we take up again is just Emmet's task of silent unattractive work, the routine of correspondence and committees and organising. We must face it as bravely and as quietly as he faced it, working on in patience as he worked on, hoping as he hoped; cherishing in our secret hearts the mighty hope that to us, though so unworthy, it may be given to bring to accomplishment the thing he left unaccomplished, but working on even when that hope dies within us.

Such speeches might fire huge audiences, but they counted for little with the hard men of Clan-na-Gael, who had listened for years to Irishmen promising revolutions that never came. John Devoy had written in 1883: "Revolutions are never sketched out nicely on paper beforehand, and it is rugged, practical men who will pull down governments and build up nations!"[17] However earnestly Pearse talked to the Irish-American leaders of his commitment, he could not break through the wall of their scepticism. He went on asserting his personal faith, even to John Quinn, who had no sympathy with his revolutionary posture. After Pearse's execution, Quinn wrote sentimentally about their meeting: "I remember his sitting near a window in my drawing room and looking out into Central Park, covered with snow, about twelve o'clock at night, and talking about his hopes and dreams for Ireland; and I remember well, and often think of it as I look at that chair and out of that window, his saying, quite simply, 'I would be glad to die for Ireland ... any time'."[18]

Despite its misgivings, Clan-na-Gael was sufficiently impressed with Pearse's oratorical skills to offer him the opportunity of extending his tour. He had little choice, for by 21 March the St Enda's College Fund had not yet reached $1,000, and departure would leave the American trip a financial failure. Willie was sending encouraging letters about the school, and urging his brother to stay on if necessary. "I hope by this you shall have got a penny or two. Be sure and stop on now as you have gone so far. It would be madness to come home too soon. Little man in bank thinks you should go on to Boston etc." Whatever Willie's intellectual shortcomings, he had more influence on his brother than anyone else, probably because his criticisms were made from a position of unquestionable loyalty. His letters to his brother are affecting. Although he was uneasy on paper, he could convey affection and trust far more warmly than could the reserved Patrick: he could send his love without a blush, and make silly jokes without reserve. His letters are in welcome contrast to Patrick's barren messages home. In one artless sentence, Willie could conjure up the family's devotion to Patrick. "I read your letter for Mother. She was delighted, nearly broke her neck running when she heard it came." Mrs Pearse did her best too, reassuring him about creditors, and letting her love shine through her erratic prose.

Dearest Paddy

The time seems so long & dreary without you how are you getting on your own dear self I am all right I paid £10 off taxes they gave me more time for £5 more I will have it by then

Encouraged by the tidings from home, Pearse decided to stay on for a short time at least. McGarrity had found him a lecturing engagement in Philadelphia, and there he went. He met a friendly reception from the McGarrity family, and, with Hobson, spent some pleasant visits with them. McGarrity wrote of them later:

> These two young men were like enthusiastic schoolboys. Needless to say, I too entered into the conversation [about the Volunteers] with the deepest interest. For a number of nights, no matter how late we returned from meetings, or personal calls on friends, we wound up in the kitchen! Here, between cups of tea we more than once prolonged the discussion of Ireland's problems till the breaking dawn proclaimed a new day.[19]

They talked also of the expected European war. Hobson, like Casement, believed that Britain would be smashed, but Pearse—however he arrived at them—was more accurate in his prognostications. "Pearse was equally certain that England was on the verge of war. He was by no means so sanguine that she was going to meet an overwhelming defeat. He was quite positive, however, that war was swiftly approaching, and that Ireland's long looked-for opportunity would follow." [The orthodox IRB thesis.]

Pearse was at his most relaxed with the youngest member of the McGarrity family.

> Sometimes he would take our little girl on his knee and hum an old song or a lullaby. His favourites were "Gallon Gay" and "Jack Smith, filly fine, Can you shoe this horse o' mine?" Often, too, he would get the child to repeat the hymn—"Daily, daily, sing to Mary"—and when she would lisp *Contempation* instead of *Contemplation*, he would laugh heartily and make her repeat the verse again. He took keen delight also in teaching her little prayers in Irish, and her lisp amused him.

With help such as McGarrity's the fund crept slowly upwards, and there were other lectures in New York and Wilmington. On 9 April, in Celtic Park, the most ambitious money-spinner of Pearse's whole tour was held—the St Enda's Field Day, on the ninth centenary of the Battle of Clontarf. The entertainment included Co. Cavan v. Co. Kildare at football and Co. Kilkenny v. Co. Cork at hurling, singing, hornpipes, reels, Irish War Pipes played by the New York Pipers' Club, and a band detachment from the First Regiment of the Irish Volunteers. The event was quite well patronized, but there were two incidents which Pearse omitted to describe in his optimistic letters home. Some would-be patrons apparently found the 50c admission fee excessive. In the words of the *Gaelic-American*,

> ... a few coarse hoodlums, led by a fellow who carried a pair of cheap gloves ostentatiously in one hand—a pair which evidently did not cost more than a quarter of a dollar, as that seemed to be the fellow's limit in everything—made a scene at the entrance to the grounds, but beyond creating some temporary excitement they did no harm to anybody or anything except their own reputations.

The other problem was posed by an uninvited football team which claimed to represent Co. Kildare, and which the committee had to put in the place of the official team "to avoid a disagreeable scene". Celtic Park was altogether less civilized than the grounds of St Enda's and Pearse was prompted to send thanks to the major of the Volunteers for "the very material help which they gave us in the difficult circumstances we had to encounter in the park".[20]

Anyway, St Enda's did quite well from Celtic Park. By 9 May Pearse had collected over $3,000. He was still worried about being so long away from home, but his mother and brother kept up the pressure on him to stay in America as long as it was profitable. "But now as you are in with the right people *get more*." Willie sent regular progress reports on the boys—and the creditors whom he was keeping at bay with money Patrick cabled from America. "You certainly should remain after Easter. I can easily keep the boys up to the idea of your coming home and then a little change re. lecturing delaying you and they will not notice time going over. Of course I am not telling them you are actually collecting money—nor do I think they think you are." Mrs Pearse:

> Dearest Paddy
>
> lumps of love to you and how are ye hope well Have you got thin or fat We are all well and things going on all right Dont be worrying about coming home do about what Willy says.... On the whole my dear poor fellow you have got on well I hope some other good friends may turn up. I think when leaving you ought to make a speech and say you are sorry you are leaving them so soon but that you might come back in the Summer I would like if possible then for you and Willy to go there for the summer

To all her suggestions, including half-conceived plans for letting St Enda's to Americans for the summer, raising money for a chapel, and advertising for American pupils, Pearse replied with unfailing courtesy. For instance:

> I will put in an advt. and try to get pupils, but very few people will send boys 3,000 miles away from home to school. I don't think there would be much chance of letting the place for the summer: furnished as we have it, for a school, it is not luxurious enough for wealthy Americans. The study-hall, classrooms and dormitories wd. only be in their way. There is no billiard table, smoke room to lounge in, or anything like what they are used to. I may put in an advt., but I don't think it will be much use. . . .
>
> You asked me in your last whether I was getting fat or thin. I think I have got a bit thin.

(A few American pupils he had already, and others were to come later.)

He also wrote manifestoes to be read out to the boys in his absence.

> . . . I want to appeal to you, and I do so most earnestly, to put all your heart into the work that remains to be done during that short month or six weeks that [remain in the] school year. . . . Let every boy do his best at his weak subjects especially. Do a six weeks' work that it will be a pleasure to yourselves to look back upon, whatever the results of the examinations may be. Show what Sgoil Eanna can do. Remember you have a great reputation. You have a great reputation now even in America. You must live up to that reputation. It would be disgraceful to have an undeserved reputation.

And ending with a militaristic note, "I do hope finally that you are making some effort to speak Irish. Remember that that rifle is still unwon. I want to give it away this summer, but it can only be given on condition that some boy wins it by a genuine effort to speak Irish."

Willie was urged on, too. "Press on the work as much as possible. Make sure that no part of the programme is lost sight of—geography, history, or any of the texts. Mathematics, too, is important. Try and keep the spirit up. I am anxious about the McGinleys, Sweeney, F. Holden, Baker, and the MacNeills. See that Brendan Holden is kept hard at work." But Willie needed no encouragement to do his best, and the financial realities had penetrated his dreamy protective shell. ". . . Money is the thing. More and more I am coming to believe that it is the only fault with the whole business. We must give people confidence. Then we may expect more boys."

Home was calling, however, and the engagements were not limitless. Pearse gave some more lectures—still in the same revolutionary vein—in Philadelphia, New York, Rhode Island and Springfield, Massachusetts, and on 7 May sailed for home on the *Baltic*. He was almost £1,000 the richer, and he had great hopes of an early return visit to collect, on an extensive lecture tour, enough money to pay off all his debts. The £1,000 was enough to keep creditors off his back for long enough to reopen the school in September, and he had made friends in America on whom he could call in emergencies. But just as important was the effect the experience had on him. He had learned to communicate powerfully with mass audiences, and he had discovered a natural aptitude for extreme rhetoric. He had met, in men like Devoy and McGarrity, revolutionaries beside whom the militarism and fanaticism of his Dublin colleagues paled into milksop petulance. Their doubts of his own capacity for action were to act as an additional, and very sharp spur to him to prove his own fixity of purpose. As they were the embodiment of the Fenian tradition, so he must be worthy to take up the torch of Irish republicanism. And most important of all, the public's recognition of Pearse as a momentous political figure added determination to his own sense of destiny; there had been little interest in the headmaster of St Enda's, and this altered his vision of his rôle. He would not neglect his school, but he came back to Ireland with a clear set of priorities. His important work from now on was not just to organize the Volunteers, but to ensure that they were not used to support Redmond. They were a weapon with which to confront the British empire, head-on. It was no longer a question of whether there should be a revolution—only a question of when.

CHAPTER SIX

PREPARATIONS

I "I HAVE TURNED MY FACE TO THIS ROAD BEFORE ME"

Until Pearse found his vocation in martyrdom, he went on industriously with the compositions which were to make his reputation as a writer. During 1913, despite all distractions, he had put a good deal of time and effort into non-political compositions. In December 1913, he published another short story, "An Mhathair" (The Mother). Like all his serious fiction, it drew deeply on the Irish-speaking west, and on Irish folk tradition; politics and personal struggles affected these stories only very incidentally. It attempts, with mixed success, to represent the religious faith of rural Ireland through its central character, a barren woman who at last becomes fruitful through a plea to the Virgin Mary who, in accordance with tradition, enters her house on Christmas Eve because a candle has been left lighted in the window. It is often powerful, for Pearse had, through the intense cultivation of his talent, reached literary maturity. From now on the best of this talent would be plied in his political writings, which probably represent his finest prose.

"The Mother" was much superior to his other prose effort of this period. Called *An Choill* (The Wood), it was his only recorded attempt at a novel, and he published two instalments in the *Irish Review*, in July and August 1914. He never finished it (whether because he was too busy with politics, or because his inspiration dried up, is not clear) but it was unpromising from the beginning.

It was an experiment in a new format—the dual-language work—concerning a young boy, Mac an Chuill (Son of the Hazel) and his relationship with "the living and dead things" of the wood where he makes his home. Weak as it is, it is additional evidence that Pearse did not have ideas capable of sustained treatment. His short pieces are best—whether stories, poems, plays or polemics—where his literary polish did not suffer for lack of an underlying complexity or subtlety of mind. Throughout his career, where others saw a web of complications, Pearse saw a single thread, and he fought to avoid tangling his vision. In politics he was naïve, and in literature he showed only one facet at a time. It was a serious hindrance to artistic achievement, but his sincerity and single-mindedness gave his writings a moral force which often transcended their intellectual and aesthetic limitations.

In January 1914, the *Irish Review* published in book form a collection of his poetry, *Suantraidhe agus Goltraidhe* (Songs of Sleep and Sorrow), a slim volume of twelve poems, seven of which had already appeared in various newspapers and journals. This collection marked the zenith of Pearse's achievement as a poet. His later verse, usually written in English, was so strongly coloured by political or sentimental considerations that little of it could compare with this earlier work. Six of the re-published poems have been discussed earlier. The seventh, "Cronan Mna Sleibhe" (Lullaby of a Woman of the Mountain) was a simple pastoral song of maternal love. The five new poems were the product of a very different inspiration. "Cad Chuige Dhibh Dom' Chiapadh?" (Why Do Ye Torture Me?) was redolent of Pearse's spiritual anguish.

> Why are ye torturing me, O desires of my heart?
> Torturing me and paining me by day and by night?
> Hunting me as a poor deer would be hunted on a hill,
> A poor long-wearied deer with the hound-pack after him?

The strength of the poem lies in one protracted image—rather than pursuing his desires, the poet has seen a bizarre reversal in the chase: only in his grave will he escape the pack, which "is the greedier of the satisfaction it has got". By this stage of his life, those human desires in Pearse which had not shrivelled from neglect had been forcibly suppressed—with one exception. He still longed for success, and that appetite had been whetted by the moderate recognition he had received in his various endeavours. Death would bring relief through oblivion and, perhaps, satisfy the hounds with his posthumous glory.

"A Chinn Aluinn" (O Lovely Head) was a lament.

O lovely head of the woman that I loved,
In the middle of the night I remember thee:
But reality returns with the sun's whitening,
Alas, that the slender worm gnaws thee to-night.

Beloved voice, that wast low and beautiful,
Is it true that I heard thee in my slumbers?
Or is the knowledge true that tortures me?
My grief, the tomb hath no sound or voice!

This poem, here quoted in its entirety, has been taken by many as proof of Pearse's love for Eveleen Nicholls, but the arguments are unconvincing. It was apparently not written until nearly five years after her death, and Pearse, where his poetry dealt with specific episodes (for example, Willie's absence in Paris), wrote during or immediately after the occasion concerned. The poem was an exercise in a common romantic convention, by which the death of the beloved provided a vehicle for morbid reflections. Pearse did not speak from personal experience of the kisses of a little boy being sweeter than the kisses of women, or the honey of their bodies; and no more can it be assumed that when he wrote of his love in the tomb he was thinking of a particular woman. (In the consumption-ridden Ireland of that period love frequently gave way to death: Willie's Mabel Gorman was dying during 1913 and 1914.) All that can with certainty be said of Pearse's poems was that they represented his current moods and preoccupations. And while he wrote these poems, his mood was black and his preoccupation was with death.

"Do Leanbh Ionmhuin" (To a Beloved Child), like "Little Lad of the Tricks", points up the contrast between childhood innocence and adult suffering, but its tone is more despairing.

Laughing mouth, what tortures me is
That thou shalt be weeping;
Lovely face, it is my pity
That thy brightness shall grow grey.

"Fada Liom do Theacht" (Long to Me Thy Coming) and "Rann do Rinneas" (A Song I Made), like "Why Do Ye Torture Me?", both deal with death, the welcome visitor.

Long to me thy coming,
Old henchman of God,
O friend of all friends,
To free me from my pain.

In "A Song I Made", death comes in regal form:

A rann I made within my heart
To the rider, to the high king,
A rann I made to my love,
To the king of kings, ancient death.

Critics have seen Pearse, reconstructed from his poetry, as everything from a saint to a chronic melancholic. His most recent biographer claims piously that these last four poems are in no way morbid, but "embody the Christian view of death as the beginning, not the end, of life". Yet Christianity, although it requires that death be accepted, does not urge that it be sought. Pearse the poet owed more to the Romantics than to Christianity, in whose institutional theology he had little interest. His mystical religion centred on Christ—the crucified Christ—as his mystical political stance centred on his own blood. William Irwin Thompson, in *The Imagination of an Insurrection*, has brilliantly analysed the imagery of the Irish revolutionary poets of this period, and places them firmly in the romantic tradition of which Byron was the chief exponent. The poetry of the ebullient Thomas MacDonagh, though it lacks the messianic *motif* of Pearse's, shares its torture and despair. Joseph Plunkett had more natural talent than either of his friends, and drew his inspiration from the Spanish mystic, St John of the Cross, rather than from any Irish literature. As Thompson says, his poetry was "filled with the thunders and seven seals of Apocalypse". Where Pearse looked to a solitary and poignant gesture, Plunkett set a cosmic stage for his sacrificial drama. Through their verse, MacDonagh, Plunkett and Pearse had publicly committed themselves to insurrection, and were well along a path from which there was no turning back without ridicule. In Thompson's words, "they shared a common desire to live a myth", a self-dramatization which was exaggerated even in a romantic age. In the case of two of them, their personal lives contributed sincerity to the pose. Plunkett was a very young man—only 28 when he died—but he was dying anyway from consumption, and he sought a more heroic end. Pearse had nothing to live for, and he believed that sacrificial death would bring him the immortality he craved. Only MacDonagh was ultimately a victim of his own romantic extravagances—he was happily married, a father, and his career in the university and Dublin's world of letters seemed set fair for success.

Pearse's only other original poetry in Irish was written in 1914 and, although still romantic in tone, was otherwise far off his usual track. He had always been interested in popular ballads. His uncle, Christy Brady, used to sing his favourite—"The Old Grey Mare"—and Pearse published a version of it in *An Macaomh*, prefaced by a stanza of his own.[1] This ballad was typical of a strong strain in Irish folk legend, which celebrated Napoleon in the belief that he would return from exile to save Ireland. Even as an adult, Pearse retained his love of Napoleon and, as Desmond Ryan said, this hero-worship was bound up with his fanatical glorification of war.[2] He had what was supposed to be a lock of Napoleon's hair in his St Enda's museum, which was full of relics of his heroes. (The most famous of these, now in the Kilmainham Museum, was the block on which, reportedly, Emmet's head was cut off.) The historical accuracy of ballads never troubled him: it was their suitability for recitation which determined their popularity with him. The stanza which he added to "The Old Grey Mare" was in keeping with the rest.

At break of the day I chanced to stray
  All by the Seine's fair side,
When to ease my heart young Bonaparte
  Came forward now to ride.
On a field of green with gallant mien
  He formed his men in square,
And down the line with look so fine
  He rode his Old Grey Mare.

His favourite recitation was "Seamus O'Brien", Sheridan Le Fanu's rollicking ballad of 1798. According to his sister Margaret, Pearse had learned it from his father who relished dramatic pieces from any cultural tradition, and Patrick recited it so well that his father always stood down in his favour.[3] It later became so popular with the St Enda's boys that they would request it on festive occasions. Ryan says Pearse used to startle his audience with the histrionic passion he put into the last lines, addressed to the British troops who had failed to run the eponymous hero to earth:

Your sabres may clatter, your carbines go bang,
But if you want hanging it's yourselves you must hang![4]

He made two modest efforts in composing poetry of this type in Irish. The first appeared in the St Enda's pupils' weekly paper, *An Scolaire* (The Student), and it also was about Napoleon. Called "O! 'Bhean an Tighe" (O! Woman of the House), it told of the poet's meeting in Paris with Wolfe Tone, who passed on to him the news of an imminent French invasion of Ireland. Every stanza had the line "Boney will be in Ireland at the dawning of the day".* The other composition, published in the first issue of the *Irish Volunteer*, was a lyric for a marching song for the Volunteers, written while Pearse still believed that they would use the Irish language. Casement had suggested that a Jacobite marching song, "Searlus Og" (Young Charles), be adapted for the Volunteers.[5] Pearse's version was called "An Dord Feinne" (The Fenian Chant), and it promised that the foreigners would be routed by a Gaelic force. In both the ballad and the song Pearse showed a gift for *pastiche*, but his adherence to Irish was ill-judged. The songs sung by the Volunteers were almost all in English, since, like the rest of the people, so few of them knew Irish, and Pearse could not graft a dying language on to an English culture. None of his writings in Irish had a wide public: his serious poetry in particular received no intelligent criticism. (MacDonagh spoke for many Irish-language enthusiasts when he said that to encourage writing in the language, criticism should only be favourable.)

Pearse's other poetic efforts during this period were published in the *Irish Review*, for which he had been sporadically producing two separate anthologies (literal translations and editions of Gaelic poems), later published as *Specimens from an Irish Anthology* and *Songs of the Irish Rebels*. The former were garnered during his Gaelic League days (some of them had earlier appeared in print), and although uniformly sad in tone, they had no political overtones. *Songs of the Irish Rebels*, as the title suggests, was an attempt to demonstrate the long-standing separatist Irish national tradition through the mouths of poets. There were three poems by Geoffrey Keating, the seventeenth-century poet who was Pearse's favourite among writers of Irish. All the poems spoke of exile or death, and breathed hatred of the foreigner. Pearse spoke of them as examples of a mystical patriotism, and certainly they had been selected with that end in view. But this exercise, much though it interested him, was something to which he grudged the time. As he wrote to W. P. Ryan in October 1913:

> I don't know when that Anthology will appear in book form. I made a collection of early Irish pieces long ago, but the modern ones I am only selecting from month to month for the [Irish] *Review*.... What I am afraid of is that someone will forestall me but I have no time to give to it. And I keep drifting more and more to politics and away from books. I feel that we of the Gaelic League generation must be ready for strong political action,

leading up to *other* action, within the next few years, whether under Home Rule or in its absence.[6]

Pearse was putting behind him those activities which did not help towards that action, and his only dramatic production of this period was a very slight piece, *Eoin* (Owen), performed at two entertainments, in the Mansion House in Dublin and in a hall belonging to a Gaelic League branch. Written originally in Irish, it was later translated into English and published by Pearse in *Fianna*, in December 1915. Like all his later plays, it was an allegorical expression of his current political attitudes. Set in 1867, on the day before the unsuccessful Fenian rising, the action revolves around a Fenian schoolmaster, whose escape from the police is ensured by the assistance of one of his pupils, shot down in a gun battle. Like a later and more ambitious play, *The Master*, it gave ammunition to those who condemned Pearse after the rising for training revolutionaries at St Enda's. Such attacks are not wholly fair, being based on an over-literal interpretation of his writings. There is no doubt but that Pearse's romantic imagination was greatly attracted by a vision of himself going out at the head of his boys to confront the Gall. But he was not an irresponsible schoolmaster, and although he inevitably created in St Enda's an environment where revolutionary politics came as second nature to the pupils, he did not attempt to involve them directly in his own activities. The Fianna circle of the IRB included several of the Dogs—Desmond Ryan, Eamonn Bulfin, Joseph Sweeney and Frank Burke. They were IRB men long before their ex-headmaster, who after his own recruitment did not make any attempt to swear in St Enda's boys. Nor did all his boys adopt his politics. Some St Enda's students (including his prize pupil, Denis Gwynn) joined the British army after the outbreak of war. MacDonagh, acknowledging the military character of the school, reacted philosophically with "Now begad, that's consistent!".[7] Nevertheless, in feeding the boys constantly with revolutionary ideals in his addresses and his plays, he had a profound influence on their political development: they were in close contact with him at the most formative period of their lives. He encouraged them in the military arts and introduced them to men like Colbert, who were less scrupulous about recruiting the very young, and he therefore bears the ultimate responsibility for their entanglement in matters beyond their innocence. It is in the nature of the young to take things literally, and the transparent message of a piece like *Owen* was not lost on them. Pearse had inspired the admiration and love of many of his boys: it was only natural that they should seek to emulate him.

If the soldier, writer and teacher sometimes tripped one another in practical matters, Pearse was nonetheless at his peak as a theoretical educationalist. He had already published, from February to March 1913, three articles on Irish education in *Irish Freedom*, one in February 1913 in the *Irish Review*, and given a lecture on the same topic in December 1912. His last statement on the subject appeared in June 1914 in the same journal. In January 1916 he was to publish a selection from these writings in a famous pamphlet called "The Murder Machine", which summarized his thoughts on, and experiences of, Irish education. St Enda's had not changed his basic beliefs in the superiority of the age-old Irish fosterage system, in the need to inculcate in children a love of truth and beauty, and in the iniquity of the Intermediate examinations. He condemned suggestions that education should be "modernised", and reiterated his conviction that the need was for a return to the eternal values of the ancient Irish. Ironically, Joseph Lee, in his *Modernisation of Irish Society*,[8] has pointed out that Pearse's educational writings place him, willy-nilly, among the theoretical modernizers of Irish society, but there is no paradox. Pearse stood at the point of departure of a centuries-long cycle in educational philosophy; the virtues he saw in the foster-teachers of old were those which now underlie *avant-garde* theories of tuition, but they were heresy to the establishment of the early twentieth century. Where Pearse really had something to say was in his recognition of children as individuals, who should be encouraged to give of their best rather than crushed by impossible demands. In one of the best-known passages in these writings, he summed up the attitude which had made him a successful schoolmaster.

> I knew one boy who passed through several schools a dunce and a laughing-stock; the National Board and the Intermediate Board had sat in judgement upon him and had damned him as a failure before men and angels. Yet a friend and fellow-worker of one discovered that he was gifted with a wondrous sympathy for nature, that he loved and understood the ways of plants, that he had a strange minuteness and subtlety of observation—that, in short, he was the sort of boy likely to become an accomplished botanist. I knew another boy of whom his father said to me: "He is no good at books, he is no good at work; he is good at nothing but playing a tin whistle. What am I to do with him?"

> I shocked the worthy man by replying (though really it was the obvious thing to reply): "Buy a tin whistle for him."

Few schoolmasters have had the intimate knowledge of their pupils that Pearse saw as his duty. All reports and letters to parents were his own, and although—in his anxiety to persuade parents to keep their sons at his school—he sometimes represented his geese as swans, there was little of the "Could do better" evasion of lesser teachers.[9] He did not pretend to be an *original* thinker in education, but he had put into practice, in hostile circumstances, the theories of men like Hyde and MacNeill and the example of the enlightened Belgian educationalists.

What Pearse was railing against, more vehemently now than ever before, was the repressive spirit of Irish education, which squeezed out pupils' individuality and made them slaves to examinations and unsympathetic teachers, who had themselves been rendered impotent by the rigid imposition of narrow curricula. But he no longer believed that example would be sufficient to change all that. He now placed all his hopes in an independent Ireland, and his pleas for the rational and free system which he hoped would follow in its wake will be recognized, by most state-educated Irish readers, as castles in the air.

> The first thing I plead for, therefore, is freedom: freedom for each school to shape its own programme in conformity with the circumstances of the school as to place, size, personnel, and so on; freedom again for the individual teacher to impart something of his own personality to his work, to bring his own peculiar gifts to the service of his pupils, to be, in short, a teacher, a master, one having an intimate and permanent relationship with his pupils, and not a mere part of the educational machine, a mere cog in the wheel; freedom finally for the individual pupil and scope for his development within the school and within the system. And I would promote this idea of freedom by the very organisation of the school itself, giving a certain autonomy not only to the school, but to the particular parts of the school: to the staff, of course, but also to the pupils, and, in a large school, to the various sub-divisions of the pupils.

There was more compassion and intelligence in Pearse's educational manifestoes than in any of his other writings. In other fields he was too often hampered by ignorance or inexperience, or governed by dangerous emotionalism, but his sincerity over education still found an answering chord in the hearts of moderate men. Parents might withdraw pupils who brought Pearse's dogma

James and Margaret
Pearse

Patrick, Willie,
Margaret and Mary

The Young Pearse

Schoolboy

Student

Student

Barrister

Miss Byrne (cousin), Patrick, Margaret, Mrs Pearse, Willie, Mary Brigid

Representative Congress of the Gaelic League, 1900 (Pearse arrowed). See key attached.

Pearse in America: 1914

Willie as Fionn in a St Enda's production

Patrick and Willie

Contemporary caricature by
Joseph Holloway

Willie, by Sean O'Sullivan

The Orator

Circa 1912-13

At O'Donovan Rossa's grave-side

August 1915

Idealized reconstruction of G.P.O. interior, by W. Paget. Connolly on stretcher; Pearse standing by with revolver; Clarke behind his left shoulder; Willie beside Pearse; Plunkett approaching from rear, in flowing overcoat; O'Rahilly on table by window, directing fire

The G.P.O. after the Rising

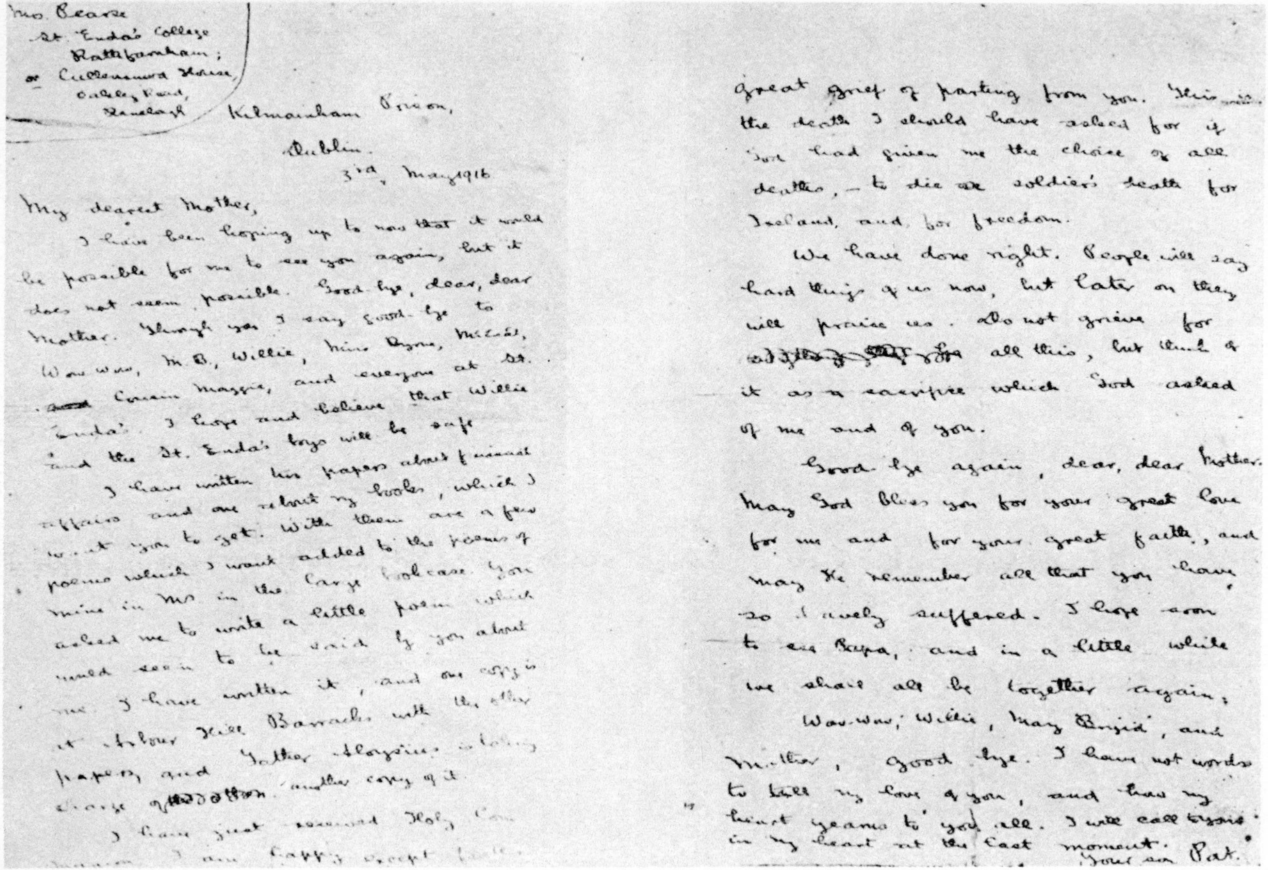

Mrs. Pearse
St. Enda's College
Rathfarnham;
or Cullenswood House,
Oakley Road,
Ranelagh

Kilmainham Prison,
Dublin.
3rd, May 1916

My dearest Mother,

I have been hoping up to now that it would
be possible for me to see you again, but it
does not seem possible. Good-bye, dear, dear
Mother. Through you I say good-bye to
Wow-Wow, M.B., Willie, Mary Byrne, Micheal,
Cousin Maggie, and everyone at St.
Enda's. I hope and believe that Willie
and the St. Enda's boys will be safe.

I have written two papers about financial
affairs and one about my books, which I
want you to get. With them are a few
poems which I want added to the poems of
mine in MS. in the large bookcase. You
asked me to write a little poem which
would seem to be said by you about
me. I have written it, and one copy is
at Arbour Hill Barracks with the other
papers and Father Aloysius is taking
charge of another copy of it.

I have just received Holy Com[illegible]
[illegible] I am happy except for the

great grief of parting from you. This is
the death I should have asked for if
God had given me the choice of all
deaths, – to die a soldier's death for
Ireland, and for freedom.

We have done right. People will say
hard things of us now, but later on they
will praise us. Do not grieve for
[illegible] all this, but think of
it as a sacrifice which God asked
of me and of you.

Good-bye again, dear, dear Mother.
May God bless you for your great love
for me and for your great faith, and
may He remember all that you have
so bravely suffered. I hope soon
to see Papa, and in a little while
we shall all be together again.

Wow-Wow, Willie, Mary Brigid, and
Mother, good-bye. I have not words
to tell my love of you, and how my
heart yearns to you all. I will call to you
in my heart at the last moment.
Your son, Pat.

Farewell letter to his mother

home, but he could still count on the support of men like Douglas Hyde (who distributed prizes at St Enda's in June 1914) and the Redmondite MP, John Horgan, who deplored Pearse the politician, but believed that he could have been the Irish Dr Arnold had he stuck to education.[10] Pearse had no more energy to expend in this direction. With the other concerns that commanded his attention for the rest of his life, it was as much as he could do just to keep St Enda's alive.

II The Struggle for the Volunteers

The euphoria generated by the overwhelming public response to the foundation of the Irish Volunteers was not long in being dispelled. Conceived initially as a corps in which Irishmen of all political persuasions would stand together, it soon found enemies. The greatest rancour was shown by the leadership of the Irish Citizen Army (ICA), notably Sean O'Casey and James Larkin. O'Casey was a bitter man, his political views shaped by his own early poverty and a resentment of those better placed. Larkin's career and morale had been crushed by his own errors of judgement in provoking the disastrous lock-out, and he was singing his swan-song before leaving Ireland. Both of them found a release in their assaults on the Volunteers.

ICA antipathy to the very idea of a volunteer force had been voiced at the inaugural meeting in the Rotunda, where a group of its members staged a hostile demonstration. Their opposition was founded on the belief that the motivation behind the Volunteers was unsympathetic to the class struggle—the Labour movement had no interest in any change in Irish society which did not involve a shift in the balance of power from capitalist to worker. Vicious attacks were launched from the columns of the *Irish Worker* on the leading spirits of the Irish Volunteers, and mainly through the vitriolic prose of O'Casey.

> Many of you have been tempted to join the much talked of movement by the wild impulse of genuine enthusiasm. You have again allowed yourselves to be carried away by words—words—words. You have momentarily forgotten that there can be no interests outside of those identified with your own class....
>
> Workers, this movement is built on a re-actionary basis.... Are you going to be satisfied with a crowd of chattering well-fed aristocrats and commercial bugs? ... Are you going to rope

Ireland's poor outside to the boundaries of the Nation? . . .[1]

There were more moderate voices among Irish socialists. Connolly, for one, took some time to join in the attack on the nationalists. But the damage had been done: Clarke wrote to Devoy, "Larkin's people for some time have been making war on the Irish Volunteers. I think this is largely inspired by a disgruntled fellow named O'Casey. By this attitude they have antagonised the sympathy of all sections of the country and none more than the advanced section."[2] The "advanced section" was the IRB, and Ryan was right to say that it had been antagonized. In *Irish Freedom* it had consistently shown a genuine sympathy with the workers' cause, receiving in return only ridicule and misrepresentation. By May 1914 Connolly had joined the hecklers. "We believe that there are no real Nationalists in Ireland outside of the Irish Labour movement. All others merely reject one part or other of the British conquest, the Labour movement alone rejects it in its entirety, and sets itself ... the reconquest of Ireland as its aim."[3] But whatever their differences, the ICA and the IRB had one very important attitude in common: they both saw Redmond under the Volunteers' bed.

Redmond was a problem for the Volunteer leaders. MacNeill, particularly, had hoped from the beginning that he would lend his support and thereby assist in maintaining the balance between moderates and extremists. At the beginning such prospects seemed remote. Redmond stood aloof at first, but he quickly became alarmed by the success of a movement outside his control. Although he engineered public attacks on the Volunteers by members of his Irish parliamentary party, the presence on the Provisional committee of such constitutionalists as Thomas Kettle and Colonel Maurice Moore made the issue complicated. Moore held out hopes that Redmond might be brought into sympathy with the aims of the organization, and in the *Irish Volunteer* in February 1914, he wrote "For the first time since the Jacobite Wars Irish Nationalists are on the side of constitutional right and Parliamentary government, and they intend to use their opportunity with courage and moderation." In the event of a German invasion of Ireland, the Irish Volunteers would be the defenders. To Moore it seemed that such a responsible attitude would guarantee the granting of Home Rule.

To the IRB men, however, such sentiments were anathema. They were already worried by the size of the new movement, which made more remote their hopes of controlling it. Their original strategy of infiltration was rendered impractical as they realized that their numbers were insufficient for nation-wide influence, and they feared that the whole movement would be sold out to the constitutionalists, who vastly outnumbered the revolutionaries. But they were professionals, and they did not easily give up. For four months of 1914, although their most distinguished new recruit was away wooing American audiences, they concentrated on entrenching themselves as firmly as possible, and trying to sabotage efforts to entice Redmond into the leadership.

New organizational steps were taken in February 1914 with the issuing of a provisional constitution, embodying the objects of the Volunteers:

1. To secure and maintain the rights and liberties common to all the people of Ireland.
2. To train, discipline, arm and equip a body of Irish Volunteers for the above purpose.
3. To unite for this purpose Irishmen of every creed and of every party and class.

Sub-committees were formed the same month, and the disproportionate number of IRB members who sat on them reflected IRB dedication. The Finance sub-committee had one IRB man out of four members—Sean MacDermott. The Country sub-committee (organizing non-Dublin Volunteers) had four out of six—MacDermott, Hobson, Macken (of the *Barr Buadh*) and Patrick Ryan. There was an IRB majority on the Uniform sub-committee too—three of the five members were Kent, Plunkett and Robert Page—but Kent stood alone among the six members of the Dublin City and County sub-committee. Their position was stronger than it seems from these figures, for several other members of the committees were closer in sympathy to the IRB than to Redmond, and Hobson was the most active—and one of the most influential—of all the Volunteer leaders.

Yet nothing could be done to prevent negotiations with Redmond, for Moore had MacNeill's ear, and was determined to bring about a *détente*. His strategy was to secure Redmond's support for a plan to present the Volunteers to the British as a Territorial army, and to this end he held secret meetings with MacNeill and Casement, seeking their support in committee. Casement was on the Provisional committee, and he was not affiliated to any party, but although he at first supported an alliance with Redmond, his pro-German sympathies eventually drew him out of the negotiations. Hobson had been involved at an early stage, and was too much the politician to blow the gaff and provoke a crisis, but he also dropped out when he went to America. It was therefore left to Moore and MacNeill, and MacNeill, jittery over the left-wing nationalist extremists, was open to influence.

During April and May 1914 there were meetings with parliamentarians (usually in Buswell's Hotel), and although the latter were furious when they discovered that MacNeill stood virtually alone and had no authority from the Provisional committee to negotiate, they continued to talk. Redmond was unhappy with the composition of the Provisional committee, and objected particularly to Pearse and Hobson (who were still in America). Eventually he promised his support in exchange for 25 seats on the committee for his nominees.

Redmond had a point in his objections to the Volunteer leadership: it was not elected, and was wholly unrepresentative of the Volunteer members. MacNeill also had good political arguments on his side in trying to force acceptance of the Redmond nominees. But to the IRB men, and the ICA, such a compromise spelt treachery. (Besides, nomination by Redmond was hardly a democratic process.) Pearse was a long way from the corridors of power, even after his return from America, and his popularity with the Volunteer rank and file was not yet great enough to buy him a place. MacNeill distrusted him politically, and had already withdrawn his sons from St Enda's for fear of Pearse's influence. Denis Gwynn, in a post-war apologia, described the man he knew: "... Most of us in Dublin who lived in the atmosphere of the Nationalist movement regarded him still as a strangely attractive visionary, gifted with great talents, but a man whose political ideas were so crude that we never expected that he would have any influence in politics."[4] In his League days, Pearse had been crude indeed, incapable of any manoeuvre other than the head-on clash, and this lack of subtlety still characterized his actions in the crisis over Redmond's demands. MacNeill was a consummate politician, who emulated his old leader, Hyde, in attempting to reconcile all sides and secure strength through compromise. But he could not steer his whole committee alongside Redmond, nor even deflect the brunt of the impact.

Redmond was impatient with the delays which followed his proposal, and on 12 June 1914 he issued an ultimatum, demanding that his nominees be accepted forthwith. On the evening of 16 June, the Provisional committee met at the Volunteer office in 206 Great Brunswick Street. MacNeill had not been idle. He had spent a large part of the day at a conference with Moore, Casement and Hobson and the latter had persuaded Casement that to exclude Redmond's nominees would result in a split fatal to the whole movement. Both Casement and Hobson, despite private reservations, spoke at the meeting for acquiescence with Redmond's demand, and their influence helped to carry through the resolution, by a majority of eighteen to nine. The dissidents included seven IRB men: Pearse, Kent, Colbert, MacDermott, Beaslai, Liam Mellows and Eamonn Martin. The other two were Michael Judge of the Ancient Order of Hibernians and Sean Fitzgibbon, who was unconnected with any party. Three IRB men, including Plunkett, voted with Hobson. MacDonagh, a member of the committee and almost certainly not yet an IRB man, had sent a letter apologizing for his absence which was so ambiguous that no one could construe it either way in the ballot.

The minority was furious at its defeat and called a meeting on the following day at Wynn's Hotel. Pearse, who had been silent at the committee, was no more prominent at this gathering. A statement was sent to the press, signed by all of them except Mellows, whose vote had been kept secret to avoid compromising his position as assistant secretary to the committee. The statement was brief:

> We, the undersigned members of the Provisional Committee of the Irish Volunteers, who opposed the decision arrived at by a majority of the Committee on Tuesday night, on the grounds that it was a violation of the basic principles which, up to the present, have carried the Irish Volunteer movement to success, at the same time feel it our duty to continue our work in the movement; and we appeal to those of the rank and file who are in agreement with us on this point to sink their personal feelings and persist in their efforts to make the Irish Volunteers an efficient, armed, National Defence Force.[5]

This was felt to be an honourable compromise. Pearse explained the policy in a letter to McGarrity a few days later:

> You will have seen that the Provisional Committee has had to swallow Redmond's twenty-five nominees. I voted against surrender, and think I was right in so voting; but I do not regard the cause as lost—far from it. We all remain in the movement, and shall be watchful to checkmate any attempt on Redmond's part to prevent us from arming. This is the real danger. The future of the movement depends upon our remaining at our

posts to see to it that the Volunteers are a real army, not a stage army.

There was now established within the committee a known minority whose objectives were very different from those of the majority. Hobson was the first casualty of the schism. His close friend, Clarke, though humble in his station in the Volunteers because of his reputation, was particularly bitter about Hobson's stand. He distrusted his motives, and even asked, "How much did the Castle pay you?" MacDermott was equally disillusioned, and Hobson quickly realized that for both of them ideology came before friendship. He resigned from the Supreme Council of the IRB and, at Clarke's instigation, was sacked from his part-time job as Dublin correspondent of the *Gaelic American*. Although he continued to play an important rôle in the Volunteers, he was seen by his erstwhile colleagues as a lackey of MacNeill's and they never trusted him again. Judge, not an IRB man himself, later wrote proudly of his attitude to Hobson. "I refused Hobson's hand that night, and said I never would take it while I lived. I blamed him even more than I blamed any of the others for the sudden *volte face*.... I believe the decision of the Committee was the result of intrigue rather than conviction, and that Hobson was the prime mover in that intrigue."[6] Hobson had put his political instincts above his personal reputation, and thus secured for himself the permanent rôle of scapegoat.

> In taking the course I did I believed and still believe that I saved the Volunteer movement from collapse. At that time it was too new and not sufficiently organised and a split would have meant that the Volunteers would have degenerated into an unarmed parade at political meetings, and we of the I.R.B. would have been back to a little secret movement meeting in back rooms, which is all we were before the Volunteers were started.[7]

It was a sad end to Hobson's influence in the IRB. He later said that had he not resigned in weariness and disgust he could have stayed on the Supreme Council, and fought those whom he thought irresponsible—interested in revolution for its own sake and careless of its prospects of success. Certainly, by resignation, he left the field open to the impetuous. He never met Clarke again and remained on bad terms with MacDermott, who though a man of charm and gaiety, attractive to women and popular with men, was at heart as implacable an ideologue as Clarke.

MacNeill and his allies had hoped only to satisfy Redmond's

ultimatum and defer the inevitable show-down. They retained their hold on the reins of the movement. The Redmond nominees included men traditionally hostile to the Volunteers, and the committee meetings of that summer were little more than faction fights. (Only two of the Redmondites, James Creed Meredith and Redmond's brother Willie, remained above the fray and tried to be co-operative.) But the time gained was important—time to set the Volunteers' house in order, and time to buy arms.

Meanwhile, the adoption of Redmond's nominees had widened the gulf between the ICA and the Volunteers. O'Casey poured scorn on the decision: "... since the Provisional Committee of the National Volunteers have placed their necks for John Redmond to rest his feet, ours is the only body which gathers inspiration from the principles of Wolfe Tone! The time is at hand for a reawakening of the rank and file of the Republican element in the Volunteers."[8] But the nine dissenters had at least secured for themselves some kind words from the *Irish Worker*, which described them as "honest men". And O'Casey over-reached himself in his animosity towards the Volunteers. He had a particular dislike for the striking Countess Markievicz, a woman in the tradition of Yeats's Maud Gonne, frustrated by a social position which denied her energies any release save on the hunting field. She had been associated with the nationalist women's theatrical movement, Inghinidhe na hEireann, during the first decade of the century, but wanted greater excitement. She had been instrumental in setting up, with Hobson, the Fianna Eireann, and although there was much resentment at a woman leading that male organization, she became president when Hobson's work elsewhere became overwhelming. A dominant personality, with the courage and assurance of her Ascendancy background, she took her suffragette principles to their logical conclusion and refused to be hampered by her sex from playing a full part in separatist movements. Under her, the Fianna (hitherto an innocuous Irish boy scout movement) became an organization for training boys to participate in a fight for freedom, and she became a member of both Cumann na mBan (the women's auxiliary of the Volunteers) and the ICA. Her identification with the workers could not be challenged: she had worked for them throughout the lock-out. But O'Casey hated her, and tried to force her to choose between her two loyalties and resign from either the ICA or Cumann na mBan. He was defeated, and resigned from the secretaryship of the ICA, thus removing the greatest bar to co-operation between the two armies.

The Ulster Volunteers had stolen a march on their southern

counterparts in a superbly managed gun-running at Larne in April 1914. 20,000 rifles and 3,000,000 rounds of ammunition had been landed in defiance of a government ban on the importation of arms into Ireland, enacted in response to the creation of the Irish Volunteers. Attitudes to Ulster were ambivalent. There were many northerners in the IRB, including MacNeill, Hobson, Denis McCullough (president of the IRB in 1915), and McCartan. They were reluctant to believe that their native province was not nationalistic at heart, and they resisted for a long time the evidence of their own ears. Pearse, too, was a firm believer in Ulster's importance for a free Ireland. As he said himself, St Enda's could not have survived without the help of three Ulster backers—Dolan, MacManus and Wilson. Many of his pupils and some of his teachers were Ulstermen, and the school drew its greatest inspiration from Cuchulainn—the Hound of Ulster.[9] Pearse was naïve about the Orangemen, and envious of their daring and strength of commitment. He was certain they could be won over to the nationalist cause, since they had in common their repudiation of England. As late as November 1913, he wrote:

> ... the rifles of the Orangemen give dignity even to their folly. The rifles are bound to be useful some day. At the worst they may hasten Sir Edward Carson's final exit from Ulster; at the best they may crack outside Dublin Castle. The Editor of *Sinn Fein* wrote the other day that when the Orangemen fire upon the King of England's troops it will become the duty of every Nationalist in Ireland to join them: there is a deal of wisdom in the thought as well as a deal of humour. Or negotiations might be opened with the Orangemen on these lines: You are erecting a Provisional Government of Ulster—make it a Provisional Government of Ireland and we will recognise and obey it.... It is unquestionable that Sir Edward Carson's Provisional Government would govern Ireland better than she has been governed by the English Cabinet....[10]

But the war came, Carson pledged his Volunteers to the service of the British army, and the spectre of partition loomed closer. Pearse could no longer offer any theoretical solutions to the Ulster problem, so he ignored it in his writings and hoped vaguely that a revolution would find the Ulstermen shoulder to shoulder with their southern brethren.

The Larne running took place before Carson's death-blow to co-operation, however, and many Irish Volunteers were excited by the audacity and spectacular success of the operation. Few of them knew that steps were already being taken to stage a similar demonstration for the nationalists. Roger Casement, Mrs Erskine Childers and some other friends unconnected with the Volunteers had put up £1,500, a modest sum which enabled their envoy, Darrell Figgis, to purchase in Hamburg 1,500 Mauser rifles and 45,000 rounds of ammunition. MacNeill was party to the plan, and in June Hobson was brought into MacNeill and Casement's counsels to organize the gun-running. Being in disgrace with many of the IRB leadership, Hobson discussed his plans with only one colleague, Patrick Ryan, one of those who had voted with him on the Redmond resolution.

The gun-running was planned to attract the maximum publicity for the Volunteers. It was already being discussed while Pearse was writing to McGarrity about the need for arms, and he was still so far removed from the real centre of power within the Volunteers that only nine days before the gun-running he was still unaware of the plan. Nonetheless, it was clear from his letter to McGarrity on 17 July that he had been engaged in intense political activity during the previous month.

> I am writing on behalf of the large and important element in the Irish Volunteers represented by the nine dissentients on the Provisional Committee—in other words, on behalf of the men who are still determined to keep the movement straight and to lend it, if they can, to a genuine national purpose. Our appeal is this: we want the American Committee [of the *Gaelic American*'s "Guns for the Volunteers Fund"] to make arrangements, if possible, to send us *at once* at least as much arms and ammunition as will arm our men in Dublin—say 1,000 rifles with a fair amount of ammunition for each. We want this request to take precedence of any other request that may have been made by MacNeill or by anyone else.... The men with whom I am acting more immediately in this are Sean MacDiarmada [MacDermott], Kent and Fitzgibbon.

Pearse went on to describe to McGarrity what was happening to the leadership of the Volunteers. Redmond, he alleged, was prepared to arm the Volunteers, but only those in Ulster, to resist the Orangemen and to impose Home Rule. (Pearse had in any case moved so far to the left that he now saw arms as quite unrelated to Home Rule. They would be needed with or without it.) He again showed himself too big a man to stoop to personal vilification. Although he was writing behind Hobson's back, he digressed from the main point of the letter to defend him, "I think they have been too hard on Hobson on your side, and regret very much to hear that he has been dropped as Dublin correspondent of the 'Gaelic American'. He has lost the acting editorship of '[Irish] Freedom', too, and is left without income of any sort. He may have to leave Dublin, which would be an incalculable loss."

The same letter made it clear that Pearse and his associates had been particularly worried by the appointment of a standing committee which was to exercise effective control of the Volunteers—the Provisional committee meeting only once a month. He and most of his political friends were out in the cold. "Of these 13, only Hobson & Fitzgibbon can be absolutely relied on: Judge (tho' a Hibernian) I believe sound and courageous; MacNeill and O'Rahilly are honest, but weak, and frightfully subject to panic. The rest will do exactly as Redmond tells them. At most we can count on only 5 out of the 13 who now rule the Volunteers; but possibly only on 2 or 3." This was not a bad analysis. MacNeill, with all his gifts, hated dissension and could be weak for the sake of peace. Pearse's fears were unfounded, however: MacNeill had been more astute than he expected, and on 26 July the gun-running took place successfully.

Hobson had been so discreet in his organizing that most of the Volunteers who were detailed to receive the arms at Howth, Co. Dublin (From the Childers's yacht), had no idea that he was behind the arrangements. Indeed, MacDermott and Clarke are reputed to have kept their own low-level information secret from Hobson, whom they believed to be in total ignorance of the plans.[11] The arms shipment had been split. Childers landed 900 guns and 26,000 rounds at Howth on 26 July and the remainder were run into Kilcoole, Co. Wicklow, on 1 August. Eight hundred Volunteers marched to Howth and started straight back for Dublin with the arms. There were two unfortunate incidents during the march. First, their way was barred by soldiers and police, but Hobson de-fused the situation by the simple expedient of detailing MacDonagh and Figgis to distract Assistant Commissioner Harrell, who commanded the forces of law, while Hobson dispersed his troops through the neighbouring fields and sent them peacefully back to Dublin with their booty. As Hobson says, either MacDonagh or Figgis could have talked Harrell blind, and they staged a *virtuoso* duet. Unfortunately, a few of the Volunteers, including Kent, got out of hand during the confrontation and fired on the soldiers: catastrophe was averted only because the soldiers thought the shots came from the onlooking crowd. The second outbreak of violence was more serious. Crowds in Bachelor's Walk, baiting the King's Own Scottish Borderers about the earlier incident, and about their kilts, provoked confusion in the ranks, and with guns and bayonets the soldiers killed three and injured 38. This tragedy was a gift to the propagandists. Seumus MacManus put its value crudely in an American newspaper sub-heading: "Every one of those dead or dying on fatal Sunday immediately worth to Ireland fully ten thousand living."[12]

There was no explosion, however. The Volunteer command was too divided for any direct retaliatory action, and the moment passed. The gun-running had nevertheless been of great assistance to the Volunteers: Pearse, although his only rôle in the episode had been to provide St Enda's as a reception centre for arms awaiting distribution, was exultant. In a letter to McGarrity he wrote: "The brutal murders of the unarmed crowd by the soldiers who an hour previously had run from the Volunteers have given public sentiment just that turn that was desirable. The army is an object of odium and derision, and the Volunteers are the heroes of the hour. The whole movement, the whole country, has been rebaptized by blood shed for Ireland."

Those injured or bereaved in Bachelor's Walk had been unwitting and unwilling victims, but Pearse, in personal matters a compassionate man, was reaching a high pitch of dehumanized enthusiasm about bloodshed. (He was not alone. MacDermott, partially crippled in 1911, and apparently doubting if he would live long, was by now also speaking of the need for a blood sacrifice, and other republicans were beginning to use the same rhetoric.) In this letter to McGarrity, Pearse ceased his injunctions to him to send arms immediately. He was still concerned that Redmond might try to send guns to Ulster nationalists, but he was delighted that most of the arms were in the hands of non-Ulstermen, in Dublin and elsewhere. He still asked for a large consignment of arms to be sent to him and his friends, but he was no longer particularly concerned with the timing. (He was unduly pessimistic about Redmond, who was having little luck in getting control of arms, but many of the guns *had* disappeared mysteriously, and there is strong evidence that MacDermott and Plunkett were among those appropriating them secretly. Pearse was not yet sufficiently trusted by the IRB leaders to be acquainted with such sharp practice.)

The European war, declared on 4 August, caused shifts in the kaleidoscope of alliances in Ireland. For one thing, there was a reconciliation between the ICA and the IRB, a development in which James Connolly was the prime mover. He had just come to live in Dublin and, already personally committed to organizing an insurrection, he decided that the war would provide the opportunity. There must be concerted action from all republicans, and he asked his colleague, William O'Brien, to put him in touch with "the right people". O'Brien takes up the story.

> ... I saw Eamon Ceannt [Kent] with whom we were well acquainted and who was a member of the executive of the Irish Volunteers as well as a leading member of the Irish Republican Brotherhood. He undertook to arrange a conference for Connolly and myself to attend....
>
> The conference arranged by Eamon Ceannt was held in the library of the Gaelic League at 25, Parnell Square on September 9th and amongst those present were: Tom Clarke, Sean MacDermott, Joseph Plunkett, P. H. Pearse, Sean T. O'Kelly, John McBride, Arthur Griffith [not in the IRB, although he had been before 1900], Thomas MacDonagh, Eamonn Ceannt, James Connolly and the present writer.
>
> Tom Clarke presided and Connolly advocated making definite arrangements for organising an insurrection, and in connection therewith, getting in touch with Germany, with a view to military support....
>
> Ultimately it was agreed to appoint two sub-committees one to endeavour to form contact with Germany and the other to organise an open organisation to be used for propaganda purposes and as a recruiting ground for the secret movement.[13]

This account naturally gives the Labour leaders more prominence than the IRB reminiscences allow. Sean T. O'Kelly attributed the initiative and the proposals for insurrection to Clarke. But he agrees with O'Brien as to the conclusions of the meeting. The open organization set up was called the Irish Neutrality League: Connolly was president, and O'Kelly secretary. Dublin Castle suppressed it after a couple of months, but the common purpose of the conspirators survived intact.

The war brought new complexities for the Volunteer leadership, too. Pearse had had an early unfounded hope that a war would allow the Volunteers to replace British garrisons in Ireland and so give them an unparalleled opportunity to "rise to the occasion". By 12 August he was worried even about the usefulness of the arms, since the Mausers were rather antiquated and the ammunition had been discovered to be explosive bullets which, on principle, they could not issue to their men. Redmond was making renewed efforts to locate the arms and deflect them to Ulster, and was intimating that he intended to offer the loyal support of the Volunteers to the British government. He had taken control of the Provisional committee, and the dissidents had no chance of being heard. Pearse wrote:

> I personally have ceased to be any use on the Committee. I can never carry a single point. I am now scarcely allowed to speak. The moment I stand up there are cries of "Put the question", etc. At the last meeting I had half determined to resign, but have decided to stick on a little longer in the hope of being useful at a later stage.
>
> I blame MacNeill more than anyone. He has the reputation of being "tactful", but his "tact" consists in bowing to the will of the Redmondites every time. He never makes a fight except when they assail his personal honour, when he bridles up at once. Perhaps I am wronging him, as I am smarting under the remembrance of what I regard as very unfair treatment of me personally and of all who agree with me at the last meeting. He is in a very difficult position, and he is weak, hopelessly weak. I knew that all along.[14]

In this letter, for the first time, Pearse clearly defined his strategy. "Now it is perfectly clear that whatever is to be done for Ireland in this crisis must be done *outside* the Provisional Committee. The men are sound, especially in Dublin. We could at any moment rally the best of them to our support by a *coup d'état*; and rally the whole country if the *coup d'état* were successful. But a *coup d'état* while the men are still unarmed is unthinkable."

Conditions on the Provisional committee were becoming intolerable. At a meeting on the evening of 9 September Pearse proposed two resolutions, the first that the Volunteer action during the war should be confined to the defence of Ireland and the second that the Volunteers should announce their intention to occupy the ports, in the event of shortages, to prevent food being exported. An anonymous correspondent in the *Gaelic American* took up the story.

> There was a big row on the Provisional Committee the other night. P- [Pearse] had heard a rumour that some members of the committee were in communication with the War Office to hand over the Irish Volunteers to the English. P- demanded to know if any members of the Committee were making terms with the War Office, and there was a silence. He repeated the question and N- [probably Nugent, the most aggressive Redmondite

> on the committee], whom you will remember as the man who employed ruffians to insult and beat women when the Suffrage Party were holding their meetings a year ago, well, this same N- answered P- "No, you cur"—or I believe some worse epithet. P- struck N-. Revolvers were drawn and anyway the air was cleared and the traitors ranged themselves together and *are now known.*[15]

There is an alternative version given by Ernest Blythe, from a report by MacDermott, in which the offending Redmondite was a priest, who struck Pearse. Whichever account is accurate, the Provisional committee was obviously becoming unworkable, and would very likely have ceased to function even without Redmond's subsequent actions.

Pearse had been right about Redmond, but wrong about the extent of MacNeill's capitulation to him. Redmond, who had earlier stated that the Volunteers should defend Ireland and not be asked to fight elsewhere, announced, on 20 September—without prior consultation with his committee—a change of heart. He hoped that a high level of voluntary recruitment would discourage the British government from extending conscription to Ireland.

> This war is undertaken in defence of the highest principles of religion and morality and right, and it would be a disgrace forever to our country, a reproach to her manhood, and a denial of the lessons of her history if Young Ireland confined their efforts to remaining at home to defend the shores of Ireland from an unlikely invasion, and shrinking from the duty of proving in the field of battle that gallantry and courage which have distinguished their race.... Your duty is two-fold.... Go on drilling and make yourselves efficient for the work and then assert yourselves as men, not only in Ireland itself, but wherever the firing line extends in defence of right, freedom and religion in this war.

Redmond's motives were of the highest, but his political judgement was defective. His speech was that of a man more in touch with opinion in London than in Dublin; he underestimated the strength of Irish antipathy to Britain. Although many Irishmen were willing to join up—over 200,000 volunteered—there were many more who now renounced any faith in the parliamentarians. Redmond had just got Home Rule on to the statute book, but it was suspended for the duration of the war, and separatist Ireland looked to a new leader. There was an immediate split in the Volunteers. MacNeill and twenty other members of the original committee issued a repudiation of Redmond in uncompromising terms.

> Mr Redmond ... has now announced for the Irish Volunteers a policy and programme fundamentally at variance with their own published and accepted aims and objects, but with which his nominees are, of course, identified. He has declared it to be the duty of the Irish Volunteers to take foreign service under a Government which is not Irish. He has made this announcement without consulting the Provisional Committee, the Volunteers themselves, or the people of Ireland, to whose service alone they are devoted.
>
> Having thus disregarded the Irish Volunteers and their solemn engagements, Mr Redmond is no longer entitled, through his nominees, to any place in the administration and guidance of the Irish Volunteer Organisation. Those who, by virtue of Mr Redmond's nomination, have heretofore been admitted to act on the Provisional Committee accordingly cease to belong to this body, and from this date until the holding of an Irish Volunteer Convention the Provisional Committee consists of those only whom it comprised before the admission of Mr Redmond's nominees.

Of the six proposals which were to be put to the next meeting of the Provisional committee, three were especially significant.

> 1. To call a Convention of the Irish Volunteers for Wednesday, 25th November, 1914, the anniversary of the inaugural meeting of the Irish Volunteers in Dublin.
>
> ...
>
> 5. To declare that Ireland cannot, with honour or safety, take part in foreign quarrels otherwise than through the free action of a National Government of her own; and to repudiate the claim of any man to offer up the blood and lives of the sons of Irishmen and Irishwomen to the services of the British Empire while no National Government which could speak and act for the people of Ireland is allowed to exist.
> 6. To demand that the present system of governing Ireland through Dublin Castle and the British military power, a system responsible for the recent outrages in Dublin, be abolished without delay, and that a National Government be forthwith established in its place.

This throwing down of the gauntlet had its anticipated effect. Redmond kept the leadership of an estimated 170,000 men, renamed the National Volunteers; MacNeill's group were left with only 10,000 (still known as the Irish Volunteers). This was a manageable number for the exercise of IRB control. The anniversary convention would determine whether the leadership was composed of the moderates or the extremists.

III The Achievement of Power

The majority of the people had gone Redmond's way, but the section of opinion represented by the tiny residue in the Irish Volunteers had no doubts but that they spoke for the soul of Ireland. The moderates among them were committed to separatism, and to non-involvement in the European war. Physical force was seen as a last resort, to be used to defend Irishmen from the threat of British conscription. But among the Volunteers were two other groups, the larger of which, numbered in hundreds, was made up of IRB men dedicated to physical force against Britain at any favourable opportunity. By the terms of their constitution this was to be a democratic decision. "The IRB shall await the decision of the Irish Nation as expressed by a majority of the Irish people as to the fit hour of inaugurating a war against England and shall, pending such an emergency, lend its support to every movement calculated to advance the cause of Irish independence, consistently with the preservation of its own integrity." Hobson, who had sworn in most members to the IRB after 1912, stated later that he had had to give many of them an assurance that they would not be required to aid an insurrection which did not have public support. The third element in the Volunteers comprised no more than a handful of IRB members, set on revolution at all costs, and quite untrammelled by their own constitution. They were mixed in their inspirations, but united in one important conviction—that they were entitled to sacrifice themselves and others for political ends. Connolly, however much he cared for civil rights, was from the same Marxist mould which produced the Bolsheviks; the triumph of labour was his end, not democracy. Clarke and Kent represented a different despotic tradition, though one equally indifferent to the will of the people. This third group was completed by four men who were to be to the fore in planning the mounting of an insurrection: Pearse, MacDonagh, Plunkett and MacDermott were exponents of a romantic morality which sanctioned the sacrifice of self and others in the pursuit of self-realization. Pearse and MacDonagh, before they succumbed to this logic, had believed that the Irish people could be revitalized and led in unity to self-government. By 1914 they had despaired of such an outcome, and henceforward they were as unconcerned as their colleagues about the popular will; the wishes of Tone and Emmet were sufficient vindication for their revolutionary convictions; the vast majority of their countrymen had ceased to be a factor in any other than military calculations. Attempts by MacNeill and Hobson during the next eighteen months to keep the revolutionary cabal in line with the avowed objects of the Volunteers (in the case of MacNeill) and the constitution of the IRB (in Hobson's case) were destined to failure. Their opponents were irreversibly committed to insurrection, and were waiting only for arms and an opportunity.

So the divisions ran deep even before the Volunteers' first convention. Complaints about the undemocratic appointment of the Provisional committee had brought its proposed date forward by a month: it was now scheduled for 25 October. Six days before this, Pearse wrote again to McGarrity to request money for arms. He outlined the circumstances in which a rising could be provoked.

> We shall have to act (1) if the Germans land either in Ireland or in England; (2) if the Government enforces the Militia Ballot Act or any other drastic way of securing recruits; (3) if the food supply becomes scarce; (4) if the Government tries to disarm the "disloyal" Volunteers; and (5) if the Government commences to arrest our leaders, who are being *pointed out to them* (if they did not know them before) by the Redmondite press. Any one of these things may happen at any moment; any one of them would precipitate a crisis,—*the* crisis; and we are not ready, for we have not arms. If the chance comes and goes, it will in all probability have come and gone forever, certainly for our lifetime.

Pearse was still being kept in the dark. Clan-na-Gael had already asked the German Ambassador in America for military assistance in an insurrection, and had financed Casement's visit to Germany, a journey with three objectives—the shipment of arms to Ireland, moral support for Irish independence, and the formation of an Irish Brigade, recruited from prisoners of war, which would support the rebels. Casement and Clan-na-Gael were pro-German, as were certain sections of the IRB, but Pearse had little sympathy with such a position. To him German domination was as odious as British, and although he was later prepared to approve the seeking of German military help, he wanted to see an *Irish* not a foreign insurrection. Hobson wanted to see an Irish kingdom, headed by a German prince, and Ernest Blythe (who was achieving new prominence in both the Volunteers and the IRB) was one of his strongest supporters.[1] Pearse became converted to this view, because he felt it would assist de-Anglicization, but he wanted no political alliance with Germany.

He had just gained promotion in the IRB, but not yet to the Supreme Council. An advisory committee of Volunteer leaders (Pearse, Plunkett and Kent) had been set up within the IRB to draw up military plans for an insurrection, Plunkett being the effective member. He had a fascination with military matters, and at this stage was the brains behind the IRB plans. Pearse had no such gifts, but remained on the committee because of his importance in the Volunteers. He was now much closer to Clarke and MacDermott, though by no means in their confidence, and by this period he seems to have seen himself at the centre of a caucus of the IRB elite. Although Clan-na-Gael was tied up in negotiations with the Germans, it had a great deal of its own money to put at the disposal of the IRB and Volunteers. Pearse was anxious to organize the spending of it.

> I would suggest that in sending the money you do not entrust the expenditure of the whole of it to MacNeill and O'Rahilly or any other two men. Not that I doubt their honesty, but simply that they are not in or of our counsels and that they are not formally pledged to strike, if the chance comes, for the complete thing. I suggest that you name certain sums to be placed at the disposal of certain men whom you know for the arming of Volunteer companies to be selected by them. This is the only way I can see of securing that the right men are armed. Thus, if T. Clarke, J. MacDermott, Hobson [Pearse apparently did not realize how far Hobson had fallen from favour among the activists within the IRB], Kent, and myself had each $2,500 at his disposal to arm the companies each is in touch with, the arms would be sure to get into the right hands, and the transaction would be perfectly *bona fide* and could be defended before the Provisional Committee. . . .[2]

Pearse did not stand high enough in the estimation of the Irish Americans to affect their policy. Although McGarrity and Devoy were sympathetic towards him, they pinned most of their hopes on Casement, whom McGarrity described as a "reincarnated Tone". Hobson, too, still had McGarrity's friendship, and had patched up relations with Devoy. Clan-na-Gael did send money to the IRB, but it continued also to send a great deal to the Volunteers—apparently without strings attached. Its resources were immense: $100,000 was sent to the two organizations between 1913 and 1916, and far more later. Despite Pearse's failure to convince it of his own importance, his optimism helped to keep the money rolling in.

> It is my matured conviction that, given arms, the Volunteers who have adhered to us as against Redmond may be depended upon to act vigorously, courageously, promptly, and unitedly if the opportunity comes. We are at the moment in an immensely stronger position than ever before. The whole body of Volunteers that has supported our stand against recruiting may be looked upon as a separatist body. In other words, the separatist organisation has been multiplied by a hundred. In Dublin we have some 2500 admirably disciplined, drilled, intelligent, and partly armed men. Nationalist Ireland has never before had such an asset. Our main strength is in Dublin, but large minorities support us everywhere, especially in the towns and in the extreme South and West. We expect to have 150 companies, representing 10,000 to 15,000 men, represented by delegates at next Sunday's Convention. This small, compact, perfectly disciplined, determined *separatist* force is infinitely more valuable than the unwieldy, loosely-held-together mixum-gatherum force we had before the split. The Volunteers we have with us now may be relied upon to the death, and we are daily perfecting their fighting effectiveness and mobilization power.
>
> It seems a big thing to say, but I do honestly believe that, with arms for these men, we shall be ready to *act* with tremendous effect if the war brings us the moment.
>
> The spirit of our Dublin men is wonderful. They would rise tomorrow if we gave the word. A meeting of Dublin officers the other night was as exhilarating as a draught of wine.[3]

The wine had gone to Pearse's head. The Volunteers were too raw to be perfectly disciplined and drilled, and few of them were ready to turn out for an unprovoked insurrection. Yet, given the arms and the right circumstances, they were potentially effective. No amount of American money could procure guns from thin air, however, and the war had made further gun-running impracticable. By December new laws made the acquisition of weapons almost impossible. By that time the Volunteers had over 2,000 guns, acquired by purchase within the country and occasional theft, but they were to remain an ill-equipped army.

Pearse's position in the Volunteers was made secure at the convention, held in the Abbey Theatre on 25 October 1914. A new alliance with the ICA, resulting from the split with Redmond, was frustrated by the refusal of the Volunteers to co-opt two members of the ICA on to the committee, or to affiliate the ICA as a whole. They were in a position of strength: Connolly, with only 200 members, was the petitioner. This was a set-back to the drive to present a united revolutionary front, and caused friction between the two sides for many months.

The convention set up a General Council (to replace the old committee) composed of 62 members. Thirty-two represented the Irish counties and nine the major cities. The remaining 21 elected were the surviving members of the original committee. MacNeill and The O'Rahilly stayed on as chairman and treasurer respectively, but the IRB was well represented in the new posts that were created. Hobson was general secretary, Kent financial secretary, Pearse press secretary, Plunkett co-treasurer, Patrick Ryan publications secretary and Seamus O'Connor musketry training officer. Hobson was a strong influence on Ryan and O'Connor (who had voted with him over the Redmond nominees), but this still left three members of the "insurrection at all costs" group in key positions. This organization was in any case too rudimentary to manage the Volunteers, and the main decisions about spheres of activity were left until the first meeting of the General Council, on 6 December 1914.

Meanwhile, Pearse did his personal reputation a great deal of good in a *cause célèbre* in November. He had been invited by the Trinity College Gaelic Society to speak, with Yeats and Thomas Kettle, at a meeting to commemorate the birth of the Young Irelander Thomas Davis, a famous Trinityman. Such an event would have attracted only mild interest, but for the intervention of Professor Mahaffy, now vice-provost. Mahaffy, in a subsequently famous letter, banned the meeting on the grounds that the speakers included "a man called Pearse"—prominent in the anti-recruiting movement. Mahaffy, as in his contest with the League fourteen years earlier, showed a genius for presenting his enemies with ammunition, and the Davis meeting, held *outside* Trinity on 20 November, received widespread publicity in the press. Yeats made a conciliatory and, according to Holloway, a fascinating speech.

> I am very sorry Professor Mahaffy is not here tonight. I am not more vehemently opposed to the Unionism of Professor Mahaffy than I am the pro-Germanism of Mr Pearse but we are here to talk about literature and about history ... it is necessary to keep always unbroken the truce of the muses. I am sorry the Vice-Provost of Trinity should have broken that ancient truce. It would have been a great pleasure to have stood on the same platform with Dr Mahaffy, who has done so much good service for

Engish literature, and with Mr Pearse, who has done such good service to Irish literature.[4]

Pearse, in his speech, talked with his usual religious symbolism about the respective gospels of John Mitchel (also a Young Irelander) and Thomas Davis. The year before he had written of Mitchel in *From A Hermitage*, describing his *Jail Journal* as "one of the holy books of Ireland; the last gospel of the New Testament of Irish Nationality, as Wolfe Tone's Autobiography is the first". Now he elevated Mitchel above Davis, although the latter was still third of the four evangelists of Irish nationalism about whom Pearse was to write at length later. Mitchel was to St John as Davis was to the more human St Luke, or, as Yeats put it in his speech, Mitchel taught hate of England, Davis love of Ireland.[5] It was a new development in Pearse to speak approvingly of hate of England. It has been suggested that this rancour was due to his personal resentment of his half-English parentage; certainly it may have made him more vehement in his rejection of England—a parallel to his sensitivity to gibes concerning his political sincerity. Holloway at least was unmoved by Pearse's performance: "... he spoke longly and drearily in English. His style of delivery is deadly monotonous. Yeats smoked his stylographic pen in listening to Pearse meander on."

The most remarkable aspect of the evening, and one which showed the way the political wind was blowing in Ireland, was the reception accorded to Kettle. A man of great talent, Kettle in his later years had grown frustrated, and was known to be a heavy drinker. He was still a Redmond supporter, and encouraged recruiting. (He was quite sincere, and his beliefs led him to die for his country in the Great War as surely as Pearse's drove him to revolution.) He arrived at this meeting, in Ryan's words, "gloriously drunk" and was booed and heckled by the crowd, who jeered his political views and ridiculed his drinking.[6] Poor Kettle was derided by many generations of his countrymen, and it says much for Pearse that in an open letter to Kettle in his *Barr Buadh* days, attacking everything for which he now stood, he had shown a grace lacking in many of his contemporaries. "If I have spoken bitterly in anything I have said to you, forgive me for it. I have never lost the affection I had for you."[7]

The publicity attending the meeting could only enhance Pearse's reputation among the Volunteers, who, whatever their differences, were all vehemently opposed to Redmond's recruiting drive. Their commitment against conscription was put on a more practical footing by Pearse, who before the General Council meeting drew up detailed plans for resistance to such an imposition. In view of Pearse's predilection for blunt tactics it seems unlikely that the scheme embodied his own ideas (it was probably concocted by the office-holders), but his flair for reducing complicated instructions into intelligible form made him an obvious man to draft such an important document. It outlined a gradual stand, escalating into guerrilla warfare, the object being minimum confrontation and maximum points of opposition throughout the country. This strategy, by tying up a large British force, would make conscription impossible to enforce.

When the General Council met, it was decided to set up a military headquarters staff. Pearse's document was released to senior men within the Volunteers, and it may have contributed to his appointment as director of military organization. MacNeill was chief-of-staff, O'Rahilly director of arms, MacDonagh director of training, Plunkett director of military operation, Hobson quartermaster and Kent director of communications. This allocation of posts played into the hands of the revolutionaries: they occupied all the positions requiring direct personal contact with officers in the field. Pearse found himself in control of the whole machinery for action, and he was not slow to make his presence felt. On 16 December he published a scheme of organization for the Volunteers to lick them into a more military shape. It owed a great deal to British army practice. The tactical units—the companies—were to consist of a maximum of 100 men under a commander. Four to eight companies would compose a battalion under a commandant, and three to five battalions a brigade. The brigadier-generals would report directly to headquarters general staff.

Pearse quickly took advantage of his new power, and IRB men were appointed to key positions throughout the country (although they were still heavily outnumbered). On 10 March 1915 he, Plunkett and Hobson were appointed as commandants unattached to any battalion and therefore responsible only to themselves, while MacDonagh, Edward Daly (Mrs Tom Clarke's brother), Kent and Eamon de Valera became commandants in charge of the four Dublin battalions. De Valera was the only one who caused Pearse any anxiety, and on the day after his appointment he questioned him as to how he would behave in the event of an insurrection.[8] De Valera, who throughout his career in the Volunteers was to act in rigid observance of military discipline, said that as a soldier he would obey any order from his superiors. Satisfied with this response, Pearse summoned de Valera to a meeting of the four new commandants to be held on 13 March.

At this meeting, at which Pearse presided, the possibility of staging a rising the following September was discussed, and military rôles assigned to each battalion.[9] Shortly afterwards MacDonagh was put at their head, in command of the Dublin Brigade. De Valera, who had earlier refused to join the IRB, eventually took the oath at MacDonagh's behest, but never attended meetings or entered the counsels of its leaders. He was clearly reliable, however, and so remained in his post.

Pearse's new responsibilities with both the Volunteers and the IRB did not tie him to desk or committee table. As director of operations he was in close touch with officers throughout the country and, although no military man, he enjoyed watching the action. He involved himself, usually as an onlooker and in a formal capacity, with drilling and exercising the troops. One of the most spectacular manoeuvres in which he was concerned was held on Easter Sunday (4 April) 1915, when a mock battle was staged for some of the Dublin County Volunteers.[10] Pearse was in command of all the Dublin forces, which launched an "assault" on the Fingal Volunteers outside the city. Operations lasted from 9:30 am to three o'clock the following morning, and the scale of the manoeuvre was an indication that Pearse was taking his new rôle seriously. However, he did not confine himself to this sphere of action. Although he loved the trappings of the soldier and dressed for his rôle carefully, with a well-fitting uniform and a sword, his pen was unsheathed more frequently. He wrote frequently for the *Irish Volunteer*, publishing a weekly column in Irish (in January and February 1915), 'Headquarters Bulletin', and other occasional articles. If the weekly 'Mo Thuairim Fein' (My Own Opinion) was little read by the largely non-Irish speaking Volunteers, the writings in English had a wider audience. The calls for unity were still there, and he was still fighting a losing battle for the language.

> I do not know who among the Gaelic Leaguers that have joined the Volunteers has been foolish enough to suggest that he "cares for the language merely as a sort of stimulant in the fight for nationhood". Certainly not I: I have spent the best fifteen years of my life teaching and working for the idea that the language is an essential part of the nation. I have not modified my attitude in anything that I have recently said or written; I have only confessed (and not for the first time) that in the Gaelic League I have all along been working not for the language merely, but for the nation.

He was near to retreat on this issue. After February 1915 he was forced to recognize the realities: the Volunteers spoke English, read English, sang English marching songs and were drilled in English. If Pearse wanted to get his message across, he would have to do so in English. All his political writings after this time were in English, and so was virtually all his literary output. The message was increasingly plainly expressed. In May 1915 he wrote, in an article called "Why We Want Recruits":

> We want recruits because we are absolutely determined to take action the moment action becomes a duty. If a moment comes—as a moment seemed on the point of coming at least twice during the past eighteen months—when the Irish Volunteers will be justified to their consciences in taking definite military action, such action will be taken. We do not anticipate such a moment in the very near future; but we live at a time when it may come swiftly and terribly. What if Conscription be forced upon Ireland? What if a Unionist or a Coalition British Ministry repudiate the Home Rule Act? What if it be determined to dismember Ireland? What if it be attempted to disarm Ireland? The future is big with these and other possibilities.

He was also making a reputation as a political pamphleteer. The previous year he had published *How Does She Stand?*, which brought together his most celebrated speeches—the two Emmet orations given in America and the Tone commemoration speech of June 1913. By February 1915 he had risen to a new stature in Dublin. In a popularity poll in a separatist paper, the *Spark*, to find the Irish nationalist whom Dublin most wished to honour, Pearse came sixth in a group headed by Griffith and MacNeill. None of his other colleagues came anywhere. He was now the IRB's greatest public asset. In June 1915 he published a more influential work—*From a Hermitage*—a collection of his *Irish Freedom* articles. *How Does She Stand?* was too much a *pot-pourri* of current revolutionary rhetoric to attract much attention—and in print the speeches lacked the power given them by Pearse's polished delivery. *From a Hermitage* was on a higher intellectual plane and it was well received even by Connolly. In the *Worker's Republic* (the *Irish Worker* had been suppressed in December 1914), he expressed his pleasure at finding Pearse "so widely sympathetic to the struggles of the workers".[11] There was only one significant change from the text of the articles as they had originally appeared.

Hyde was by now attracting the scorn of the IRB, who finally took control of the Coiste Gnotha and drove him to resignation after 22 dedicated years as president. (MacNeill was his replacement.) Pearse was obviously aware of the IRB campaign, and of the abuse aimed at Hyde by Sinn Fein, which had been an implacable critic for years. In August 1913, when Pearse had first written about troubles in the Gaelic League, he had been politically uncommitted, and had launched a Philippic against Griffith and the new wreckers. Griffith's denunciation of Hyde

> has been written by a man who has never worked under you or with you at all, who has never been an active member of the Gaelic League, who has never sat on any important Gaelic League committee, who has never taken part in the deliberations of the Ard-Fheis, who has never been a member of the Coiste Gnotha, who does not even speak the language in which you and I and our friends have been doing our work all these years, who has never been privy to any of our counsels, who knows nothing whatever of what your influence and status with your colleagues are, who knows, in fact, absolutely nothing of the inside of the Gaelic League except what has been conveyed to him by persons who have broken their faith to you and to their colleagues (reliable informants, truly—I had almost written informers), and who is about as qualified to form an estimate of your character and influence as he is of the character and influence of, let us say, the Prime Minister of Hungary. The fact that your critic is an able man and, as I believe, a true man, makes him on this occasion none the less ridiculous.[12]

In preparing *From a Hermitage* for pamphlet publication, Pearse had excised this passage, and one other phrase—"I love and honour Douglas Hyde above all the men who are leading us Irish today"—was shortened to "I love and honour Douglas Hyde". These omissions surely showed a change of priorities, but Pearse would not desert his old heroes in time of trouble. Although IRB colleagues like Clarke were now plotting Hyde's downfall, Pearse retained an independent conscience, and stood with Hyde against them. "O ye of little sense, know ye not when ye have got a good captain for a good cause? And know ye not that it is the duty of the soldier to follow his captain, unfaltering, unquestioning, 'seeing obedience in the bond of rule'? If ye know not this, ye know not the first thing that a fighting man should know."

Well though this speaks of Pearse's loyalty, this last paragraph has a certain irony: he was already working behind MacNeill's back to subvert the stated policy of the Volunteers. Nor was he to show himself any more capable of unquestioning obedience in the IRB.

Pearse also found time during that period of intense activity to write another play for the St Enda's boys. Even the Volunteers could not curb the theatrical preoccupations of the Pearse brothers and their friends MacDonagh and Plunkett. The latter pair had, with the financial help of Edward Martyn, set up their own Irish Theatre in 1914, in Hardwicke Street Hall, Dublin. In May 1915 a double bill of *Iosagan* and a new play, *The Master*, was staged there by St Enda's. *The Master* was set in pre-Christian Ireland, and centred on two protagonists, Ciaran (played by Willie), the Christian master of a small forest school, and Daire, the King (Eamon Bulfin) who has come to challenge Ciaran to prove the superiority of the new religion. Daire threatens to kill Ciaran's favourite pupil, little Iollan, unless Heaven intervenes, and such is the strength of the child's faith that the Archangel Michael appears to defend him. Ciaran, whose faith has been defective until now, acknowledges this revelation and falls dead. The affinity of Ciaran with Pearse is striking. Ciaran had spent much of his life searching for glory, and was now trying to subdue his pride by giving up the world—without success.

> ... I see that all my wayfaring has been in vain. A man may not escape from that which is in himself. A man shall not find his quest unless he kill the dearest thing he has. I thought that I was sacrificing everything, but I have not sacrificed the old pride of my heart. I chose self-abnegation not out of humility, but out of pride: and God, that terrible hidden God, has punished me by withholding from me His most precious gift of faith. Faith comes to the humble only.... Nay, Lord, I believe this is but a temptation. Thou, too, wast tempted. Thou, too, wast forsaken. O valiant Christ, give me Thy strength! My need is great.

Written when Pearse had recently espoused a new religion—physical force—this convoluted self-reproach is a rich vein of clues to his inner struggles. He had come to his new beliefs at bewildering speed, and self-analysis was too strong a habit for him not to question his own motives, however loudly (like Ciaran) he might preach his new gospel. He had rejected the obvious temptations of the world, represented by Daire—"the little, foolish, mean, discordant things of a man's life"—and had sought instead things "remote and Holy and perilous". But he was uncertain, and in the play, it took the shining innocent faith of the young child to bring him a certain sign that his new religion represented the truth.

Whether or not Pearse ever had the truth of his new faith revealed to him through an intermediary history does not record, but by setting his inner torment down on paper, and having it acted out—by Willie, in public—he seems to have laid the ghost of his doubts. After *The Master* these doubts appear in his literary work only in the past tense. It is almost certain that from mid-1915 onwards, Pearse felt secure and had no more fears about the righteousness of his cause. There was no looking back.

The year at St Enda's had not all been plain sailing. Pearse was still burdened with debt, although American proceeds and further occasional contributions and loans from McGarrity had kept the school afloat. Now that he was facing the likelihood of his own death, however, he was distressed at the state in which he would leave his personal affairs. In November 1914 he had deposited with his solicitor a statement of his financial affairs, listing the friends who had lent him money and asking Clan-na-Gael, in the event of his death, to pay at least one, Stephen Barrett, whose signature was on a bill standing at £275. "... I do so because I know them to be the noblest and most generous Irish organisation in the world, because I know them to sympathise with my attempt at St Enda's College, and because I know that they will be zealous to vindicate the honour and good name of one who shared with them great ideals and mighty hopes."[13]

His business creditors had by now received a total of 4s.6d. in the pound, and were expressing dissatisfaction. More distressingly, although most of his friends could survive non-repayment of their debts without too much hardship, the ex-headmistress of St Ita's was badly in need of the money she had put into the venture. A letter to her in December 1915 showed the strain against which Pearse was labouring beneath the dashing exterior proper to his new position of power.

> I can easily imagine that your position is very difficult in these trying times, and I only wish I could do something substantial towards reducing my debt to you and thus making things easier. The old struggle as regards the finances of St Enda's goes on always, or rather the strain increases from month to month and from week to week. I have never enough in the bank to enable me to pay anything off the old liability, and I see no prospect of being able to make a further payment all round until I am able to resume my American lectures at the end of the war. I can earn or collect at the rate of $100 a week in America, but there is no use in going out again until the war is over. Besides, my

> place is obviously here during the present crisis.
>
> I am almost ashamed to mention the only thing I can do. Out of my infinitesimal private a/c which I keep open in the Royal Bank by lodging in it occasional guineas which I earn for literary or semi-literary work, I think I could manage to send you £5, as I expect to get that sum in a few days from a publisher; and I might be able to follow this up by other small instalments from time to time.[14]

Private concerns apart, Pearse had been revelling in the glories of his new position. In general, he was guaranteed respect and enthusiasm from his audiences. But in May 1915, he saw the other side of the coin—crowd hostility. Pearse, de Valera and Blythe were among Volunteer leaders who travelled to Limerick, where a parade of about 1,000 Irish Volunteers from Dublin and Cork were to lend strength to Volunteer recruitment. Pearse's "Why We Want Recruits" had been published in the *Irish Volunteer* the previous day, and he must have had high hopes of a successful outing. In the event, Limerick showed that Redmondite propaganda was having a powerful effect. Many Irishmen were joining the war effort, and their families were greatly consoled by the separation allowance, which guaranteed them a reasonable living standard while their men were away. The Volunteers were jeered and stoned by sections of the crowd, chiefly the families of British army men. Blythe was with Pearse.

> Later, in Daly's house, I met Pearse and the other leaders. Before long news came that an angry threatening crowd was around the station and that the Volunteers would have to fight them on their way to the train. It was evident that Pearse was very disturbed. When a messenger came in to say that an officer had given orders to a company of the Limerick battalion to load their rifles lest the mob should try to take them from them, he was sent a hasty order to unload immediately. Much later I understood what caused the anxiety I read on Pearse's face. His plans were made or were already in the making, and would be ruined if the Volunteers were to kill or wound some of the Limerick people.[15]*

Fortunately, the Volunteers managed to get to their train without a major confrontation, although one of them bayoneted a member of the crowd. The recruiting mission had been a complete failure, but Pearse had learned his lesson. His enthusiasm for the Volunteers was unabated, but he no longer believed that there was any chance of carrying the country at large with them. His best efforts in the future were to be channelled into secret planning within the IRB. And Blythe was right about Pearse's sudden anxiety in Limerick. He was no guerrilla tactician, but it was clear to him that another similar episode, perhaps with more drastic results, could rob the Volunteers of their remaining prestige—one civilian death would be fatal to the insurrection. An uncompromising directive was issued to all Volunteers by their director of organization in June, forbidding any unauthorized discharge of firearms, on pain of suspension and discipline.

Pearse's fears of precipitate action did not affect his preparation for what was to be the apogee of his oratorical career—the tribute at the graveside of O'Donovan Rossa. Rossa, one of the narrowest and most bitter of the old Fenians, but equally one of the most courageous and indomitable of them, had died after a long illness in America, and he was to be buried at Glasnevin Cemetery in Dublin. The funeral was arranged as a gigantic propaganda exercise, to be held on 1 August 1915. From the point of view of the revolutionaries, the most important aspect of the funeral was to draw together the ICA, the IRB and the Volunteers. Clarke stood at the centre of the web of organizing sub-committees, whose members included most of the important names in separatist Ireland—prominent among them being Griffith, Connolly, MacNeill and Markievicz. Clarke was in no doubt about who should deliver the panegyric—Pearse was the man. Pearse never relied on spontaneity in his speeches, and he retired with Willie and Desmond Ryan to the west, where he spent his time corresponding with Volunteer headquarters, finishing a collection of short stories, and writing and re-writing his script.[16] He wrote to Clarke for advice on how far he should go in what he said, and received the instruction, "As far as you can. Make it as hot as hell, throw all discretion to the winds."[17]

So, while hundreds of people laboured in Dublin perfecting arrangements for the procession and funeral, Pearse sat in Rosmuc, blowing ever more heat into his inflammatory phrases. The speech in his pocket, he set off for Dublin, and was brought down to earth by a meeting with a dissolute Gael. Ryan wrote of it:

> In the carriage half way to Dublin a truculent and drunken countryman lurched into the carriage blowing foul smoke-clouds over all the ladies and flourishing a bottle of whisky with an invitation to us all to take a swig. Pearse came down from Heaven where he weaved the phrases of his Oration with an imperious

> order to the countryman to behave himself and stop smoking in a non-smoking carriage under pain of instant removal. The countryman issued a general invitation to us all to light up and not mind the Pig. And until he left the carriage many stations onward he kept up a chorus of "Don't mind the Pig, enjoy yourselves!" Sometimes he turned to Pearse and addressed him by name as "You pig, pig, pig!" Pearse sat in fist-clenched silence, his face flushed while Willie laughed quietly, warning his brother with looks to say no more to the infuriated combination of clay pipe, wild hat and whisky-bottle at his elbow. We reached Dublin on the very eve of the Rossa funeral and found it electrified with the preparations for the lying in state and the march to Glasnevin. All the peace of the hills and lakes fell from us suddenly.[18]

The funeral was no anti-climax. Between the Volunteers and the ICA there were thousands of uniformed men, and the public swelled the numbers at Glasnevin to the hundreds of thousands. It was Pearse's greatest test and he rose to the occasion, with a speech which was his masterpiece. In his idealization of the rather unattractive figure of Rossa, as Ryan says, he sketched himself, and heralded the approaching revolution. His peroration was open defiance of Dublin Castle.

> This is a place of peace, sacred to the dead, where men should speak with all charity and all restraint; but I hold it a Christian thing, as O'Donovan Rossa held it, to hate evil, to hate untruth, to hate oppression, and, hating them, to strive to overthrow them. Our foes are strong and wise and wary; but, strong and wise and wary as they are, they cannot undo the miracles of God who ripens in the hearts of young men the seeds sown by the young men of a former generation. And the seeds sown by the young men of '65 and '67 are coming to their miraculous ripening to-day. Rulers and Defenders of Realms had need to be wary if they would guard against such processes. Life springs from death; and from the graves of patriot men and women spring living nations. The Defenders of this Realm have worked well in secret and in the open. They think that they have pacified Ireland. They think that they have pacified half of us and intimidated the other half. They think that they have foreseen everything, think that they have provided against everything; but the fools, the fools, the fools!—they have left us our Fenian

> dead, and while Ireland holds these graves, Ireland unfree shall never be at peace.[19]

The effect of Pearse's eloquence upon his listeners was conveyed in the Souvenir of the funeral.

> Cold, lifeless print cannot convey even an idea of the depth and intensity of feeling in which his words were couched. Calm and deliberate, in soft yet thrilling accents, his oration was almost sublime. Here was no rhetoric, no mathematical oratory; it was the soul of a patriot breathing words of love and devotion, of hope and truth and courage, no threnody, but a paean of triumph such as might have come from out the tomb by which we were.... For some moments after Mr Pearse had finished there was an intense, an all pervading, silence, then we who are accustomed to stand subdued in the home of Death gave forth round after round of cheers which surely must have gladdened the spirits of Rossa and his colleagues, O'Mahony, Stephens, and O'Leary, who lie so near.

A more telling assessment of Pearse the orator has analysed his success—and this is the time for such an assessment, for he never again attained the splendour of his Rossa speech. Stephen McKenna wrote after Pearse's death:

> ... he was certainly a powerful orator if the orator is the man that holds and convinces or drives his hearers. I suppose the people of Dublin never heard quite such speeches as he gave them. He poured out, certainly, the gospel of nationality as they heard it speaking of itself in their own hearts, in that vague first yearning which it's the craft of the orator to turn into self-conscious will and act. But, like Habbakuk in the French story, Pearse was capable of anything: a great audience, panting with actuality, longing, one would swear, for definite guidance, for policies and personalities, would find itself dreaming with him for a quarter of an hour at a time, over the lovely lapse of falling water; he would tell us how Mitchell missed in Australia the perpetual tinkling of streams that had been music to him in Ireland, how Colum-cille had loved Ireland as a waterfall land —"Only thy government, Eire, displeased me, thou Waterfall Land"—he would croon to us in that peculiar voice of his about birds and mountains and misty lakes and of the ancient Irish love of colour in costume and of bodily beauty in hero and in hero's Lady-love. A poet, a philosopher, a mystic, one would say, not a leader of the people in the hard tussle of politics, in

> the desperate onslaught upon a brutally unsensitive organization like the Parliamentary machine. Yet he did lead and the people followed. They hung on his slow, melodious words, dreamed his dream and very largely did his will.[20]

This evokes well the appeal of Pearse, but it misrepresents his audiences. He could stir their emotion, shape and direct them for as long as his words lasted, but there were still few among them whom he could impel to action. And standing before vast crowds, he was still a solitary man of solitary ambition. Over Rossa's remains, while complying fully with Clarke's mandate, he had momentarily carried listeners into the heart of his own personal vision. Ryan has the last word.

> Beside the grave he stood, impressive and austere in green, with slow and intense delivery, and as he cried aloud upon the fools he threw back his head sharply and the expression seemed to vivify the speech which ended calmly and proudly. He walked home alone, and sat in his study: at last he had spoken the just word he sought to immortalise a man less great than himself.[21]

IV The IRB at Work

The British authorities in Ireland were in an impossible dilemma by the summer of 1915. Reports of heavy casualties from the front line were beginning to curb Irish enthusiasm for the war effort, and the anti-enlistment philosophy was being preached from platforms and in the separatist press. The Castle spies knew the dangerous men, and they were all well aware that the Rossa funeral was IRB inspired, and likely to have a seditious effect on public opinion. But the Volunteers were armed and could not be suppressed without massive bloodshed. Neither could they be ignored. There were sporadic suppressions of offending papers, and occasional deportations or imprisonments of men who had committed themselves too publicly to the anti-enlisting cause. MacDermott and Blythe were among those in prison for short terms at the beginning of the summer. Such action tended to rebound on the harassed authorities. Dangerous though MacDermott was at liberty, the detention of IRB and ICA men only tended to increase their popularity, unite their leaders and push even the moderates closer to action.

Although the authorities never really saw him as a great threat,

Pearse had attracted attention by his Rossa speech, and he suffered swift retaliation. They struck at his Achilles heel—his finances. Sir John O'Connell, solicitor to the Woodbyrne estate (including the Hermitage), was warned by the lord chancellor that Pearse was "in a very dangerous position", and in mid-August he demanded immediate payment of the outstanding half-year's rent. A writ was issued for £288 plus costs. Pearse wrote in desperation for McGarrity's help.

> ... We are all convinced that it is part of a move to discredit me in the eyes of the public. It is their way of hitting at me. They will represent me as a bankrupt and discredited man who takes refuge in "advanced" politics and hides his failure to meet his creditors by preaching sedition.
>
> Now the effect of this will be not only to smash St Enda's but to impair most seriously, if not fatally, my public influence and utility. I shall be involved in protracted bankruptcy proceedings, with public examinations by hostile counsel, etc., etc., and it will be impossible for me to give the cause at this supreme moment any useful help. I am down and out.

Pearse was not exaggerating: his utility to the IRB was based wholly on his public reputation, for he had little to offer as a counsellor or organizer. Bankruptcy would finish him, and he was in agony over the disgrace he might suffer. "I must hold St Enda's for the sake of the cause. I could bear to see it go down gloriously by my imprisonment for a political offence, but to see it go down squalidly as the result of such a plot will be heartbreaking."

The Irish Americans knew little of Pearse's newly-acquired importance, so they had a cablegram from Clarke in his support (camouflaged against the censor). "If at all possible, Garrity should attend to Paddy's communication regarding school—it is both urgent and vital. Ask Garrity to cable Paddy at once, even if he can't see his way."[1] McGarrity saw his way, and £300 was lodged in time with Pearse's bank. Pearse's gratitude was intense—a compensation, it seems, for the peremptory tone in which he habitually clothed his petitions for financial aid. He could not stand appearing obsequious while he was in a position of weakness, but anybody who helped him weather a crisis was a noble ally to whom he could address fulsome thanks without demeaning himself. McKenna noted this.

> Pearse was a very generous man himself in little things and big, and that trait seemed to make him all the more sensitively

> grateful for any help, or even any encouragement, he got from others. He was always begging for the sake of the language, of the school, of the entire work of Ireland: in return for some slight help I was myself happy enough to be able to give him from time to time he sent me notes of thanks couched in such perfervid phrases as filled me with shame.[2]

St Enda's was saved, and with it Pearse's reputation. On 6 September he held an Aeridheacht and Volunteer Display at the Hermitage, featuring among other attractions a Cumann na mBan display, shooting competitions, Volunteer drill competitions, marches, and pipe bands. Participants included, as a gesture of solidarity, both the ICA and the Hibernian Rifles (the armed section of a small break-away group from the AOH who eventually joined forces with the insurrectionists). Holloway was there and, as usual, the darker significance of the occasion completely eluded him. Although he noted that all but the youngest boys were dressed in Volunteer uniform, he found the event worth recording only as "a glorious day's outing". To Pearse it was a show of strength.

In its own, less public way, the IRB was also showing it meant business. In May, its lapsed advisory committee on military affairs was reformed as the Military committee, briefed to draft specific plans for an insurrection. Its composition remained the same—Pearse, Kent and Plunkett. The latter took a great delight in his work and, on a trip to Germany to seek arms in April 1915, he entered into the cloak-and-dagger spirit of the thing in his manoeuvres to avoid detection. He had initially met an unenthusiastic response from the Germans. (Casement was still preoccupied with his crumbling plans to form an Irish Brigade—an idea which Pearse disliked, because it required that the men break their oath in the British army—and he denounced plans for an insurrection as folly, though he offered to join in if the IRB insisted on going ahead.) Though Plunkett's mission failed, it had begun with high hopes, and at one stage the Military committee believed that it might have a German arms shipment by September 1915—a good moment to strike, it felt, since the arrests and deportations had inflamed public opinion by this time.

The summer came and went and brought no arms, and no insurrection. Contingency plans had been made, and Pearse had secretly sent instructions to Volunteer officers throughout the country as to how they were to act in the event of war breaking out in Ireland. MacNeill did not discover that this had been done until early in September, and he became seriously worried. Hobson had long suspected that the IRB would seek to make use of the Volunteer organization to its own ends, and he tried to persuade MacNeill to call a special convention to clarify policy. MacNeill, afraid of confrontation, chose to avoid it, and as Hobson later said "after that we were standing on a powder barrel". The two factions within the Volunteers were becoming more remote from each other. Hobson was still bearing the main burden of work, though MacNeill attended most meetings and was officially editor of the *Irish Volunteer* (Hobson was the actual editor). Hobson had recruited to the paper two able military tacticians, J. J. (Ginger) O'Connell and Eimar O'Duffy, and, while Pearse and his colleagues were framing plans for open confrontation, these two wrote about the projected guerrilla campaign which was to follow the imposition of conscription. Although Pearse and MacDermott, particularly, tried to persuade the Volunteer executive to change its strategy, they were unsuccessful, and the split in the movement widened.

In September Pearse was further promoted, during a change of personnel on the eleven-man Supreme Council of the IRB. MacDermott (whose place while he was in prison had been taken by Diarmuid Lynch) had been released, and he and Clarke were re-instated as treasurer and secretary respectively. Pearse and McCartan were elected as new members. A new president was needed, as the incumbent, Deakin, always inactive, now wanted to retire from the IRB completely. McCullough, a Belfast member of the Supreme Council, relates how the new president was chosen.

> I was sitting beside Sean and I said "Sean, we will have to have a chairman. Who are we going to have?" I said, "I'm going to propose Pearse."
>
> "Oh, for the love of God, don't be stupid, don't be foolish," he said.
>
> "Why?" I said, "he is an excellent man."
>
> "We couldn't control him," he said.
>
> "And who are you going to have?"
>
> "Now leave that to Tom and myself. We will get all that fixed."
>
> And then he came along and proposed me. I said, "That's absurd. I couldn't do this. I couldn't take that job. I live in Belfast and you people are in Dublin here and things are going to happen here and how could I possibly be of any value?"
>
> "That's all right," he said, "we can fix that, you must take it," and under pressure I took it. I said,

"Very well, if I must take it I'll make myself available at an hour's notice if you send me a wire anytime you want me."[3]

His services were never required. Clarke and MacDermott had been running the IRB virtually by themselves for a long time, and the last thing they wanted was an active president to queer their pitch. At the Supreme Council a policy of insurrection was formally adopted, despite the reservations of McCartan, whose policy echoed Hobson's.

He said "Who are we ... to call a rising? Before you commit a nation to war, you should have the support of the people. We haven't the support of the people. We should gain that first." So I was in the chair, and I said, "Well, what are we organised for? 'Tis obvious this country will never do it unless we start it. It is our job to start it," I said, "to organise for it and trust the people afterwards." And he was volubly opposed.... I said Dr McCartan must get a hearing. They wouldn't listen to him.[4]

At this meeting the Military Committee became the Military Council, and its numbers were raised to five by the addition of Clarke and MacDermott. Pearse's rôle continued to be a logical extension of his Volunteer position. He dispatched Lynch to inspect suitable arms landing-places on the south-west coast. Plunkett was off on another trip, this time to America to gain help from Clan-na-Gael in procuring German arms.

On 31 October 1915, the second convention of the Irish Volunteers was held, again in the Abbey Theatre. The executive reported on its activities.

The Director of Organisation reported that a special scheme of organisation had been drawn up to suit the particular needs of the Volunteers, which had been followed with success. Its object was to combine flexibility with cohesion. The organisation of the smaller units was almost complete; that of the larger units was progressing satisfactorily. To keep the work of organisation going visits of inspection were necessary, and the Director had personally visited the better organised districts, while the Headquarters Organisers had been working in all parts of the country, and this work was going on undeterred by the periodical imprisonments of individual organisers.[5]

The headquarters staff were re-appointed to their old positions. (O'Connell was added in November as chief of inspection.) There was no discussion of the policy of the Volunteers, only a re-affirmation of the objectives of the previous convention, which were as vague as the IRB could have desired—it could make what it liked of the Volunteer commitment to "secure the abolition of the system of governing Ireland through Dublin Castle". Pearse's report to the convention necessarily avoided all mention of the most important aspect of his work, the continual elevation of IRB men to officers' positions throughout the country. Even Willie, now an IRB brother, had been promoted to captain. But the convention gave no fresh help to the IRB. Although it numbered fourteen out of the twenty members on the executive, MacNeill's position had been re-affirmed and he and Hobson were still securely in control. Pearse, as director of organisation, went as far as he dared in his appointments and in his speeches, which urged the Volunteers to lose their lives rather than their arms.

In their struggles to swing the Volunteers to a more aggressive posture, the revolutionaries from the IRB enjoyed little support from their recent ally, James Connolly. The honeymoon between the ICA and IRB was suspended when Connolly was disappointed in his hopes for a summer insurrection, and for some time he talked little of unification of forces in the republican cause. He was also disappointed by the forces of international socialism, however, and so for a time he stood alone.

> We have ere now looked hopefully to the British Trade Union Congress, but our hopes are gone. The British Empire is ruled by the most astute ruling class in the world; the British working class is the most easily fooled working class in the world.
>
> God help the poor Irish as long as they remain yoked to such a combination.

The British authorities gave the factions another push towards unity. The arrest of an Irish Volunteer organizer provoked the ICA to suggest talks with the Volunteer leaders. MacNeill, O'Connor, MacDermott and Pearse met several times with Connolly and two of his colleagues, but Connolly's insistence on a pledge of joint action if there were any further arrests prevented any agreement. MacNeill could not accept such a proposal. The abortive Volunteer-ICA talks were replaced with IRB-ICA meetings, at which Pearse was in company with Clarke, MacDermott, MacDonagh and Thomas Ashe, but no decisions were made either way. Connolly was still more impatient about insurrection than the IRB and could not accept its vague schedules. He was developing more sympathy towards, and belief in, the IRB leaders, however, and Pearse had certainly fallen under his spell by now. He had read *Labour in Irish History* several times, and read the *Workers' Republic* regularly. His earlier flirtation with the distressed workers' cause in 1913 had been consolidated by some serious study, and he was especially interested in the economic writings of James Fintan Lalor, one of the Young Irelanders. (Lalor's ideology had for years been a staple in the diet of those who supported nationalism *and* socialism.)

At a meeting in the Labour headquarters (Liberty Hall) in November 1915, to commemorate the Manchester Martyrs, Connolly gave voice to his growing impatience.

> He [Connolly] said in closing that the saying "England's difficulty is Ireland's opportunity," has been heard on a thousand platforms in Ireland. England was in no small difficulty, but since England got into difficulties the phrase had never been heard or mentioned. If Ireland did not act now the name of this generation should in mercy to itself be expunged from the records of Irish history.[6]

There was no cessation of hostilities within Volunteer headquarters. O'Connell was in his new post, and he had little time for the manner in which his associates played soldiers. Pearse wrote a glowing account of further manoeuvres of the Dublin brigade, which was sharply contradicted in a report by O'Connell. The only thing learned from the manoeuvres, he claimed, was how little the brigade knew. He wrote later, "... the effect of my review may be guessed from the fact that never from that time on ... did Pearse or MacDonagh ... take command of a side in a manoeuvre ... the fact is that Pearse and MacDonagh, Plunkett also, believed that the art of war could be studied in books."[7]

It was not surprising that a real soldier should despise the amateurism of the revolutionaries: though Plunkett had a certain flair for planning, their lack of experience rendered negligible their chances of military success. The insurrection was being designed with a different objective, however—they were interested only in an effective demonstration: Pearse's concern was to make a better showing than Tone, Emmet, the Young Irelanders or the Fenians. De Valera claimed much later that at the meeting of the Dublin commandants in March 1915 (with Daly, Kent, MacDonagh and Pearse), he was the only one who expected to survive a rising.[8] The work of infiltration of the Volunteers, of procuring arms, and of attempting to unite with the ICA was a means only to give the insurrectionists strength to hold off the inevitable defeat as long as possible, and so prolong the demonstration.

Relations between the ICA and the IRB continued to fluctuate, depending on Connolly's mood. In December he was enthusiastic. "... [There] is growing the feeling of identity of interests between the forces of real nationalism and of Labour which we have long worked and hoped for in Ireland."[9] But Pearse went too far even for Connolly in an article of December 1915, published in *Spark*. It was unsigned, and Connolly may not have known who was responsible. Called "Peace and the Gael", of anything Pearse ever wrote it is to many the most offensive, for in it his glorification of war reached a level which suggested a deranged view of the world. He may well have been inspired in its composition by the IRB's definite selection of a date for the proposed insurrection—Easter Sunday, 1916. It began on a triumphant note. "When we are old (those of us who live to be old) we shall tell our grandchildren of the Christmas of 1915 as the second Christmas which saw the nations at war for the freedom of the seas; as the last Christmas, it may be, which saw Ireland, the gate of the seas, in the keeping of the English." Of the heroism of the European war, he wrote, "It is good for the world that such things should be done. The old heart of the earth needed to be warmed with the red wine of the battlefields. Such august homage was never before offered to God as this, the homage of millions of lives given gladly for love of country." Connolly was prepared to sacrifice a few lives for the sake of the workers in Ireland, but that was as far as he went. "No, we do not think that the old heart of the earth needs to be warmed with the red wine of millions of lives. We think anyone who does is a blithering idiot. We are sick of such teaching, and the world is sick of such teaching."[10]

This hurt Pearse deeply, for he felt that Connolly should have agreed with every line. He had made a gesture in the article to the labour movement, for though his social education was recent and self-conscious, he had elevated the workers' cause into an emotional dogma. Deploring the "exploitation of the English masses by cruel plutocrats", he welcomed the war because it might kindle "in the slow breasts of the English toilers a wrath like the wrath of the French in 1798 ...".

Labour's leader had rejected Pearse's bloody offering, and his language was moderated henceforth. Such hymns to slaughter were strangely incongruous in a man who could not bear the sight of suffering,[11] and who was sickened by the sinking of the *Lusitania*. Even if he had been able to overcome his squeamishness, it is unlikely he would have been personally effective in combat: though he wore his officer's sword, he was incapable of slicing a loaf of bread. He never had occasion to use the revolver he carried after the decision on Easter as the deadline for rebellion, nor were the services of his newly appointed bodyguard—Con Colbert—required. (All members of the Military Council were provided with bodyguards at the meeting where the insurection policy was adopted.)

The decision to prepare for an insurrection was conveyed to Hobson unofficially by McCullough in December 1915, but in such vague terms that he did not take it very seriously. Although he knew there was some plot being hatched, he was still concerned to save the Volunteers and the IRB from infringing their own constitutions. Even MacNeill was aware of the need to impose some restraint on his more hasty subordinates. In the *Irish Volunteer*, at the end of December, he wrote:

> One or two instances of what may be called unwise impatience among Irish Volunteers have come to my knowledge.... Now, no man has a right to seek relief of his own feelings at the expense of his country.... We have convicted our enemies of trampling upon law and order.... We Irish Volunteers are the Defenders of law and order and loyalty. There is no reason why we should be impatient, but rather that we should go forward confidently. Our conscience is clear. Our cause is good.

It was not the IRB which was likely to display the most impatience, however. Connolly's demands for action reached a crescendo in January 1916: "... the time for Ireland's battle is NOW the place for Ireland's battle is HERE ...".[12]

He had several more conferences with the Volunteers, represented this time by Pearse and MacNeill only, and had met resistance from both to his calls for immediate insurrection. It was clear that Connolly was meditating a solo venture by the ICA, and a particularly explosive issue of the *Workers' Republic* persuaded the Military Council that it was time to tell Connolly of the plan. On 19 January, at the behest of Clarke and MacDermott, Connolly was persuaded to come to a meeting. (The Supreme Council, at a meeting in the same month, had fixed the date of its next meeting for Easter Sunday, an indication of its grip on affairs. Clarke and MacDermott made it clear that they did not wish to discuss plans with the Supreme Council and Pearse said very little about anything. Even the IRB president was kept very much in the dark. So in dealing with the Military Council, Connolly was dealing with the *de facto* rulers of the IRB.) The meeting was a remarkable affair. Connolly simply disappeared from Liberty Hall on 19 January and did not reappear until three days later. It was thought at the time that he had been kidnapped, but this has since been disproved. He was a difficult man to convince, and it took the Military Council a long time to extract a promise that he would add his forces to those of the IRB for the planned Easter Sunday insurrection. Finally he was sworn into the IRB and co-opted on to the Military Council which was now in sole charge of the operation.

Although Pearse remained the important front-man of the Military Council and continued to relay instructions to the forces in the field, he had little to do with their planning. In McCullough's opinion (and this is borne out by other evidence), the council was inspired by Clarke and dominated by MacDermott and Plunkett. Connolly had some involvement in the planning—Plunkett used to consult him. He was happy with the new arrangement, and changed his tone in the *Workers' Republic.*

> In solemn acceptance of our duty and the great responsibilities sketched thereto, we have planted the seed in the hope and belief that ere many of us are much older it will ripen and blossom into action.
>
> For the moment and hour of that ripening, that fruitful and blessed day of days, we are ready.[13]

The Military Council made contact with Clan-na-Gael in February, and Devoy notified the German authorities that action was planned for Easter Saturday, and arms should be sent to Limerick on the Friday or Saturday. On 12 February, McGarrity had a message from Pearse confirming that rifles were needed between Good Friday and Easter Sunday. It was not until 9 March that Clan-na-Gael could send Pearse and Clarke the information they awaited: "Will send 20,000 rifles, 10 machine guns, small boats to place near Tralee [Co. Kerry], between 23rd and 25 April."[14]

While the arrangements progressed, there was further trouble at Volunteer headquarters. MacNeill was being pressed by his lieutenants, Hobson, O'Connell and Sean Fitzgibbon (director of recruiting—not a headquarters post) to compel the revolutionaries to state a clear-cut policy in line with Volunteer strategy. He had already been deceived by Pearse, who told him that Connolly had been persuaded out of immediate insurrection, but gave him no further information. MacNeill was suspicious, and in mid-February he took action of a sort, which O'Connell later recorded.

> On one occasion he set out his views in great detail in a letter to Pierce. This letter Pierce read at a meeting of the Executive. On this occasion MacNeill was not able to be present, and we all took it that the letter in question was so to speak MacNeill's contribution to the discussion. There was no discussion. The excuse put for this being that this was a carefully prepared document, and that the rest of us not having had a like opportunity of systematising our ideas and putting them on paper would be at a disadvantage in considering the subject. There was a majority of this opinion and so the matter ended—with promises of full investigation later. To me, at least, it was quite plain that discussion was the last thing to be desired by some of the Executive and that no stone would be left unturned to postpone and prevent it.[15]

MacNeill's letter contained a reiteration of his view that no one should let his personal feelings override the judgement of the whole executive, but he was playing to different rules. What the IRB Military Council was planning was a deliberate exploitation of its position in the Volunteers to lead its men into an insurrection "unprepared and unaware of what they were being let in for" (Hobson). MacNeill's absence had made it possible to evade the issue, but a direct confrontation was still sought by the Hobsonites. MacNeill was pressured into calling, at last, a meeting specifically to clarify Volunteer policy, and into preparing a memorandum on Volunteer policy, to which he would demand dissent or assent. MacNeill baulked at such directness when the meeting took place: as Hobson later said, he "had many great qualities, but he would not face up to a row".[16]

When the meeting (held in March) began, MacNeill slipped the memorandum into a drawer, and the show-down evaporated.[17] There were questions about whether an insurrection was being planned, and Pearse and MacDermott explicitly denied any intention of mobilizing the Volunteers without the agreement of the executive. Embroidering their innocence, they reproached their questioners for their suspicious natures. Hobson did not believe a word of it, but with MacNeill in the chair, there was nothing more to be said. MacNeill hoped that his civilized arguments would carry sufficient weight to deter the revolutionaries, but they took them in their stride.

Although MacNeill's memorandum was not specifically discussed, the point of view it embodied was well known to the conspirators within the Volunteer leadership, and was substantially the same as expressed in the earlier letter which Pearse had read to a meeting of the IRB executive. His arguments, as one might expect from a scholar of his standing, were based on sound premises and were skilfully developed. The purpose of the Volunteers, he claimed, was to defend Ireland if conscription or any other unacceptable measures were imposed. Should this eventuality not arise, the presence in Ireland of a strong armed force, probably augmented by Irish veterans of the front, would ensure that no post-war British government could renege on the promise of Home Rule as a result of Unionist pressure. No insurrection could hope to succeed, and indeed there was strong evidence to suggest that the British authorities in Ireland were hoping to provoke a rising which would justify them in taking strong measures against the Volunteers, who were otherwise impregnable. This being the case, such action would be morally wrong.

> To enter deliberately on a course of action which is morally wrong is to incur the guilt not only of that action itself but of all its direct consequences. For example, to kill any person in carrying out such a course of action is murder. The guilt of murder in that case falls on those who have planned and ordered the general course of action or the policy which makes such action inevitable.
>
> The success which is calculated or estimated must be success in the operation itself, not merely some future moral or political advantage which may be hoped for as the result of non-success.[18]

There were trenchant blows at two of the chief elements in the the revolutionaries' logic. Firstly, at the precept that war made action desirable, because in the past "Ireland has always struck her blow too late", or "in military matters the advantage lies with the side that takes the initiative (or the aggressive)": "To put forward these or any other dogmas of the kind without associating them with the actualities, or so as to overrule the actualities, would be a proof of mental incapacity. To act on them would be madness, to act on them without otherwise justifying the action would be criminal." Secondly, he dealt with the emotive conviction that it would be a disgrace to pass up the opportunity provided by the war: "We shall be cowards if we fear any disgrace except the disgrace of doing what we know to be wrong and not doing what we know to be right."

Perhaps unknowingly, MacNeill had identified justifications for insurrection held severally by the members of the Military Council. The first assertion he rejected was that of the IRB traditionalists, the opportunistic maxim that motivated Clarke and MacDermott more fundamentally than the council's other members, and which Connolly had so recently challenged them to live up to: "England's difficulty is Ireland's opportunity." A greater spur to Pearse was the second conviction; he was being driven to insurrection less by strategy than by the spectre of humiliation. His pride, which he himself acknowledged as his major flaw, required that he live up to his own bombast and his own contempt for the passivity of his generation. Plunkett, Kent and Connolly shared this belief, though to a lesser extent. (None of them had committed himself publicly as far as Pearse.) But consistency of motivation was unnecessary to the revolutionaries: it was enough that they all have a drive to action, and that they work in concert to achieve it.

MacNeill's logic was wasted and the piece of paper it had produced would have been equally wasted, even had he been prepared to show his distrust of his subordinates by forcing them to accept or deny its propositions. They were all beyond persuasion, and even the honourable and truthful Pearse was prepared to deceive his chief-of-staff to protect a righteous cause. The rules of debate no longer applied: his emotions protected his reason from irreconcilable intrusions.

Hobson, in a later recollection, tells a story which illustrates the Pearse of early 1916: "I remember having a discussion with Pearse in a Dublin restaurant at this time, which ended with Pearse saying, as he rose from the table, 'I cannot answer your arguments, but I feel that we must have insurrection'."[19] Connolly, on the other hand, had class warfare as an intellectual talisman.

> About the same time, and in another Dublin restaurant, I had a similar conversation with James Connolly. His conversation was full of clichés derived from the earlier days of the Socialist movement in Europe. He told me that the working class was always revolutionary, that Ireland was a powder magazine and that what was necessary was for someone to apply the match. I replied that if he must talk in metaphors, Ireland was a wet bog and that the match would fall into a puddle.[20]

MacNeill and Hobson made an effort to assert themselves with the rank and file of the Volunteers by appearing at a parade on St Patrick's Day, but they had been too remote for too long. It was Pearse and the other crucially placed IRB officers who now controlled the organization.

In the months leading up to the planned insurrection, Pearse had been augmenting his literary reputation and in January 1916 he published his second collection of Irish short stories, *An Mhathair agus Sgealta Eile* (The Mother and Other Stories). It included three new tales, written the previous summer, and as a folio they did him more credit than the *Iosagan* collection, produced more than eight years previously. They did not later reach the same popularity, largely because the *Iosagan* stories were about children, and therefore suitable for schools, while these were adult reading without the subtlety to enjoy a lasting popularity with adult audiences. All three of the new offerings dealt with religion. In "Na Boithre" (The Roads), a child running away from home has a vision of the passion and death of Christ. In "An Gadaidhe" (The Thief), a child is tortured by guilt because he has stolen a doll to comfort his sick sister. Cloying to the adult palate, they yet raise issues too complex for young children. The third new story was probably the best he ever wrote. "An Dearg-Daol" (The Black Chafer) concerns a woman, cursed by a priest, whose company brings death and disaster to a peasant family. The question is left open as to whether the misfortunes are caused by accident or the curse. The chief virtue of the story lies in its representation of human misery and isolation, which Pearse was by now skilful in conveying. He thought the story his best, and regretted, with his new-found social concerns, that he had never before written about the hard life of the people.

The Mother was well received in literary circles, but Pearse was now too prominent politically to separate his two *personae*. His old colleague, Cathal O'Shannon, now also in the IRB, reviewed the stories in the *Workers' Republic*. He spoke for many of Pearse's admirers, and echoed his own religious imagery. "In the one [literature] he is a master. In the other [politics] an Apostle. And yet—and yet—high as many of us appreciate his writing is it not to-day as one of the Apostles of Revolution, Insurrection Incarnate itself, that we love him best and need him most?"[21]

With the date of the insurrection fixed, Pearse had little time left, but by dint of frenetic activity, he succeeded in writing four new pamphlets and preparing a fifth ("The Murder Machine"). The urgency of these new pamphlets required that he give up one of his commitments—*The Wandering Hawk*, an adventure story for boys which appeared from February 1915 to January 1916 in *Fianna.* The episodes he completed are a curious amalgam of Irish revolutionary sentiment and the elements of the English school story. Entertainingly written, its purpose was didactic—to recommend the principles of Wolfe Tone to the young. But there were more important things to be said about Tone, and said to a more influential audience.

The new pamphlets were more than affirmations or repetitions of what had gone before, they were a deliberate attempt to lay down a book of law for Irish nationalists. Pearse had not been a good lawyer, and spurned the whole profession, but it was as a lawyer that he framed his political testaments. His concern was to establish precedents for his intended action from a survey of the casebook of Irish separatism. Although their outlines were blurred by religious imagery (the predecessors he cites were "Fathers", speaking "gospel") his arguments, and the arrangement of evidence on which they were based, were for all the world like the case for the defence. His compulsion to establish "legal" justification for what he was about to do marked him apart from his colleagues, whose conviction ran deep enough to swamp any inner doubts they may have once had. Pearse had to prove his case, not only to others, but finally to himself. But he had a secondary purpose. As men like Tone, Davis, Mitchel and Lalor had created precedents for him, so he would continue the line for the benefit of future generations. His casebook would lay down the tradition up to 1916, and those who survived him would have a standard work on nationalism by which they could check their own consciences. The pamphlets were a *tour de force* of partisan interpretation of history, brilliantly conceived and intelligently executed, but the logical footwork and bold generalizations necessary to such an exercise confounded later analysis. Where MacNeill wrote like a scholar, with an academic concern for realities, Pearse dealt in universals which could be applied to any time and any situation. The Irish people, with their unique reverence for their history and their men of letters, were bequeathed a conundrum over which they could argue for generations.

The first of the new pamphlets, "Ghosts" (his debt to Ibsen for the title was acknowledged), reviewed a separatist tradition in Ireland reaching back to those who resisted the Norman invasion in 1169. Pearse attributed to the political and military figures of earlier generations a philosophy of nationality which had not developed until the nineteenth century.

> I make the contention that the national demand of Ireland is fixed and determined; that that demand has been made by every generation; that we of this generation receive it as a trust from our fathers; that we have not the right to alter it or to abate it by one jot or tittle; and that any undertaking made in the name of Ireland to accept in full satisfaction of Ireland's claim anything less than the generations of Ireland have stood for is null and void, binding on Ireland neither by the law of God nor by the law of the nations.

On to the modern concept of nationality Pearse grafted his own contribution, its elevation to a religion. The people are in "the image and likeness of God". (Although Pearse was still assiduous in the practices of his baptized religion, he had long since succumbed to his own unorthodox, more colourful interpretation of its basic tenets. Besides, IRB membership brought with it automatic excommunication, which he had ignored: he was unlikely to be any more worried at the prospect of accusations of blasphemy.)

> Like a divine religion, national freedom bears the marks of unity, of sanctity, of catholicity, of apostolic succession. Of unity, for it contemplates the nation as one; of sanctity, for it is holy in itself and in those who serve it; of catholicity, for it embraces all the men and women of the nation; of apostolic succession, for it, or the aspiration after it, passes down from generation to generation from the nation's fathers.

For the first time, Pearse named those ghosts who had left behind them "*a body of teaching*", which constituted their claim as fathers of the nationalist religion—Tone, Davis, Mitchel and Lalor. Parnell was a fifth: "less a political thinker than an embodied conviction; a flame that seared, a sword that stabbed".

Pearse carried his religious parallels to their logical conclusion, and there was no room for a fifth evangelist. From this point, Pearse's political writings concentrate on the first four named. The manner in which he chose them is a guide to his rapid political development over five years. Tone was the hero in the first year at the Hermitage (1910-11), because he was in the same mould as the beloved Emmet and had a vital additional attribute—his autobiography. Mitchel joined the canon within a year, when his *Jail Journal* became another favourite book. Although Pearse had always had an affection for Davis, the cultural nationalist, his enthusiasm was subdued until late 1914, when Pearse spoke at the centenary celebrations. Lalor was a very late discovery, born of a determination to find a teacher who could reconcile Pearse's nationalism with his nebulous ideas of social justice. The trail to Lalor's writings led through the columns of the labour press, and though Pearse never seemed to reach an easy command of the ideology of his hastily assimilated fourth evangelist, he nevertheless afforded him a place alongside the nationalist teachers. In "Ghosts" he was preaching the simple doctrine of separatism, and he quoted the gospels as the expression of a natural law. Though Tone, Davis and Mitchel were pure nationalists, Lalor went much further. "Ireland her own—Ireland her own, and all therein, from the sod to the sky. The soil of Ireland for the people of Ireland, to have and to hold from God alone who gave it—to have and to hold to them and to their heirs for ever, without suit or service, faith or fealty, rent or render, to any power under Heaven." Little wonder that Connolly was impressed by "Ghosts", which he said "ought to be spread by the thousand":[22] Pearse had built a bridge between their doctrines.

"Ghosts" was finished on Christmas Day 1915, and the preface made clear its purpose—to justify to present and future generations the forthcoming insurrection. "There is only one way to appease a ghost. You must do the thing it asks you. The ghosts of a nation sometimes ask very big things; and they must be appeased, whatever the cost."

Its argument was developed further in the next pamphlet, "The Separatist Idea", written in January 1916, which was a lengthy examination of Tone's view of nationality. "Now, the truth as to what a nation's nationality is, what a nation's freedom, is not to be found in the statute-book of the nation's enemy. It is to be found in the books of the nation's father." Tone merited treatment before the other evangelists. "He stands first in point of time, and first in point of greatness. Indeed he is, as I believe, the greatest man of our nation; the greatest-hearted and the greatest-minded."

In tracing Tone's gradual progress towards republicanism Pearse could justify, by implication, his own history. He had been twitted long enough over his failure to commit himself to revolution and republicanism before he was 33. Tone was a splendid vindication, for Pearse could demonstrate that he had been no quicker to adopt these doctrines, but that he too, like Pearse, could in the end represent himself as having always been a separatist at heart. It was not enough that Tone was a separatist; to establish a consistent line through the other fathers, he must also carry the seeds of socialism. Here too, the quotes provided evidence. "Our independence must be had at all hazards. If the men of property will not support us, they must fall: we can support ourselves by the aid of that numerous and respectable class of the community—*the men of no property*." This, said Pearse, was the origin of "modern Irish democracy", although in fact it represented little more than Tone's disenchantment with the failure of his class to rally to his revolutionary call. Yet it set the seal of historical respectability on Pearse's new social ideas. Emmet and Tone alike were scientific in their methods. "Both were extraordinarily able men of affairs, masters of all the details of the national, social, and economic positions in their day; and both would have been ruthless in revolution, shedding exactly as much blood as would have been necessary to their purpose."

Pearse must have felt the need for reassurance on the violent aspects of revolution. It was one thing to shout exultantly about the heroism of a distant war, quite another to contemplate the sacrifice of political bystanders at home. But then there was the final justification:

> That God spoke to Ireland through Tone and through those who, after Tone, have taken up his testimony, that Tone's teaching and theirs is true and great and that no other teaching as to Ireland has any truth and worthiness at all, is a thing upon which I stake all my mortal and all my immortal hopes. And I ask the men and women of my generation to stake their mortal and immortal hopes with me.

Pearse had yet to consider the other three evangelists. "The Spiritual Nation" was written at the beginning of February, and it treated of the philosophy of Thomas Davis. He, like the other two, was subordinate to Tone. "I have said that all Irish nationality is implicit in the definition of Tone, and that later teachers have simply made one or other of its truths explicit." Davis's contribution was to express the spiritual tradition "which is the soul of Ireland", and incidentally to justify Pearse's cultural nationalism, which Tone would have found quite incomprehensible.

> The spiritual thing which is the essential thing in nationality would seem to reside chiefly in language (if by language we understand literature and folklore as well as sounds and idioms), and to be preserved chiefly by language; but it reveals itself in all the arts, all the institutions, all the inner life, all the actions and goings forth of the nation. It expresses itself fully and magnificently in a great free nation like ancient Greece or

> modern Germany; it expresses itself only partially and unworthily in an enslaved nation like Ireland.

The Irish nation could survive as long as the repositors of the Gaelic tradition remained. Had "the last unconquered Gael" died, the nation would have died with him, for the nation would have lost its soul. "Any free state that might thereafter be erected in Ireland, whatever it might call itself, would certainly not be the historic Irish nation." Where Tone had accepted that Ireland must be free,

> Davis, accepting that and developing it, stated the truth in its spiritual aspect, that Ireland must be herself; not merely a free self-governing state, but authentically the Irish nation, bearing all the majestic marks of her nationhoood. That the nation may live, the Irish life, both the inner life and the outer life, must be conserved. Hence the language, which is the main repository of the Irish life, the folklore, the literature, the music, the art, the social customs, must be conserved.

Pearse's quotes from Davis illustrate this conviction.

> The language of a nation's youth is the only easy and full speech for its manhood and for its age. And when the language of its cradle goes, itself craves a tomb....
>
> A people without a language of its own is only half a nation. A nation should guard its language more than its territories—'tis a surer barrier, and more important frontier, than fortress or river.

Though it was easier to demonstrate Davis's cultural nationalism, it was also necessary to prove him a separatist, and this was a more difficult task, for Davis wrote little about political action. The rest of the pamphlet is a skilful analysis of Davis's writings, selected and interpreted to fit the separatist tradition. To prove Davis a revolutionary was beyond even Pearse's ability, but he argued that he would have fought if necessary.

> That Davis would have achieved Irish nationhood by peaceful means if he could, is undoubted. Let it not be a reproach against Davis. Obviously, if a nation can obtain its freedom without bloodshed, it is its duty so to obtain it. Those of us who believe that, in the circumstances of Ireland, it is not possible to obtain our freedom without bloodshed will admit thus much.

It was also difficult to portray Davis as a democrat.

> If we accept the definition of Irish freedom as "the Rights of Man in Ireland" we shall find it difficult to imagine an apostle of Irish freedom who is not a democrat. One loves the freedom of men because one loves men. There is therefore a deep humanism in every true Nationalist. There was a deep humanism in Tone; and there was a deep humanism in Davis. The sorrow of the people affected Davis like a personal sorrow. He had more respect for aristocracy than Tone had (Tone had none), and would have been less ruthless in a revolution than Tone would have been. But he was a democrat in this truest sense, that he loved the people, and his love of the people was an essential part of the man and of his Nationalism.

The case for Davis the democrat had to rest there, since the argument had perforce to be somewhat tenuous. There were no such problems with the next and last pamphlet.

"The Sovereign People", written in March 1916, dealt with Lalor and Mitchel and their social attitudes. ". . . the nation's sovereignty extends not only to all the men and women of the nation but to all the material possessions of the nation, the nation's soil and all its resources, all wealth and all wealth-producing processes within the nation. In other words, no private right to property is good as against the public right of the nation."

He went further.

> It is for the nation to determine to what extent private property may be held by its members, and in what items of the nation's material resources private property shall be allowed. A nation may, for instance, determine, as the free Irish nation determined and enforced for many centuries, that private ownership shall not exist in land; that the whole of a nation's soil is the public property of the nation. . . . A nation may . . . determine that all sources of wealth whatsoever are the property of the nation, that each individual shall give his service for the nation's good, and shall be adequately provided for by the nation, and that all surplus wealth shall go to the national treasury to be expended on national purposes, rather than be accumulated by private persons.

Pearse embraced no coherent socialist doctrine—indeed for years he had a deep distrust of socialists and syndicalists. Although he believed that a nation had the right to impose state socialism, he could not bring himself to recommend it. His sympathy for the workers' cause did not lead him to any desire for class conflict;

the nation's rulers should be truly representative of the people—not just of one triumphant class; the nation should be governed in the interests of *all* the people, and its rulers should be elected by universal adult suffrage. Yet the most rousing passage concerned the oppressed masses whom he described in terms which echoed Marxist rhetoric and obscured his own stated abhorrence of class-warfare.

> It is, in fact, true that the repositories of the Irish tradition, as well the spiritual tradition of nationality as the kindred tradition of stubborn physical resistance to England, have been the great, splendid, faithful, common people—that dumb multitudinous throng which sorrowed during the penal night, which bled in '98, which starved in the Famine; and which is here still—what is left of it—unbought and unterrified. Let no man be mistaken as to who will be lord in Ireland when Ireland is free. The people will be lord and master. The people who wept in Gethsemane, who trod the sorrowful way, who died naked on a cross, who went down into hell, will rise again glorious and immortal, will sit on the right hand of God, and will come in the end to give judgement, a judge just and terrible.

Lalor was Pearse's acknowledged inspiration here. He wrote little, but he was both a social-democrat and a revolutionary (although his major concern was with the small tenant-farmer rather than with the landless labourer or urban worker, whose plight was much worse). Lalor's nationalism had made him acceptable to many of those who feared socialism from other sources, and his often vaguely-worded pronouncements could be distorted to suit later generations espousing much more extreme doctrines. "Not to repeal the Union, then, but the conquest—not to disturb or dismantle the empire, but to abolish it utterly for ever ... not to resume or restore an old constitution, but found a new nation and raise up a free people, and strong as well as free, and secure as well as strong, based on a peasantry rooted like rocks in the soil of the land." His doctrine of ownership was that which Pearse had reiterated in "Ghosts": "... I hold and maintain that the entire soil of a country belongs of right to the entire people of that country, and is the rightful property, not of any one class, but of the nation at large, in full effective possession, to let to whom they will, on whatever tenures, terms, rents, services, and conditions they will...."

Lalor made it clear that his objective was to get rid of landlords, whose property was in Ireland but whose loyalty was to England.

Yet his words were taken up by John Mitchel (another of the Young Irelanders), John O'Mahony (of the Fenians), James Connolly and many others, who used them out of context. Pearse wrote of him with feeling, but his words lacked the lasting power of Tone's and Davis's, and Pearse seemed more attracted to him as a man of action (he had led a desperate fiasco of his own in 1849). He could not stir the emotions as could the other fathers, although his inspiration came from the same source. "The Lord God must have inspired the poor crippled recluse, for no mortal man could of himself have uttered the things he uttered."

Mitchel had similar credentials. "Mitchel was of the stuff of which the great prophets and ecstatics have been made. He did really hold converse with God; he did really deliver God's word to man, delivered it fiery-tongued." In fairness to Pearse, he may not have realized that Mitchel later spoke with an equally fiery tongue in favour of the south in the American Civil War (and defended slavery). Of all the fathers, Mitchel is the least attractive, for he was consumed by hatred of his political enemies rather than by love of his people. Pearse recognized but approved this. "Mitchel's is the last of the four gospels of the new testament of Irish nationality, the last and the fieriest and the most sublime. It flames with apocalyptic wrath, such wrath as there is nowhere else in literature." But he justified the hatred, rather speciously, as an inevitable complement of love, and as a hatred of English misgovernment rather than the English people. But Mitchel's vengeful passion blazed through Pearse's *apologia.*

> ... Can you dare to pronounce that the winds, and the lightnings, which tear down, degrade, destroy, execute a more ignoble office than the volcanoes and subterranean deeps that upheave, renew, recreate? ... In all nature, spiritual and physical, do you not see that some powers and agents have it for their function to abolish and demolish and derange—other some to construct and set in order? But is not the destruction, then, as natural, as needful, as the construction?
>
> ...
>
> The vengeance I seek is the righting of my country's wrong, which includes my own. Ireland, indeed, needs vengeance; but this is public vengeance—public justice. Herein England is truly a great public criminal. England! all England, operating through her Government; through all her organised and effectual public opinion, press, platform, pulpit, Parliament, has done, is doing, and means to do, grievous wrong to Ireland. She must be

punished; that punishment will, as I believe, come upon her by and through Ireland; and so will Ireland be *avenged*.

The gentle Pearse of ten years earlier would not have had the stomach for this, but Mitchel had accepted the gospels of Tone, Davis and Lalor, and added a further dimension, which set the precedent for Pearse's new militarism.

This denunciation of woe against the enemy of Irish freedom is as necessary a part of the religion of Irish nationality as are Davis's pleas for love and concord between brother Irishmen. The Church that preaches peace and good-will launches her anathemas against the enemies of peace and good-will. Mitchel's gospel is part of the testament, even as Davis's is; it but reveals a different facet of the truth. A man must accept the whole testament; but a man may prefer Davis to Mitchel, just as a man may prefer the gospel according to St Luke, the kindliest and most human of the gospels, to the gospel of St John.

And, with the end of "The Sovereign People", Pearse summed up the contributions of the four evangelists.

Tone is the intellectual ancestor of the whole modern movement of Irish nationalism, of Davis, and Lalor, and Mitchel and all their followers; Davis is the immediate ancestor of the spiritual and imaginative part of that movement, embodied in our day in the Gaelic League; Lalor is the immediate ancestor of the specifically democratic part of that movement, embodied to-day in the more virile labour organisations; Mitchel is the immediate ancestor of Fenianism, the noblest and most terrible manifestation of this unconquered nation.

It was not in Pearse the writer to end on an anti-climax, and composing the last words of the pamphlet at the end of March 1916, he brought his political writings to a triumphant cadence.

At the end of a former essay I set that prophecy of Mitchel's as to the coming of a time when the kindred and tongues and nations of the earth should give their banners to the wind; and his prayer that he, John Mitchel, might live to see it, and that on that great day of the Lord he might have breath and strength enough to stand under Ireland's immortal Green. John Mitchel did not live to see it. He died, an old man, forty years before its dawning. But the day of the Lord is here, and you and I have lived to see it. And we are young. And God has given us strength and courage and counsel. May He give us victory.

As he said in his preface, written on the 31st, "For my part, I have no more to say."

He wrote to his publisher with a plea. *"I want to ask you as a personal favour to me to rush these two last pamphlets through . . . so timing things as to have the 'Sovereign People' the last of the series, on sale by Monday, April 17th.* I ask you to do this for me, and you will later appreciate the reason and regard it as sufficient. *If any extra cost is involved I will see it paid."*

Though this ended Pearse's political output, he had a need to express himself in other ways, and while drafting the pamphlets he had also made his last poetic and dramatic statements—all in the same conclusive way.

From this period, his important poems were all written in English. "The Rebel" was a rather crude expression of the anger of a man determined to end the oppression of his people, and ended somewhat hysterically:

> And I say to my people's masters: Beware,
> Beware of the thing that is coming, beware
> of the risen people,
> Who shall take what ye would not give.
> Did ye think to conquer the people,
> Or that Law is stronger than life and than
> men's desire to be free?
> We will try it out with you, ye that have
> harried and held,
> Ye that have bullied and bribed, tyrants,
> hypocrites, liars!

Another, "The Fool", was his rejoinder to those who might believe him to have frittered away his talents and opportunities in the vain pursuit of dreams.

> I have squandered the splendid years that
> the Lord God gave to my youth
> In attempting impossible things, deeming
> them alone worth the toil.
> Was it folly or grace? Not men shall
> judge me, but God.

And to exonerate himself before God, as well as his people:

> O wise men, riddle me this: what if the
> dream come true?

What if the dream come true? and if
  millions unborn shall dwell
In the house that I shaped in my heart, the
  noble house of my thought?
Lord, I have staked my soul, I have staked
  the lives of my kin
On the truth of Thy dreadful word. Do
  not remember my failures,
But remember this my faith.

This plea, to be judged by motives rather than by actions, was the final settling of his religious accounts. For Pearse, although he had abandoned the doctrines (though not the practices) of conservative Irish Catholicism and adapted his deeply-felt religion to his own needs, was not so free from his background that he did not have fears about how his God might judge his deeds. Some of his companions in insurrection, like MacDonagh, were free-thinkers; others, like Connolly, had abandoned religious practices. None had Pearse's depth of commitment to Catholicism, or his obsessive need to bedeck word and action with a profusion of religious images, to demonstrate to friends, enemies and himself that God was truly on the side of the Gael.

His last play, *The Singer*, represented the culmination of his religious nationalism. It was never performed in his lifetime, and would scarcely have attracted much attention if it had, but Plunkett spoke truly when he said, "If Pearse were dead, this would cause a sensation." Written in late 1915, it portrays a revolutionary leader, MacDara, who goes off at the end of the play to sacrifice himself for the freedom of Ireland. He departs, grieving that the sacrifice has not been left to him alone, for sixteen men, including his young brother, had gone out before him. "The fifteen were too many.... One man can free a people as one Man redeemed the world. I will take no pike, I will go into the battle with bare hands. I will stand up before the Gall as Christ hung naked before men on the tree."

It is commonly denied that Pearse's plays, and *The Singer* in particular, are autobiographical, largely because to take them as such is embarrassing to his admirers; extravagances of language, and messianic utterances, are more comfortably explained away as dramatic licence, as are the doubts and self-questionings of *The Master* and *The Singer* (for MacDara, like Ciaran, has suffered a religious crisis in which he lost his faith). Obviously, the analogy between Pearse and his characters is imperfect; MacDara and

Ciaran have both travelled far and had wide experience; MacDara loves his foster-sister, Sighle (although that love he finds only after many years' absence, when he returns and judges her beauty to be "holy". The stilted dialogue which characterized all Pearse's plays is at its worst in the love-scene, for MacDara's resolution of his love is to acknowledge and sacrifice it in a higher cause). These divergences notwithstanding, the parallels are too pronounced to be ignored. MacDara is a poet, an orator and a revolutionary leader, who wishes only the opportunity to die for his people. His young brother, Colm, follows his political lead, and when they have both gone, the women are left to grieve—the allotted portion of the Pearse women. On the surface the play is a clumsy *pastiche* of classical tragedy, a struggle between love and *virtus* obeying Racinian rules, but its force lies wholly in its deeper reflection of the reality of its author's intention. Had Pearse not suffered MacDara's fate, the play would have failed.

His political, poetic and dramatic testaments safely completed, Pearse had little left to write of a personal nature. One more task had been accomplished: he had explained and justified himself, to his contemporary and his future publics. He had now to find an explanation and a justification in which his devoted simple mother, incapable of understanding his other work, could find consolation. Facing death, and knowing that he would probably take Willie with him, he composed his most famous poem, "The Mother". It was not a particularly good poem, but its associations gave it a potent tragic dimension, and its effect on Margaret Pearse was profound.

> I do not grudge them: Lord, I do not grudge
> My two strong sons that I have seen go out
> To break their strength and die, they
>   and a few,
> In bloody protest for a glorious thing,
> They shall be spoken of among their people,
> The generations shall remember them,
> And call them blessed;
> But I will speak their names to my own heart
> In the long nights;
> The little names that were familiar once
> Round my dead hearth.
> Lord, thou art hard on mothers:
> We suffer in their coming and their going;
> And tho' I grudge them not, I weary, weary

Of the long sorrow—And yet I have my joy:
My sons were faithful, and they fought.

There is bathos in the image of Margaret Pearse's two sons going out to fight: the heavy, balding schoolmaster with a sword he could not use, and the inarticulate, long-haired slight young man whose talent had been dissipated in the service of causes he could barely understand. But as always, Pearse's eloquence could raise him beyond squalid reality. In the flesh he might not measure up to the heroic figures who peopled his imagination, but in his prose he surpassed them, and became what he wanted to be. By the beginning of April he could truly claim that he had said it all. Now his commitment was ready for testing in action.

V The Lead-up to Insurrection

Preparations for Easter Sunday became more intensive from the beginning of April, and in these preparations Pearse, as director of organization of the Volunteers, was invaluable to the IRB Military Council. The brigade commandants already had instructions to make ready for a great mobilization at Easter, and had been warned that they would be involved in extensive manoeuvres. On 3 April, Pearse issued "General Orders" for the manoeuvres, which were to last for three days.

Political tension was growing. Hobson's early scepticism about the insurrection plans, of which McCullough had told him, was shaken by these recent manifestations of activity. The Castle authorities, true to the warning in MacNeill's memorandum, seemed eager to goad the Volunteers into illegal action—Blythe and Mellows had been arrested prior to deportation. In addition, MacNeill had heard from America that an Easter deadline was common knowledge there. He asked his University College Dublin colleague, MacDonagh, if such plans were being made, and was assured that the rumours were false—and again reproached for his lack of trust. In fact, MacDonagh was not yet in the confidence of the conspirators, and may not have known the truth. MacNeill believed him, but he was left with a sense of unease which was heightened by Hobson, who told him that he thought the revolutionaries were abusing their position in the Volunteers to their own ends.

MacNeill called another meeting in his house on 5 April, which was attended by all the headquarters staff except Plunkett, who was in hospital. Hobson proposed and had accepted a resolution that all important orders emanating from headquarters should in future be invalid unless counter-signed by MacNeill, Hobson, O'Rahilly, O'Connoll, Fitzgibbon and O'Connor. What they did not realize was that plans were already so far advanced that the insurrection could go on in spite of this restriction. Both Volunteer and Volunteer/IRB men in the field were now clear about their Easter orders, even if most of them did not know they would be required to fight. Even McCullough, president of the IRB and theoretical leader of any provisional government set up in an IRB revolution, did not know what was going on. Worried by rumours, he came down from Belfast to see Tom Clarke. "I said to Tom, 'What in the name of God is going to happen?' He said, 'I declare to God I know nothing more than you do. All I know is I have orders to report to Ned Daly on Sunday morning and have my arms and equipment and I have them ready.' He brought out an old revolver that would have killed him if he had fired it. And he said, 'I'm turning out.'"[1]

McCullough assumed from this that Clarke knew nothing, and went on believing it for many years afterwards. Clarke (though he left most of the practical arrangements to MacDermott) knew a great deal and, like the other members of the council, was determined that this insurrection should not suffer the fate of earlier abortive risings, ruined by informers. The charade he acted out for his president's benefit was a side-show to the pantomime staged for MacNeill by Pearse and his colleagues in the higher echelons of the Volunteers. Some of them hoped, right up to the end, that they might persuade MacNeill to march out with them, and that hope coloured all their dealings with him throughout the April preparations.

By the middle of April, there was a great deal of heart-searching at Dublin Castle: how best to meet the new militancy in the Volunteer propaganda? There was a difference of view between the civil and military authorities. The chief secretary, Augustine Birrell, and the under-secretary, Sir Matthew Nathan, although somewhat hampered by a lack of political subtlety in their lord lieutenant (Lord Wimborne), had pursued a policy of appeasement in Ireland, and were on friendly terms with Irish constitutionalist and literary leaders. They were aware of the existence in Ireland of a revolutionary group and, naturally, took a close interest in reports of subversive activities, but they opposed attempts to provoke a confrontation, and underestimated the likelihood of rebellion. Although General Lovick Friend (who commanded the

British army in Ireland) and Major Ivor Price (military intelligence officer) were less sanguine about holding off revolution with kid gloves, Nathan was still convinced, as late as 10 April, that the possibility of violence was remote. "Though the Irish Volunteers element has been active of late, especially in Dublin, I do not believe that its leaders mean insurrection or that the Volunteers have sufficient arms if the leaders do mean it."[2]

He was short of information about the extremists. Most of them, especially Clarke (whom the authorities later identified correctly as the insurrection's Grey Eminence), were closely watched by government spies—who were generally ill-informed about their strategy, however, and unable to infiltrate the tightly controlled IRB network. Price and Friend were deeply perturbed at the Volunteers' increasingly warlike posture, and their obvious success in absorbing a steady trickle of arms. There was also reason to believe that disaffected elements were manufacturing bombs and hand-grenades. (Although Dublin Castle had no information about St Enda's, Bulfin and Ryan and their young IRB comrades were hard at work in their bomb factory in the basement.) But the civil authorities were not yet prepared, despite pressure from their military colleagues, to run the risk of trying either to disarm or disband the Volunteers. MacNeill had made it very clear that such an attempt would meet armed resistance, and Birrell and Nathan had no taste for bloodshed. So although by 17 April they had information that an arms landing was fixed for Easter Saturday, and an insurrection for Easter Sunday, they discounted it as rumour and merely conveyed a warning to county inspectors in the south-west to watch the coastline.

Inadvertently, they had information more correct than even that of the IRB Military Council, which had notified the German authorities that the arms shipment should not arrive before Easter Sunday (lest it provoke the British to strike first). It was some time before they discovered that the message had been delivered too late to be passed on to the *Aud*, already heading for Ireland with its arms and no radio receiver. Sir Roger Casement (who was still hoping to prevent an insurrection) accompanied the gun-running ship, aboard the submarine U19.

The Military Council was well aware that its activities were under scrutiny by military intelligence, and they soon found a way to turn the Castle's reputation for vigilance to their advantage. The news was broken that a document had been smuggled out by a clerk in the Castle, giving details of an order of General Friend to disarm the Volunteers and arrest most of their leaders. MacNeill was told of it. "The document, which I afterwards ascertained to be not genuine, was planted on me by a carefully thought out method. I was first told of its existence and that certain persons expected to be able to secure it or a copy of it. Printed copies were got out early in Holy Week." The paper became public property when a copy was read at a meeting of the Dublin Corporation. Although the Castle authorities denounced it as a complete fabrication, and Hobson had severe doubts as to its authenticity, MacNeill believed in it and had copies circulated throughout the Volunteer organization.

There is still controversy over the provenance of the document, but there can be little serious doubt. Plunkett, now out of hospital, had dreamed up the gambit to incite the Volunteers in general and MacNeill in particular, and had arranged for the printing. It was he who arranged for it to be "planted" on MacNeill, and he who raised it at meetings of the headquarters staff. Hobson, writing of it later, was understandably bitter. "Most of us were bending all our energies to outwitting the common enemy, but Plunkett devoted his talents to outwitting his friends. It must, however, be remembered that he was in a very advanced stage of T.B. and that his condition was far from normal."[3]

MacDermott was in on the subterfuge, but it is by no means certain that all the Military Council knew that the document was a forgery. MacDonagh, co-opted on to the council as its seventh member a few days before the document was first produced, insisted on its authenticity at a meeting with his command on the Wednesday before Easter—and he was not a man who was happy with deceit. Indeed his main fault as a conspirator was his inability to keep his mouth shut. At the same meeting (an informer reported to the Castle), MacDonagh said to his men, "... we are going on Sunday.... Boys, some of us may never come back."

The Volunteers were on their guard against the threat implicit in the document, and so the work of the Military Council was facilitated. Instructions continued to be sent out to hand-picked IRB men, who were now being told the true purpose of the "manoeuvres". McCullough heard of it by accident. Although he had a promise from Pearse that he would be given two weeks' notice of an insurrection, the council had decided that paucity of members made Ulster a non-runner, and had therefore kept the Belfast contingent—and the IRB president—in ignorance. Furious at the apparent duplicity of his close friend MacDermott, McCullough spent some days hunting him down. He finally found him, and was enraged by MacDermott's attempts to put off talking to him.

> "You'll see me now! You have been avoiding me for the last two days. I want to know what's happening, and I'm entitled to know. I bloody well want to know," and I turned the key in the door. "Now," says I, "you have got to tell me."
>
> "All right," says he. "I'll tell you what's going to happen," and he told me what had been arranged. He told me a cock and bull story of probably a German submarine coming up the Liffey, and that the Germans were going to send us at least 250 officers, and other things. I don't remember what the rest was, but it was all to me as I say a cock and bull story. And to me says he, "Well, what are you going to do? What do you think of it?" And I said,
>
> "Well, Sean, in truth," I said, "it looks to me like murder and suicide."
>
> "And what are you going to do?"
>
> "Well," I said, "if you are going to turn out what can I do but turn out my men and do my best. But," said I, "if I live through this, Sean, I'll have something to say to you and Tom Clarke." And he laughed, and threw his head back and said,
>
> "I don't think you need bother about that because probably neither of us will live through it."[4]

McCullough had reacted as MacDermott hoped. A major part of the council's strategy was to force upon those outside their counsels an acceptance of the inevitability of insurrection. It was this hope that kept them talking to MacNeill, who, they believed, could be brought out to join them if he once accepted there was nothing he could do to prevent the coming battle.

On Holy Thursday O'Connell and Eimar O'Duffy, the two military strategists of the Volunteers, came to Hobson to tell him they were certain that the Volunteers were going to be led into action the following Sunday by certain officers acting on Pearse's instructions. The three went to MacNeill's house and roused him from bed, and they all set off for St Enda's, where they arrived at 2:00 am on Good Friday. MacNeill recalled:

> I told Pearse what I knew of these orders and that they showed the intention of an immediate rising. Then for the first time I learned by Pearse's admission that the rising was intended. I told him that I would use every means in my power except informing

> the govt, to prevent the rising. He said I was powerless to do so, and that my countermand would only create confusion. I said that the responsibility in that case was not mine, but his. I then reproached him with keeping me in the dark as to his purpose. He justified this action on two grounds, first because ... he and those with him feared to approach me on the subject, and secondly because the Volunteers were none of my making, that they really originated from another organisation and found it advisable to make use of me. I contested both points, and ended the argument by leaving with the repeated declaration that I would do all that was honestly possible to prevent the rising.

At the same meeting Pearse told Hobson that as a sworn member of the IRB he was bound to help with the insurrection, to which Hobson retaliated by referring Pearse to the IRB constitution's requirement of popular support. MacNeill and his colleagues left St Enda's, and Hobson and O'Connell were given authority to cancel all orders for any Volunteer activity over the weekend. O'Connell set off for Cork, carrying his instructions directly to the field, and Hobson went to work to draft the countermand of all Pearse's orders for the rest of the country.

Pearse had not accepted MacNeill's word as final and he left home to consult his council colleagues. Later on Good Friday morning he arrived at MacNeill's house with MacDermott and MacDonagh, and MacDermott had an interview with MacNeill in his bedroom. According to MacNeill's account of the meeting, MacDermott told him that an arms shipment was due at any time, and MacNeill recognized that this would inevitably force a confrontation between the Volunteers and the army. "If that is the state of the case," he said, "I'm in with you." But MacDermott, when he went down to Pearse and MacDonagh, told them that MacNeill had abdicated as chief-of-staff. MacNeill denies making any such statement, and it was certainly in keeping with MacDermott's usual methods that he should have been prepared to stiffen the resolve of his colleagues by deceiving them. He had in any case already achieved his objective: Hobson, busily writing out orders in the Volunteer office and organizing the destruction of its records, received a note from his chief-of-staff telling him to take no further action. In Hobson's view this was an example of MacNeill's characteristic vacillation: certainly, MacNeill's behaviour throughout Holy Week was not distinguished by any great tenacity or clarity of purpose. Hobson was left helplessly fuming in his office, while MacDermott circulated throughout the country yet another order, signed by MacNeill, stating that Volunteers should stand ready to defend themselves against suppression by the army.

Pearse, like the rest of the Military Council, had a great deal to occupy him during these frenzied days. The meetings themselves were time-consuming, but, additionally, the paper-work always came down heavily on the director of organization, and fresh orders confirming the mobilization had to be issued from St Enda's. With MacNeill's supposed resignation, Pearse was by common consent chief-of-staff of the Volunteers, and his orders were so signed. Captain W. J. Pearse was drafted in to help: Willie had for some time been on his brother's staff. He wrote on Patrick's behalf to Sean T. O'Kelly, also a captain under Pearse's command.

Dublin Brigade: Easter Manoeuvres, 1916

You will report yourself to me at temporary Headquarters, Beresford Place, at the hour of 4 p.m. on Sunday next, 23rd inst. (Easter Sunday) and hold yourself in readiness to act on the Staff of Commandant P. H. Pearse, Acting G.O.C. Dublin Brigade, during the Easter manoeuvres.

You will provide yourself with a bicycle, a Street map of Dublin City, a road map of the Dublin District, and a field message book. You will carry full arms and ammunition, full service equipment (including overcoat) and rations for eight hours.

You will acknowledge receipt of this order by returning, by hand, to me at St Enda's College, Rathfarnham, the annexed form duly filled in and signed.

William Pearse
Capt.
Acting Chief of Staff[5]

Patrick Pearse was too embroiled in the complexities of these days to consider the position he was putting Willie in by nominating him acting chief-of-staff. Despite his poem to his mother about the sacrifice of her two sons, he hoped in less dramatic moments that Willie would survive him.

If the Military Council had (temporarily, as it turned out) wheedled MacNeill over to its side, it knew better than to attempt similar tactics with the redoubtable Hobson. Quite apart from the irritation he was feeling over the trickery he could see all around him, he had said his piece at a Cumann na mBan meeting on Palm

Sunday: to sacrifice the innocent for personal glory was utterly wrong. On Friday evening, he was kidnapped by his IRB colleagues, and kept under guard until Easter Monday, when he was released and urged to join the insurrection. Consistent to the last, he refused to be railroaded into support of an action he condemned, and by his intransigence he removed himself from Irish politics for good. His dedication for his whole adult life to the cause of Irish independence had been more single-minded and practical than that of any of his contemporaries. If the common denominator in men like Pearse, MacDonagh and Plunkett was an excess of imagination, Hobson's lack of the quality was an impediment; his failure to predict the long-term effect the rising would have on Irish popular opinion was an error of judgement for which he paid dearly. O'Rahilly, when he realized later in the evening that Hobson had been taken, burst in on Pearse in his study at St Enda's, waving a revolver and shouting, "Whoever kidnaps me will have to be a quicker shot!" He was eventually calmed by a lengthy interview and persuaded to leave.

Prospects for the rising looked good by the evening of Good Friday. MacDermott also had orders to issue—MacCurtain and MacSwiney, commandants in Cork, replied, "Tell Sean we will blaze away while the stuff lasts." The stuff was to be more limited than the plotters had hoped: the *Aud* had arrived too soon, Casement was captured, and the arms had gone down with the ship, which its German captain had scuttled. Pearse was summoned from St Enda's very late in the evening, to a conference in Liberty Hall, where he heard from Connolly about the *Aud*—news which he and MacDermott passed on to MacNeill on Saturday morning. MacNeill was further convinced by this information that a bloody reckoning must result, and saw no reason to change his orders of the previous day. He received another visitor that morning—Joseph Plunkett, who came to persuade him to put his name to a proclamation. MacNeill refused to sign anything without seeing it, for he was still wary of the Military Council's wiles. He was called on later in the day by O'Rahilly and Fitzgibbon, supporters of the Hobson policy, who wanted to find out from MacNeill what was going on (the whole period is characterized by groups and individuals operating on partial information). They brought disturbing news.

Fitzgibbon, who had been sent by Pearse earlier in the week to make arrangements concerning the arms landing, had been assured that the whole affair had MacNeill's blessing. Pearse had pushed his luck too far: he had chosen Fitzgibbon for the mission because he had been prominent and successful in the Kilcoole gun-running of 1914, but Fitzgibbon had never joined the IRB, and was loyal to his chief-of-staff. He also told MacNeill that the Castle document was a forgery, and this double revelation of treachery was too much. MacNeill, convinced by O'Rahilly and Fitzgibbon that it was not too late to call off the rising, went with them to St Enda's to tax Pearse with his deceit, and to announce his intention yet again to countermand his orders. (Pearse had arrived home shortly before, exhausted by the events of the previous couple of days, to be met by his worried sister Margaret. She was no doubt perturbed by all the comings and goings, but was much soothed by Patrick's assurance that he had found time to receive communion.)[6] Pearse dropped all pretence, and challenged MacNeill: "We have used your name and influence for what they were worth, but we have done with you now. It is no use trying to stop us: our plans are all made and will be carried out."

Although Pearse asserted that he had no chance of having his orders obeyed, MacNeill determined to draft a new set of instructions to the field. He called a meeting at a friend's house, summoning everyone he thought might be able to assist him. There was some harassment by Plunkett and MacDonagh, but Griffith, Fitzgibbon, O'Rahilly and others were there to advise the agitated MacNeill, who finally composed an order which went some way to resolving the confusion in the Volunteers' ranks—temporarily. "Volunteers completely deceived. All orders for special action are hereby cancelled, and on no account will action be taken." This was despatched by messenger to field officers, and the countermand published in the *Sunday Independent* of Easter Sunday.

The unknown factor in everybody's calculations was the attitude of the Castle. The revolutionaries, convinced that the capture of Casement would lead to their arrest, were dead set on early action. MacNeill believed that such trouble could yet be averted. In fact, the conspirators were right: plans for their arrest and internment in England had already been prepared. Wimborne had summarized his policy in a letter to Birrell.

> The evidence is now sufficient for any measure we think desirable.... The whole lot of them could be arraigned for associating with the King's enemies and there is our internment policy safely in port. I am afraid if you stir up the hornets' nest and leave the hornets that we may have serious trouble.... I want to implicate as many of the Sinn Feiners [a commonly used generic title for revolutionaries—although Sinn Fein had no part

in the rising] as I can with the landing—the invasion, in fact. It has changed everything, and justifies our altering our attitude.[7]

But the Castle saw no need for unseemly haste: MacNeill's countermanding order reassured them of the unlikelihood of immediate insurrection, so they held their hand.

The Military Council had not given up hope of salvaging the situation. Fearful of arrest, the Pearse brothers had left St Enda's for the night. Desmond Ryan witnessed their departure. "It was amusing to watch Pearse's submissive affection to his mother. Even on Easter eve, when she said good-bye to him at the Hermitage gate and he was marching down into Dublin, ready to tackle the greatest British Army known to history, she had said: 'Now, Pat, above all, do nothing rash!' and he had dutifully replied: 'No, mother.'"[8]

Patrick Pearse had given up hope of adhering to the original military plan—to occupy crucial buildings in Dublin and hold them against attack. He walked to Liberty Hall with Connolly for a conference, and on the way they met an IRB colleague. Pearse, despondent, said they would have to retreat to the west, but Connolly corrected him—on the contrary, they were going to fight in the streets of Dublin. Connolly, yet again, was a lonely voice urging immediate action, for Pearse and MacDonagh had agreed that the countermanding order necessitated a short delay for reorganization. They had to prevent Connolly from bringing out the ICA in an unconvincing demonstration which could only end in their annihilation and put paid to any plans for a bigger rising. Pearse talked the situation over with MacDermott, MacDonagh and Plunkett that night, after midnight, and, believing that the rising should be postponed, they called a meeting of the Military Council the following morning.

The meeting was held at Liberty Hall. In the event, it was Tom Clarke who proved most difficult to convince in favour of even a day's postponement. He was sure that to go ahead with the original plans, to the original timetable, would be the least confusing action for the men in the field, and that once the news of the rising was out, MacNeill's veto would be ignored by the Volunteers at large. He was overruled and, to his grief, found even MacDermott voting against him. Two decisions were taken. First, to allay suspicion, dispatches should be sent confirming MacNeill's countermand. Second, the rising would take place a day late, on Easter Monday, and further dispatches sent on Sunday night would convey that information to the officers outside Dublin. At 1 pm the first messages were sent out. The Pearse brothers returned, apprehensive and dejected, to St Enda's. The long-appointed moment had come and gone, and the fierce elation for which the revolutionaries had long been preparing themselves had dissolved into confusion and doubt. At 5:05 pm Patrick Pearse sent a note to MacNeill. "Commandant MacDonagh is to call on you this afternoon. He countermanded the Dublin parades to-day with my authority. I confirmed your countermand as the leading men would not have obeyed it without my confirmation."

MacDonagh was uncomfortable at this meeting: MacNeill found him uncharacteristically reserved. But he persuaded MacNeill that the insurrection was finally cancelled, and left—his deceit heavy on his shoulders. He was of too generous a nature to leave MacNeill's position open to misinterpretation, and after he left he wrote a statement with a twin purpose: to justify them both in their personal decisions.

> I have had a long conversation with MacNeill and Sean Fitzgibbon upon many aspects of the present situation. I hope that I have made clear to them my loyalty to Ireland, my honour as an Irish Volunteer, and also—a thing which I could not for obvious reasons state definitely—my intention to act with my own Council, and the position of that Council.
>
> My future conduct may be different from anything now anticipated by MacNeill and Fitzgibbon, two honest and sincere patriots, though, I think, wrong in their handling of the present situation and in their attitude to military action. They and my countrymen must judge me on my conduct. I have guarded secrets which I am bound to keep. I have, I think, acted honourably and fairly by all my associates. I have had only one motive in all my actions, namely, the good of my country.

At 8 pm Pearse dispatched couriers bearing a simple message for delivery during the night.

> We start operations at noon to-day, Monday. Carry out your instructions.
>
> P. H. PEARSE

CHAPTER SEVEN

THE RISING

I EASTER MONDAY

Even on the eve of insurrection, Pearse was not free of mundane duties. He spent some of his last hours in the Hermitage arranging his papers and settling, as far as possible, his complicated personal affairs. A letter to Mrs Bloomer, written that evening, was a fitting postscript to a decade of financial juggling: "I enclose you chq. £5 as a further instalment. Wishing you a very happy Easter."[1]

He left home on Easter Monday morning with Willie, already rather weary, and they were seen cycling through Dublin, Patrick's greatcoat bulging over his kit and provisions.[2] For his last dramatic performance he had paid his usual attention to costume. While many comrades-in-arms were carelessly turned-out, Pearse carried a repeating pistol, ammunition pouch and canteen, and wore his smart green Volunteer uniform with a matching slouch hat and a sword. While the Dublin troops were assembling at pre-arranged points around the city, the brothers made their way to Liberty Hall, to meet the core of the newly-formed provisional government —Connolly, Clarke, Plunkett and MacDermott.

Two appointments had been made from among the seven members of the Military Council. The previous day all their signatures had been affixed to the proclamation which MacNeill had refused to sign unread. Clarke's name led the rest, in deference to his acknowledged seniority among the revolutionaries. It was now certain that MacNeill would not be available in name or person to fill the two posts of president of the provisional government and commander-in-chief of the army of the Irish Republic (a hybrid of Volunteers, ICA and Hibernian Rifles). It was desirable that the same man occupy both positions. MacDonagh and Kent would be isolated from headquarters, in their respective outposts at Jacob's Biscuit Factory and the South Dublin Union (a workhouse), and were anyway small beer politically. That left a choice of five.

Connolly was ruled out as unacceptable for either position—his political *credo* would set an unfortunate tone, and public opinion was important for the time being, even if none of the conspirators survived to see the implementation of a government programme of any colour; and the Volunteers, who were numerically by far the more important wing of the army, had a right to a Volunteer as their nominal head. Plunkett was dying from consumption. MacDermott and Clarke had avoided taking military rank, and although the latter had unassailable claims on the presidency, he was still prompted by his nature and experience to shun the limelight so long as there was a better-equipped public personality to hand. Pearse was the obvious candidate. (No attention was paid to the Military Council's unfortunate sleeping partner, Denis McCullough, *ex officio* president of the Irish Republic. At that moment McCullough was vainly trying to find some support in Belfast, to obey stale and unconfirmed orders from Connolly and Pearse to transport his men to join in the Western insurrection.)

The revolutionaries had made some small provision for the day of victory, however unlikely. A provisional civil government, less abhorrent to the people than they were, had been selected—Alderman Tom Kelly, Arthur Griffith, William O'Brien, Mrs Sheehy-Skeffington and Sean T. O'Kelly (Sinn Fein, Sinn Fein, Labour, Suffragette-socialist and Sinn Fein respectively). It is most unlikely that any of these prominent citizens knew of the august rôle for which they had been chosen—except O'Kelly, who was secretly a member of the IRB, and was to suffer some anguish after his arrest lest the British authorities should have discovered his "importance": in case Tom Kelly refused the chair, Sean T. was to direct the civil government.

Pearse found himself president and commander-in-chief (or, as he described himself throughout, "Commandant-General, Commanding in Chief, Army of the Irish Republic") more because of an accident of circumstances than because his confederates recognized his right to the laurels. Connolly, styled commandant of the Dublin Districts, was effectively the military *supremo*, with the c-in-c's automatic endorsement. Pearse had considerable personal advantages for the role of president, however. He had drafted the proclamation, and would be in his element writing all further missives to the Irish people, whose moderate majority would be marginally more likely to accept propaganda from a man of Pearse's academic and literary standing, than from a felon like Clarke. And Pearse had the demeanour for the job, unlike any of the other front-runners; for all his inadequacies as a soldier-statesman, he at least looked the part. At 36, even with the onset of middle-age spread, and his eye disfigurement, his imposing height and his solemn, noble features were enhanced by a carefully cultivated stately bearing.

The Dublin City Volunteers were mobilized on MacDonagh's orders as brigade commandant. Apart from MacDonagh's and Kent's units, the 2nd and 4th respectively, Ned Daly's 1st battalion was to occupy the Four Courts, de Valera's 3rd battalion Boland's Mill, and a fifth battalion was to operate in North County Dublin, outside the city. A further group of about 60 Volunteers, most of whom had spent months training at the Plunkett's house at Kimmage (a virtual arsenal), was to man the headquarters at the General Post Office (GPO). They were to be joined by a section of the ICA, which had been split into three: the second section, under Michael Mallin and Constance Markievicz (Connolly's two lieutenants) was to occupy St Stephen's Green with a group of the Fianna, and the other was assigned to make an attempt on Dublin Castle. Carefully though Plunkett had drawn up his plans, they were intentionally only defensive, and the only question in doubt was how long the insurrectionists could hold out against the British army. Plans for the rest of the country were already in chaos, and no one could begin to calculate whether there would be any rising outside Dublin.

Pearse arrived at Liberty Hall on a sunny Monday morning to complete with his colleagues the arrangements for the headquarters contingent. Just before noon they stepped out to survey their troops and lead the march on the GPO. Other commandants were discovering elsewhere in the city that the confusion of the previous week had taken a heavy toll of Volunteers before a shot was fired: many of them were too frightened or too bewildered to turn up. The headquarters forces, by any estimate, numbered less than 150 men.

Morale was boosted by the unexpected arrival of The O'Rahilly, who had spent his weekend driving around the east and midlands thinning the ranks with MacNeill's cancellation, but had decided to yield to the inevitable. He leaped from his touring car and is reported to have run up the steps with the first memorable line in the drama: "Well, I've helped to wind up the clock—I might as well hear it strike." Any optimism Pearse felt at O'Rahilly's entrance was swiftly dispelled by an equally unexpected arrival—his sister, Mary Brigid. Long excluded from family counsels, she had learned late of her brother's activities and came to remonstrate. To the general embarrassment she bustled up to the commandant-general and cried, "Come home, Pat, and leave all this foolishness!"[3] Connolly shattered the painful tableau with a bellowed command to the men to form fours, and Pearse, ignoring his sister as best he could, silently moved to his side to head the column.

Dublin was quite accustomed to shows of strength by its part-time armies, and any urgency in the march to the GPO was in the hearts and minds of the knowing participants (many of the rankers anticipated nothing more taxing than a route march). Behind Pearse, Connolly, a squat figure in impeccable uniform and highly-polished leggings, strode beside the emaciated Plunkett, his chief-of-staff, whose throat was enveloped in bandages and whose hands glittered with rings. Close to death, he was flamboyant to the last, and had unsheathed his sabre before the group advanced. Clarke walked apart from the column, a spare grey man, side-by-side with his friend MacDermott, who leaned heavily on his cane. The "uniforms" of the troops were in most cases no more than some token badge of their military calling—a cap, a bandolier, a pair of puttees—quite often worn with a best Sunday suit. They carried an exotic assortment of rifles, shotguns, picks and spades, and some made shift with the traditional Irish implement of insurrection, the home-made pike.

Dublin's GPO, recently refurbished, was a fine century-old building, with a classical columned portico rising to the top of its three generous storeys. A few clusters of citizens watched incuriously as the procession came to a halt before its objective (selected largely because it was the acknowledged centre of Dublin—city businesses often advertised themselves as "so many paces from the GPO"). The O'Rahilly's motor car probably excited more admiration than the patchwork army.

Connolly shouted "Left Turn, Charge!" and the troops poured in, scattering panic-stricken staff and customers alike, who rushed for the door. The only identifiable foemen, a British lieutenant and an elderly policeman, were taken prisoner by Plunkett's young *aide-de-camp*, Michael Collins, an ex British civil servant who was to prove himself in action as an excellent soldier. At Pearse's order, a party was sent to the upper storeys, where they found a guard of seven soldiers, impressively armed with rifles, but no ammunition. Downstairs, Connolly was already in action and his voice boomed around the building as he detailed men to smash the windows, fortify them and barricade the doors. Quite apart from tactical considerations, the men's morale was boosted by the activity: Connolly (an ex member of the British army) was emerging as a natural field commander. Plunkett, although he occasionally roused himself to study the strategic state-of-play, lay on a mattress for days, too ill to act. Pearse bore himself well from the beginning, but had little to offer in the way of tactical instructions.

He was to spend most of the week doing what he always did—writing, talking and thinking.

Pearse's first talk was with Clarke and MacDermott, for whom the insurrection was, throughout, a game of policies rather than bullets. As they discussed upstairs the implications of the morning's activities, Connolly down below realized that in the excitement of leaving Liberty Hall an important symbol had been left behind—the flags. Finding Sean T. O'Kelly, Pearse's aide, with nothing to do he sent him off to retrieve them. (O'Kelly was little needed by Pearse, and he was to spend most of the week running errands for all and sundry.) The flags were essential props for the proclamation of an Irish Republic, due to be staged at the first possible moment.

Two flags were raised over the GPO in the place of their British equivalents. One was green, with a golden harp in the centre, and bore the legend "Irish Republic", in gold and white Irish lettering. The other, green, white and orange, was the tricolour later adopted as the nation's official flag. Connolly emerged to admire the effect and to set men pasting up copies of the proclamation in the area. Pearse's rôle was preordained: as president and as orator, it was his job to announce to the citizens of Dublin that they had a new government. For several years he had spoken almost exclusively to sympathetic audiences: the few hundred random bystanders in Sackville Street were a very different proposition. Incredulous, amused and hostile by turns, they offered no encouragement. Stephen MacKenna, one of his few supporters outside the GPO recorded the scene.

> . . . very pale he was, very cold of face, as he scanned the crowd, the indifferent-seeming crowd that at times and in places warmed only to show positive hostility. I saw him . . . read the Proclamation of the Irish Republic: but for once his magnetism had left him; the response was chilling; a few thin, perfunctory cheers, no direct hostility just then; but no enthusiasm whatever; the people were evidently quite unprepared, quite unwilling to see in the uniformed figure, whose burning words had thrilled them again and again elsewhere, a person of significance to the country.[4]

But Connolly, at least, was moved. Taking Pearse's hand he said, "Thanks be to God, Pearse, that we've lived to see this day." And as the posting of the proclamation on the columns of the GPO began, the unlikely allies turned and re-entered the building.

The proclamation was mainly Pearse's work, approved in

discussion with the rest of the Military Council, and amended slightly. In its opening paragraphs it echoed Emmet's proclamation of 1803, which had borne the banner:

THE PROVISIONAL GOVERNMENT
TO
THE PEOPLE OF IRELAND

Though the appeal to the Irish people could be couched in similar terms in 1916, it had to offer more than the simple commitment to establish "a free and independent republic in Ireland". A provisional government including James Connolly could not avoid mention of its social responsibilities, and the proclamation therefore dealt not only with the separatist tradition, but also with the more recent concept of the sovereign people: nor was it devoid of a religious overtone.

POBLACHT NA h-EIREANN
THE PROVISIONAL GOVERNMENT
OF THE
IRISH REPUBLIC
TO THE PEOPLE OF IRELAND

IRISHMEN AND IRISHWOMEN: In the name of God and of the dead generations from which she receives her old tradition of nationhood, Ireland, through us, summons her children to her flag and strikes for her freedom.

Having organised and trained her manhood through her secret revolutionary organisation, the Irish Republican Brotherhood, and through her open military organisations, the Irish Volunteers and the Irish Citizen Army, having patiently perfected her discipline, having resolutely waited for the right moment to reveal itself, she now seizes that moment, and supported by her exiled children in America and by gallant allies in Europe, but relying in the first on her own strength, she strikes in full confidence of victory.

We declare the right of the people of Ireland to the ownership of Ireland and to the unfettered control of Irish destinies, to be sovereign and indefeasible. The long usurpation of that right by a foreign people and government has not extinguished the right, nor can it ever be extinguished except by the destruction of the Irish people. In every generation the Irish people have asserted their right to national freedom and sovereignty; six times during the past three hundred years they have asserted it in arms. Standing on that fundamental right and again asserting it in arms in the face of the world, we hereby proclaim the Irish Republic as a Sovereign Independent State, and we pledge our lives and the lives of our comrades in arms to the cause of its freedom, of its welfare and of its exaltation among the nations.

The Irish Republic is entitled to, and hereby claims, the allegiance of every Irishman and Irishwoman. The Republic guarantees religious and civil liberty, equal rights and equal opportunities to all its citizens, and declares its resolve to pursue the happiness and prosperity of the whole nation and of all its parts, cherishing all the children of the nation equally, and oblivious of the differences carefully fostered by an alien Government, which have divided a minority from the majority in the past.

Until our arms have brought the opportune moment for the establishment of a permanent National Government, representative of the whole people of Ireland and elected by the suffrages of all her men and women, the Provisional Government, hereby constituted, will administer the civil and military affairs of the Republic in trust for the people.

We place the cause of the Irish Republic under the protection of the Most High God, Whose blessing we invoke upon our arms, and we pray that no one who serves that cause will dishonour it by cowardice, inhumanity, or rapine. In this supreme hour the Irish nation must, by its valour and discipline, and by the readiness of its children to sacrifice themselves for the common good, prove itself worthy of the august destiny to which it is called.

Signed on behalf of the
Provisional Government:
THOMAS J. CLARKE,
SEAN MAC DIARMADA, THOMAS MACDONAGH,
P. H. PEARSE, EAMONN CEANNT,
JAMES CONNOLLY, JOSEPH PLUNKETT.

Within the Post Office Connolly's dynamism had established him firmly as the source of orders and the solver of problems. Pearse, lacking any common language with the soldiers, was completely out of his depth: though the men were bolstered up by his air of calm confidence, Connolly looked to more practical types, like O'Rahilly, for support. The contrast was not lost on their subordinates. Michael Collins later described his reaction. "Of Pearse and Connolly I admire the latter most. Connolly was a realist, Pearse the direct opposite. There was an air of earthy directness about Connolly. It impressed me. I would have followed him through hell had such action been necessary. But I honestly doubt very much if I would have followed Pearse—not without some thought anyway."[5]

Another of the GPO complement, W. J. Brennan-Whitmore (ex British army), was sent by Connolly with a small group of men to set up an outpost between the GPO and Amiens Street Station—work which involved long hours of labour in breaking through party walls to provide an "inside thoroughfare" through the block, and improvising a barricade across the distressingly wide street. Relating the episode ten years later, Brennan-Whitmore could still remember his exasperation at the "acquisitive element" in the civil populace, who helped themselves to those portions of the barricade—bicycles, particularly—that took their fancy, as soon as the hard-worked insurgents turned their backs. Brennan-Whitmore had a highly-developed sense of military etiquette, and was less than inspired by Pearse's visit to his newly-established area headquarters when the work was done. Pearse chatted with him for ten minutes or so about the general situation, and went back across the street to the GPO: "In no sense could his visit be described as an inspection". He had greater satisfaction from Connolly, who saluted, nodded a greeting and reprimanded him on the inadequacies of the barricade: Pearse's gratitude for any effort in the cause inhibited his critical faculty.

Within an hour after the issuing of the proclamation, rumours were already rife throughout headquarters, rumours about German submarines, Turkish landings, and Volunteer victories throughout the country. There was also speculation, anticipatory relish mixed with awe, about how long it would take to provoke the British army into action. Shortly after one o'clock they had their answer, when a company of Lancers on horseback (who had been in the area on a routine mission) charged down Sackville Street in formation, sabres drawn and carbines holstered. They met a ragged volley of fire, for not all the Post Office troops were disciplined enough to await the orders of Connolly and O'Rahilly. Four Lancers were hit, and the rest of the company fled in disorder. There was jubilation inside the GPO at the proven mortality of the enemy; but the rebels had committed themselves completely now, and the next time they would face more than British arrogance: the work of strengthening the defences continued. The group had now been joined by the Rathfarnham Volunteer company, which included the Dogs (on whose breasts Mrs Pearse had pinned miraculous medals), and their numbers had been swollen to almost 200. Foraging parties were sent out to commandeer food, bedding and medical supplies, many of them offering in return receipts promising compensation by the Irish Republic—received with ill grace by local shop and hotel managers. Desmond Fitzgerald, a young poet and O'Rahilly's adjutant (who had shared his doubts about the insurrection), was later sent out by Pearse to pay cash for these supplies, for Pearse, who was to bear the nominal responsibility for leaving large parts of Dublin in ruins, was still concerned to do the correct thing and show the rebels to be men of honour in all their dealings.

There were already several casualties in the post office—victims of over-zealous window-breaking and untrained handling of firearms—and the Pearse brothers had shown themselves properly concerned and distressed by them. Willie (Pearse's other aide) was by his brother's side throughout most of the rising, and though he exhibited the same calmness, he looked sad and pale. His temperament was wholly unsuited to the atmosphere of war, but his convictions, however vicariously acquired, did not betray him.

There was exciting news within the next hour from the dispatch riders who were arriving from the other commands in the city. The small ICA party detailed to attack Dublin Castle was thought to be in control there. All the other men were in their pre-arranged positions, sealing off the main routes to the GPO, and Daly's men had shot two more Lancers (a different detachment) and captured the rest. Other news was equally encouraging, although it was already clear that there were fewer than 1,000 armed rebels in the whole of Dublin. It seemed that the British forces were also seriously under strength. At noon on Easter Monday they had only about 400 fighting men available (many were out of town at Fairyhouse races). By 5 pm recalls and summons for reinforcements had brought their strength up to more than 4,000.

The Dublin Castle bonus was soon shown to be an unfounded rumour. Indeed, it was increasingly difficult to separate truth from hearsay, and some of the outpost commanders confused things further with a plethora of progress reports.

Although Connolly and Pearse were happy with general progress, O'Rahilly, still resentful of the way his colleagues had deceived him, denied them the support of his optimism—there was no chance of holding out for more than 24 hours, he said. Still, he was an effective officer, and under his control the upper floor had been well fortified. His adjutant had managed to establish (with the help of Cumann na mBan and prisoners) an efficient canteen. Pearse was deeply grateful to him for having joined in the rising with such a will, but O'Rahilly could not easily forgive him, his friend, for his lack of trust. There was only a superficial unity within the GPO. The Volunteers and the ICA had a deep mutual antagonism which was hard to overcome, though Connolly's charisma helped to keep the peace. Clarke had little to offer, now that Irish guns awaited British targets, except a fierce delight in having accomplished his long-standing ambition. His best energies were devoted to assailing MacNeill and Hobson, in their absence, for having issued the orders that had so reduced the fighting forces. It was not that early successes had dazzled any of the leaders; they were still aware of the ultimate hopelessness of the battle. Connolly had predicted before leaving Liberty Hall that all the men would be slaughtered, and Plunkett, Clarke and Pearse, although they believed they could have lasted longer with more troops, implied throughout that there would have been no hope of victory in any case.

Desmond Fitzgerald, who spent many hours talking to Plunkett and Pearse, recorded that the moral issues which had so long tortured Pearse were still not banished from his mind.

> Plunkett could forget in conversation, the facts that surrounded us. Sometimes when there were only the two of us together we would talk about literature and writers, and he would ask questions about writers who were friends of mine. But with Pearse it was different. Even when he spoke of what might have been, one felt that the major part of his mind was turning over what actually was. Time and again we came back to one favourite topic which could not be avoided. And that was the moral rectitude of what we had undertaken. These can hardly be called discussions for only the one side was taken. We each brought forward every theological argument and quotation that justified the Rising. And if one of us could adduce a point that the other two had not been aware of it was carefully noted. I remember asking to have such points repeated and for exact references. One of the reasons for this was that in talking with others this question so often arose, and any quotation that seemed to be authoritative and that favoured us, was comforting to the questioners. During those talks I probably persuaded myself that we were only interested in being able to give some reassurance to others. But looking back since then I know quite well that as far as I was concerned I was also seeking for reassurance for myself. Certainly none of the three gave voice to any argument that might call the rightness of our action into question, unless

it was that we had an immediate refutation ready for it.

This religious preoccupation was a feature of the rising which Pearse had turned over time and again in his writings. Most of the rebels were Catholics, and the more sophisticated among them had some difficulty in reconciling their actions with their religion. Yet the task was made easier by the divided attitude of their church. Firmly as the bishops always set their face against political violence, there were always priests who felt sympathy with Irish revolutionaries—some were even in the IRB—and could help to keep theoretically excommunicated men within the Catholic Church. But few of the rebels could have been as earnest in their practice of religion as Pearse, and few had to go to such lengths to appease their own consciences. One of Pearse's early acts in the Post Office was to send for a curate from the nearby Pro-Cathedral to hear confessions from the men.

By mid-afternoon, a new phenomenon forced its attention on the rebels: looting. There had already been unpleasantness from the crowds in Sackville Street, intensified as queues of women lining up outside the GPO to collect their British army separation allowance were told that with the establishment of an Irish Republic the allowances had ceased. Up to now the insurgents had been subject to ridicule and occasional abuse, but now the insults came thick and fast, and the mob turned ugly. They had already seen supplies being requisitioned without interference, since the police had absented themselves from the area, and there was nothing between the people of the nearby slums, who made up the majority of the crowd, and the goods in the high-class shops of Sackville Street but the glass in the display-windows. Once the first window was broken the crowd went wild. As the rebel leaders gazed in mounting horror, the sovereign people trampled each other in their lust for the possessions they could never afford to buy.

Pearse, despite his sympathy for the poor, had virtually no first-hand experience of their ways, and had expected them to be at worst passive supporters of the rebellion, at best participants. The riots of the 1913 lock-out had been largely precipitated by police brutality, and Pearse had had no difficulty in ennobling, in his imagination, the exploited masses, while he deplored the conditions in which they were forced to live. Connolly had long worked closely with representatives of the urban poor, but he was quite unprepared for the extremes of behaviour so typical of any mob once it senses the absence of restrictions; the materialism on which his political philosophy was based gave him no clue to the frantic smash-and-grab party he now witnessed. The stream of slum-dwellers running across Sackville Street with their pathetic trophies goaded MacDermott into action. He limped out of the post office and turned on a section of the crowd the eloquence which had won him numerous recruits to the IRB during his years as an organizer, but it was too late for words. His appeals to the looters not to disgrace the fight for Irish freedom went unheard.

Connolly took a more aggressive step, sending the diminutive figure of Sean T. O'Kelly at the head of a small party to dissuade the crowds with batons, but as fast as they cleared them from one shop another was invaded. When he arrived back to report defeat, Connolly growled that he would order another sortie to shoot looters down, but he did not. Pearse, standing beside Desmond Fitzgerald with a tragic face, backed up Connolly's strong line and said that anyone caught looting was to be shot. But when Fitzgerald told him later that one culprit had been caught, Pearse's heart failed him and he sighed, "Ah, poor man, just keep him with the others".

There was a steady trickle of new recruits during the afternoon and evening (including 30 of the Hibernian Rifles), as the news of the rebellion spread, but few of them brought much elation to their new leaders. Too many of them, like O'Rahilly and Fitzgerald, believed that the call to arms had been ill-advised, and came out of duty, convinced that death was inevitable. Louise Gavan Duffy, who had suffered from Pearse's impetuosity while she taught at St Ita's, rebuked him for his action, but helped to run the canteen efficiently all week. The Cumann na mBan contingent in the post office were assigned to the traditional female rôles of feeding the men and caring for the wounded; several Citizen army women were aiding Countess Markiewicz in St Stephen's Green.

Reports of all this strange activity had brought other curious onlookers. Joseph Holloway, his routine shattered by the Abbey's cancellation of its matinée, spoke of the events of the day to Pearse's old enemy, Father Dinneen, and feared for the effect the rebellion might have on his beautiful city. Bulmer Hobson, released from captivity at O'Rahilly's insistence, stood in Sackville Street, a wry memory stirring, as he watched the looters, of Connolly's insistence on the revolutionary nature of the working class. Despite the distractions the preparatory work went on. A telephone line was set up with outposts across the street, and attempts were being made to reactivate disused wireless equipment in a telegraphy school nearby. (The efforts with the wireless were partially rewarded: later in the week, nearby ships picked up communiqués from the rebels, and so early news of the rising reached the waiting sympathizers in America more quickly than might otherwise have been the case.) Reports coming in by dispatch riders—they were still free to travel most streets without interference—told of successful skirmishes with British troops elsewhere. The first real indication that the authorities were taking things seriously came with a printed proclamation from Lord Wimborne, couched in less colourful terms than that of the IRB.

> Whereas an attempt, instigated and designed by the foreign enemies of our King and Country to incite rebellion in Ireland, and thus endanger the safety of the United Kingdom, has been made by a reckless, though small body of men, who have been guilty of insurrectionary acts in the City of Dublin:
>
> Now, we, Ivor Churchill, Baron Wimborne, Lord-Lieutenant General and Governor-General of Ireland, do hereby warn all his Majesty's subjects that the sternest measures are being, and will be taken for the prompt suppression of the existing disturbances, and the restoration of order:
>
> And we do hereby enjoin all loyal and law-abiding citizens to abstain from any acts or conduct which might interfere with the action of the Executive Government, and, in particular, we warn all citizens of the danger of unnecessarily frequenting the streets or public places or of assembling in crowds.

In the absence of troops and police, Wimborne's injunctions had no effect on the crowds, whose enjoyment of their unparalleled freedom of action continued unabated until the shops were emptied. Francis Sheehy-Skeffington, a well-known pacifist (and husband of the woman selected to sit on the provisional government), found himself another lost cause in trying to dissuade the crowds from looting. A couple of shops caught fire but were swiftly extinguished by the Dublin fire brigade.

The rebel leaders were under no illusion that retaliation from the authorities would be long delayed. By Monday night they had disposed their forces as best they could in and around the GPO, and established that the defensive picket was well dug-in in buildings around the perimeter of the city centre. They had little left to do but wait and try to sleep—a luxury denied them throughout the week, except in short snatches. The initiative lay with the British army.

II The General Post Office

On Tuesday morning, the worst handicap suffered by the rebel leaders was the shortage of dependable information. Rumours continued unabated, but only the sound of machine-gun fire from the south of the city showed that the British troops were becoming active (the rebels had no such sophisticated weapons). As copies of the *Irish Times*, the only Dublin newspaper issued that morning, became available, it was clear that censorship was already fully in operation. Other than Lord Wimborne's proclamation, there was only one reference to the rising.

> SINN FEIN RISING IN DUBLIN
>
> Yesterday morning an insurrectionary rising took place in the city of Dublin. The authorities have taken active and energetic measures to cope with the situation. These measures are proceeding favourably. In accordance with this official statement, early and prompt action is anticipated.[1]

To men desperate for news of their comrades throughout the country the *Irish Times* was no help. Ironically, an earlier edition had carried extensive information on the previous day's events, but it was so promptly and efficiently suppressed that no copy of it was discovered for public comment until 60 years later. It was perhaps as well that the first edition of the paper was unavailable, for it would have confirmed fears that virtually all insurgent activity was confined to the capital. Morale, rendered unstable by the long wait, would have suffered grievously from such a revelation. As it was, the leaders were still free to make encouraging assertions about uprisings outside Dublin, and forthcoming German aid, even if they were not prepared to indulge in quite such flights of fancy as did their men. A favourite rumour was that Jim Larkin was on his way with 50,000 Irish-American fighting men.

Pearse fell to work early in the morning, composing a communiqué for the *Irish War News*, a four-page Republican newspaper, printed at Liberty Hall and issued only once, on Tuesday morning. Having announced the main events of Monday, including the appointment of a provisional government, he went on to produce a news report which owed more to the interests of propaganda than of truth.

> At the moment of writing this report, (9:30 a.m., Tuesday) the Republican forces hold all their positions and the British Forces have nowhere broken through. There has been heavy and continuous fighting for nearly 24 hours, the casualties of the enemy being much more numerous than those on the Republican side. The Republican forces everywhere are fighting with splendid

gallantry. The populace of Dublin are plainly with the Republic, and the officers and men are everywhere cheered as they march through the streets. The whole centre of the city is in the hands of the Republic, whose flag flies from the G.P.O. Commandant-General P. H. Pearse is commander-in-chief of the Army of the Republic and is President of the Provisional Government. Commandant-General James Connolly is commanding the Dublin districts. Communication with the country is largely cut, but reports to hand show that the country is rising, and bodies of men from Kildare and Fingal have already reported in Dublin.

Just before writing this bulletin, Pearse had in fact had news that the south and the west were quiet, but he cherished a hope that news of the Dublin successes would rouse Volunteers throughout the country. A messenger had already been dispatched to Wexford to urge action, and Pearse's optimism was such that by mid-morning he had translated this hope into a statement to some of his men that Wexford had risen. His attitude was ambivalent. He was torn between his desire to be the main—possibly the only—sacrificial victim, and the contradictory desire to put up the most impressive demonstration possible. By Tuesday he was already depressed at the thought that prolonged resistance would mean all the rebels, both men and women, being killed in action or shot afterwards by the British. Like the other leaders, he had little idea of what treatment to expect from their eventual captors, and could predict by turns release or annihilation for the rank and file.

As time wore on, and the British troops failed to make any obvious progress towards Sackville Street, Pearse came to believe that the rebels had a chance of holding out for longer than had been anticipated. Connolly had a firm conviction, shared by many of his colleagues, that the forces of British capitalism could never bring themselves to destroy property, and that the battle would therefore involve only a straightforward shoot-out with light weapons. The Post Office and the surrounding buildings were now so well defended that any such enemy advance could be long held off, so Pearse instructed Fitzgerald to ration food to allow for a three-week siege. The unfortunate result of this logic was to keep the weary men underfed, and so to lower their resistance to the hardships of the following days.

It was already clear that current British activity was concentrated on rebel outposts. They had succeeded in clearing the area around Dublin Castle, and had driven the ICA from St Stephen's Green itself into the overlooking building of the Royal College of Surgeons. Several of the smaller units had already been dislodged and communication with the strongholds of the other commandants was seriously dislocated.

The scene outside the GPO was even less edifying than the previous day. Discarded plunder littered the street, and since most of the shops had been cleared out, pubs had become the main target. Drunken Dubliners carried liquor bottles about with them, most of them indifferent to the British sniper fire that was coming occasionally from some distant buildings, including Trinity College. There was a steady trickle of casualties. Sheehy-Skeffington appeared again, pasting up notices calling unsuccessfully for a vigilante committee to control the looters. Neither Connolly nor Pearse showed any more determination in the matter of punishing the looters, who were drifting away to stores in the side-streets which had not already been picked over. As though disappointed at the ease with which the fire brigade had done its work the previous day, they staged an impromptu display with large quantities of fireworks from Messrs Lawrence's, whose building soon went up in flames.

The British still did not come. The GPO garrison was steadily growing, as men driven back from outposts in the north rejoined the headquarters group. A final-year medical student, James Ryan (who had, like O'Rahilly, spent Saturday night and Sunday delivering MacNeill's veto in the country), arrived to take charge, with a captured British army doctor, of the casualty unit. For the rest, apart from the construction of more barricades to impede the British advance, and sporadic bomb-making, there was little to do but wait. Pearse, during the afternoon, was back at a desk drafting his second manifesto to the citizens of Dublin. Like his earlier announcement, it was designed to stir the souls of the Irish people, but it was also an attempt to shame the looters into abandoning their ignoble pleasures. It proved about as effective as Sheehy-Skeffington's abortive efforts.

He emerged from the Post Office to read the declaration, and although the rebels' measure of success made him a more interesting figure than the previous day, the crowds soon became bored and went off looking for more spectacular entertainment. But Pearse read on.

THE PROVISIONAL GOVERNMENT
TO THE
CITIZENS OF DUBLIN

The Provisional Government of the Irish Republic salutes the

Citizens of Dublin on the momentous occasion of the proclamation of a

SOVEREIGN INDEPENDENT IRISH STATE,

now in course of being established by Irishmen in arms.

The Republican forces hold the lines taken up at twelve noon on Easter Monday, and nowhere, despite fierce and almost continuous attacks of the British troops, have the lines been broken through. The country is rising in answer to Dublin's call, and the final achievement of Ireland's freedom is now, with God's help, only a matter of days. The valour, self-sacrifice and discipline of Irish men and women are about to win for our country a glorious place among the nations.

Ireland's honour has already been redeemed; it remains to vindicate her wisdom and her self-control.

All citizens of Dublin who believe in the right of their country to be free will give their allegiance and their loyal help to the Irish Republic. There is work for everyone: for the men in the fighting line, and for the women in the provision of food and of first aid. Every Irishman and Irishwoman worthy of the name will come forward to help their common country in this her supreme hour. Able-bodied citizens can help by building barricades in the streets to oppose the advance of British troops. The British troops have been firing on our women and on our Red Cross. On the other hand, Irish Regiments in the British Army have refused to act against their fellow-countrymen.

The Provisional Government hopes that its supporters—which means the vast bulk of the people of Dublin—will preserve order and self-restraint. Such looting as has already occurred has been done by hangers-on of the British Army. Ireland must keep her new honour unsmirched.

We have lived to see an Irish Republic proclaimed. May we live to establish it firmly, and may our children and our children's children enjoy the happiness and prosperity which freedom will bring.

Signed on behalf of the Provisional Government,

P. H. PEARSE,

Commanding in Chief the Forces of
the Irish Republic,
and President of the
Provisional Government.

Manifesto written and delivered, Pearse began again his morale-building tours with Willie, congratulating the men on their hard work and trying to dispel the nervous tension. He had already achieved a personal ambition to put up a better show than had Emmet in his two-hour fight, and he talked of this triumph throughout the week. Tom Clarke, although not given to the theological discussions which so preoccupied Pearse, spent much of the afternoon and evening of Tuesday telling his life story to James Ryan and his sisters Mary (MacDermott's fiancée and later Mrs Richard Mulcahy) and Phyllis (later Mrs Sean T. O'Kelly). He wanted, he said, to explain to those who had a chance of surviving him what had driven him to this action. So he talked for hours about his IRB history, his part in the dynamiting campaign, his fifteen years in prison and his work in Dublin for over eight years building up an effective revolutionary organization and moulding protégés like MacDermott. It was unusual enough for Clarke to feel the need to justify himself, but he certainly expressed no doubts about the culmination of his life's work.[2]

For the rest of Tuesday evening, the main distractions came from snipers, distant machine-guns, the Sackville Street fire, and reports that British reinforcements were arriving in the city. By nightfall, the British troops numbered over 6,500, martial law had been declared, and—more ominous for the rebels—artillery had arrived for use on occupied buildings. Intelligence showed that a British force was approaching Sackville Street from the north around midnight, suggesting imminent attack and preventing the men from getting any solid sleep. But the night passed with only the now familiar sound of gunfire, leaving the garrison to face Wednesday morning in a state of exhaustion.

The British did not hold their hand much longer. By 8 am on Wednesday, the gunboat *Helga* had come up the Liffey and shelled the deserted Liberty Hall. Its rapid destruction shook the confidence of the GPO men, who could no longer accept Connolly's pronouncements about the sanctity of property. Connolly was resourceful in his optimism, and he assured Willie Pearse that this intensified action proved that the British were expecting imminent German landings. Sackville Street, although it still had not seen open confrontation between the two armies, was becoming a more and more dangerous place to be, and there were few brave enough to defy martial law and risk death in the interests of idle curiosity. Skeffington had not reappeared. He had been arrested the previous evening by a deranged British officer, Captain Bowen-Colthurst, who had him shot on Wednesday morning with two other, equally innocent, victims. (Bowen-Colthurst—a Corkman—was later committed for a short period.)

The Ryan girls, who stayed in the Post Office on Tuesday night, saw Pearse the following morning. MacDermott, unable even in these circumstances to refrain from teasing one of his favourite butts, led them to the president sitting at a desk. "Now, here are two nice girls to see you," he said to the embarrassed Pearse, who was known to the sisters as a chronically shy man whose squint prevented them from knowing whether he was avoiding their gaze.[3] Poor Pearse, as tongue-tied as ever despite his splendid uniform and heroic position, passed them quickly over to O'Rahilly for instructions.

Throughout the city British strategy was the same: house-to-house searches were followed by the advance of infantry and artillery, forming a noose around the main rebel concentration. By the afternoon, guns were lobbing incendiaries into Sackville Street from Trinity, igniting the buildings within their range. Men on the roofs of the GPO and its neighbours were visited by their commandant-general and his brother, both seemingly oblivious to the flying bullets. Pearse made encouraging speeches to his troops, and Willie, gazing around him at the advancing fires and the litter of Sackville Street, made his contribution. "A curious business. I wonder how it will end? I know a lot of good work has been done, but there is a great deal more to do."[4]

Despite the increasing danger, some couriers succeeded in getting through from other commands, although others, like Sean T. O'Kelly, once sent off on missions were unable to return. Pearse read out dispatches from other commandants, who were all under heavy fire, but reported a high state of morale among their men. Even the casualties and the growing fears of annihilation were compensated for by occasional successes and the growing feeling that, at worst, they had made a mark on history.

Pearse spent some time late on Wednesday evening composing a war bulletin. His exhaustion showed in his prose, which carried little of the power of his earlier efforts. Usually meticulous in his attention to detail, he even got the date wrong (it was to be printed on Thursday, though that did not prove possible, and Thursday was the 27th).

Irish Republic
War Bulletin

Thursday morning, 28th April, 1916

The main positions taken up by the Republican Forces in Dublin at 12 noon on Easter Monday, 24th instant are all still held by us. Our lines are everywhere intact and our positions of great strength.

The Republican Forces have at every point resisted with extraordinary gallantry.

Commandant-General Pearse, Commander-in-Chief, and Commandant-General Connolly, commanding in Dublin, thank their brave soldiers.

Despite furious and almost continuous attacks from the British forces our casualties are few. The British casualties are heavy.

The British troops have repeatedly fired on our Red Cross and even on parties of Red Cross women nurses bearing stretchers. Commandant-General Pearse, commanding in chief for the Republic, has notified Major-General Friend, commanding in chief for the British, that British prisoners held by the Republican forces will be treated as hostages for the observance on the part of the British of the laws of warfare and humanity, especially as regards the Red Cross.

Commandant-General Pearse, as President of the Provisional Government, has issued a proclamation to the citizens of Dublin, in which he salutes them on the momentous occasion of the proclamation of an Irish Republic, and claims for the Republic the allegiance and support of every man and woman of Dublin who believes in Ireland's right to be free. Citizens can help the Republican Forces by building barricades in the streets to impede the advance of the British forces.

Up with the barricades!

The Republican Forces are in a position to supply bread to the civil population within the lines occupied by them.

A committee of citizens known as the Public Service Committee has been formed to assist in the maintenance of public order and in the supply of food to the civil population.

The Provisional Government strongly condemns looting and the wanton destruction of property. The looting that has taken place has been done by the hangers-on of the British forces.

Reports to hand from the country show that Dublin's call is being responded to, and that large areas in the West, South, and South-East are now in Arms for the Irish Republic.

(Signed)
P. H. PEARSE,
Commandant General

His statements about country-wide risings were almost as inaccurate as before. IRB men throughout the country had been provided with vague plans along Dublin lines, requiring them to concentrate their forces in major buildings, but they had been told to work out their own tactical details. Those few who managed to find enough men prepared to fight with them virtually had to improvise as they went along. The 5th Dublin Battalion was the most successful. Operating in Counties Dublin and Meath, it had some modest success in capturing a handful of police barracks and forcing the surrender of a police column. Its commandant, Thomas Ashe, and his number two, Richard Mulcahy, never had more than 44 men under their command, yet they kept their guerrilla war going longer than the more impressive static show-down in Dublin. Galway had been more thoroughly roused by Liam Mel lows, whose fight began on Tuesday. With about 500 badly-armed men he held out until Saturday, having been forced into a defensive position early in the week. In Wexford there was more success. The Enniscorthy Volunteers took over their town on Thursday, in response to orders from Connolly, and later seized Ferns. They kept going until Monday, 1 May. The unfortunate Denis McCullough gave up in Ulster, when he found himself almost without men, or any means of transporting those few he had to the rendezvous in the west. As he said later, he could theoretically have commandeered transport, but lacked the confidence to commandeer as much as a hen. The insurgents outside Dublin, like those inside, often bungled, and were obviously amateurish, but frequently showed remarkable tenacity and courage.

Pearse's other composition of Wednesday evening—a message to Mrs Pearse—was determinedly cheerful, pandering to a mother's worries with little regard for the truth. (It did not arrive for some weeks.)

> We are all safe here up to the present (6.30 Wednesday evg.). The St Enda's boys have been on duty on the roof ever since we came in, but have been relieved this evening and will spend tonight on the ground floor with me. They are all in excellent spirits, though very sleepy. We have plenty of the best food, all our meals being as good as if served in a hotel. The dining room here is very comfortable. We sleep on mattresses and some of us have sheets, blankets, pillows and quilts. The men have fought with wonderful courage and gaiety, and, whatever happens to us, the name of Dublin will be splendid in history for ever. Willie and I hope you are not fretting, and send you all our love.
>
> P.

To which Willie, melancholy and worried, could add little. "Have really nothing to say. We are still here. Don't worry. I saw a priest again (Confession) and was talking to Fr. Bowden also.

Willie" (Pearse may not have known it, but one St Enda's old boy had been killed. Pearse had sent the youth, Gerald Keogh, on an errand late on Monday, and he had been on his way back, towards dawn on Tuesday, with two companions, when he was shot down.)

Later, in conversation with Desmond Ryan, Pearse showed that his expressed belief that Dubliners would give moral support to the rising had given way in the face of the evidence of his own eyes and ears. He had to face reality, and assure himself that his name would yet have a glorious niche in Irish history, despite the temporary hostility of public opinion. "When we are all wiped out, people will blame us for everything, condemn us. But for this the war would have ended and nothing have been done. In a few years they will see the meaning of what we tried to do."[5] His exultancy shone through. "Emmet's two-hour insurrection is nothing to this! ... They will talk of Dublin in future as one of the splendid cities like they speak to-day of Paris! Dublin's name will be glorious for ever!"

Pearse's efforts to add heroic tone were not appreciated by all his men. Collins wrote sharply of this later. "... I do not think the Rising week was an appropriate time for the issue of memoranda couched in poetic phrases, nor of actions worked out in a similar fashion. Looking at it from the inside ... it had the air of a Greek tragedy about it, the illusion being more or less completed with the issue of the before mentioned memoranda."[6]

It was a fair criticism, but Pearse had not a great deal else to offer. The dignity of his rank—an important element in the maintenance of the "professional army" illusion—did not permit him to soil his hands on the endless jobs for which men were so badly needed. The commandant-general could hardly have built barricades, tunnelled through buildings, or stood guard, and there is no reason to believe that he ever fired a shot throughout the whole rising. He was neither a soldier nor a tactician, so his time was best spent in addressing his men, showing himself free of fear and full of confidence, and vindicating their actions through his written words. He knew his own inadequacies and never tried to meddle; as long as Connolly was in control, Pearse the soldier was redundant, and he fully acknowledged Connolly's authority and supported it throughout. He rose to the occasion not with the military prowess of a Cuchulainn, but certainly with all the courage and nobility of bearing of Tone and Emmet. But with lack of sleep, and the weight of personal responsibility for the death and injury all around him, he was kept going only by nervous energy.

The British cordon was tightening. Insurgents on the perimeter had held up its advance for some days, but by Thursday morning they no longer posed much of a threat. The British army had set its sights on the rebel headquarters and took little further interest in the outposts, although sporadic skirmishes continued. The British had certain disadvantages. Their men were less desperate than the rebels, and although a more potent fighting force both numerically and by training, they were unaccustomed to street fighting. Reinforcements from England, composed of two brigades of about 10,000 men, arrived on Wednesday and Thursday, but these men were tired from their travels, and not completely fighting fit. But the weight of numbers was certain to tell in the long run, especially as it was backed up by heavy artillery, and it was clear by Thursday morning that the Post Office could not long hold out.

As the British infantry drew steadily nearer, rifle and artillery fire increased their tempo and effectiveness. More garrisons around Sackville Street were abandoned as the fire spread (the barricades helped it to creep across streets). There was serious danger that the flames might spread to the Post Office block itself. Connolly, searching for new expedients in his tours of surrounding buildings, saw little hope of improving the position. The insurgents managed to repel the advancing infantry, but pulverizing machine-gun fire had caused damage inside the building which added choking dust to their other troubles, like the stench from two dead horses left after the attack on the Lancers. The rebels' guns were by now being fired so frequently that only lubrication with sardine oil kept them in use. Casualties were still low, compared with those of the British, but this was small consolation in the face of the real threat—advancing fire. By the afternoon the GPO was feeling the frightful heat of the blaze across the road, and a shell had scored the first direct hit on the building. The two commandants reacted in characteristic form. Pearse addressed a speech to all the available men, paying tribute to their courage and strength in terms which he was to re-echo in his last manifesto, written in the suffocating heat of Thursday night and Friday morning. He could still move the hearts of his supporters, and the men responded with a perceptible, if temporary, lifting of spirits. Connolly was driven to defiant action, and led 30 men out of the beleaguerd Post Office to set up an outpost in a building to the west. Halfway there, helping to build a barricade, he received his first injury, a slight wound in the arm. He managed to slip back to have the wound dressed without his men noticing, and led them on to their destination. As they arrived there, Connolly set off back towards the

Post Office and was hit by a bullet which smashed his left ankle. In agony, he dragged himself along to within sight of headquarters, and was carried into the infirmary on a stretcher. Even with injections of morphine the pain was unspeakable, and Connolly was lost as military commander.

With Plunkett still ill, from Thursday evening the mantle of command fell on Pearse, Clarke and MacDermott (as the other members of the provisional government present), with O'Rahilly as adviser. They maintained resistance as well as possible, but a military genius could have done little at this stage, as the British advance into neighbouring streets became more obvious: the garrison in the Imperial Hotel opposite was driven out by incendiary shells, and most of them were captured on Friday morning.

During the night the heat in the GPO building had become so intense that water hoses were in constant use to soak down the inflammable material inside. The exhausted sweat-soaked men knew that the building could not survive long, and Pearse's last manifesto showed the same realization. It was notable also for its generosity. His debt to Connolly was fully acknowledged, and, like MacDonagh five days earlier, he spared a thought for the reputation and self-respect of Eoin MacNeill (who had spent the week of the insurrection in another agony of indecision, having to be dissuaded by his family and Hobson from joining his old comrades).

Headquarters, Army of the Irish Republic.
General Post Office,
Dublin.
28th April, 1916. 9.30 a.m.

The Forces of the Irish Republic, which was proclaimed in Dublin, on Easter Monday, 24th April, have been in possession of the central part of the Capital, since 12 noon on that day. Up to yesterday afternoon Headquarters was in touch with all the main outlying positions, and, despite furious, and almost continous assaults by the British Forces all those positions were then still being held, and the Commandants in charge, were confident of their ability to hold them for a long time.

During the course of yesterday afternoon, and evening, the enemy succeeded in cutting our communications, with our other positions in the City, and Headquarters is today isolated.

The enemy has burnt down whole blocks of houses, apparently with the object of giving themselves a clear field for the play of Artillery and Field guns against us. We have been bombarded during the evening and night, by Shrapnel and Machine Gun fire, but without material damage to our position, which is of great strength.

We are busy completing arrangements for the final defence of Headquarters, and are determined to hold it while the buildings last. I desire now, lest I may not have an opportunity later, to pay homage to the gallantry of the Soldiers of Irish Freedom who have during the past four days, been writing with fire and steel the most glorious chapter in the later history of Ireland. Justice can never be done to their heroism, to their discipline, to their gay and unconquerable spirit, in the midst of peril and death.

Let me, who have led them into this, speak, in my own, and in my fellow-commanders' names and in the name of Ireland present and to come, their praise, and ask those who come after them to remember them.

For four days, they have fought, and toiled, almost without cessation, almost without sleep, and in the intervals of fighting, they have sung songs of the freedom of Ireland. No man has complained, no man has asked "why?". Each individual has spent himself, happy to pour out his strength for Ireland and for freedom. If they do not win this fight, they will at least have deserved to win it. But win it they will, although they may win it in death. Already they have won a great thing. They have redeemed Dublin from many shames, and made her name splendid among the names of Cities.

If I were to mention names of individuals, my list would be a long one.

I will name only that of Commandant General James Connolly, Commanding the Dublin division. He lies wounded, but is still the guiding brain of our resistance.

If we accomplish no more than we have accomplished, I am satisfied that we have saved Ireland's honour. I am satisfied that we should have accomplished more, that we should have accomplished the task of enthroning, as well as proclaiming, the Irish Republic as a Sovereign State, had our arrangements for a simultaneous rising of the whole country, with a combined plan as sound as the Dublin plan has been proved to be, been allowed to go through on Easter Sunday. Of the fatal countermanding order which prevented these plans from being carried out, I shall not speak further. Both Eoin MacNeill and we have acted in the best interests of Ireland.

For my part, as to anything I have done in this, I am not afraid to face either the judgment of God, or the judgment of posterity.

(Signed) P. H. PEARSE, Commandant
General, Commanding-in-Chief, the
Army of the Irish Republic and
President of the Provisional
Government.

Pearse's was not the only rousing speech of that morning. The indomitable Connolly, rising above his excruciating pain, demanded to be transferred to a bed with castors, and from early Friday morning he was back in the main hall of the Post Office cheering his men on. For the first time he felt the need for literary composition and he dictated to his secretary, Winifred Carney—who had been with him throughout the week and refused to leave—an address which O'Rahilly read to the assembled rebels. It echoed Pearse's earlier bulletins and speeches in its wild claims about the success of the rising, and its defiant ending had the old Connolly ring. "Courage, boys, we are winning, and in the hours of our victory let us not forget the splendid women who have everywhere stood by us and cheered us on. Never had man or woman a grander cause, never was a cause more grandly served."

Although both Pearse and Connolly could write stirring prose, their efforts of that Friday demonstrated the difference in their temperaments. For all Pearse's intoxication with the *idea* of purifying bloodshed, and his delight at the success of his demonstration, he did not enjoy the actuality. He suffered for the death and injury he had brought on the men, and the citizens of his own city caught in the cross-fire of Sackville Street. He was kept going by the impetus of his rôle—to break now would be to betray the sacrifices already made. Connolly, on the other hand, was an essentially practical man who thrived on action and whose spirits were lifted by the ruthless realities of warfare. Throughout Friday, the last day in the Post Office, Pearse was controlled but unhappy, while Connolly had regained his former verve.

By mid-morning, many of the surrounding fires had burned themselves out, but that was of little comfort to the insurgents. The British artillery was by now well within range, and the shelling of the Post Office began in earnest. It became obvious that evacuation could not be long delayed. Fitzgerald persuaded Pearse to order the women out of the building, before escape became impossible. Many of them agreed to leave after strong protests, and Pearse made a moving speech of gratitude, thanking them for their bravery and devotion. Although he almost changed his mind when Mac-

Dermott objected that they would be safer inside, Fitzgerald kept him to his decision and the women left, to be arrested nearby. Women might get through the British cordon, and the wounded also (for whom other arrangements were being made), but there was no safe passage for the rest of the garrison. The only plan was to remain in the Post Office as long as possible, and then attempt to escape through the adjoining Henry Street, which the British had in their sights although it was barricaded against the advance of their troops.

During the afternoon, the shells fell so frequently that the fires could no longer be contained with the leaky water hoses. Pearse was almost helpless with exhaustion, and asked James Ryan for a sleeping draught in the hope of snatching an hour's sleep before the evacuation, but before the soporific could take effect, he was summoned by the announcement of a newer and more serious fire. The draught had made his condition worse, and he could do little to help. For the first and last time in the week he lost his composure, and stood flushed and excited, shouting at Plunkett, who was now temporarily revived and courageously trying himself to restore order. The problems of divided and amateur command were solved by O'Rahilly, who took over effective control of the fire-fighting.

By late afternoon, O'Rahilly was in charge of a concerted attack on the flames, which had taken a firm hold on the upper storeys. His men struggled to save the ground floor with sandbags and water, while Pearse, Plunkett, Clarke, MacDermott, and O'Rahilly gathered at Connolly's bedside to work out plans for the evacuation. There was only one chance of sparing the men a hopeless gunfight in the open: a large factory in Parnell Street offered a possible fortress, and it was agreed that when the evacuation became necessary, the only senior military leader left—O'Rahilly—would take an advance party across the adjacent Henry Street and up Moore Street, which led into Parnell Street, in an attempt to occupy the building and secure it for the main party. (The scheme was hopeless from the start—the factory was already in British hands.) At 8 pm the position was clearly desperate. The ceilings of the upper floors were collapsing, and the ammunition stores were exploding. In the hot and dust-laden atmosphere of the ground floor, the whole garrison, now joined by fugitives from the last local outposts, was crowded together uncomfortably. Pearse announced the plan, and ordered the men to stand by for withdrawal.

Desmond Fitzgerald was leaving with the wounded, all of whom, except Connolly, were being evacuated to Jervis Street Hospital nearby. (With the help of the captured British doctor and Father

Flanagan, the Pro-Cathedral curate—who, despite his misgivings about the rebellion, had ministered to the insurgents for 48 hours, and arranged safe conduct for the wounded—they reached the hospital. Flanagan carried with him several pathetic scrawled messages from rebels to their families.) As Fitzgerald prepared for his final departure, his close friend O'Rahilly, also ready to set off with his party of 30 men, came up to say good-bye. He was under no illusions about his chances of survival, but he preferred to go out laughing. As he took Fitzgerald's hand he said,

> "Good-bye, Desmond. This is the end now for certain. I never dreamed it would last as long. The only thing that grieves me is that so many of these lads are good Gaelgeoiri (Irish speakers). But never mind, when it comes to the end I'll say—'English speakers to the fore, Irish speakers to the rear, charge'." Then as he turned to go he said with a smile—"But fancy missing this and then catching cold running for a tram."

He was fatally wounded within ten minutes, leading the hopeless charge up Moore Street, though he lingered some time before dying. More than twenty of his men were also hit.

Lieutenant Mahony, the British army doctor, had come back to the GPO, from safety, to minister to Connolly, whose ankle needed further treatment. He was a witness of the last scene in the post office, as Pearse ordered the main party out. At this moment of disaster, he was fully in command of himself and his men, and his particular gift of leadership, the gift of instilling calm, came to his aid. Mahony was impressed. "I could see no panic, no obvious signs of fear—and in the circumstances that would have been excusable, for parts of the building were already an inferno and the roof and ceilings had already given way in places. To me, in that hasty moment, it seemed that Pearse, in the way he held them all together, was a gifted leader and a man supremely fitted to command."[7]

Pearse's last instruction to his men was to "go out and face the machine-guns as though you were on parade". As they left they sang a song which had given them great comfort at the worst times in the week—"The Soldier's Song" (the Irish version later became the national anthem of independent Ireland).

> Soldiers are we, whose lives are pledged to Ireland;
> Some have come from a land beyond the wave;
> Sworn to be free, no more our ancient sireland
> Shall shelter the despot or the slave.

Tonight we man the *bearna baoghail*
In Erin's cause, come woe or weal;
'Mid cannon's roar and rifle's peal
We'll chant a soldier's song.

Pearse had ordered the men to follow O'Rahilly's route, but as they set off, news met them of the fate of O'Rahilly's men. Disorder broke the ranks: some followed Pearse's instructions and ran into gun-fire in Moore Street; others, led by Michael Collins, looked for refuge in Henry Street. Plunkett, Clarke and MacDermott arrived in time to see the chaos, and shouted for order and courage. Plunkett's sword was drawn and his illness forgotten as he called on the men to be brave and go forward into the hail of bullets. The remnants scattered and found their way into houses in Henry Street and Moore Street.

Pearse and Connolly were left in the Post Office, both refusing to move until the last man was clear. At last Connolly was borne out into the street, still accompanied by Winifred Carney, and with one of the stretcher-bearers, a Fianna boy, insisting on acting as a shield for his commandant. The street was full of thick black smoke, which hampered British marksmen and machine-guns. Pearse turned and ran back into the Post Office to check that it was completely empty, and stood there, face red and swollen from the heat, as the small party which had accompanied the wounded tumbled back into the GPO through a hole in the wall. Willie was with them. Together they left the ruins of their headquarters.

III SURRENDER

Connolly had been taken to Cogan's grocery shop in Moore Street, where he found a party including Plunkett, Clarke and MacDermott. The street was a little safer by the time Pearse arrived with the last evacuees, for some of the barricades had been adjusted to screen latecomers from bullets. The British did not slacken their fire but they hesitated to close with the rebels (whose strength they over-estimated by anything up to a factor of ten). Inside the shop, the men were given food by Mrs Cogan, who, like many of the families in the area, showed sympathy to her uninvited guests. Connolly and Plunkett were both suffering badly from the rigours of the withdrawal. Pearse ordered parties of men to tunnel through walls, away from the British headquarters to the north, and to investigate the possibilities of occupying the buildings between Cogan's and Henry Street. Then, exhausted, he went upstairs with Willie and they stretched out side by side on a table and spent their last night together.

It was clear from early on Saturday that there was no hope. The scouting party had not returned, and the new headquarters was apparently cut off from all outside support. There were seventeen wounded men in the house, all injured in the flight from the GPO (except one British prisoner-of-war whom Plunkett's brother George had brought in from the dangers of the street). There were two Cumann na mBan nurses to care for them, and they also cooked for the whole contingent when they awoke in the morning. After breakfast, the party moved through the holes bored through the adjoining houses until they reached a fish shop, at 16 Moore Street. They could go no further, because Connolly's foot had turned gangrenous, and they could subject him to no more pain. He was put to bed in the back room of the house, and Pearse, Willie, Clarke, MacDermott and Plunkett gathered round him in consultation. Across the room lay four of the wounded, attended by the Cumann na mBan nurses, Julia Grenan and Elizabeth O'Farrell, and by Winifred Carney. The leaders could not agree on a course of action. 21-year-old Sean MacLoughlin, whose resourcefulness the previous night had won him a field commission, was called and asked for suggestions on escape. He offered to lead a diversionary attack on the British positions to give the remaining Irish forces a chance to make a dash towards the Four Courts, where Ned Daly was still in occupation. On close questioning, he said that at best such an operation would cost 20 to 30 lives. After some discussion Pearse said that the plan was worth trying, and MacLoughlin went back to find volunteers to tunnel through to the point from which the diversionary charge was to be launched.

While the tunnelling went on, Pearse witnessed from a window the death of three civilians—a Moore Street publican and his wife and daughter, shot while carrying a white flag. Pearse had up till now held out against the provisional government's majority opinion in favour of surrender, but this sight affected him deeply. When MacLoughlin came back to report the tunnel complete, in company with MacDermott (both of them shaken by the discovery of O'Rahilly's riddled body), he was told to order an hour's ceasefire, and the five leaders went back into conference. Later evidence suggests that Clarke backed Pearse against the majority. He had all his old horror of prison, and wanted to die a free man, with a gun in his hand. But the other three had had enough. Plunkett felt that the demonstration had already exceeded all reasonable hopes. Mac-

Dermott was determined to avoid further civilian casualties, and Connolly was tormented by a vision of his boys being burned to death. Pearse, though he was anxious to prove himself as determined and courageous as the most die-hard among his men, was by now wavering, and he agreed to accept the majority view.

On a small piece of cardboard, probably a picture backing, he recorded the decision.

H.Q. Moore Street.

Believing that the glorious stand which has been made by the soldiers of Irish freedom during the last five days in Dublin has been sufficient to gain recognition of Ireland's national claim at an international peace conference, and desirous of preventing further slaughter of the civil population and to save the lives of as many as possible of our followers, the members of the Provisional Government here present have agreed by a majority to open negotiations with the British Commander.

P. H. PEARSE,
Commandant General
Commanding in Chief
Army of the Irish Republic.

29 April, 1916.

(The belief that Ireland could claim a place at an international peace conference was wholly fallacious—founded on a strange notion that three days of combat bought such a right. This had long been one justification for a defensive strategy, designed to prolong the fight. There was still some room for optimism.)

Willie went out with the news to Desmond Ryan, in an adjoining room. He was obviously glad that there was some chance of saving the men from slaughter. He borrowed a safety razor for his brother, for Pearse, expecting to treat directly with the enemy, wished to be as spruce as possible. In the headquarters room, the decision was announced to MacLoughlin and the women. MacLoughlin asked Elizabeth O'Farrell to provide a white flag, and Clarke, controlled until now, burst into tears: MacDermott wept too. Nurse O'Farrell was given a verbal message to take to the Dublin commander, Brigadier-General Lowe, proposing the negotiation of terms. She reached the barrier between Moore Street and Parnell Street safely and was sent under guard to the officer in command. There was a brief battle of words, for he insisted on referring to the Irish Republican army as "the Sinn Feiners", and further insisted (for British informants had confused Connolly with Pearse) that Pearse would have to be brought to the parley on a stretcher. Nurse O'Farrell was then escorted to Tom Clarke's tobacconist's shop while Colonel Owens wrote to Lowe.

> We have been engaged with Sinn Feinners in Moore Street and Moore Lane and from reliable information received from Major Morrogh—Royal Irish Regiment who observed from the back of Sackville Street Club about 100 Sinn Feinners he located in a white house at the southern end of Moore Lane.
>
> On receipt of this information I ordered the Gunner Officer to put five shells into the house the result being that a Red Cross Nurse of the enemy has come in with a verbal message from the self-called Commander Pearse—Republican Force to the effect that he wishes to treat with the Commandant of the Forces. We have detained the nurse here and are proceeding with the operations of searching and closing in.
>
> R. L. OWENS
> Lt. Col.
> Comdg. 3rd Bn. R.I. Reg.
>
> Parnell's Monument
> Sackville Street
> Time 12.10 p.m. 29th '16.[1]

(The popular determination to talk and write of the "Sinn Fein Rebellion" was perhaps understandable, since the open and vociferous separatist propaganda issued by Sinn Fein was designed to lodge itself firmly in the public imagination. Indeed, the organization's leader, Arthur Griffith, had offered his services in the rising half-way through Easter week, but Connolly had refused him, saying he had more to offer as a propagandist, and should stay alive to write for Ireland.)

The message was sent to Dublin Castle, where it arrived at 12.35 pm and was forwarded to Lowe. He came to the shop to interview Nurse O'Farrell shortly afterwards and sent her back to Pearse with a note.

> 29 April '16
> 1.40 p.m.
>
> A woman has come in and tells me you wish to negotiate with me.
>
> I am prepared to receive you in Britain Street at the north end of Moore Street provided that you surrender unconditionally.
>
> You will proceed up Moore Street accompanied only by the woman who brings you this note under a white flag.
>
> N. W. M. LOWE

Nurse O'Farrell also gave Pearse a 30-minute time limit imposed by Lowe.

Although there was little alternative, unconditional surrender was a bitter pill to swallow: the provisional government had hoped to negotiate release for its surviving rank and file. Pearse scrawled a note asking for terms for his men and unconditional surrender for himself, and received back a terse reiteration of Lowe's original message. There was a brief council of the leaders and, sadly and silently, Pearse shook hands with his comrades in arms, all of whom, except MacDermott and Willie, were in tears. MacDermott had already shed his tears at the sight of the white flag: for Willie, the moment was too big for weeping. Pearse set off with Nurse O'Farrell to walk to the top of Moore Street. As he left the room, Nurse Grenan noticed that at the head of Connolly's bed hung a large picture of Robert Emmet.

Lowe's staff officer, Major de Courcy Wheeler, later described the surrender. "Commandant-General Pearse walked up Moore Street, surrendered to General Lowe at the junction of Moore Street and Parnell Street and handed over his arms and military equipment to myself. These consisted of his sword, automatic pistol in holster, with pouch of ammunition, and his canteen, which contained two large onions. His sword was retained by General Lowe."[2] Nurse O'Farrell recorded their conversation.

Lowe: The only condition I make is that I will allow the other Commandants to surrender. I understand you have the Countess Markievicz down there.

Pearse: No, she is not with me.

Lowe: Oh, I know she is down there.

Pearse: Don't accuse me of speaking an untruth.

Lowe: Oh, I beg your pardon, Mr Pearse, but I know she is in the area.

Pearse: Well, she is not with me.

As Pearse was driven off to Parkgate, British headquarters, one of the soldiers standing by remarked (betraying a widely held belief that the rebels were in the pay of the Germans): "It would be interesting to know how many marks that fellow has in his pocket." Pearse was taken to see the British commander-in-chief, General Sir John Maxwell, who had arrived to deal with the rebellion early on Friday morning. The meeting was short, for Pearse had already conceded everything. His orders to his subordinates were brief, and quickly typed.

> In order to prevent the further slaughter of Dublin citizens, and in the hope of saving the lives of our followers now surrounded and hopelessly outnumbered, the members of the Provisional Government present at Headquarters have agreed to an unconditional surrender, and the Commandants of the various districts in the City and Country will order their commands to lay down arms.
>
> P. H. PEARSE.
> 29 April, 3.45 p.m., 1916.

He was left under Wheeler's guard.

> I was handed a loaded revolver with orders to keep it pointed at the General and to shoot if he made an effort to escape. I was locked in the room alone with General Pearse, who smiled at me across the table and did not seem in the least perturbed. I was on this duty for only fifteen minutes when I was sent for by General Lowe. Another officer was sent to relieve me. I did not see General Pearse again.

Later that evening Pearse was transferred to Arbour Hill Detention Barracks.

Copies of the surrender order were taken to Nurse O'Farrell to be relayed to certain sections of the Irish troops. Connolly, under instruction from Lowe, had already been carried out to surrender on his own account. He was taken to the military hospital at Dublin Castle. There was some difficulty in the Moore Street headquarters in persuading all the men to obey the surrender order, but Clarke and MacDermott rose to the occasion. Clarke, although he had been the last of the leaders to give in, reminded them of his own life-long struggle for Irish independence and said, simply, that if he was satisfied, so should they be. MacDermott absolved them of shame.

> We surrendered not to save you but to save the city and the people of this city from destruction. You would have fought on. No matter, I am proud of you. You made a great fight. It was not your fault that you have not won the Republic. You were outclassed, that is all. They had the men, the munitions, the force. But this week of Easter will be remembered, and your work will tell some day.

Nurse Grenan recorded the last scene in Moore Street before the men marched out. "... a number of the boys gathered in the back drawing room and knelt to say the Rosary. This was a picture that will never fade in my memory. They knelt holding the rifles, that they were so soon to surrender, in their left hands, the beads in their right; tears ran down many a cheek, and the responses were said chokingly."

Led by Willie Pearse—who carried the white flag—and young MacLoughlin, the Moore Street contingent marched towards the Parnell Monument. They were disarmed and taken to the forecourt of the Rotunda Hospital. MacDermott endured with dignity one of the gibes of the captors, when an officer, observing his limp, said, "You have cripples in your army". "You have your place, sir," replied MacDermott, "and I have mine, and you had better mind your place, sir."

They all spent the night in the open outside the Rotunda, an experience which did little for the health of Plunkett and MacDermott. With the prisoners from the Four Courts, they numbered about 400. Ned Daly, still well entrenched in his command, had been reluctant to give up, but in tears he had insisted to his still more reluctant men that Pearse's orders must be obeyed. Other commandants gave more trouble. More isolated from the Sackville Street battle-ground than Daly, they little realized the trials the headquarters garrison had been through, and they were proud of their own success and confident of holding out longer. Most of them did not receive their orders until Sunday. Mallin, at St Stephen's Green, gave no answer: de Valera, protocol-conscious as ever, refused to accept orders from anyone but his own immediate superior, MacDonagh. When Nurse O'Farrell, who carried most of the surrender orders, reached Jacob's factory, MacDonagh declined to accept orders from a prisoner, who might be acting under duress. He claimed that his men could hold out for several more weeks, and insisted, as the new commander-in-chief, on meeting Lowe personally. At their meeting, shortly after noon, Lowe (who had been courteous and considerate throughout), saluted MacDonagh, and agreed on an armistice until 3 pm, giving MacDonagh safe conduct to negotiate with the other commandants. He returned to Jacob's Factory and told his men that one glorious week had achieved all that had been hoped for. Then he too burst into tears and, still distressed, left to consult with Eamonn Kent in the South Dublin Union. With their joint decisions to surrender, the Dublin rising came effectively to an end.

There was similar difficulty in arresting the impetus of the North County Dublin Battalion and the Wexfordmen. Richard Mulcahy had been sent to see Pearse that Sunday morning to verify his orders, and arrived at Arbour Hill.

Inside the prison, on the right, the door of the second or third cell was noisily opened by a soldier who shouted harshly, "Get up!" Pearse, in his uniform, was lying on bare trestle boards at the back of the cell; on a small table alongside was a glass of water and some biscuits. He arose and moved quietly a few steps towards us.

Slightly behind my left shoulder was the officer and, behind him, the soldier. When movement ceased I turned to the officer and said I wished to speak to Commandant Pearse alone. I was not surprised that this request was refused, and that in a manner which alerted me to the full realities of the position. I was in the presence of my Commander-in-Chief: both of us in the hands of the British Army authorities: I could be nothing but the most perfect soldier: it was a moment for standing to attention....

"Is this your order, sir?" I asked, as I held it out before him. Pearse answered "Yes." "Does it refer to Dublin alone or to the whole of Ireland?" "It refers to the whole of Ireland." "Would it be of any use," I asked, "if a small band of men who had given a good account of themselves during the week were to hold out any longer?" And Pearse replied "No." My lips moved to frame a "Beannacht De agat" [God bless you] but the sound was stifled, absorbed in the solemnity of my salute which closed the scene.

The same day, Captains Seamus Doyle and Sean Etchingham came from Enniscorthy on the same mission.

... The cell-door was banged open and we went in accompanied by a Tommy, while a group of officers waited in the corridor outside ... just inside the door was a small table on which were a stetson hat, a pannikin of water and a broken military biscuit. At the far end, lying on a mattress, covered with a greatcoat was the first president of the Irish Republic. He rose up and advanced to meet us; it seemed to us that he was physically exhausted but spiritually exultant. His uniform was complete except for the Sam Browne belt which they had taken from him. The Dublin Brigade, he said, had done splendidly—"five days and nights of almost continuous fighting". Amongst the dead, he told us, were The O'Rahilly and Tom Weafer (an Enniscorthy man).... "No," he was not aware that we in Wexford were out.

Writing materials were brought in and the order to the Wexford men to lay down arms was written. While the Tommy was outside submitting the order for inspection to the officers Pearse whispered to us to hide our arms in safe places. "They will be needed later," he said.

The order was brought back and handed to us and we said farewell.

Except for a scattering of snipers in Dublin, the surrender was complete.

IV Court-martial and Execution

The emergence of Patrick Pearse as "the wretched 'Commandant' of the insurgents" (Birrell), was a matter of bewilderment to the British authorities. They had been right for many years in seeing Tom Clarke as the centre of revolutionary activity in Ireland, but their obsessive concern with him had blinded them to potential danger in others, However loudly men like Pearse and Connolly might preach sedition, they did not break the hypnotic spell exerted on the authorities by Clarke and his ex-Fenian colleagues. The Castle, with all its spies, had played into Clarke's hands, and left his more respectable recruits free to go about the business of insurrection.

The rising had brought downfall to the moderates in the administration. Birrell and Nathan, to the manifest joy of the Unionists, had no option but to resign, and the conduct of the courts-martial was left to the strong man, Sir John Maxwell. Although Wimborne lingered for a few days more (until he was forced to go), he had neither the inclination nor the strength to soften the wrath of Maxwell, who was determined to mete out to the rebels the "stern justice" called for by the *Irish Times.* Under the Defence of the Realm Act, he quickly instituted Field General Courts-Martial for the summary trial of all prisoners.

Pearse remained in Arbour Hill from Saturday to Tuesday. Cheerless though his cell was, he was in better circumstances than many. His GPO comrades (minus MacDermott, who had to be conducted under slower, separate escort) had been taken through enraged Dublin crowds, who showered them with rotten vegetables to remove any lingering doubts of their hostility. They marched through a gauntlet of abuse to Richmond Barracks, where they found crowded quarters. Liam O Briain, who had been in Stephen's Green with Mallin and Markiewicz, was with them.

My best friend, Sean MacDermott, was there—poor, lame Sean,

affectionate, gay, handsome, warm-hearted.... The first thing he said to me was "What's that you have under your arm?" It was the old quilt I brought with me from the College of Surgeons. "Give it to Plunkett," he said, "he's very sick." Joe Plunkett was lying on the floor near him, trying, and failing to rest. For a couple of days following he had the old quilt, sometimes under him as a bed, sometimes under his head as a pillow. Plunkett was wearing a Volunteer uniform and top-boots, as were his two brothers, George, and Sean. Sean MacDermott was dressed just as when I had last seen him, ten days before. After spending two years preparing for this great occasion he hadn't spent a minute's thought on what he would wear for the event.

Tom Clarke was sitting there just as we had seen him twenty times in his shop in Parnell Street, with the same clothes, the same look, quiet, silent, with the suspicion of a smile on his lips now and then. Tom was very satisfied with himself and the situation....

There was a dreamy-eyed young man with rather long hair who looked like an artist and was wearing a Volunteer uniform: he was Willie Pearse....*[1]

Even in the comparative calm of the Barracks, sleep held its own terrors for the veterans of the Post Office.

After a while Sean fell asleep with his head on Tom's chest. Young Pearse was turning from side to side on my left, very disturbed though he was fast asleep. I don't think Tom slept at all—nor did I for a long while. It was clear that the other two, in their dreams, were back in the G.P.O. Sean would start a little and we would hear a mutter from him saying "The fire! The fire! Get the men out!" Then you would hear Tom's quiet voice saying gently, "Quiet, Sean! We're in the barracks now. We're prisoners now, Sean." In the same way Pearse would utter a little moan "The fire! The fire!" now and again.*

There were no observers of Patrick Pearse's last days; his solitary confinement left him fittingly remote from his friends. On Monday, 1 May, free of the interruptions of the previous day and conscious that time was short, he threw himself into a frenzy of creation. He wrote to his mother in tones which echoed the poem he had earlier composed to equip her for the coming grief. (The letter was used by the prosecution at his court-martial; the prosecutor underlined significant passages, as below.)

Arbour Hill Barracks,
Dublin.
1st May, 1916.
My dear Mother,

You will I know have been longing to hear from me. I do not know how much you have heard since the last note I sent you from the G.P.O.

On Friday evening the Post office was *set on fire* and we had to abandon it. We dashed into Moore Street and remained in the houses in Moore Street on Saturday evening. We then found that we were surrounded by troops and that we had practically no food.

We decided in order to prevent further slaughter of the civilian population and in the hope of saving the lives of our followers, to ask the General Commanding the British Forces to discuss terms. He replied that he would receive me only if I surrendered unconditionally and this I did.

I was taken to the Headquarters of the British Command in Ireland and there I wrote and signed an order to our men to lay down their arms.

All this I did in accordance with the decision of our Provisional Government who were with us in Moore St. *My own opinion was in favour of one more desperate sally before opening negotiations, but I yielded to the majority*, and I think now the majority were right, as the sally would have resulted only in losing the lives of perhaps 50 or 100 of our men, and we should have had to surrender in the long run as we were without food.

I was brought in here on Saturday evening and later all the men with us in Moore St. were brought here. Those in the other parts of the City have, I understand, been taken to other barracks and prisons.

All here are safe and well. Willie and *all the St Enda's boys are here*. I have not seen them since Saturday, but I believe they are are well and that they are not now in any danger.

Our hope and belief is that the Government will spare the lives of all our followers, but we do not expect that they will spare the lives of the leaders. We are ready to die and we shall die cheerfully *and proudly*. Personally I do not hope or even desire to live, but I do hope and desire and believe that the lives of all our followers will be saved including the lives dear to you and me (my own excepted) and this will be a great consolation to me when dying.

You must not grieve for all this. We have preserved Ireland's honour and our own. *Our deeds of last week are the most splendid things in Ireland's history*. People will say hard things of us now, *but we shall be remembered by posterity and blessed by unborn generations*. You too will be blessed because you were my mother.

If you feel you would like to see me, I think you will be allowed to visit me by applying to the Headquarters, Irish Command, near the Park. I shall I hope have another opportunity of writing to you.

Love to W.W., M.B., Miss Byrne, X.X. and your own dear self.

P.S. I understand *that the German expedition which I was counting on actually set sail but was defeated by the British.*[2]

(It was, of course, Friday and not Saturday evening they spent in Moore St. WW was "Wow-Wow", a pet name for sister Margaret; MB was Mary Brigid; Miss Byrne was a family friend; the illegible initials XX may have referred to Margaret Brady, his cousin—or perhaps the first copier of the manuscript was baffled by Gaelic characters referring to the gardener, Micheal Mac Ruadhri. The original is untraceable. Pearse was wrong—Willie and the St Enda's boys were not in Arbour Hill.)

It was more affectionate than his usual letters home, but Pearse was still crippled by his old reserve. Desperate to express emotions the only way he knew, he composed poems to the two people he had loved, inarticulately but devotedly, through all his life.

"To My Mother"

My gift to you hath been the gift of sorrow,
My one return for your rich gifts to me,
Your gift of life, your gift of love and pity,
Your gift of sanity, your gift of faith
(For who hath had such faith as yours
Since the old time, and what were my poor faith
Without your strong belief to found upon?)
For all these precious things my gift to you
Is sorrow. I have seen
Your dear face line, your face soft to my touch,
Familiar to my hands and to my lips
Since I was little:
I have seen
How you have battled with your tears for me,

And with a proud glad look, although your heart
Was breaking. O Mother (for you know me)
You must have known, when I was silent,
That some strange thing within me kept me dumb,
Some strange deep thing, when I should shout my love?
I have sobbed in secret
For that reserve which yet I could not master.
I would have brought royal gifts, and I have brought you
Sorrow and tears: and yet, it may be
That I have brought you something else besides—
The memory of my deed and of my name
A splendid thing which shall not pass away.
When men speak of me, in praise or in dispraise,
You will not heed, but treasure your own memory
Of your first son.

And to Willie, who, he believed, would soon be released from prison.

"To My Brother"

O faithful!
Moulded in one womb,
We two have stood together all the years,
All the glad years and all the sorrowful years,
Own brothers: through good repute and ill,
In direst peril true to me,
Leaving all things for me, spending yourself
In the hard service that I taught to you,
Of all the men that I have known on earth,
You only have been my familiar friend,
Nor needed I another.

Neither of these poems, nor the letter, was given to Mrs Pearse, although Pearse sent everything he wrote on 1 May to Maxwell asking that they be handed on.[3] A third poem, a copy of which he gave to a Capuchin priest, was given to Mrs Pearse on the day of his execution. It was a reiteration of the theme of "The Mother" (I do not grudge them, Lord), amended in the light of his hopes for Willie's survival.

"A Mother Speaks"

Dear Mary, that didst see thy first-born Son
Go forth to die amid the scorn of men
For whom He died,

Receive my first-born son into thy arms,
Who also hath gone out to die for men,
And keep him by thee till I come to him.
Dear Mary, I have shared thy sorrow,
And soon shall share thy joy.

As ever, he had more prosaic concerns. Seventeen months earlier he had deposited with his solicitors instructions about his literary and financial affairs, and he now rewrote them in essence.[4] Painstakingly, he detailed the location and condition of all his literary effects, giving directions for the work necessary to prepare them for publication. Two points were of special interest. The memory of Dinneen's assault on "Poll an Phiobaire" was still with him—ten years later—and he asked that the title be changed to "An Uaimh" (The Cave). He also referred to his fragmentary autobiography, which he said had been written with a little *dichtung* (poetry) mingled with the *wahrheit* (truth). (There is no evidence as to the date of the autobiography's composition.)

His financial affairs, though in better shape than before the American trip, were still too complex to handle in detail. Ironically, on Easter Monday an industrious Inland Revenue official had sent Pearse a note threatening to distrain his property for non-payment of income tax.[5] There were still many large traders' bills outstanding in addition to the money owing to Dolan, MacManus and other benefactors. In this statement he drew attention once again to the bill countersigned by Stephen Barrett, and asked Clan-na-Gael to ensure that he bear no part of the loss. Mrs Bloomer was also singled out as a priority. Otherwise, Pearse's financial status was summed up in one paragraph.

> Apart from the sorrow which failure must necessarily bring on my mother and family, and from my own sorrow in separating from them, I have had but one source of personal regret in embarking on this enterprise. It is this: that its failure will involve loss, more or less considerable, to various persons, including traders and personal friends, to whom I am under financial obligations in connection with St Enda's and St Ita's Colleges. I desire to express my grief that these generous friends and these traders and business firms who trusted me should lose by my failure. I was gradually paying off the whole burden of debt, having already paid off 25% of it, and I should have paid off the whole had the call to take action for my country not come. That call, I believe rightly, I held to be imperative and that its obligation overshadowed all minor obligations. I am grateful beyond my power to

put into words to all those who, by active help or by generous forbearance, enabled me to carry on the noble work of St Enda's College; and I wish that I had been allowed to repay them better.

On Tuesday morning he was taken to Richmond Barracks for his court-martial. (Clarke and MacDonagh were tried the same morning.) As Emmet had inspired the framing of the proclamation of the Irish Republic, so Tone was the inspiration for Pearse's speech from the dock. The two testimonies should be read together.
First, Tone:

> I mean not to give you the trouble of bringing judicial proof to convict me, legally, of having acted in hostility to the Government of his Britannic Majesty in Ireland. I admit the fact. From my earliest youth I have regarded the connection between Ireland and Great Britain as the curse of the Irish nation, and felt convinced that, whilst it lasted, this country could never be free or happy. My mind has been confirmed in this opinion by the experience of every succeeding year, and the conclusions which I have drawn from every fact before my eyes. In consequence, I determined to apply all the powers which my individual efforts could move in order to separate the two countries.
>
> That Ireland was not able, of herself, to throw off the yoke, I knew. I therefore sought for aid wherever it was to be found. In honourable poverty I rejected offers which, to a man in my circumstances, might be considered highly advantageous. I remained faithful to what I thought the cause of my country, and sought in the French Republic an ally to rescue three millions of my countrymen from ... [here interrupted]

Next, Pearse—showing the same need to justify the use of foreign aid, and the same poetic licence in the description of his developing militance for Irish freedom.

> ... My object in agreeing to an unconditional surrender was to prevent the further slaughter of the civil population of Dublin and to save the lives of our gallant followers who, having made for six days a stand unparalleled in military history, were now surrounded and (in the case of those under the immediate command of Headquarters) without food. I fully understand now, as then, that my own life is forfeit to British law, and I shall die very cheerfully if I can think that the British Government, as it has already shown itself strong, will now show itself magnanimous enough to accept my single life in forfeiture and give a general

amnesty to the brave men and boys who have fought at my bidding.

In the second place I wish it to be understood that any admissions I make here are to be taken as involving myself alone. They do not involve and must not be used against anyone who acted with me, not even those who may have set their names to documents with me. (The Court assented to this.)

I admit that I was Commandant General Commanding in Chief the forces of the Irish Republic which have been acting against you for the past week, and that I was President of their Provisional Government. I stand over all my acts and words done or spoken in those capacities.

When I was a child of ten I went down on my bare knees by my bedside one night and promised God that I should devote my life to an effort to free my country. I have kept that promise. As a boy and as a man I have worked for Irish freedom, first among all earthly things. I have helped to organise, to arm, to train, and to discipline my fellowcountrymen to the sole end that, when the time came, they might fight for Irish freedom. The time, as it seemed to me, did come, and we went into the fight. I am glad we did. We seem to have lost. We have not lost. To refuse to fight would have been to lose; to fight is to win. We have kept faith with the past, and handed on a tradition to the future.

I repudiate the assertion of the prosecutor that I sought to aid and abet England's enemy. Germany is no more to me than England is. I asked and accepted German aid in the shape of arms and an expeditionary force. We neither asked for nor accepted Germany gold, nor had other traffic with Germany but what I state. My aim was to win Irish freedom: we struck the first blow ourselves but should have been glad of an ally's aid.

I assume that I am speaking to Englishmen, who value their freedom and who profess to be fighting for the freedom of Belgium and Serbia. Believe that we, too, love freedom and desire it. To us it is more desirable than anything in the world. If you strike us down now, we shall rise again and renew the fight. You cannot conquer Ireland. You cannot extinguish the Irish passion for freedom. If our deed has not been sufficient to win freedom, then our children will win it by a better deed.

He did not fail to make an impact in court. One of his three judges, who had no option but to sentence him to death, was moved to pay him a tribute that evening. The Countess of Fingall was his hostess.

> ... General Blackader, who was President of the Courts-Martial, used to dine with us sometimes.... He came to dinner one night greatly depressed. I asked him: "What is the matter?" He answered: "I have just done one of the hardest tasks I have ever had to do. I have had to condemn to death one of the finest characters I have ever come across. There must be something very wrong in the state of things that makes a man like that a Rebel. I don't wonder that his pupils adored him."[6]

After the court-martial, Pearse was transferred yet again, this time to a death cell in Kilmainham, where he wrote his account of his speech, one more poem, and letters to his mother and Willie. He had done everything in his power to explain his actions, and the last poem, "The Wayfarer", was reminiscent of earlier days. Remembering, perhaps, his last holiday in Rosmuc in the summer of 1915, which had been filled with joy as well as anxiety about events to come, he made his farewell to life's pleasures.

"The Wayfarer"

The beauty of the world hath made me sad,
This beauty that will pass;
Sometimes my heart hath shaken with great joy
To see a leaping squirrel in a tree,
Or a red lady-bird upon a stalk,
Or little rabbits in a field at evening,
Lit by a slanting sun,
Or some green hill where shadows drifted by,
Some quiet hill where mountainy man hath sown
And soon would reap; near to the gate of Heaven;
Or children with bare feet upon the sands
Of some ebbed sea, or playing on the streets
Of little towns in Connacht,
Things young and happy.
And then my heart hath told me:
These will pass,
Will pass and change, will die and be no more,
Things bright and green, things young and happy;
And I have gone upon my way
Sorrowful.

He still hoped to see his mother and brother before he died. His faith in the latter's survival was intact; he had no idea that Willie too had been court-martialled, that very afternoon. There can have been little evidence against Willie, whose rôle during Easter Week had been almost wholly passive, but he had been tried in the very early stages, when clemency was smothered by the tribunal's righteous desire to make examples of the leaders. And when it came to identifying leaders of revolutions, the authorities now knew that little reliance could be placed on personal appearances or occupation. They had netted a university lecturer (MacDonagh), a wealthy poet (Plunkett), a trade-unionist (Connolly), a "headmaster and barrister" (so Pearse was described in court), a corporation official (Kent), and a bewildering assortment of intellectuals and professional men, together with the full-time subversive, Clarke. (Ironically, Clarke's right hand man, MacDermott, had not yet been sifted out from the mass of detainees.) In the welter of contradictory orders that preceded the rising, Willie had set his name to papers as "Acting Chief of Staff", and it is probable that the court had knowledge of this fact—anyway he was as likely a senior officer as some of the others, on a brief acquaintance. Observers report that he adopted an exultant attitude, and claimed that he was involved in the plans for insurrection from the first. He was sentenced to death.

Patrick Pearse remained alone in his cell until late on Tuesday night. He had asked to see a Capuchin priest, Father Aloysius, who was collected from his Friary about 11 pm. (The Capuchins were traditionally sympathetic to the revolutionaries.) The soldier who called for him had intended collecting Mrs Pearse from Rathfarnham, but a few persistent snipers prevented them from getting through, and Father Aloysius was taken directly to Kilmainham. He ministered to both Pearse and MacDonagh, for all the leaders—with the almost certain exception of Clarke—returned to their Church at the end. Pearse was pleased at such news as Father Aloysius was able to give him.

> "You will be glad to know that I gave Holy Communion to James Connolly this morning," I said to Pearse when I met him. "Thank God," he replied, "It is one thing I was anxious about."
>
> Pearse assured me that he was not in the least worried or afraid; and that he did not know he deserved the privilege of dying for his country....
>
> I told Pearse that I would go to Rathfarnham at the earliest possible moment to break the news myself to his mother. Then

he made his confession. After that I gave Holy Communion to him.

Before the priest's arrival, Pearse had been writing his last two letters.

Kilmainham Prison,
Dublin.

3rd May, 1916.

To
William Pearse.

Dear old Willie,

Good-bye and God bless you for all your faithful work for me at St Enda's and elsewhere. No one can ever have had so true a brother as you.

P.

The second was finished after Father Aloysius's departure, within an hour of his execution.

Kilmainham Prison,
Dublin.

3rd May, 1916.

Mrs Pearse,
St Enda's College,
Rathfarnham;
or Cullenswood House,
Oakley Road,
Ranelagh.

My Dearest Mother,

I have been hoping up to now that it would be possible to see you again, but it does not seem possible. Good-bye, dear, dear Mother. Through you I say good-bye to Wow-Wow, M.B., Willie, Miss Byrne, Micheal, Cousin Maggie, and everyone at St Enda's. I hope and I believe that Willie and the St Enda's boys will be safe.

I have written two papers about financial affairs and one about my books, which I want you to get. With them are a few poems which I want added to the poems of mine in MS, in the large bookcase. You asked me to write a little poem which would seem to be said by you about me. I have written it, and one copy is at Arbour Hill Barracks with the other papers and Father

Aloysius is taking charge of another copy of it.

I have just received Holy Communion. I am happy except for the great grief of parting from you. This is the death I should have asked for if God had given me the choice of all deaths,—to die a soldier's death for Ireland and for freedom.

We have done right. People will say hard things of us now, but later on they will praise us. Do not grieve for all this, but think of it as a sacrifice which God asked of me and of you.

Good-bye again, dear, dear Mother. May God bless you for your great love for me and for your great faith, and may He remember all that you have so bravely suffered. I hope soon to see Papa, and in a little while we shall all be together again.

Wow-wow, Willie, Mary Brigid, and Mother, good-bye. I have not words to tell my love of you, and how my heart yearns to you all. I will call to you in my heart at the last moment.

Your son,
Pat.

There was an attempt to bring Willie to say good-bye to his brother before Patrick faced the firing-squad in the prison's stone-breakers' yard. Willie saw his mother and Margaret in the early hours of Thursday morning, shortly before his own execution, and told them what had happened. "Last night," he said, "I had a terrible experience. I was in prison over there (indicating across the road) when a guard of soldiers came and brought me here. About half way over we heard shots. The men looked at each other, and one said: 'Too late.' I think they were bringing me here to see Pat, but we heard only the volley that took him."

CHAPTER EIGHT

AFTERMATH

I The Political Legacy

Pearse was shot at 3.30 am on 3 May. So were Clarke and MacDonagh. Willie Pearse, Daly, Plunkett and Michael O'Hanrahan (a writer and friend of MacDonagh's, who fought with him in Jacob's Factory) died the following day. Major John MacBride died alone on 5 May. (His rank was a memento of the Irish Brigade, with whom he fought on the side of the Boers. He was married to Yeats's love, Maud Gonne.) Eamonn Kent, Con Colbert, Michael Mallin and Sean Heuston (whose tiny force had held the Mendicity Institution for two days against enormous odds) were executed on 8 May, and Thomas Kent (who fought a pitched battle with police on 2 May at his family home in County Cork) on 9 May. Sean MacDermott, who had at last been identified, is said to have fought hard for his life at his court-martial, demanding that the prosecutor prove that he had signed the proclamation. He and James Connolly (medically unfit for trial until 9 May) were shot on 12 May.

General Maxwell had not intended to stop at fifteen executions; 97 others had been condemned to death, following a piece of straightforward military logic. The casualties of the rising were high: although only about 60 rebels had been killed during Easter Week, 132 soldiers and police, and over 300 civilians had also died. Maxwell knew little of Ireland, and he had a mandate from the highest level to pacify it, with firmness, as a matter of urgency. He was no monster, but a soldier—not a politician. He set out to do the job the only way he knew—with exemplary executions and swingeing prison sentences on all known subversives. Interested parties with more subtle minds and better local knowledge spoke up early. John Dillon, who had been in Dublin during the rising, had written to his chief, John Redmond, as early as Sunday 30 April, with a prophetic warning.

> You should urge strongly on the Government the *extreme* unwisdom of any wholesale shooting of prisoners. The wisest course is to execute *no one* for the present.... If there were shootings of prisoners on a large scale the effect on public opinion might be disastrous in the extreme. *So far* feeling of the population

in Dublin is *against* the Sinn Feiners. But a reaction might very easily be created.

Redmond had quickly expressed in the House of Commons his abhorrence of the rising, but grew alarmed at the long-drawn-out executions, and exerted great pressure on Asquith to stop them. Asquith at first acted indirectly, sending a message to Maxwell *via* a third party to say that he was "a little surprised and perturbed by the drastic action of shooting so many rebel leaders". He acted more decisively, at Redmond's request, to save the life of Eoin MacNeill, who had precipitated his own arrest to show solidarity with the rebels and, perceptively, to ensure himself a future in Irish politics. MacNeill survived, but Maxwell was not prepared to accept from Asquith anything but a direct order; he ignored even a strong telegram from the prime minister before the last three executions, which stated that he hoped the shootings (other than in some quite exceptional cases) would cease. Maxwell was consistent in pursuing one of only two courses of action open to him. The moderate course suggested by Dillon, and the early release of detainees, would perhaps have restored friendly relations between the Castle and the Irish people. Had Maxwell been allowed to take his hard line to its conclusion, had he removed the seditious elements permanently —or at least until the episode was a dim memory—the peaceable majority might have reconciled itself quickly to the absence of a small part of its generation. But a compromise came, and it came late.

On 11 May, the leaders of the Irish parliamentary party, in a Commons debate, reflected the accelerating change in Irish public opinion. Redmond appealed for clemency, and Dillon, moved to bitterness by the twelve executions and by new details on the murder of Sheehy-Skeffington, made a powerful speech in defence of the rebels. "I admit they were wrong; I know they were wrong; but they fought a clean fight, and they fought with superb bravery and skill, and no act of savagery or act against the usual customs of war that I know of has been brought home to any leader or any organized body of insurgents." The Irish people, now reading more accurate accounts in their newspapers of the conduct of the heavily outnumbered rebels, felt a reluctant respect which Dillon shared. "... I declare most solemnly, and I am not ashamed to say it in the House of Commons, that I am proud of these men." And perceiving accurately that the electorate would come to make a choice between the constitutional Home Rulers and the revolutionaries, he called for "an absolute and final stop" to the executions. "You are letting loose a river of blood, and, make no mistake about it, between two races who, after three hundred years of hatred and of strife, we had nearly succeeded in bringing together."

Neither Dillon nor Redmond could save MacDermott and Connolly, arguably "quite exceptional cases". Maxwell was obdurate, and explained his policy to the prime minister.

> In view of the gravity of the Rebellion and its connections with German intrigue and propaganda and in view of the great loss of life and destruction of property resulting therefrom, the General Officer Commanding in Chief, Irish Command has found it imperative to inflict the most severe sentences on the organizers of this detestable Rising and on the Commanders who took an actual part in the actual fighting which occurred. It is hoped that these examples will be sufficient to act as a deterrent to intriguers and to bring home to them that the murder of His Majesty's subjects or other acts calculated to imperil the safety of the realm will not be tolerated.

Asquith did not intervene further over these two executions—a grave error of judgement. The circumstances of Connolly's execution particularly outraged public sensibilities: he had to be carried on a stretcher to the place of execution, and was shot sitting on a chair. The Irish people had read terse statements of the executions over a period of eight days; in a famous phrase, it was "as though they watched a stream of blood coming from beneath a closed door".[1]

Asquith succeeded in preventing any further executions, although imprisonments and internment *en masse* continued. After visiting Ireland from 12 to 19 May, he concluded that some effective form of government must be found, and put Lloyd George in charge of negotiations with the Unionists and Home Rulers to try and find a formula. The talks with these two irreconcilables broke down within two months. The royal commission on the rebellion reported in June, and heavily censured Nathan and Birrell for taking a soft line and allowing sedition to grow unchecked. With the old government discredited, the constitutionalists frustrated, and conciliation spent, the revolutionaries had scored their first political success.

Others were to follow. The Irish National Aid and Volunteers' Dependants' Fund, whose committee included Mrs Tom Clarke and Mrs Pearse, kept the memory of the executed and imprisoned men alive. With the release of all the internees in December 1916, and the prisoners in 1917, Sinn Fein, under Arthur Griffith (whose political respectability had been assured by his abortive effort to join the insurrection), staged a come-back. After initial electoral successes, Griffith gave way as leader to Eamonn de Valera, the senior surviving commandant of the rising, who was elected for East Clare in July 1917 on the platform of the proclamation. In the general election of 1918, Sinn Fein won 73 of the 105 seats, and effectively annihilated the Home Rulers. Although they had drawn up virtually no policy, Sinn Fein's success marked a new defiance in Ireland, which—though aided by the conscription threat—was chiefly based on an uncritical acceptance of the principles of the 1916 rebels. Simultaneously came a revitalization of the IRB, achieved largely by Michael Collins who, in his capacity as secretary to the Dependants' Fund, made use of its national network of contacts to set up an effective secret army.

Sinn Fein's birth certificate, said Sean T. O'Kelly, had been "written with steel in the immortal blood of martyrs in 1916".[2] For the moment the only dispute over the martyrs' testaments was between those who believed that the Irish Republic could be achieved through negotiation and passive resistance, and those, like Cathal Brugha, who believed that there was need for further bloodshed. There was more serious controversy later, after the success of the war of independence, when Irish plenipotentiaries to Downing Street agreed to take home with them a Free State and an oath of allegiance to the Crown—a provision of the treaty unacceptable to many.

The words of the 1916 revolutionaries were quickly brought into action in the debate which followed, and although the Free Staters (Mulcahy among them) made attempts to prove that Pearse would have accepted the treaty,[3] the rhetoric of the rising's leaders was more suited to use by the Republicans, and they soon established their right to mobilize the martyrs in their favour. Their heroes had claimed the right of a minority to determine, in defiance of the ballot-box, the future of the Irish people—a precedent and a comfort for the Republican side during the civil war, which took over where the debate left off. The Republicans lost the war, but found political respectability in 1926, when de Valera founded the Fianna Fail party—a minority strengthened by its virtual monopoly of the hallowed dead. Yet it was the same precedent of 1916, and the same justification of physical force, when the IRA opposed de Valera's new pragmatism after he came to power in 1932.

The debate as to where the dead men of 1916 would have stood on the divisive issues of modern Irish history can of course never be resolved. But Pearse and his friends had left, by their words and their actions, a political legacy which could be construed as a defence of the die-hards. The Republic proclaimed at Easter 1916 proved to be unattainable: partition could not be avoided; Pearse's Gaelic Ireland had died half-formed; Connolly's socialism was too strong for his conservative heirs. The major political parties eventually saw the inevitability of compromise: the majority of the people of Northern Ireland were in favour of partition; the imposition of compulsory Irish did not restore the language in all its glory; socialism proved repugnant to the people at large. Yet independent Ireland produced intransigent minorities, whose refusal to compromise should hardly have come as a surprise to generations accustomed to the taunt "Where were you in 1916?" Children in a free Ireland were nurtured on the writings and deeds of the men of 1916, and condemned by their own government when as adults they put into action the logic of force they absorbed from them. The self-styled ideological descendants of Pearse and Connolly still refuse to compromise over partition. They have a dubious precedent for the manner of their warfare, for Pearse and his comrades stood for an open confrontation (however hopeless) in which non-combatants died by accident rather than design. But taken out of context, there is ample material to support the most intractable political stance. Pearse, in May 1915, wrote an article on the founding of the Irish Volunteers:

> We have no misgivings, no self-questionings. While others have been doubting, timorous, ill at ease, we have been serenely at peace with our consciences. The recent time of soul-searching had no terrors for us. We saw our path with absolute clearness; we took it with absolute deliberateness. "We could do no other." We called upon the names of the great confessors of our national faith, and all was well with us. Whatever soul-searchings there may be among Irish political parties now or hereafter, we go on in the calm certitude of having done the clear, clean, sheer thing. We have the strength and peace of mind of those who never compromise.

Very soon afterwards, he and his fellows had entered the ranks of "great confessors of our national faith". Sean O'Faolain, during the civil war, shut himself up in his room to write Republican propaganda, and began to suffer the effects of isolation from reality.

> By now I was the mad mole who thought he had made Mont Blanc. I was the mouse in the wainscotting of the Vatican who believed that he told the Pope every night what His Holiness must tell the world every morning. I was Ireland, the guardian

of her faith, the one solitary man who would keep the Republican symbol alive, keep the last lamp glowing before the last icon, even if everybody else denied or forgot the gospel that had inspired us all from 1916 onwards. I firmly believed in the dogma that had by now become the last redoubt of the minority's resistance to the majority: that the people have no right to do wrong. Like all idealists, I was fast becoming heartless, humourless and pitiless.[4]

II The Legacy to the Family

With the deaths of Pat and Willie, Mrs Pearse and Margaret were left alone to grieve at St Enda's, besieged by debt. The estrangement with Mary Brigid had been aggravated by her opposition to her brothers' new militarism, and, although Mrs Pearse continued to support her, she could be of no assistance to them in their new trials. Her nervous condition was exacerbated by the family tragedy; unlike her mother and sister, she did not yet have the consolation of believing that her brothers had been martyred to glorious purpose. She praised them later, but never shared in the political and social honours heaped on her mother and sister.

Patrick had known his mother well, and even from the grave he could channel and moderate her grief through the poetry he had left her. Her sense of loss was intense, but so was her pride in her sons' death—in a cause which she had adopted loyally and wholeheartedly. (Ryan records her laughing response to a critic of the Irish Volunteers' guerrilla policy: "My good woman, don't argue with me about ambushes. Why, you will find ambushes in the Bible.")[1]

After their executions she had a week of near-madness, from which she emerged determined to keep them alive in the memory of their countrymen. Her grief would still overwhelm her in unguarded moments: sometimes, she told Desmond Ryan, "The long sorrow came upon her with a terrible intensity as she walked the Dublin streets by herself. She would look round and see people looking at her for she had called out: 'Pat and Willie! Pat and Willie!' "

During May she and Margaret tried to persuade the authorities to hand over the bodies of Pat and Willie for burial in consecrated ground. Dillon worked manfully for them, and stirred Asquith's compassion with a letter. "You know, I suppose, the deep feeling which exists in Ireland on this matter. I may say that in my deliberate opinion this poor lady, Mrs Pearse, has been cruelly treated. She had but the two sons—and the second—Willie Pearse—with whom I had a slight acquaintance—was a most inoffensive creature and in no sense a Leader amongst the rebels."[2] Although Asquith agreed initially to the request, Maxwell induced him to change his mind, pointing out that it would create an unfortunate precedent. "Irish sentimentality will turn these graves into martyrs' shrines to which annual processions, etc., will be made which will cause constant irritation in this country." Besides, it would be difficult to disinter the bodies, which had been buried without coffins in quick-lime in Arbour Hill. Maxwell also refused the family request to have Pearse's last writings, some of which he found objectionable.

The letters of sympathy which flowed in after the execution were mixed in the condolences they offered. Mrs Pearse's niece, Mary Kate Shovelton (who had been away from Ireland for many years) learned with horror about the rebellion from the hostile English press.

> Until I saw Pat's name in the paper on Sunday I never for one moment thought that he was mixed up in this terrible business. Each day I have lived in terror, and today to read in bald print that my own dear Pat had been shot was too awful. How on earth has it all come about? and what awful madness possessed him? Still, whatever I think, I know that he was possessed by none but the highest ideals, and my love remains unchanged.[3]

Even Mary Hayden could not wholly applaud her old friend's actions. "I regret very much that I saw so little of him lately, but I suppose it could not be well helped; he was heart and soul in a cause which, deeply as I sympathise with everything done for Ireland, I could not in conscience help. I do wish though that I had seen him even once in the last few months."[4] Other letters took a different line. One priest wrote to urge Mrs Pearse the course she quickly adopted.

> ... retain "The Hermitage", and thus continue the good work to which your dear martyred son devoted his great talents. Ireland, I have no doubt, will yet build a monument to his memory, but no monument were it to reach even to the skies can do him greater honour than the perpetuation of those noble ideals to which his best years were dedicated, and his life-blood ungrudgingly given. St Enda's is a national sanctuary, consecrated by the glorious work he initiated, and it would be a pity to see it return to profane uses....[5]

Such advice had a profound effect on Mrs Pearse and Margaret, appealing as it did to their sense of duty to their dead.

Even to contemplate running the school without its guiding spirit was awesome enough. The financial problems made things worse. Although Pearse had left statements on his financial affairs, he had died intestate, and his property was therefore divided equally among Mrs Pearse, Willie and his two sisters. With Willie's death, his quarter-share went equally to the three survivors, and the total was pitifully small, a tenth of James Pearse's legacy sixteen years earlier. The deeds of Cullenswood House were held as security for various loans, and the few remaining assets were valued at £187.13s.1d. Debts (and these excluded loans from friends) came to £2,259.0s.7d.[6] After the deduction of costs, 1s.3d. in the £ could be paid to creditors who, as a fellow revolutionary remarked wryly years later, constituted the majority of Pearse's mourners in 1916.[7]

Yet the financial omens were not all bad. In addition to contributions from well-wishers, and more substantial help from the Dependants' Fund, there were loyal old boys, ex-masters and friends of St Enda's to help re-open it in the autumn of 1916. The Fund paid the bill signed by Stephen Barrett which had so worried Pearse,[8] and left Mrs Pearse clear to open in Cullenswood House. Others were kind. M. H. Gill refused to accept any money from Pearse's estate, writing that "in the circumstances we could not think of retaining it".

When St Enda's re-opened, MacDonagh's brother Joseph became headmaster, and, with the release of the internees at Christmas, old boys Frank Burke and Brian Joyce returned as teachers. Joseph MacDonagh was re-arrested in a new purge late in 1917, and his place was taken by the ex-Chemistry master, Peter Slattery, later replaced in his turn by Frank Burke, who stayed on as headmaster until the school was finally closed down.

The experiment was not a success. Although money was available from Ireland, America and elsewhere, there were endless rows between the Pearses and the fund-raising committees, as well as among the members of the committees themselves. Money was raised by the Save St Enda's Committee in America to buy the Hermitage in 1920, and Mrs Pearse, on a tour of the States in 1924, raised over $10,000. But there were often strings attached to the money, and Mrs Pearse and Margaret bitterly resented the control exercised by the various committees over the financial and educational affairs of the school.

There were good reasons for excluding the Pearses as far as possible from the important business of the school. Although they were good-hearted and industrious, they had exercised no control of any kind while Pat and Willie were alive. Mrs Pearse had been purely a house-keeper, and Margaret's contribution to the teaching was kept within strict limits. With staff shortages, they became involved beyond their competence. One pupil who attended St Enda's in 1917 recalls being taught endless catechism, and little else, for the religious zeal of both Mrs Pearse and Margaret reached new heights after 1916.[9] Parents sympathetic to the memory of the Pearse brothers soon found that the school could not keep up its pre-war standards. A letter from Mrs Pearse to a dissatisfied father illustrates the problem. Where Pearse's letters to parents were models of intelligence and perception, his poor mother could substitute only her down-to-earth common sense.

> I assure you if you go into details you will find us most reasonable with regard to the boys not having learned I must say I have heard my daughter say several times she wished they would apply themselves better to study I know I heard her say one of them was so giddy and careless I don't know which. She will write to you all particulars on her return from her holidays. With regard to keeping them at home, I personally think that would be a great mistake, but this is for yourself to judge. My idea would be to give them a right good scolding and tell them you would take them away at the Xmas holidays if they did not do better.[10]

However clear it might be to committees and staff that the school must be run by professionals, such an idea broke Mrs Pearse's heart. She wrote about her loss of control as a disaster both for her and the school.

> My dear boys always held they would not be slaves, and now their devoted and dearly beloved Mother is expected to be a slave in her own house that home of such happy memories to her that home her heart was centered in and that she gave all she possessed to save *it* for the Irish Nation and to give them a chance to save it as a memorial to her loved ones....
>
> But if this sacrifice of mine made in good faith to keep it for the country can not be carried out on my sincere ideas better not be carried out at all.[11]

The disunity between the family and the governing committees seriously weakened St Enda's. Even good teachers could not work well in such an environment, and the old boys themselves realized that Patrick Pearse had been an essential and irreplaceable part of the school. It limped along until 1935, always operating at a loss, and suffering by competition with other more successful colleges. Numbers were low, ranging between about sixteen and thirty. When the school finally closed, it was tacitly admitted by many of those who had helped in its running that it should have died with its founder.

St Enda's was not the only area in which Mrs Pearse was out of her depth. She was a simple woman, ill-equipped for the burdens of her new prominence. Her understanding of politics had always been negligible: and after his death her only criterion was what she felt Pat would have wished. With the Irish *penchant* for heaping political honours on the widows and children of the famous dead, she did not remain long out of the political arena. Pearse's standing as president and his voluminous writings earned him the position of posthumous spokesman for the 1916 rising, and Mrs Pearse was elected to Dail Eireann in 1919 as the most glorious among Irish mothers. During the war of independence she suffered the indignities of her notoriety from the Black and Tans, who wrecked Cullenswood House and even the little cottage in Rosmuc. Her spirit pulled her magnificently through these encounters, and she missed no opportunity to shame her tormentors; but in the row over the treaty courage was not enough. She followed trustingly the political lead of Liam Mellows and Eamon de Valera, seeing in the latter the political successor of her son. And she made speeches to prove that Pearse would have opposed the treaty. No one is equipped to judge where Pearse would have stood on this or any later issues: it is enough to say that those who knew him were divided on the question. The Dogs split politically at this time, and Desmond Ryan in particular later expressed his regret that Mrs Pearse became involved. But she had no doubts.

> I rise to support the motion of our President for the rejection of this Treaty. My reasons for doing so are various, but my first reason for doing so is on my sons' account. It has been said here on several occasions that Padraic Pearse would have accepted this Treaty. I deny it, and on his account I will not accept it. Neither would his brother Willie accept it, because his brother was part and parcel of him ... if I accepted that Treaty ... I feel in my heart—and I would not say it only I feel it—that the ghosts of my sons would haunt me.[12]

Her support of de Valera led her to take sides in the civil war, where again she had to endure raids on her home—this time by Free State soldiers. Although she did not keep her seat in the Dail, she became a senator, and a member of the Fianna Fail executive.

In America, and for years in Ireland, she made what she humorously described as her "Pat and Willie speech", and thus unwittingly she helped make them the property of a political party rather than of a united country.

There were those who said of Mrs Pearse and her daughter that they thought they owned 1916. Certainly, their emergence as the most famous of the bereaved caused much resentment. Mrs Tom Clarke, who knew that her husband had been the main force for insurrection, was bitter when Pearse overshadowed him: she was one of many who blamed Mrs Pearse and Margaret for helping to distort the truth. Mrs Pearse herself indulged in acrimonious debate with those who questioned her son's primacy. When Devoy maintained his belief in Clarke as *the* rebel, Mrs Pearse told him never to mention her sons' names again[13]—an emotional reaction for which she could hardly be blamed. She was fed constantly on exaggerated tributes to her sons. Patrick Pearse was represented as the greatest of the patriot dead, and a fit subject for canonization. His mother could hardly be expected to see him in a lesser light. Margaret was equally susceptible, and equally vitriolic in her attacks on anybody who deviated from the true path—Patrick's path, as interpreted by the less imaginative minds who followed. She always wrote her name in Irish, but that was almost the limit of her knowledge of the language: yet she had no hesitation in branding "traitor" any individual who opposed its compulsory imposition.[14]

Sad though the 1920s were for those who wanted to see Patrick Pearse as a unifying rather than a divisive figure, the subsequent history of the family was even more depressing. Mrs Pearse died in 1932, leaving the St Enda's house and grounds to Margaret and, at her death, to the nation—as a memorial to Pat and Willie. Legal technicalities upset that provision of the will, so that Margaret inherited the Hermitage absolutely. There were several years of unedifying legal squabbles between Margaret and Mary Brigid over the other assets, and over the royalties on Patrick Pearse's writings (which brought in a small but steady income over the years). When, in 1935, Mary Brigid published a volume of assorted reminiscences, called *The Home-Life of Patrick Pearse*, Margaret claimed part of the proceeds on the grounds that his autobiographical fragment—quoted in the book—was their joint property. In pique, Mary Brigid withdrew the book. Relations never became good. Although Margaret, conscientious to the last, tried to see that Mary Brigid was well looked after, the old antipathy persisted until the latter died in 1947.

Nor were Margaret's last days happy. When she inherited her

mother's seat in the senate and on the Fianna Fail executive, she closed St Enda's, but insisted on living virtually alone in that huge building until she died. She was never free of money worries, and the house fell gradually into decay. Pressure from property developers and would-be legatees made her decide to leave the Hermitage away from the nation, and only the devoted work of Eamonn de Barra (whose admiration for her brother and affection for the family made him her chief support for many years) and the timely intervention of de Valera led her to change her mind at the last moment. St Enda's, vandalized and falling apart, eventually went to the Irish people, but not before many of Pearse's private papers had been destroyed by a fall of wet plaster from the ceiling of his study. Margaret died in 1969.

His family, in their innocence, had helped damage Patrick's political reputation and, in equal innocence, they tarnished his personal memory. His concern about the friends to whom he owed money was never made public, for it was thought discreditable for a national hero to be in debt. Stephen Barrett, for instance, was told by the bank that his bill had been paid, but he never knew that Pearse had remembered him at the last. Mrs Pearse did try to make amends to Joe Dolan. When she could afford it, in 1930, she wrote to ask him how much he was owed, and received a pathetic and noble letter from an old bed-ridden man.

> My total advance to Padhrig [sic] go ndeanidh Dia trocaire ar a anam [may God have mercy on his soul] was £1100. I never expected to see any of it and I preserved no record or evidence of it.
>
> ...
>
> If there is anything over in your hands after you have made full provision for your own and Miss Pearse's future I will be very thankful to get it as my means are quite reduced.[15]

She managed to find £600 for him.

The secrecy which surrounded the settling of Pearse's debts made him appear to have reneged on his friends. Family susceptibilities also led to his being labelled a snob. His autobiography had included a wholly truthful account of his humble origins, but the manuscript was amended for publication by Mary Brigid to give an impression of bourgeois respectability. To those who knew something of the truth, it appeared that he had written dishonestly. Of course, accusations of faithlessness or snobbery were made in whispers, and among a very few. The Pearse family were not the chief offenders in the distortion of the Pat and Willie story; their political canonization was undertaken by others whose emotions ruled their intellects. They created a legend which bore little relation to the truth, a legend the effects of which they could hardly have anticipated.

III The Legacy of Patrick Pearse

When Patrick Pearse was shot, few, other than his family and pupils, mourned the passing of a friend. Though there were many who respected him, he could not inspire the intimate love given to happier spirits, like the garrulous MacDonagh and the laughing MacDermott. Nor, though he was quite well-known, was he missed by the *literati* as a loss to poetry and drama—certainly not as Plunkett and MacDonagh were missed (to a large extent, perhaps, because his best work was written in Irish). Intellectually, few would have put him on a par with Connolly. George Russell (AE), wrote to Nathan: "I knew many of those now dead and had a genuine liking for them. They had no intellect. Connolly was the only one with a real grip on his mind. They were rather featherbrained idealists."[1] His political views were often distrusted by those of his countrymen who were aware of them. Yeats had shown insight before the rising. "Pearse is a dangerous man; he has the vertigo of self-sacrifice."[2]

His reputation was not long in the making. Emotion about the executed men quickly reached a high pitch, and the poets and writers reflected the new national spirit. It was inevitable that attention would be concentrated on the signatories of the proclamation—and primarily on the writers among them. Pearse, Connolly, MacDonagh and Plunkett appeared in the work of dozens of good and bad poets. Yeats and AE led the best.

Yeats:

"Oh words are lightly spoken,"
Said Pearse to Connolly,
"Maybe a breath of politic words
Has withered our Rose Tree;
Or maybe but a wind that blows
Across the bitter sea."

"It needs to be but watered"
James Connolly replied,
"To make the green come out again
And spread on every side,
And shake the blossom from the bud
To be the garden's pride."

"But where can we draw water,"
Said Pearse to Connolly,
"When all the wells are parched away?
O plain as plain can be
There's nothing but our own red blood
Can make a right Rose Tree."

AE:

Their dream had left me numb and cold,
  But yet my spirit rose in pride.
Refashioning in burnished gold
  The images of those who died
Or were shut in the penal cell.
  Here's to you, Pearse, your dream not mine,
But yet the thought for this you fell
  Has turned life's waters into wine.

And the lesser poets had their impact on public opinion, too.

Schoolmaster of all Ireland! May God give
Eternal rest to your most gallant soul.
You have more pupils now upon your roll
Than ever at St Enda's, and the new
Outdo the old in prouder love of you;
Learning with kindled hearts your lesson high,
Who taught your boys how Irish boys should live,
And taught your countrymen how men should die.[3]

Even Father Dinneen spoke kindly of Pearse in his verse, remembering in bewilderment the energetic, clever, talented man who wouldn't hurt a child or an animal.[4]

It was not only the poets who gave Pearse pride of place. In the rabid Irish-American press he was quickly established as the greatest of the martyrs. Both the *Irish World* (now growing as militant as its sister paper) and the *Gaelic American* had received garbled accounts of the rising within a few days of its outbreak, and printed confused and heavily padded reports on 29 April. The latter published a large photograph of Eoin MacNeill who, it assumed, was at the head of the rebels. But news of the proclamation of the Irish Republic had reached other parts of America by the time these newspapers were on the streets. Pearse's new political importance attracted a letter written on 29 April, from the Kutztown National Bank, Pennsylvania.

Hon Patrick Henry Pearse
Dublin

My dear Mr. Pearse

I notice your appointment as the First President of Ireland! Kindly allow me to congratulate you upon this auspicious event! I am making a collection of autographs of notables. I should be pleased to receive a few lines from you for this collection; sincerely hoping I may have a favourable response I am

Very Sincerely
O. P. GRIMLEY
Cashier.[5]

O. P. Grimley cannot have lived long in hope of a response; the *Gaelic American* had information on the first executions in the issue of 6 May. There was still confusion about who had actually "led" the rising. On 13 May, the *Gaelic American* described Clarke as "the strongest man among the twelve martyrs". The *Irish World* was still preoccupied with MacNeill, who was on his way to London, they thought, "to meet a martyr's fate". But in the ensuing weeks Pearse's position as president, and the weight of his literary output, gained him first place among the patriots. His last letter to his mother and "A Mother Speaks" were widely published, and his writings and speeches (particularly the American speeches) were quoted and requoted. By 10 June, in the *Irish World*, his pre-eminence was beyond doubt when they called a mass meeting to collect funds: "to sustain the Mother of P. H. Pearse and the Widows, Orphans and Relatives of the other Irish Martyrs". Pearse's name led all the rest on the inscribed tombstone (a Celtic cross) pictured on the front page of the *Gaelic American*. His 1914 visit to America was useful for propaganda purposes, since newspaper files held treasures of his political statements for reproduction.

No one with an eye for political survival in the new Ireland could afford to question Pearse's right to speak for his country. MacNeill regained prominence, like Griffith, by retrospective acceptance of the rising—aided by Pearse's testimonial written in Easter Week. De Valera stood for Pearse's Ireland. Only those prepared to stay out of Irish politics, like Hobson, dared state a contrary opinion. He wrote of Pearse later.

He was a sentimental egotist, full of curious Old Testament theories about being the scapegoat for the people, and he became convinced of the necessity for a periodic blood sacrifice to keep the National spirit alive. There was a certain strain of abnormality in all this. He did not contribute greatly to the hard grind-

> ing work of building up the movement, but as soon as we had succeeded in getting a small organisation and a handful of arms he seized the opportunity to bring about the blood sacrifice.[6]

In the tragic divisions which befell Ireland during the ten years after Pearse's death, it was he whose name appeared most often, with Mrs Pearse's *imprimatur*, in Republican propaganda. Pearse had stood for a Republic, and there were plenty of extracts from his writings to prove it. His deliberate and all-embracing canon of Irish history, his book of law, was plundered for acceptable rulings. Again, it took Sean O'Faolain to sum it up in retrospect. "... if men do not balance feelings and intelligence they lose command of both—and worse still, of their object. I fear that in 1922 our realists said goodbye to too many of their feelings. I cannot say that we idealists said goodbye to our intelligence, because, alas, if we had any worthy of the name I saw but little sign of it in those disheartening days of civil war."[7]

Pearse's writings were still a weapon in the 1930s. *An Phoblacht*, a Republican organ, sought to dislodge de Valera from his new pragmatism with quotations from the pages he had once used in his own climb to power, passages urging the sacrifice of expedient to principle. Pearse's mausoleum was built by republican hands, for his appeal was wholly for the idealists, for those who stood for the achievement of the impossible. He had written, as late as April 1916, an article sketching his idea of a free Ireland. Its legislators would be honest and capable. Its educational system would help every man and woman to become a perfect citizen.

> In a free Ireland there will be work for all the men and women of the nation. Gracious and useful rural industries will supplement an improved agriculture. The population will expand in a century to twenty millions; it may even in time go up to thirty millions. Towns will be spacious and beautiful (as the semi-free Anglo-Irish of the 18th century planned to make Dublin), but, since the country will chiefly rely on its wealth and agriculture and rural industry, there will be no Glasgows or Pittsburghs.
>
> Literature and art will flourish. The Tain and the Fionn-story will come again in mighty dramas. The voice of a people that has been dumb for many centuries will be heard anew; and it will make such music as has not been heard since Greece spoke the morning song of the free people.[8]

That was Pearse's independent Ireland. It goes without saying that he did not envisage partition. Nor could he guess that the modernization and mechanization of Irish agriculture would tend to increase the average size of farm holdings and, as an inevitable corollary, start a new wave of emigration—the cities (in the absence of a massive industrial expansion) could not absorb all the labour the vanishing small-holdings left idle.

The Irish tragedy of which O'Faolain speaks—the inability to combine pragmatism and idealism—has made selective appreciation of Pearse's qualities difficult. Sean O'Casey, who retained an affection for Pearse, had grave doubts about his influence on the workers of Dublin, and brought down a storm of abuse on his own head when, in 1926, the Abbey produced his play, *The Plough and the Stars* (the Citizen Army flag). Demonstrating the futility of death—even noble death—it dramatized the effect of Pearse's words on the emotional tenement dwellers of his Dublin. The reaction of Fluther Good, a carpenter, to the stirring oratory of Pearse at the grave of Wolfe Tone shows how O'Casey, after the civil war, felt about the rhetoric of blood.

> Fluther:
> Jammed as I was in th' crowd, I listened to th' speeches pattherin on th' people's head, like rain fallin' on th' corn; every derogatory thought went out o' me mind, an' I said to meself, "You can die now, Fluther, for you've seen th' shadow-dhreams of th' past leppin' to life in th' bodies of livin' men that show, if we were without a titther o' courage for centuries, we're vice versa now!" Looka here. (*He stretches out his arm under Peter's face and rolls up his sleeve.*) The blood was BOILIN' in me veins!

Not until recently have Irish writers again questioned the Pearse myth seriously. The idealists sought to put him beyond criticism. With a very few exceptions, everything written on him for 50 years after his death was designed to prove his sanctity, his vision, and the validity of even his wildest prognostications. The pragmatists, despairing of making him their own, tried to ignore him.

In the 1920s, Pearse's fame spread to the schoolchildren. With the achievement of Irish independence in 1922, the educators, anxious to promote the Irish language and its literature, were hampered by the paucity of suitable material. Pearse helped to fill the gap. His stories, poems and editions of Gaelic texts appeared on the syllabi, and gradually his English writings also achieved some prominence. *The Story of a Success* (an edition of his *Macaomh* writings) was set for the Kilkenny County Council scholarship, where examinees were asked questions like "Why would you like to visit Sgoil Eanna?" Students at training colleges were even required to study and regurgitate the seventeen-year-old Pearse's *Three Lectures on Gaelic Topics.*

His popularity with the department of education in the 1920s merely made the *name* of Pearse familiar to schoolchildren, but with Fianna Fail in power in 1932, a new spirit possessed the educators. Forgetful, it would seem, that the battle for an independent Ireland had already been won, and that revolution was no longer necessary, the *ideals* of Pearse (and to a very much lesser extent, of the more acceptable of his colleagues) became a faith for the primary schools, and for those of the secondaries ready to accept it. At the top of the department of education, some new men appeared—men stamped in the mould of the Cork Republicans of the civil war. In its notes for teachers, the department recommended Pearse's "The Singer", and provided a list of suitable songs in English, packed with Irish rebel ballads like "Who Fears to Speak of '98?" The teachers were instructed not only to teach excellent Irish, but to establish "the Gaelic outlook".

> The teaching of the Irish language itself is ... not an end in itself. The aim is broader and more difficult. It is to restore, as far as is practicable, the characteristically Gaelic turn of mind and way of looking at life. That Gaelic attitude, of course, gives us our individuality as a nation, without it we become an amorphous or a hybrid people and in these modern days of foreign penetration by newspaper, book and cinema, the need for a vivid conception of our duty in this regard is more urgent than ever.... Prayers and ordinary salutations and expressions breathing a high spirituality, a vivid awareness of the presence of God, and a deep spirit of resignation to his will are dominant elements in the Gaelic outlook on life.

This doctrine was almost pure Pearse, as expressed in "The Spiritual Nation", but "resignation to the will of God" had replaced the socially-advanced arguments of "The Sovereign People". (Connolly had been quietly forgotten by the majority of Irish politicians, and attempts by a socialist minority to have his ideas realized in the new State were firmly resisted. Although Sinn Fein, in 1919, had adopted a diluted version of the social principles of Pearse and Connolly, they were later dismissed by the Free State Minister, Kevin O'Higgins, as "pure poetry"; they remained anathema to both the majority parties.) The non-social ideals were still the property of Fianna Fail, which suppressed the IRA, ignoring that organization's debt to Pearse. The notes for teachers dealing with history made the objective clear.

> The continuity of the separatist idea from Tone to Pearse should be stressed. The events leading up to the Rising of 1916 and to the struggle that followed it will be so fresh in the minds of all teachers that there can be no difficulty in dealing with them vividly, or with the great language movement that was the inspiration of the leaders.

The teachers were recommended to study Pearse's *Collected Works* as an aid in this great effort. Each of them should be busy "imbuing the minds of his pupils with the ideals and aspirations of such men as Thomas Davis and Patrick Pearse". (Fintan Lalor was not mentioned.)

The schoolteachers of Ireland, struggling with overcrowded classrooms, inadequate facilities, poor pay and, often, their own weakness in the Irish language, tried hard to satisfy the ubiquitous inspectors. They might not be able to cultivate the Gaelic outlook but they could, without too much difficulty, impose on their pupils the ideals of Patrick Pearse, subtly described in the most popular history text-book as "The greatest of these leaders [of 1916] and one of the noblest characters in Irish history".[9] The schools, and particularly the Christian Brothers, dinned into successive generations—frequently with a liberal use of the cane—a veneration for this greatest of Irishmen. The human being disappeared under the weight of glorification: Pearse's admirers could no more see his flaws than he could see Tone's.

Since the fiftieth anniversary of the 1916 rising, there has been an attempt to re-assess Pearse and his associates. Better conditions in the schools, new text-books and a less partisan department of education have helped to modify the legend. In a powerful if intemperate article in 1972, Father Shaw described the damage done by an uncritical acceptance of the policies of the tiny revolutionary cabal.

> In the commonly accepted view of Irish history the Irishman of today is asked to disown his own past. He is expected to censure as unpatriotic the common Irishmen who were not attracted by the new revolutionary ideas, but who adhered to an ancient tradition. Irishmen of today are invited at least implicitly to apologize for their fellow-countrymen who accepted

loyally the serious guidance of the Church to which they belonged. Irishmen of today must despise as unmanly those of their own country who preferred to solve problems, if possible, by peaceful rather than by violent means.[10]

In his anger, Father Shaw made the same mistake as the propagandists he was attacking. No doubt intending to correct the balance, he painted Pearse in dark colours, contrasting starkly with the bright unsullied tints in which he had hitherto appeared: he too forgot the human being. Pearse can only be assessed accurately in the light of his own experiences and attitudes. Desmond Ryan, who loved him, and whose *A Man called Pearse* (1917), fanned the flames of the man-without-fault legend, wrote in his maturity a fine evaluation of the man behind the name.

> ... the Devil's Advocate will urge, provoked more by the successors of Pearse than Pearse himself, that though Pearse has been vindicated by results and by history, that his own temperament coloured his views, and ponder how far personal disillusion and ambition shaped his acts and outlook. Only very simple-minded admirers or very dishonest politicians can ignore this question, and to ignore it today is no service to Pearse or to truth. There was a disconcerting side to Pearse, especially in his earlier years. No honest portrait can hide certain shadows: a Napoleonic complex which expressed itself in a fanatical glorification of war for its own sake, an excess of sentiment which almost intoxicated him both on the platform and in private ventures, a recklessness in action and the narrow outlook of a very respectable Dubliner who has never left his city or family circle for very long. This is the very worst that the Devil's Advocate will be able to advance against Patrick Pearse. He had no petty vices nor meannesses, and to live with him was to fall under his persuasive spell. He was a recluse and a mystic, and no reader of the above list of possible grounds for criticism against Patrick Pearse should fail to correct them by Pearse's own personal defence in his poems, *The Rebel* and *The Fool*, and his play, *The Singer*, all written in answer to his own heart-searchings on the eve of the Insurrection. The testimony of his friends is unanimous: they all loved him even when his faults stood out before their eyes. Pearse towered over the Ireland of his time, a man who meant what he said and died and lived for it....
>
> There were strange contradictions in this great man, a man so great that it goes against the grain to have to search for the flaws in him as one remembers how he soared over the provincial

and Anglicised Ireland of his early years and confounded the time-serving politicians of his later days, and with open eyes walked to death with all his hopes in ruin around him.[11]

A less affectionate observer, the novelist James Stephens, wrote an equally perceptive appraisal:

> As to Pearse, I do not know how to place him, nor what to say of him. If there was an idealist among the men concerned in this insurrection it was he, and if there was any person in the world less fitted to head an insurrection it was he also.
>
> Men must find some centre either of power or action or intellect about which they may group themselves, and I think that Pearse became the leader because his temperament was more profoundly emotional than any of the others. He was emotional not in a flighty, but in a serious way, and one felt more that he suffered than that he enjoyed.
>
> ...
>
> It was not, I think, that he "put his trust in God", but that when something had to be done he did it, and entirely disregarded logic or economics or force. He said—such a thing has to be done and so far as one man can do it I will do it, and he bowed straightaway to the task.[12]

Yet neither of these analyses took into account Pearse's two major failings. Through his adult life he had been consistently disappointed in the response of his countrymen to the visions he laid before them, yet this never led him to question his own judgement. He wrote, acted and died for a people that did not exist; he distorted into his own image the ordinary people of Ireland, who lacked his own remarkable qualities, but who had perceptions and complexities of their own that he could never understand. His vanity smothered any evidence that might cast doubt on his convictions, or on the course of action that sprang from these convictions. If Pearse gave his contemporaries the key to a new self-respect, it was also the key to a Pandora's Box of troubles quite alien to his view of the world.

Ryan has described the rising as "the triumph of failure",[13] and it is a fitting epitaph for Pearse, whose achievements never measured up to his inflated aspirations. He failed, like many others, to save the living Irish language. He failed to inspire a new and glorious epoch in Gaelic literature. He failed, through his arrogance, to maintain a successful school. He failed to bring about a free, united and Gaelic Ireland. But he achieved, triumphantly, his greatest ambition of all:

> I care not though I were to live but one day and one night provided my fame and my deeds live after me.

SOURCES AND REFERENCES

The source material for this book was so extensive that I have had to cut references drastically to keep them to a manageable level. At the beginning of each section of these notes I list the main sources (see key below) for the section of the text it represents. The *numbered* notes lead to sources which are less frequently used. Where they duplicate "main source" entries, it is because I have felt the material to be especially important, controversial, or difficult to trace. I apologize for the arbitrariness of this method. Where an entry seems incomplete, cross-checking with the bibliography will provide fuller details.

ACS: *An Claidheamh Soluis*
BB: *Barr Buadh*
BOW: Board of Works (Pearse Family Papers)
DDA: Dublin Diocesan Archives
de B: Eamonn de Barra (Pearse Family Papers)
FL: *Fainne an Lae*
FLD: Folk-lore Department
FCMB: Gaelic League; Finance Committee Minute Book
GLMB: Gaelic League; Minute Book of the Coiste Gnotha
Home-Life: Pearse, *The Home-Life of Patrick Pearse*
JPP: James Pearse Papers (NLI)
Kerr: Kerr, *The Gaelic Revival* (thesis in UCD Library)
Last Words: Mac Lochlainn, *Last Words*
Mahaffy: Stanford and MacDowell, *A biography of an Irishman*
MP: Mrs Margaret Pearse Papers (NLI)
MNP: MacNeill Papers (NLI)
Mulcahy: Mulcahy Papers (UCD)
Murder Machine: *see* Pearse, *Collected Works: Political Writings*
NLI: National Library of Ireland
PA: Pearse's Autobiographical Fragment (de B)
PCMB: Gaelic League: Minute Book of the Publications Committee
PPP: Patrick Pearse Papers (NLI)
PRO: Public Record Office of Ireland

Remembering Sion: Ryan, *Remembering Sion*
TCD: Trinity College, Dublin
The story of a success: *see* Pearse, *Collected Works: St. Enda's and its Founder*
"They were schoolboys": *Christian Brothers Westland Row Centenary Record*
UCD: Archives Department, University College, Dublin
WPP: William Pearse Papers (NLI)

Chapter One: Beginnings

i. James and Margaret
JPP; PA; Births, deaths and marriages records, Dublin and London; *Thom's Directories*; *Irish Builder*.

1. de B: PA
2. *ibid*
3. de B: Devine to Pearse (26.12.1877)
4. Barrett MSS (NLI); Lennon to Sighle Barrett, 14.5.58
5. JPP: correspondence of James Pearse and Margaret Brady
6. de B: PA

ii. Childhood
Home-Life; JPP; *Remembering Sion*; *Thom's Directories*.

1. *Home-Life* p. 31
2. *ibid* p. 37
3. JPP: Mrs Pearse to James Pearse (16.9.year undated)
4. ACS 19.5.06
5. de B: Conditions of Partnership
6. de B; James Pearse to Archdeacon Kinane (13.1.1883)
7. JPP: Entry dated 4.9.1889 in Account Book
8. Dublin Exhibition Catalogue
9. JPP: *passim*

iii. School
Home-Life; "They were schoolboys".

1. *Home-Life* p. 26
2. O'Faolain, *Vive Moi* p. 95
3. Ryan, *Remembering Sion* p. 64
4. Pearse, "The Murder Machine"
5. Curran, *Under the Receding Wave* p. 60

6. O'Neill, "Patrick Pearse"
7. Curran, *op. cit.* p. 37
8. ACS 5.10.07
9. *ibid*
10. Gaelic League Membership Book (NLI)
11. BOW
12. O'Neill, "A Translation by P. H. Pearse", in *Samhain*, La Samhna, 1917, p. 2
13. BOW
14. *Home-Life* p. 141
15. FL 28.5.98

iv. The Gaelic League
FL; GLMB.

1. O'Casey, *Drums under the Windows*, p. 410
2. Ryan, *op. cit.* pp. 104-5
3. O'Casey, *op. cit.* p. 410
4. GLMB 3.11.1897
5. MNP: Pearse to MacNeill (20.12.1897)
6. FL 29.1.1898
7. *ibid* 8.1.1898
8. *ibid* 5.3.1898
9. *ibid* 16.4.1898
10. *Shan Van Vocht* 6.6.1898
11. *Irish Monthly* June 1898
12. *New Ireland Review* June 1898

CHAPTER TWO: ASPIRATIONS

i. The Coiste Gnotha
MNP; FL; GLMB; ACS.

1. *Home-Life* p. 137
2. O'Casey, *op. cit.* p. 428
3. FL, "Cuairt ar Arainn na Naomh", 19.11.1898
4. Holloway diaries, 5.1.1899
5. FL 14.1.1899
6. Walsh, *Old Friends*, p. 9
7. Fathers of the Society of Jesus, *A page of Irish History*, p. 478
8. *ibid* p. 503
9. Budgen, *Further recollections of James Joyce* p. 10

10. GLMB 4.7.1899
11. Henry Morris Letter Book: Pearse to Henry Morris (30.8.1899)
12. ACS 6.5.1899

ii. The League and the Pan-Celts
GLMB; ACS; FL.

1. MNP: Hyde to MacNeill (n.d.)
2. FL 19.8.1899
3. MNP: Borthwick to Hyde (15.1.1900) (copy)
4. MNP: Hyde to MacNeill (n.d.)
5. Doyle MSS: Pearse to Doyle (31.8.1901)
6. Later published in *Os Cionn na Fairrge agus Aisti Eile*
7. MNP: O'Growney to MacNeill (2.3.1899)
8. Ryan, *op. cit.* p. 93
9. *ibid*
10. O'Rahilly Thomas F., *Early Irish History and Mythology*, Dublin, 1946, p. 261
11. O'Neill, "Patrick Pearse"

iii. The League's New Horizons
Kerr; Mahaffy.

1. Doyle MSS: Pearse to Doyle (12.7.1900)
2. *ibid* (25.7.1900)
3. Quoted in ACS 21.4.1900

iv. The Publications Committee
GLMB; PCMB.

1. Doyle MSS: Pearse to Doyle (2.7.1900)
2. DDA: Pearse to Walsh (22.11.1900)
3. *ibid* (19.12.1900)
4. *Leader* 22.2.02
5. *Banba* June 1903
6. *Leader* 1.3.1902
7. *ibid*

v. New Responsibilities
Thom's Directories; Ryan, *Remembering Sion*; ACS; GLMB.

1. *Irish Builder* 15.9.1900
2. *Freeman's Journal, Irish Independent* 8.9.1900
3. de B: Brady's Will
4. de B: PA

5. PRO: Calendar of Wills and Probate
6. TCD: Attendance Book, Constitutional and Criminal Law Classes, 1889-1901
7. ACS 6.4.1907
8. O Ceilleachair, *An Duinnineach* p. 198
9. PPP: Glynn to Pearse (n.d.)
10. MNP: O'Hickey to MacNeill (23.10.1901)

vi. An Claidheamh Soluis
ACS; MNP.

1. Greene David H., *J. M. Synge* p. 104
2. ACS 26.4.1902
3. Later published in *Os Cionn na Fairrge agus Aisti Eile*
4. ACS 16.8.1902
5. MNP: O'Hickey to MacNeill (11.4.1902)
6. Holloway diaries, 1908, p. 1254
7. *ibid*, 1906, p. 273
8. *Banba* April 1903
9. Hayden diaries, 7.3.1903
10. Doyle MSS: Pearse to Doyle (25.2.1903)
11. *ibid* (27.2.1903)
12. Hyde, *Mise agus an Connradh* p. 101

CHAPTER THREE: JOURNALIST

i. The New-Style Claidheamh
ACS; FCMB; Gaelic League Annual Reports.

1. Hyde, *Mise agus an Connradh* pp. 123-4
2. O'Kelly MSS: Pearse to O'Kelly
3. Circular with ACS November 1903
4. *Home-Life* p. 77
5. *ibid* pp. 77-8

ii. Issues
ACS; MNP.

1. ACS 27.8.1904
2. ACS 7.1.1905
3. *ibid*
4. ACS 26.11.1904
5. ACS 19.11.1904
6. ACS 19.1.1907

7. ACS 11.5.1907
8. MNP: MacCumhaill to MacNeill (20.5.1907)
9. "From a Hermitage"
10. ACS 16.11.1907
11. GLMB
12. DDA: O'Farrelly to Walsh (28.11.1907)
13. ACS 10.12.1904
14. ACS 7.1.1905
15. ACS 26.6.1909
16. ACS 7.8.1909
17. *ibid*
18. ACS 18.7.1903
19. ACS 27.8.1904
20. ACS 7.12.1907
21. Wall Maureen, "The Decline of the Irish Language"
22. FLD: Hyde, Memoirs
23. O Ceallaigh Sean T., *Sean T.*, Dublin, 1963, I, pp. 64-5
24. ACS 20.5.1905
25. Clery Arthur, "Patrick Pearse's Only Case", in Walsh, *Old Friends*
26. Irish Law Reports 1905
27. ACS 23.9.1905
28. ACS 30.12.1905

iii. Discord

ACS; GLMB.

1. ACS 21.3.1903
2. ACS 11.3.1905
3. O'Casey, *op. cit.* pp. 501-2
4. O'Hegarty, "P. H. Pearse"
5. ACS 27.8.1904
6. ACS 10.9.1904
7. ACS 23.12.1905
8. Gwynn Stephen, *Experiences of a Literary Man* p. 283
9. ACS 28.7.1906
10. O Ceilleachair, *An Duinnineach* p. 137
11. PPP: Dinneen to Pearse (n.d.)
12. *Leader* 22.2.1908
13. ACS 23.5.1908
14. Quoted *ibid*
15. ACS 30.5.1908
16. *ibid*
17. FLD: Hyde, Memoirs

iv. Prose and Poetry

ACS; PCMB.

1. de B: Hyde testimonial (2.10.1905)
2. ACS 13.6.1903
3. *Amhrain Chuilm de Bhailis*, Dublin, 1904
4. ACS 9.5.1903
5. "Litridheacht Nua-Dheanta", in *St Stephen's*, June, 1901
6. ACS 24.8.1904
7. Lady Gregory, *Seventy Years 1852-1922*, London, 1974, p. 549
8. ACS 6.2.1904
9. ACS 10.2.1906
10. ACS 26.5.1906
11. *ibid*
12. ACS 2.6.1906
13. ACS 28.11.1908
14. French, "J. O. Hannay and the Gaelic League"
15. ACS 6.10.1906
16. George Moore had attempted to encourage the modernization of Irish fiction by allowing the Gaelic League to translate and publish some of his stories. The League showed little enthusiasm; they were not ready for him. Cf. Moore, *The Untilled Field*, London, 1914, p. vi
17. ACS 26.5.1906
18. *Irish People* 5.5.1906
19. *ibid* 12.5.1906
20. *Banba* June 1906
21. ACS 23.5.1908
22. UCD Archives: Pearse to Editor *An Connachtach* (16.1.1908)
23. ACS 21.11.1908
24. Later published in *Os Cionn na Fairrge agus Aisti Eile*
25. ACS 1.9.1906
26. Later published in *Os Cionn na Fairrge agus Aisti Eile*
27. ACS 21.12.1907

v. The Irish Theatre

1. ACS 28.1.1905
2. *ibid*
3. ACS 22.4.1905
4. ACS 16.6.1906
5. ACS 9.2.1907
6. ACS 2.3.1907

7. *ibid*
8. ACS 6.4.1907
9. *ibid*
10. *ibid*

vi. The Schools
ACS

1. O'Hegarty P. S., "P. H. Pearse"
2. ACS 12.11.1904
3. ACS 13.1.1906
4. NLI Ms 10,192: Pearse to O'Kelly (4.7.1905)
5. Pearse Margaret, "Patrick and Willie Pearse", in *Capuchin Annual*, 1943
6. de B: Hyde testimonial (2.10.1905)
7. ACS 26.1.1907
8. ACS 5.1.1907
9. ACS 6.1.1906
10. *ibid*
11. ACS 25.11.1905
12. ACS 26.1.1907
13. ACS 28.7.1908
14. MNP: Beaslai to MacNeill (4.4.1908)
15. ACS 4.4.1908
16. ACS 13.4.1907

Chapter Four: St Enda's

i. Plans
Thom's Directories; *The Story of a Success*; MNP.

1. DDA: O'Nowlan to Walsh (14.1.1906)
2. A useful summary by Padraig O Snodaigh, "Willie Pearse: Artist" is in *Leabhran Cuimhneachain*
3. Pearse Margaret, *op. cit.*
4. Registry of Deeds, No. 282, Chapman to Pearse, Book 66 of 1908
5. Ryan, *op. cit.* p. 126
6. DDA: Walsh to Pearse (29.7.1908), Pearse to Walsh (15.7.1908, 17.11.1908, 16.12.1908)
7. Delaney Joyce, *No Starch in my Coat*, London, 1971, p. 8
8. Glenavy, Beatrice Lady, *Today We Will Only Gossip*, London, 1964, p. 91

9. *ibid* p. 92
10. MacManus MSS (NLI): Pearse to MacManus (4.3.1908)

ii. The First Year

ACS; *Remembering Sion.*

1. ACS 12.9.1908
2. ACS 3.10.1908
3. WPP: correspondence of William Pearse and Mabel Gorman (1908-1912)
4. PPP: Hayden to Pearse (n.d.)
5. Holloway diaries, 22.3.1909
6. *An Macaomh* June 1909
7. Holloway diaries, 22.6.1909
8. ACS 3.7.1909
9. O Criomhthain, *An t-Oileanach* pp. 216-7
10. Holloway diaries, 16.8.1910
11. ACS 21.8.1909
12. ACS 4.9.1909
13. Oral recollection of Geraldine Dillon
14. Le Roux Louis, *La Vie de Patrice Pearse* p. 114
15. Oral recollection of Sheila O'Sullivan
16. ACS 7.11.1908
17. Oral recollection of Geraldine Dillon
18. MNP: Ryan to MacNeill (Friday, n.d.)

iii. 1909-1910

Remembering Sion; *Story of a Success*; PPP and de B: Rolls and Accounts.

1. *An Macaomh* December 1909
2. *ibid*
3. Ryan, *op. cit.* p. 158
4. Reddin, "A Man Called Pearse"
5. O Conaire Padraic Og, "Cuimhni Scoil Eanna"
6. Pearse Margaret, *op. cit.*
7. Ryan, *op. cit.* p. 147
8. Mac Garry, "Memories of Sgoil Eanna"

iv. The Hermitage 1910-1912

Remembering Sion; *Story of a Success*; PPP and de B: Rolls and Accounts.

1. *An Macaomh* December 1910

2. Ryan, *op. cit.* p. 119
3. WPP: Draft letter in sketching book
4. Ryan, *op. cit.* p. 114
5. Ryan, *op. cit.* p. 115
6. Padraic Og O Conaire, the distinguished writer, was a notable exception
7. Yeats, *Autobiographies* p. 505
8. Bloomer MSS: MacDonagh to Bloomer (17.6.1910)
9. Colum Mary, *Life and the Dream* p. 151
10. Bloomer MSS: MacDonagh to Bloomer (23.7.1910)
11. *Home-Life* p. 153
12. *ibid* p. 154
13. Nic Shiubhlaigh Maire, *The Splendid Years* pp. 145-6
14. Holloway diaries, 7.4.1911
15. *Irish Review* May 1911
16. Mac Garry, *op. cit.*
17. Casement MSS: Pearse to Casement (15.6.1911); Inglis, *Roger Casement* p. 192
18. Parminter Geoffrey, *Roger Casement*, London, 1936, pp. 93-4

v. Finances

Alec Wilson papers; Holloway papers; PPP; de B: Dolan correspondence.

1. de B: Pearse to Dolan (1.2.1909)
2. Hutton MSS: Pearse to Hutton (18.8.1909)
3. Holloway diaries, 15.7.1910
4. Ryan Desmond, "St Enda's—Fifty Years after"
5. Wilson MSS: Pearse to Wilson (23.6.1912)
6. PPP: M. H. Gill to Pearse (29.9.1911)
7. PPP: Bolands Ltd to Pearse (15.8.1912)
8. PPP: Martyn to Pearse (2.9.1912)
9. Ryan, *Remembering Sion* p. 126
10. Stephens, *The Insurrection in Dublin* p. 79

CHAPTER FIVE: POLITICS

i. 1910-1912

Remembering Sion; Le Roux, *Tom Clarke*; O Snodaigh, *Comhghuallithe*.

1. O Luing Sean, *Art O Griofa* p. 134
2. Ryan, *The Pope's Green Island* p. 291
3. Gwynn Denis, "Patrick Pearse"

4. PPP: MacCartan to Pearse (27.5.1910)
5. Ryan, *Remembering Sion* pp. 110-11
6. In Hobson MSS
7. Hobson interviewed by F. X. Martin (11.12.1960)

ii. An Barr Buadh
Remembering Sion; Le Roux, *Tom Clarke*; *BB*.

1. Hobson interviewed by F. X. Martin (11.12.1960)
2. *Irish Freedom*, March 1912
3. Gwynn Stephen, *John Redmond's Last Years*, London, 1919, p. 65
4. BB 5.4.1912
5. BB 27.4.1912
6. Blaghd Ernan de, *Slan le hUltaibh* p. 102
7. Mulcahy MSS: Mulcahy
8. Gwynn Denis, "Patrick Pearse"
9. BB 16.3.1912
10. O Cearnaigh Peadar in Burca Seamus de, *The Soldier's Song*, 2nd ed. Dublin, 1958, p. 94
11. Ryan, *op. cit.* p. 126

iii. 1912-1913
Alec Wilson papers; PPP and de B: Accounts and Rolls; *Story of a Success*

1. PPP: Leslie to Pearse (n.d.)
2. MacManus MSS (NLI): Hyde to MacManus (n.d.)
3. PPP: MacDonagh to Pearse (30.8.1912)
4. Ryan, *op. cit.* pp. 159-60
5. A selection of these can be found in the Henderson MSS
6. Holloway diaries, 25.2.1911
7. Nic Shiubhlaigh, *op. cit.* p. 151
8. BOW: Mrs Pearse to Margaret (n.d.)
9. Holloway diaries, 24.11.1913
10. *Home-Life* p. 75
11. Reddin, "A Man Called Pearse"
12. Mulcahy MSS: Sinn Fein Minute Books (22.5.1913), P7/2/2 (no. 5)
13. O'Casey, *op. cit.* p. 618
14. *ibid*
15. Holloway diaries, 14.6.1913

iv. The Volunteers and the IRB

Irish Freedom; Martin, *Irish Volunteers*; *The Irish Volunteer*. O Snodaigh, *Comhghuaillithe*

1. "How does She Stand"
2. "From a Hermitage"
3. Parks, *Thomas MacDonagh*
4. BB 11.5.1912
5. *Home-Life* p. 79
6. Nic Shiubhlaigh, *op cit.* pp. 148-9
7. MacNeill, "How the Volunteers Began", in *The Irish Volunteers* (*ed.* Martin), p. 72
8. Hobson MSS
9. *ibid*
10. Inglis, *Roger Casement* p. 248
11. FLD: Hyde, Memoirs
12. *Irish Worker* 21.2.1914
13. Dudley Edwards and Ransom (*eds.*), *James Connolly: Selected Political Writings*, London, 1973, p. 150

v. The American Tour

Gaelic American; de B; McGarrity papers

1. PPP: Keogh to Pearse (1.3.1910)
2. Reid, *The Man from New York* p. 123
3. *ibid* p. 212
4. Dudley Edwards, "American Aspects of the Rising", in Edwards, *1916*, p. 154
5. Gaelic American 24.1.1914
6. Hobson MSS
7. *Devoy's Post-Bag*: Hobson to Devoy, 4.7.13
8. de B
9. *Gaelic American* 7.3.1914
10. PPP: text of October 1912 appeal
11. *Irish World* 25.4.14
12. Dudley Edwards, *op. cit.* p. 189
13. McGarrity note in Hobson MSS
14. *Gaelic American* 28.2.1914
15. "Oration on Robert Emmet"
16. "Second Oration on Robert Emmet"
17. O Luing Sean, *John Devoy*, Dublin, 1961, p. 194
18. Reid, *The Man from New York* p. 233
19. McGarrity, "Twenty Years Ago in America"
20. NLI microfilm n5914 p6431: Pearse to Nolan (27.4.1914)

Chapter Six: Preparations

i. "I have turned my face to this road before me"

1. *An Macaomh* May 1913
2. *Remembering Sion* p. 124
3. Oral recollection of Margaret Pearse to Eamon de Barra
4. Ryan, *The Man Called Pearse* p. 187
5. *Irish Volunteer* 7.2.14, 27.2.15
6. Quoted in Ryan, Desmond, "St Enda's—Fifty Years After"
7. *Remembering Sion* p. 166
8. Lee, Joseph, *The Modernisation of Irish Society, 1848-1918*, Dublin, 1973, pp. 141-9
9. de B: Letter Book
10. Horgan, *From Parnell to Pearse*

ii. The Struggle for the Volunteers
Irish Volunteer; Martin, *Irish Volunteers*; O Snodaigh, *Comhghuaillithe*; McGarrity papers; Hobson MSS

1. *Irish Worker* 24.1.14
2. *Devoy's Post Bag*, ii, pp. 445-6
3. *Irish Worker*, 30.5.14
4. Gwynn, Denis, "Patrick Pearse"
5. Martin, *Irish Volunteers* p. 144
6. Judge, M. J., "The Inner History of the Volunteers", in *Irish Nation*, Vol. i
7. Hobson MSS
8. *Irish Worker* 20.6.14
9. Ryan, "Pearse, St Enda's College, and the Hound of Ulster"
10. "From a Hermitage"
11. Mulcahy MSS; Mrs Clark P7/D/2, 14
12. *Los Angeles Examiner*
13. *Labour News* 1.5.37
14. McGarrity MSS; Pearse to McGarrity 3.8.14
15. *Gaelic American* 10.10.14

iii. The Achievement of Power
Irish Volunteer; Martin, *Irish Volunteer*; Hobson MSS; O Snodaigh, *Comhghuaillithe*

1. Blaghd, Ernan de, *op. cit.*, p. 116
2. McGarrity MSS; Pearse to McGarrity, 19.10.14
3. *ibid*
4. Holloway diaries, 20.11.14

5. *ibid*
6. *Remembering Sion* p. 165
7. BB 25.5.12
8. Longford, *Eamon de Valera* p. 24
9. *ibid*
10. O'Neill, *De Valera* p. 42
11. *Workers' Republic* 3.7.15
12. *Irish Freedom*
13. de B
14. Bloomer MSS; Pearse to Bloomer, 3.12.15
15. Blaghd Ernan de, *op. cit.* pp. 165-6
16. *Remembering Sion* pp. 183-93
17. Le Roux, *Tom Clarke*
18. *Remembering Sion,* pp. 192-3
19. O'Donovan Rossa—Graveside Oration
20. Daly Martin, *Memories of the Dead* p. 18
21. *Remembering Sion* p. 193

iv. The IRB at Work

McGarrity papers; O Snodaigh, *Comhghuaillithe*; Lynch, *The IRB*; Hobson MSS

1. Cronin, *The McGarrity Papers* p. 59
2. Daly, *Memories of the Dead* p. 19
3. Mulcahy MSS: McCullough to Mulcahy, P7/D/14-15
4. *ibid*
5. Martin, *Irish Volunteer* p. 199
6. *Workers' Republic* 27.11.15
7. Hobson MSS: O'Connell memoirs
8. Longford, *Eamon de Valera* p. 24
9. *Workers' Republic* 18.12.15
10. *ibid* 25.12.15
11. *Remembering Sion, passim*
12. *Workers' Republic* 15.1.16
13. *ibid* 29.1.16
14. Cronin, *op. cit.*, p. 60
15. Hobson MSS: O'Connell memoirs
16. *ibid*
17. O Snodaigh, *Comhghuaillithe* p. 146
18. Martin, "Eoin MacNeill and the 1916 Rising", *Irish Historical Studies*, xii (1961)
19. Hobson, *Ireland Yesterday and Tomorrow* p. 74
20. Hobson MSS
21. *Workers' Republic* 5.2.16

22. *ibid* 18.3.16

v. The lead-up to Insurrection

O Snodaigh, *Comhghuaillithe*; Martin, "Eoin MacNeill"; O Broin, *Dublin Castle*; Hobson MSS

1. Mulcahy MSS; McCullough P7/D/14-15
2. O Broin, *Dublin Castle* pp. 72-3
3. Hobson MSS
4. Mulcahy MSS; McCullough P7/D/14
5. O'Kelly MSS
6. Pearse Margaret, "St Enda's", in *Capuchin Annual*, 1966
7. O Broin, *op. cit.* p. 84
8. *Remembering Sion* p. 129

Chapter Seven: The Rising

i. Easter Monday

Fitzgerald, *Memoirs*; Ryan, *The Rising*; Lynch, *The IRB*

1. Bloomer MSS: Pearse to Bloomer 23.4.16
2. Father Aloysius, "Easter Week 1916", in *Capuchin Annual*, 1966
3. Eyewitnesses have said only that it was a sister of Pearse, but there can be little doubt about it being Mary Brigid rather than Margaret. M.B. was in the city that day (*Home-Life*, p. 122); she loathed her brothers' military activities (evidence of Frank Burke) whereas Margaret was sympathetically disposed (*ibid*)
4. Daly, *Memories of the Dead* p. 19
5. Taylor Rex, *Michael Collins*, London, 1958, p. 77

ii. The General Post Office

Lynch, *The IRB*; Fitzgerald, *Memoirs*; *Last Words.*

1. *Irish Times* 25.4.16
2. Ryan James, "The G.P.O.", in *Capuchin Annual*, 1966; Mulcahy MSS; Mrs Mulcahy
3. *ibid*
4. Ryan, *The Rising* p. 143
5. *ibid*, p. 145
6. Taylor, *Michael Collins*, London, 1958, p. 77
7. Quoted in Caulfield, *The Easter Rebellion* p. 329

iii. Surrender

Last Words; Grenan and O'Farrell articles; Ryan, *The Rising*

1. NLI MS 15,000 (4)
2. *Last Words* pp. 13-14

iv. Court-Martial and Execution

O Broin, *Dublin Castle*; *Last Words*

1. O Briain, *Cuimhni Cinn* pp. 151-2
2. MS Asquith 43, fols, 149-50
3. *ibid*
4. MS Asquith 43, fols, 145, 153-4
5. Kilmainham Museum: Harrison to Pearse 24.4.16
6. Elizabeth Countess of Fingall, *Seventy Years Young*, London, 1937, p. 375

CHAPTER EIGHT: AFTERMATH

i. The Political Legacy

O Broin, *Dublin Castle*

1. Elizabeth Countess of Fingall, *Seventy Years Young*, p. 376
2. *Official Report of the Dail Debates on the Treaty of 6 December, 1921*, p. 135
3. Mulcahy MSS: Mulcahy
4. O'Faolain, *Vive Moi* p. 164

ii. The Legacy to the Family

BOW papers; MP:

1. *Remembering Sion*, p. 131
2. MS Asquith 43, Dillon to Asquith, 24.5.16
3. MPP: Shovelton to Mrs Pearse 3.5.16
4. MP: Hayden to Mrs Pearse 20.6.16
5. MPP: Nevin to Mrs Pearse 19.5.16
6. Holloway Papers: Maher to Holloway 13.4.17
7. Oral recollection of Liam O Briain to Sheila O'Sullivan
8. Barrett MSS (NLI)
9. Oral recollection of R. Dudley Edwards
10. MP: Mrs Pearse to ? (illegible) n.d.
11. MP: Mrs Pearse to Fr ? (illegible) 2.3.20
12. Quoted in *Remembering Sion*, p. 132
13. Ryan, *Devoy's Post Bag*, II, p. 439

14. de Barra Eamonn, "A Valiant Woman", in *Capuchin Annual*, 1969
15. MP: Dolan to Mrs Pearse 15.1.30, 22.1.30

iii. The Legacy of Patrick Pearse

1. O Broin, *Dublin Castle* p. 168
2. Lady Gregory *Seventy Years* p. 549
3. MP: Anon
4. O Ceilleachair, *An Duinnineach* p. 234
5. PPP: Grimley to Pearse 29.4.16
6. Hobson MSS
7. O'Faolain, *Vive Moi* p. 151
8. Pearse, "The Heart's Desire", *Spark*, April 1916
9. Carty James, *A Class-Book of Irish History*, London, 1946, p. 111
10. Shaw Francis, "The Canon of Irish History—a Challenge", in *Studies*, Summer 1972
11. *Remembering Sion*, pp. 342-3
12. Stephens, *The Insurrection in Dublin* pp. 78-90
13. Ryan, *The Rising* p. 257

SELECT BIBLIOGRAPHY

For any study of Pearse and his context, there are many more sources than will be found listed here; this bibliography names only those items which have provided useful information in appreciable quantities. Where a source has been consulted on one or two matters only, and has made no further impact on the general argument, it has usually been cited in the relevant section of the notes, not here. An excellent general bibliography of the period is appended to F. S. L. Lyons's *Ireland Since the Famine*, London, 1971.

There is a lot of material about Pearse scattered through journals and newspapers published since his death. Much of it is derivative, of dubious accuracy, or otherwise valueless to the historian (except, perhaps, as an illustration of the process of glorification outlined in the last chapter). I have used my discretion in excluding many such items from this list—which should not, however, be taken as an absolute arbiter of what is worthwhile and what is not; the absence of any work should not be seen, necessarily, as a condemnation.

PUBLISHED MATERIALS

Works by Patrick Pearse

Collected Works of Padraic H. Pearse (ed. Desmond Ryan), Dublin, n.d., but published 1917-22

Plays, Stories, Poems: Most of the literary works. English translations by Pearse and Joseph Campbell of the pieces originally in Irish

Political Writings and Speeches: The important pamphlets, orations and articles

Scribhinni: The Irish texts of the plays, poems and stories. Much of the material from *An Barr Buadh* is included, with deletions in some cases

Songs of the Irish Rebels and Specimens from an Irish Anthology; *Some Aspects of Irish Literature*; *Three Lectures on Gaelic Topics*: Various compositions from numerous sources between 1898 and 1914

St Enda's and Its Founder: Includes Pearse's *The Story of a Success*—a re-working of articles from *An Macaomh* (the school's journal)—and Desmond Ryan's *The Man Called Pearse* (*q.v.*). Some Pearse/St Enda's miscellania in the appendices

Poll an Phiobaire, Dublin, 1906

In First Century Ireland, Dublin, 1935

Maingin Sceal, Dublin, 1936: Translations into Irish of children's stories

O Pheann an Phiarsaigh, Dublin, n.d.: Miscellania from *ACS*

Os Cionn na Fairrge agus Aisti Eile, Dublin, [1936]

An tAithriseoir (ed. with Tadhg O Donnchadha), 2 vols, Dublin, 1900, 1902

Bodach an Chota Lachtna (ed.), Dublin, 1906

Bruidhean Chaortainn: Sgeal Fiannaidheachta (ed.), Dublin, 1908

An Sgoil: A Direct Method Course in Irish, Dublin, 1913

A comprehensive and detailed bibliography of Pearse's writings will be found in Raymond J. Porter's *P. H. Pearse* (*q.v.*). A useful general bibliography is James Carty's *Bibliography of Irish history, 1912-21*, Dublin, 1936

Books and Pamphlets

Blaghd Earnan de, *I: Trasna na Boinne*, Dublin, 1957
II: Slan le hUltaibh, Dublin, 1971
III: Gaeil ar Muscailt, Dublin, 1973

Bourke M., *The O'Rahilly*, Tralee, 1967

Brown T. N., *Irish-American Nationalism*, Philadelphia and New York, 1966

Budgen Frank, *Further recollections of James Joyce*, London, 1955

Caulfield Max, *The Easter Rebellion*, London, 1964

Christian Brothers Westland Row Centenary Record 1864-1964

Coffey Thomas M., *Agony at Easter: The 1916 Irish Uprising*, London, 1969

"Coilin", *Patrick H. Pearse: A Sketch of his Life*, Dublin, 1917

Colum Mary, *Life and the Dream*, New York, 1947

Coogan T. P., *Ireland since the Rising*, London and New York, 1966

Cronin Sean, *The McGarrity Papers*, Tralee, 1972

Cuimhni na bPiarsach: Memories of the Brothers Pearse (ed. Brothers Pearse Commemoration Committee), Dublin, 1966

Curran C. P., *Under the Receding Wave*, Dublin, 1970

Daly Martin (pseud. of Stephen MacKenna), *Memories of the Dead*, Dublin, 1917

Dublin Exhibition Catalogue 1882
Edwards Owen Dudley and Ransome Bernard (eds), *James Connolly: Selected Political Writings*, London, 1973
Edwards Owen Dudley and Pyle Fergus (eds), *1916: The Easter Rising*, London, 1968
Fathers of the Society of Jesus (eds), *A page of Irish history: the story of University College, Dublin, 1883-1909*, Dublin, 1930
Fitzgerald Desmond, *The memoirs of Desmond Fitzgerald*, London, 1968
Gaelic League Annual Reports, 1898-1909
Glenavy Lady Beatrice, *Today we will only gossip*, London, 1964
Greaves C. Desmond, *The life and times of James Connolly*, London, 1961
Hayes James, *Patrick H. Pearse: Storyteller*, Dublin, 1919
Hobson Bulmer, *Ireland Yesterday and Tomorrow*, Tralee, 1968
Holt Edgar, *Protest in Arms*, London, 1960
Horgan J. J., *From Parnell to Pearse*, Dublin, 1948
Hyde Douglas, *Mise agus an Connradh*, Dublin, 1937
Imtheachta an Oireachtais, 1898-1909
Inglis Brian, *Roger Casement*, London, 1973
Joy Maurice (ed.), *The Irish Rebellion of 1916 and Its Martyrs: Erin's Tragic Easter*, New York, 1916
Lee Joseph, *The Modernisation of Irish Society 1848-1918*, Dublin, 1973
Le Roux Louis N., *La Vie de Patrice Pearse*, 1932
——, *Patrick H. Pearse*, (translated and adapted by Desmond Ryan), Dublin, 1932
——, *Tom Clarke and the Irish Freedom Movement*, Dublin and Cork, 1936
Larkin Emmet, *James Larkin*, London, 1965
Leabhran Cuimhneachain Arna Fhoilsiu ar Ocaid Bronnadh Eochar Scoil Eanna ar Uachtaran na hEireann Eamon de Valera, Dublin, 1970
Loftus Richard J., *Nationalism in Modern Anglo-Irish Poetry*, Wisconsin, 1964
Longford the Earl of, and O'Neill Thomas P., *Eamon de Valera*, London, 1970
Lynch Diarmuid, *The IRB and the 1916 Rising*, Cork, 1957
Lynd Robert, *Ireland a Nation*, London, 1919
McCay Hedley, *Padraic Pearse: a New Biography*, Cork, 1966
MacDonagh Thomas, *Literature in Ireland*, Dublin, 1920

Mac Giolla Choille Breandan (ed.) *Intelligence Notes, 1913-16*, Dublin, 1966
McHugh Roger, *Dublin, 1916*, London, 1966
MacKenna Stephen (pseud. Martin Daly), *Memories of the Dead*, Dublin, 1916
Mac Lochlainn Piaras F. (ed.), *Last Words*, Dublin, 1971
Martin F. X. (ed.), *The Irish Volunteers, 1913-1915*, Dublin, 1963
——, *The Easter Rising, 1916 and University College, Dublin*, Dublin, 1966
——, *The Howth Gun-Running 1914*, Dublin, 1964
——, *Leaders and Men of the Easter Rising: Dublin 1916*, London, 1967
Martin F. X. and Byrne F. J., *The Scholar Revolutionary*, Dublin, 1975
Metropolitan School of Art, Dublin, *Annual Report and Distribution of Prizes*, 1899-1912
Miller W., *Church, State and Nation in Ireland*, Dublin, 1973
Murdoch Iris, *The red and the green*, London, 1965
Murphy John A., *Ireland in the Twentieth Century*, Dublin, 1975
Nic Shiubhlaigh Maire, *The Splendid Years*, Dublin, 1935
Nowlan Kevin B. (ed.), *The Making of 1916: Studies in the History of the Rising*, London, 1969
O Briain L., *Cuimhni Cinn: cuimhni an Eiri Amach*, Dublin, 1951
O'Brien Conor Cruise (ed.), *The Shaping of Modern Ireland*, London, 1960
——, *States of Ireland*, London, 1972
O'Brien William and Ryan Desmond, (eds), *Devoy's Post Bag, 1871-1928*, 2 vols, Dublin, 1948, 1953
O Broin Leon, *Dublin Castle and the 1916 Rising*, Dublin, 1966
O'Casey Sean, *Drums under the Windows*, London, 1963
O Ceallaigh Sean T., *Sean T*, Dublin, 1963
O Ceilleachair Donncha and O Conluain Proinsias, *An Duinnineach*, Dublin, 1958
O Cuiv Brian (ed.), *A View of the Irish Language*, Dublin, 1969
Diarmuid O Donnabhain Rosa, 1831-1915: souvenir, Dublin, 1915
O Flaimghaile Tomas, *For the Tongue of the Gael*, London, 1896
O Luing Sean, *John Devoy*, Dublin, 1961
——, *Art O Griofa*, Dublin, 1953
O'Neill Tomas and O Fiamrachta Padraig, *De Valera*, Dublin, 1968
O Searcaigh Seamus, *Nua—Sgribhneoiriua Caedhilge*, Dublin, 1933
——, *Padraic Mac Piarais*, Dublin, 1938

O Snodaigh P., *Comhghnaillithe na Reabhloide, 1913-1916*, Dublin, 1966

Parks E. W. and Parks Aileen W., (ed.) *Thomas Macdonagh: the man, the patriot, the writer*, Georgia, 1967

Pearse James, *England's Duty to Ireland as it appears to an Englishman*, Dublin, 1886

Pearse Mary Brigid, (ed.) *The Home-Life of Padraig Pearse*, Dublin, 1935

Porter Raymond J., *P. H. Pearse*, New York, 1973

Reid B. L., *The Man from New York*, Oxford, 1968

The Royal Commission on the Rebellion in Ireland, London, 1916

Royal Hibernian Academy of Arts Exhibition Catalogues, 1906-1913

Royal University of Ireland Calendars, 1898-1901

Ryan Desmond, *The man called Pearse*, Dublin, 1919
(ed.) *The 1916 Poets*, Dublin, 1963

——, *Remembering Sion*, London, 1934

——, *The Rising*, Dublin, 1969

——, *The Sword of Light: From the Four Masters to Douglas Hyde*, London, 1939

Ryan W. P., *The Pope's Green Island*, London, 1912

Sinn Fein Rebellion Handbook, Dublin, 1917

Stanford W. B. and MacDowell R. B., *A Biography of an Irishman*, London, 1971

Stephens James, *Insurrection in Dublin*, Dublin, 1st ed. 1917

Thompson William I., *The imagination of an insurrection: Dublin, Easter, 1916*, London, 1967

Thom's Directories 1860-1912

Walsh Louis J., *Old Friends: Being Memories of Men and Places*, Dundalk, 1934

Williams T. Desmond, *The Irish Struggle 1916-1926*, London, 1966

Yeats W. B., *Autobiographies*, London, 1955

Newspapers and Periodicals

Banba

Barr Buadh, An

Capuchin Annual, Articles on the 1916 Rising, especially in issues 1936, 1940, 1941, 1942, 1966

Catholic Bulletin, 1916-1918

Claidheamh Soluis, An, 1899-1916 (incorporating Fainne an Lae from 4.8.1900)

Fainne an Lae (*see* An Claidheamh Soluis)

Freeman's Journal
Gaelic American
Irish Builder
Irish Freedom
Irish Peasant
Irish Review
Irish Volunteer
Irish Worker
Irish World
Irisleabhar na Gaedhilge: Gaelic Journal, Jan 1899, June 1900
Leabharlanna, An, June 1905
Leader
Macaomh, An
Peasant
St Stephen's, June 1901
Samhain, La Samhna 1917
Sinn Fein
Southern Cross, Buenos Aires
Spark
United Irishman
Workers' Republic

Articles

Aloysius Fr, "Personal Recollections", in *Capuchin Annual*, 1966

Barra Eamonn de, "A Valiant Woman: Margaret Mary Pearse", in *Capuchin Annual*, 1969

Beaslai Piaras, "Moods and Memories", in *Irish Independent*, October 1961-June 1965

Boland Eavan, "Aspects of Pearse", in *Dublin Magazine*, Spring 1966

de Burca Feargus, "An Piarsach fe mar Chuireas aithne air", in *Leabhran* (*q.v.*)

Clery Arthur E., "Pearse, MacDonagh and Plunkett: an appreciation", in *Studies*, June 1917

——, a review of Pearse's political writings and speeches, in *Studies*, June 1922

Curran C. P., "Griffith, MacNeill and Pearse", in *Studies*, Spring 1966

Dillon Geraldine, "The Irish Republican Brotherhood", in *University Review*, 1960

Dore Eamonn, "Sean MacDermott as I knew him", in *Leitrim Guardian*, Christmas 1968

Duffy Louise Gavan, "In the GPO: Cumann na mBan", in *1916 and University College, Dublin* (ed. Martin, *q.v.*)
Fallon Wm. G., article in *Sunday Press*, 14.4.1963
Fanning Ronan, "Leadership and transition from the politics of revolution to the politics of party: the example of Ireland 1914-1939", lecture delivered at XIV International Congress of Historical Sciences, San Francisco, August 1975
French R. B. D., "J. O. Hannay and the Gaelic League", in *Hermathena*, Spring 1966
Grenan Julia, account of the 1916 Rising, in *Catholic Bulletin*, June 1917
Gwynn Denis, "Patrick Pearse", in *Dublin Review*, Jan-March 1923
Hally P. J., "The Easter 1916 Rising in Dublin: the military aspects", in *Irish Sword*, 1966, 1967
Kilcullen James, "Appreciation: Headmaster of St Enda's", in *Eire-Ireland*, Summer 1967
Lemass Sean F., "I remember 1916", in *Studies*, Spring 1966
Mac an tSaoir, "Padraig Mac Piarais—I", in *Comhar*, Bealtaine 1962
——, "Padraig Mac Piarais", in *Comhar*, Mean Fomhair 1962
MacDonagh D., "Patrick Pearse", in *An Cosantoir*, August 1945
McGarrity Joseph, "Twenty Years Ago in America", in *An Caman*, 31 March 1934
MacGarry Milo, "Memories of Sgoil Eanna", in *Capuchin Annual*, 1942
McGill P. J., "Padraic Pearse in Donegal", in *Donegal Annual*, 1966
McLoughlin S., "Memories of the Easter Rising 1916", in *Camillian Post*, Spring 1948
MacNeill E., "Recollections of Pearse", in *New Ireland*, 14.6.1919
MacSheain Sean, "Mo Chuimhne ar Chuairt an Phiarsaigh ar Theilionn", in *Donegal Annual*, 1966
Martin Augustine, "To Make a Right Rose Tree", in *Studies*, Spring 1966
Martin F. X., "Eoin MacNeill on the 1916 Rising", in *Irish Historical Studies*, March 1961
——, "The McCartan Documents, 1916", in *Clogher Record*, 1966
——, "1916—Myth, Fact and Mystery", in *Studia Hibernica*, 1967
——, "The 1916 Rising—coup d'etat or a 'bloody protest'?", in *Studia Hibernica*, 1968
——, "The origins of the Irish rising of 1916", in *The Irish Struggle, 1916-1926* (ed. Williams), London, 1966

O Braonain Cathaoir, "Poets of the Insurrection II—Patrick H. Pearse", in *Studies*, Sept. 1916

O'Brien Frank, "An Piarsach Og agus Conradh na Gaeilge", in *Studia Hibernica*, No. 9

O Conaire Padraic Og, "Cuimhni Scoil Eanna", in *Cuimhni na bPiarsach* (*q.v.*)

O'Farrell Elizabeth, account of the 1916 Rising, in *Catholic Bulletin*, April 1917

O'Hegarty P. S., "P. H. Pearse", in *Irish Commonwealth*, St Patrick's Day 1919

O Neill Eamonn, "Patrick Pearse: some other memories", in *Capuchin Annual*, 1935

O Snodaigh Padraig, "Willie Pearse: Artist", in *Leabhran Cuimhneachain* (*q.v.*)

Pearse Senator Margaret M., "Patrick and Willie Pearse", in *Capuchin Annual*, 1943

——, "St Enda's", in *Capuchin Annual*, 1942

Plunkett Geraldine, "Joseph Plunkett—origin and background", in *University Review*, 1958

Reddin Kenneth, "A Man Called Pearse", in *Studies*, June 1943

Ryan Desmond, "Pearse, St Enda's College, and the Hound of Ulster", in *Threshold*, 1957

——, 6 articles on the Rising in *Irish Press*, 24.4.1961-29.4.1961

——, "St Enda's—Fifty Years After", in *University Review*, 1958

Ryan James, "General Post Office Area", in *Capuchin Annual*, 1942

Shaw Fr Francis, "The Canon of Irish History—A Challenge", in *Studies*, Summer 1972

"They were Schoolboys: The Pearse Brothers at the 'Row'", in *Christian Brothers Westland Row Centenary Record 1864-1964*

Thornley David, "Patrick Pearse", in *Studies*, Spring 1966

——, "Patrick Pearse and the Pearse Family", in *Studies*, Autumn-Winter 1971

Travers Fr Charles, "Sean MacDiarmada, 1883-1916", in *Breifne*, 1966

Wall Maureen, "The decline of the Irish language", in *A view of the Irish language* (ed. O Cuiv), Dublin, 1969

UNPUBLISHED MATERIALS

ARCHIVES DEPARTMENT, UNIVERSITY COLLEGE, DUBLIN

Mulcahy Papers: particularly interviews with Mrs Tom Clarke,

Denis MacCullough and Mrs Mulcahy, and the Sinn Fein Minute Book

EAMONN DE BARRA

Pearse Family Papers (photocopies in UCD): includes Patrick Pearse's fragment of autobiography

BOARD OF WORKS

Pearse Family Papers

BODLEIAN LIBRARY, OXFORD

Asquith Papers

CHRISTIAN BROTHERS' SCHOOL, NORTH RICHMOND STREET, DUBLIN

Brother Allen's collection: includes many interesting St Enda's memorabilia

CUSTOMS HOUSE, DUBLIN

Births, marriages and deaths records

DUBLIN DIOCESAN ARCHIVES

Laity boxes, 1900-1916

FOLK-LORE DEPARTMENT, UNIVERSITY COLLEGE, DUBLIN

MSS of Hyde's memoirs

KILMAINHAM MUSEUM

Miscellaneous letters and memorabilia

KING'S INNS LIBRARY

Miscellaneous papers concerning Pearse's student career

LAND VALUATION OFFICE, DUBLIN

Records, 1906-1912

REV. PROFESSOR F. X. MARTIN

Transcripts of interviews with Bulmer Hobson

NATIONAL LIBRARY OF IRELAND

The most important sources are:

Bloomer Papers
Doyle Papers (J. J.—letters from Pearse)
Gaelic League: Minute Books of the Coiste Gnotha
Minute Book of the Finance Committee
Minute Book of the Publications Committee
Hayden Diaries
Hobson Papers
Holloway Diaries
Holloway Papers

Hutton Papers
McGarrity Papers
MacNeill Papers
O'Kelly Papers (MSS 8469, 10.192)
James Pearse Papers
Mrs Margaret Pearse Papers
Patrick Pearse Papers
Pearse Letters (MS 5049)
Pearse: MSS Eoghan Gabha (MS 15.004)
William Pearse Papers
Scoil Eanna: Account Book, 1908-12
Attendance Book, 1915-1916
Roll, 1915-16
Alec Wilson Papers

Less important items in the following:

Berkeley Papers
Bourke Papers
Casement Papers
Ceannt Papers
Doyle (Miss C. M.) Papers
Gaelic League: Letter Book
Henderson Papers (Press cuttings and theatre programmes)
Hyde's Diaries
Morris (Henry) Letter-book
Moore (Maurice) Papers
Pearse (Proofs of ACS articles, MS 13.824)
Pearse (Draft war bulletin—MS 8499)
Whelan Papers (James, MS 10.218)

Miscellaneous 1916 material in MS 10.605, 15.00 and 15.453

NATIONAL MUSEUM, IRELAND
Miscellaneous Pearse Papers and memorabilia

PUBLIC RECORD OFFICE OF IRELAND
Calendar of Wills and Probate

REGISTRY OF DEEDS, DUBLIN
Indices and registers, 1860-1910

ST AGATHA'S CHURCH, NORTH WILLIAM STREET, DUBLIN
Marriage Records

ST ANDREW'S CHURCH, WESTLAND ROW, DUBLIN
Baptism Register

SOMERSET HOUSE, LONDON
Births, deaths and marriages records

TRINITY COLLEGE, DUBLIN, LIBRARY
Attendance Book: Constitutional and Criminal Law Classes, 1889-1901

UNIVERSITY COLLEGE, DUBLIN, LIBRARY
Kerr, Donall, *The Gaelic Revival*, unpublished thesis for National University of Ireland, 1949

GLOSSARY

of Irish terms as used in the text

Aeridheacht An outdoor entertainment
Ard-Fheis Representative Congress
Banba Poetic name for Ireland (from a queen of the Tuatha De Danann)
bearlachas Anglicism (*e.g.*, in criticizing someone's Irish, "that's *bearlachas*")
bearna baoghail Gap of Danger
Cailin Girl
Cathleen ni Houlihan Poetic name for Ireland (C. the daughter of H.—a more correct Irish form is *Caitlin ni Uallachain*)
Claidheamh Soluis, An The Sword of Light
Clo-Chumann Printing Association
Cluithcheoiri na hEireann Irish Players
Coiste Gnotha Executive Committee
Craoibhin Aoibhinn, An The Delightful Little Branch (Hyde's assumed name)
Cumann na mBan Women's Organization
Cumann na Saoirse Society of Freedom
Emhain Macha location near Armagh town
Fainne an Lae Dawn (literally *Ring of the Day*)
feis (*pl.* feiseanna) festival, entertainment or (see *Ard-Fheis*) convention. An occasion for singing, dancing, story-telling, *etc.*
Gaeltacht District, or districts, where Irish was the vernacular.
Gall Foreigner. Hence applied in succession to each of Ireland's invaders.
Inghinidhe na hEireann Daughters of Ireland
Oireachtas Assembly or Synod. The Gaelic League's term for its annual assembly and festival. Now used for the combined Dail and Senate.
Rann Rhyme
Scoil Eanna St Enda's School
Seoinin (*anglicised*, Shoneen) Flunkey; an aper of English manners
Sgoil, An The School
Shan Van Vocht Poetic name for Ireland (The Poor Old Woman)
Tain (abbr. *An Tain Bo Cuailgne*) Cattle-Raid (*The Cattle Raid of Cooley*)

Tir na nOg The Land of the Young
7 (*Shorthand for* agus) and (*cf.* &)

There were varying systems of Irish spelling until its recent standardization. While the text of the work consistently uses one system only, there are necessary variations from this norm within quotations. Adherence to one school or another of dialectal pronunciation often affected spelling—*e.g.* Coiste / Coisde, Padraic / Padraig, Scoil / Sgoil.

INDEX

This Index is necessarily selective, since many characters appear throughout. **Bold** figures indicate a description or significant activity. WRITINGS are at the end of the Index.

Ir. Vols=Irish Volunteers League=Gaelic League
PP=Patrick Pearse

WRITINGS OF PATRICK PEARSE

to which the text specifically refers: